More Than Conquerors
in Cultural Clashes

Rick Deighton

More than Conquerors in Cultural Conflicts

Library of Congress Control Number: 9014932207
ISBN Number: 978-1-939456-13-7

Published by Search for the Truth Publications
3275 Monroe Rd.
Midland, MI 48642
www.searchforthetruth.net

Printed in the USA

CONTENTS

REVIEWER COMMENT
BY REGGIE THOMAS

"When your first chapter arrived I decided that even though I am now packing and making last minute preparations to fly to Haiti that I would take the time to read Chapter one. It was interesting, inspiring, and challenging to read it. You have done an excellent job, as usual, in writing a very scholarly chapter, as well as an easy reading chapter. I tried to read it as an unbeliever seeking information. Reading it this way, I can tell you truthfully that I was tremendously challenged and helped to believe in the truth of God's Word, as opposed to the false fairy tales of unbelievers. I only offer one suggestion for improvement. In the early part of the chapter as you presented a very brief appeal to the lost sinner to find salvation in Jesus, I think it was too brief. I suggest you give a fuller, more complete presentation of the plan of salvation here. Later on in the chapter your own personal testimony is a powerful presentation and very convincing. If in the earlier part you gave a complete presentation of the plan of salvation, then I think when the reader reaches your own personal testimony, it would be even more powerful."

In Christian love, Reggie

~

"I know I have previously sent you my thoughts on Chapter I, but after re-reading I want to add two thoughts:

1). You mention that you fear that you are so eager to get your message across that you may come across too strong or too passionate and without enough love. Rick, dismiss this fear from your mind. After re-reading chapter 1, I can testify that I never felt more Christian love than I felt coming from your pen!!!!!!!!!

2). Reading Sandy's Appendix brought tears to my eyes as I felt more than ever the Christian love coming through your pen and from Sandy's heartfelt testimony.

In Christian love, Reggie

DEDICATION

I want to begin this dedication with a confession – that I neglected to put a dedication in our second published book. Yes, my name is on the cover, but I often say "our books" because they would not exist without Della. When God gave me a helper (helpmate), He gave me the perfect fit to help me transfer my thoughts scratched out on scratch paper, backs of envelopes, etc. to a clear, legible form. Since our college days Della has faithfully typed and transformed my scribbling into theme papers, tracts, booklets and now two books prior to "More Than Conquerors in Cultural Clashes". I gave a small dedication to Della in "Ready to Give an Answer", but "Is the Bible Without Any Errors?" should have been dedicated to Della also. I neglected to give credit where credit is due and honor to whom honor is due. I confess my negligence and ask your forgiveness, Della Lu. I love you, Della Lu, and I thank God for you. So belatedly I dedicate the first two books to you.

Now, however, we both agree that the dedication for "More Than Conquerors in Cultural Clashes" is to Sandy Joy, our office manager for both Deighton Lighting and Overseas Outreach, but more importantly, our own adopted daughter. (You can read Sandy's Story in Supplement 1 of Chapter 1.) We have loved you from the first time we saw your picture as a sweet two-month-old baby, then as we actually held you as our own at eight months. We have watched you grow in wisdom and stature (to all of 5'1"), taught you to love Jesus, baptized you, and observed you as you handled rejection and deep grief with grace and forgiveness (as a shining example to us and others). Your sweet spirit comes through in such a warm, pleasant, friendly manner when you pick up the phone and say, "Deighton Lighting – this is Sandy." Your people skills with customers, friends, and Idaho Power representatives are not inferior to your office skills with typing, computer, internet and organizing files of information. I really meant it when I told you recently about the book, "I couldn't be doing this without you." So, "More Than Conquerors in Cultural Clashes" is dedicated to Sandra Joy (Deighton) Smith. God has richly endowed you with the gifts and abilities to complement and enhance the way He has gifted each

of us – all to His honor and glory. We thank God for you – deeply and sincerely!

Now, readers, I should also rightly mention that Sandy helped a great deal with "Is the Bible Without Any Errors?" in preparing it for publication. "Ready to Give an Answer" was published before she came to work for us.

As an additional note – we have been asked if it is possible to love an adopted child as much as our own biological child. (Randy is our son – we love him deeply.) To answer this question, I want to clarify that Sandy's temperament, personality and skills are so similar to Della's that some people say she's a duplicate, although she doesn't look exactly like Della. Once Della said to Sandy, "Well, you probably inherited that from me." Sandy replied, "Mom! I wasn't born from you!" Della responded, "Oh, yeah. I forgot!"

If you are considering adoption, we highly recommend it. It is a wonderful option! You may rescue a child for Jesus and discover that He blesses you abundantly with a lifelong co-worker and companion for life's journey. Also, your adopted child may become the source of the fun and frolic of beautiful grandchildren!

ACKNOWLEDGEMENTS

~

Every author is dependent on the writings and insights of previous authors. I am most grateful for the men of God who wrote Scripture by the inspiration of the Holy Spirit, and I am deeply grateful for the dedicated translators who have faithfully labored to convey the words and meaning of the original languages into understandable English. I am especially grateful to the following publications for all their excellent journalism and input for this book, MORE THAN CONQUERORS IN CULTURAL CLASHES: *Citizen Magazine, AFA Journal, The Times and the Scriptures, Answers Magazine, Acts & Facts Magazine, Creation Magazine,* Ray Hawk's email messages, Victor Knowles' *One Body Magazine* and *Knowlesletter.* I am also indebted to many other authors and film makers for giving me their tremendous help and insightful comments in articles, pamphlets, book, and DVD's. We have an extensive list of recommended reading and watching items in the Reference Section.

Thanks to Reggie Thomas for writing the introduction to this book. Reggie is the founder of White Fields Overseas Evangelism, who, with his team has planted hundreds of churches worldwide. Reggie is now in his mid 80's and still preaching God's Word in churches and at conferences, as well as on the shorter mission trips. I'm honored to be one of the American evangelists who works with Reggie, and I'm grateful that he has taken time from his busy schedule to review More than Conquerors in Cultural Clashes and write the introduction. To give you a better scope of White Fields Overseas Evangelism, here is the summary on the back of the October 2013 prayer letter: "We praise God that during this year 2013 there have been 2,755 souls who have accepted Jesus as Savior and Lord and obeyed Him in Christian baptism. White Fields Overseas Evangelism is associated with 439 native evangelists worldwide. These evangelists are all looking to White Fields for support. At the present time we are only able to support 129 of these Native Evangelists. We need more supporters. It is a great thrill to report to you that these Native Evangelists have written to us that during January –September they along with our American Evangelists have baptized 2,755 souls. Thank the Lord!!!"

Thanks to Gary Strubhar for writing the foreword to this book. He has been my long-time friend and mentor. I learned a great deal from him as his associate minister for a congregation in Gresham, Oregon (now River Hills Church) – but also I was learning from him before that time about generosity, kindness, boldness and balance. Not only did I learn from his clear, well-illustrated teaching and preaching style but even more from his heartfelt generosity, his balance of tough and tender love, and his lifestyle evangelism. His humor rolls out of his mouth and eyes from the wellspring of the joy of the Lord in his heart. Sandra, his wife and co-worker in ministry for 54 years, is the ideal complement to him in ministry. (We have joked about how similar Sandra and Della are in their temperament types and how similar Gary and I are in ours.) Gary is a cancer survivor, but has Parkinson's disease, which forced his resignation from public preaching and teaching several years ago (and nearly broke his heart), but he is still writing tracts and ministering person to person with individuals. Sandra has struggled with polio most of her life – but theirs is a triumphant faith. They prefer praising God to griping and grumbling. They believe and practice *"casting all your care upon Him because He cares for you." 1 Peter 5:7* Gary and Sandra have an exemplary record in ministry for our Lord Jesus, but their greatest record of ministry and brightest shining legacy is their family. Their son and two daughters with their spouses and children love the Lord Jesus fervently and serve Him joyfully. What a legacy!!!

We have recent friends, who have become our co-workers in the Kingdom of God. Two of them are Chris and Carolyn Benjamin. Chris came to our Northwest Science Museum meeting in Nampa on July 5, 2013, with his brother, Jason, to help us evaluate how to best move forward with this monumental project. On July 28th Chris and his wife, Carolyn, came to my presentation at Minnehaha Church in Vancouver, Washington. We had the privilege of sharing lunchtime with them and getting acquainted. Both are multi-talented servants of our Lord Jesus. We learned that Carolyn is an accomplished artist, who puts her paintings on display in various settings – and she volunteered to provide the artwork you

Acknowledgements

see at the beginning of each chapter of this book. The painting of the rose she could use for two purposes and had already started on it, but the rest of the paintings she especially created to illustrate the themes covered in these chapters. When she sent us the email pictures, we were both thrilled with the results. Della said, "Look at these! She is really gifted!" I agree! Carolyn recognizes that her artistic gift comes from God, and in generosity she is giving to Him through this project. (To her credit, she has also diligently developed the artistic flair God gave her.) Carolyn, our gratitude exceeds our ability to express it adequately!

Thanks to Paul Sudhakar who designed the cover for this book. Paul is a brilliant young man from South India, who was one of my students at the seminar on Christian Evidences, which I taught last spring at New Hope Church in Kharkov, Ukraine. (New Hope Church ministers to international students from many nations.) Paul is not only brilliant, he is talented with technology and owns his own on-line business – including designing graphics. Last spring he won first prize in the world for designing a space station that would house 20,000 people. NASA hired him! I asked Paul if he would design a book cover for me and how much it would cost. He told me that since this is for the Kingdom of God, he would design it for free. He sent us four samples. I heard Della saying, "Wow! Wow!" as she looked at the samples he sent. When we forwarded the one we chose to Bruce Malone, he replied in just a few moments by saying, "That is a really sharp cover! It is probably the most eye-catching cover I've seen in a long time. I wouldn't change anything." Paul, we cannot possibly express adequately our appreciation for your generous contribution to this book. Thank you so much for using the wonderful talent God gave you in a way that glorifies Him and blesses us!

Finally, I am deeply grateful for the encouragement and helpful insights from our dedicated and discerning reviewers. THANK YOU SO MUCH! You are a treasure! I spearheaded this book project, but without your keen insights, suggestions, and encouragement it would be lacking in clarity, pertinence, and power. My gratitude to you is deeper than I can adequately express!

Yours & His, Rick

UNIQUE PERSPECTIVE

~

I believe God has prepared me for years to write this book from a unique perspective. In fact, this may be the major reason why God gave me life and put me here on this earth. In our August prayer letter for Overseas Outreach I wrote: *"Please pray for publication of "More Than Conquerors in Cultural Clashes" soon. We have now finished the manuscript except for some finishing touches, refining from suggestions for improvement by our reviewers, and waiting for permissions to quote. My prayer is that this book will challenge, inspire, and encourage fellow believers to stand up, straighten up and speak up for Jesus, while demolishing strongholds of deception and degradation. Will you pray with me for God to use this book as a spark for revival and spiritual awakening?"*

Note 1: Here are a few reasons that God has uniquely prepared me for this task:

1. God placed in my heart a love for reading when I was still a child, so I have been reading widely since I was a youth.

2. I grew up in a mixed family. My mother was a nominal believer and sent me to Bible classes, but my father, older brother, and all my uncles on my father's side were atheists, agnostics, evolutionists, and Biblical skeptics. At a very young age I declared myself an atheist when I said, "I don't believe in God! I've never seen Him!" I am **so** thankful that God by His amazing grace, and through a dramatic answer to my first earnest, personal prayer, drew me out of that web of unbelief into His kind, loving arms.

3. When I was a senior in high school I read *Masters of Deceit*, by J. Edgar Hoover, former director of the FBI, as a project for a book report. It was an insightful look at the deceptive tactics of Marxism. This foundation has given me a clear perception of what has been happening in our nation for

so many years. I'm appalled that many Americans seem to be so ignorant of Marxism that they don't recognize it in our schools, universities, journals, and government offices all the way to the Supreme Court, Congress, and the White House.

Ronald Reagan once quipped:
"Who is a communist?
– someone who reads Marx and Engles.
Who is an anti-communist?
– someone who understands Marx and Engles!!!"

4. I've had an excellent foundation in Bible, Theology, Apologetics, Philosophy, Preaching and Teaching Ministry, Missions, and Writing Ministry at Boise Bible College and Ozark Bible College.

5. While in my fifth year of Bible College I read *None Dare Call it Treason,* and wrote an essay about if for a contest. Although I did not win the first prize I had hoped for, I did win a prize and learned valuable information.

6. While preparing to go to Germany as a missionary and church planter, I served for four years (1966-1970) as preaching minister for a church in Eugene, Oregon – about half way between Seattle and San Francisco on Interstate Hwy. I-5. This was during extreme turbulence of the riots on campuses and the rise of the hippy movement. Reaching out to students on the University of Oregon campus was as much a continuing education for me as it was effective evangelism for touching them.

7. We founded Alpine Christian Mission and served seven years doing outreach in Germany and Switzerland. Learning to understand and relate to German/Western European mentality was also a continuing education.

8. I have served as Missions Professor for one year at Boise Bible College, as well as serving as associate minister of preaching at a local church.

9. For over thirty years I've served as a bi-vocational missionary, and we founded Overseas Outreach after being

invited by Reggie Thomas to serve with him as an associate evangelist for White Fields Overseas Evangelism. For the past fifteen years I've observed firsthand the devastation of Marxism /Evolutionism in former Soviet Union nations.

10. We own and operate our own business, Deighton Lighting (I'm not good at sewing, so I didn't try tent making. Besides, this way I get to share the light all the time).

11. I've taught Christian Evidences in camps in Estonia and churches in Latvia. I've taught a one week modular course in Christian Evidences and Creation Science and Evangelism at Zaparozia Bible College in Ukraine, and repeatedly for Tavrisky Christian Institute in Ukraine and Georgia.

12. Sergei Golovin invited me to come to Crimea as a presenter for the Man and the Christian Worldview Symposium in the spring of 2001. God opened many doors and I have taught at these symposiums and Creation Conferences for about twelve years. Now I often teach "Worldview" and "Building Lasting Relationships" lessons on both Christian and secular campuses in Ukraine.

13. Since December 14, 2012, Della and I have been married for fifty years. This gives some credibility to teaching on "Building Lasting Relationships" and for my chapter, "Phony Matrimony vs. Merry Marriage."

14. Bruce Malone of Search for the Truth Ministries has published my (our) two former books, *Ready to Give an Answer* and *Is the Bible Without Any Errors?* We have confirmation that they are touching hearts and lives of readers, - not only English readers, but Russian and Georgian as well.

15. Reggie Thomas, Founder of White Fields Overseas Evangelism and a living legend in missions and church planting world-wide, has gladly agreed to write the introduction for *More than Conquerors in Cultural Clashes*.

16. I served as associate minister with Gary Strubhar in Gresham, Oregon, and he has graciously reviewed the manuscript

for *More than Conquerors in Cultural Clashes*. Recently he wrote concerning Chapter 6:

"Dear Fellow Kingdom Co-worker,

Rick, you are a bold witness and author! You are spot- on with your analysis of the current 'mess we are in.' You have the facts and the truth from Scripture, applied timely to the enemy's strategies. Please reserve several copies of your coming new book. Every soldier in the Lord's army needs the information in chapter 6! (yes, 1-6) Bold, winsome, wise, witnesses are so needed in today's culture. You are truly a bold, Spirit-filled witness, and author. You represent the heart of God just as the O.T. prophets did. Bless you for your zeal. The 'world' is truly the enemy of the Cross. We are facing bold spiritual warfare and it's past time that every serious believer gets informed and bold about the issues at hand. We are the Light of the world. If we are dim lights, we influence nobody. But when we are bold and not timid, those who oppose us will know they are in 'darkness' whether or not they admit it. Gary S."

Would you consider partnering with us to give *More than Conquerors in Cultural Clashes* a wide distribution to Americans?

Note 2: Additional Resources Available Upon Request

More than Conquerors in Cultural Clashes is actually two books in one:

Volume One, which you now hold, is mostly my own writing with some quotations interspersed. If you want an overview of the heart of the cultural war going on in America - please continue reading Volume One with an open heart and mind.

Volume Two, the Companion Volume for *More than Conquerors in Cultural Clashes* is validation, documentation, and clarification for the positions I express in Volume One. There are appendixes for every chapter containing extra validation for what is written. This section will be especially important to those of you who are more skeptical, but I think everyone will find much interesting reading, as well as documentation, in Volume Two. Also, in the last pages of this companion volume you will find an extensive reference section for books and DVDs entitled "Recommended Reading and Watching." We had intended to include all of this in one volume, but it became too extensive to be practical. Our publisher and our own knowledge of the fast pace lifestyle of most Americans gives us the distinct impression that most people simply do not have time to read all of this additional documentation. But, if you are like me, and would like to have the documentation, you need only write to us and send a donation of any amount to Overseas Outreach and we will send you the photocopy Volume Two of *More than Conquerors in Cultural Clashes* in 8 ½ x 11 format. Send your request to: Overseas Outreach, Rick & Della Deighton, P.O. Box 1224, Nampa, ID 83653-1224.

Note 3: Questions

There are 10 questions after each chapter to help accommodate using this book for small group studies. Actually, I should clarify that since Chapter 1 and Chapter 7 are much longer than the other chapters, each of them has 20 questions. You will find 10 questions in the middle of each of these chapters as well as the 10 questions at the end of the chapter. Since there are also 10 questions at the end of the Final Thoughts, this makes a total of 100 questions – perfect for a 10 week series for a small group. (If you want to use it for a 13 week series for a quarter, you have plenty of material in Section 2 to use as verification and validation of the points emphasized in the main text.)

Note 4: Personal Motivation

If you are reading the book alone, the questions can help motivate you to actually study, remember, and apply the lessons in order to become a more active and bold witness for our Lord Jesus Christ. I offer you the opportunity – in fact, I challenge you – to get serious about gaining confidence to be **who** you are in Christ. Are you winning in the spiritual warfare going on inside you? Are you making a positive difference in the cultural clashes in our country?

In your county? In your city? In your own family? If not – why not? Do you really want to hear our Commander in Chief say to you, 'Well done, good and faithful servant!"? Are you living and serving as a good soldier of our Lord Jesus, or are you a coward? Are you AWOL in the heat of the battle? This book can help you, and Jesus can transform you if you are willing, but only you can supply the personal motivation and application. What will you do? If you just shake your head and say, "What is this world coming to?" – you missed the point! This world is going to hell! You already knew that! What are you doing to rescue as many souls as possible from that pit? That is the question. Transformation of our nation will happen one soul at a time!

Here is my wish for all of you: *"May the God of hope fill you with all joy and peace as you trust in him, so that you may overflow with hope by the power of the Holy Spirit." Romans 15:13 (NIV)*

To this clarification I want to add these questions from Chapter 4:

How do You Handle Criticism?

(Humbly Listening or Proudly Rejecting?)

Ravi Zacharias tells of a furious man he knew who came storming out of a counseling session and asked him: "Do you know what he said to me? He said that I don't handle criticism well!!!" Need I comment?

In the same broadcast, Ravi quipped, "The depravity of man is the most easily verifiable truth – but the most strongly resisted." He illustrated this with an example of a reaction he got from a woman in an academic setting. During the question session following his presentation, an irate lady with a shrill voice was strongly opposing Ravi's point about human beings having a flawed nature – as the Word of God teaches. Jeremiah 17:9 says, *"'The heart is deceitful above all things, and desperately wicked; who can know it?"* As she became more intense with her argument, her anger became more evident, her face more red and her voice more shrill, Ravi resisted the temptation to say what he felt like saying – "Sit down and be quiet – you just proved my point!"

Ravi had already presented truth, so he responded with compassion instead of logic. He could have embarrassed her before the whole crowd. I'm not sure I would have resisted that temptation, but in this case I realize that his compassion was better than logic. I want to be more like this in speaking the truth in love. There is a time to confront – a time to speak – but also a time to be silent. In this case his silence was an act of love while letting the truth already spoken sink in. After all, our purpose is to win people, not arguments.

Friend, how do you handle criticism – by humbly listening or proudly rejecting? Will you be wise enough to honestly, humbly consider these passages from God's wisdom literature?

"He who corrects a scoffer gets shame for himself, and he who rebukes a wicked man only harms himself. Do not correct a scoffer, lest he hate you; rebuke a wise man, and he will love you. Give instruction to a wise man, and he will be still wiser; teach a just man, and he will increase in learning. 'The fear of the Lord is the beginning of wisdom, and the knowledge of the Holy One is understanding'. . . Open rebuke is better than love carefully concealed. Faithful are the wounds of a friend, but the kisses of an enemy are deceitful." Proverbs 9:7-10, 27:5-6

"It is better to hear the rebuke of the wise than for a man to hear the song of fools." Ecclesiastes 7:5

Bottom line note: Some years ago when Alexander Solzhenitsyn spoke to a gathering of Harvard students, warning them of the consequences of adopting Marxism, they mocked him. Were those brilliant students demonstrating wisdom or foolishness? Remember that intelligence and wisdom are not the same. You can have a head full of information and a heart full of rebellion and foolishness. I remember my Dad speaking of the "educated fools" – those with a bushel of information without a thimble full of practical good sense (no wisdom of how to use it).

WERE THE LEADERS OF
ISRAEL AND ROME IN JESUS' TIME WISE?

Is it possible to accumulate information (knowledge, science) while at the same time crucifying Truth and Wisdom? The religious leaders of Israel in Jesus' time had a vast accumulation of Biblical and secular knowledge, yet they manipulated the crucifixion of Truth Himself.

Jesus had said to the religious leaders: *"You search the Scriptures, for in them you think you have eternal life; and these are they which testify of Me." John 5:39*

Some years after Jesus' death, burial and resurrection, the apostle Paul wrote, *"However, we speak wisdom among those who are mature, yet not the wisdom of this age, nor of the rulers of this age, who are coming to nothing. But we speak the wisdom of God in a mystery, the hidden wisdom which God ordained before the ages for our glory, which none of the rulers of this age knew; for had they known, they would not have crucified the Lord of glory." 1 Corinthians 2:6-8*

FOREWORD

BY GARY STRUBHAR

~

Retired minister, college professor, elder,
Servant with 40 years of kingdom fellowship with Deighton's
The Strubhar's now live in Roseburg, Oregon

~

For more than 35 years Thomas Kinkade painted legendary landscapes of light. "Thomas Kinkade, painter of light" became his registered trademark. Rick Deighton may not be as famous as Thomas Kinkade, but Rick is a spreader and promoter of light. The famous painter said every original painting comes from what he first draws. Rick also draws----conclusions ---about our current culture. Doesn't that seem natural, since he built and operates Rick Deighton Lighting? His passion for turning darkness to light is not a new idea; he has lived the life of a light-bearer for decades! I know from working with him, he is not ashamed of Jesus or His message. Rick knows God did not give us a spirit of fear and timidity, but of power, love and sound mind. His kind is especially needed in our generation. He has never met a stranger with whom he couldn't begin a pleasant, positive conversation.

Never in the last 400 years have we witnessed such an attack on Christian morals and values! From Hollywood to your neighborhood, from every government school and college to the local and national media---it's one constant stream of belittling and outright attack on the "Light."

Jesus' words to Nicodemus are equally true now as then: "*This is the crisis we're in: God-light streamed into the world, but men and women everywhere ran for the darkness. They went for the darkness because they were not really interested in pleasing God. Everyone who makes a practice of doing evil, addicted to denial and illusion, hates God-light and won't come near it, fearing a painful exposure. But anyone working and living in truth and reality welcomes God-light so the work can be seen for the God-work it is."* [*The Message. Jn.3:19-21*] The apostle John gives us further light: *"He [Jesus] created everything there is. Nothing exists that he didn't make. Life itself was in him, and this life gives light to everyone. The light shines through the darkness, and the darkness can never extinguish it."* [*Jn. 1:3-5*] And so the crisis continues! Rick's pertinent expose' is more than a reaction to the evils of our day. It is a resource book crammed full of evidence of the decay around us. Dark days are upon us; evil is more tolerated, excused, and even laughed at. Light-bearers are scoffed and scorned and insulted as inferior or ignorant. But remember, modern (and ancient) culture has always opposed the good news of God. The apostle Paul instructs us to *"take no part in the worthless deeds of evil and darkness; instead, rebuke and expose them". This is why it says, 'Wake up from your sleep, climb out of your coffins, Christ will show you the light.'* [*NLT and Message Eph. 5:11-14*]

So here's the crisis and here's our assignment. Let Rick Deighton's passion, observations, research, and warnings help shine through your life, words, and witness. Inform yourself and others about the rebellion, the 'tolerance,' the violence, the attack on marriage, purity, and purpose. Rick does a masterful job of integrating Scripture, quotes, illustrations, real-life personal illustrations, and testimonies. All this done in an easy to read, contemporary style. He will remind you of a prophet, and this is what America needs----now. And if you only have time to read part, please read his chapter 4 and his powerful closing remarks.

Commit yourself to the practical action steps in each chapter so we can do more than react, we can be light! *Be no longer inhibited; be inhabited!*

INTRODUCTION BY REGGIE THOMAS

~

It is a wonderful privilege and a great honor to be asked to write the introduction for this particular book "MORE THAN CONQUERORS IN CULTURAL CLASHES" written by my good friend and co-laborer in the Lord, Rick Deighton. In introducing this book please take note of what Chief Justice Roy Moore has written. Judge Moore was sued by the ACLU for displaying the Ten Commandments in his courtroom foyer. He was stripped of his judgeship and removed from the bench for refusing to remove the Ten Commandments from his courtroom. The people of Alabama have re-elected him as Judge for the Supreme Court of Alabama. The following is a poem written by Judge Roy Moore

America the Beautiful,
or so you used to be.
Land of the Pilgrims' pride;
I'm glad they'll never see.

Babies piled in dumpsters,
Abortion on demand,
Oh, sweet land of liberty;
your house is on the sand.

Our children wander aimlessly
poisoned by cocaine
choosing to indulge their lusts,
when God has said abstain

From sea to shining sea,
our Nation turns away
From the teaching of God's love
and a need to always pray.

We've kept God in our temples,
how callous we have grown.
When earth is but His footstool,
and Heaven is His throne.

We've voted in a government
that's rotting at the core,
Appointing Godless Judges;
who throw reason out the door,

Too soft to place a killer
in a well deserved tomb,
But brave enough to kill a baby
before he leaves the womb.

You think that God's not angry,
that our land's a moral slum?
How much longer will He wait
before His judgment comes?

Introduction

How are we to face our God,
from Whom we cannot hide?
What then is left for us to do,
but stem this evil tide?

If we who are His children,
will humbly turn and pray;
Seek His holy face
and mend our evil way:

Then God will hear from Heaven;
and forgive us of our sins,
He'll heal our sickly land
and those who live within.

But, America the Beautiful,
if you don't - then you will see,
A sad but Holy God
withdraw His hand from Thee.

~~Judge Roy Moore~~

This poem by Judge Moore says it all so well. Those of us who are adult Americans never thought things would be as they now are:

*millions of babies murdered by abortion on demand----

*drugs addicts by the millions filling our jails and prisons---

*lesbianism and homosexuality approved by our President----

*prayer and Bible reading forbidden in school where condoms are handed out freely---

Yes, our beloved America is sick and we are in danger of God judging us with fire and brimstone as He did to Sodom and Gomorrah!

Rick Deighton fearlessly exposes the errors, sins, evil and foolish ways of America. Rick is a true scholar and yet he writes in easy to understand ways in PRESENTING TRUTH, DEFENDING TRUTH, AND EXPOSING ERROR. You will love this book because Rick will help you to prepare to be a bold witness for Jesus Christ and to be ready to give clear answers to tough questions. And as you complete reading the book I pray that you will help to spread the news about this marvelous book to all Americans.

In Christian love,
Reggie Thomas, Evangelist,
White Fields Overseas Evangelism

CHAPTER 1:

PURPOSE & PASSION

Chapter 1: Purpose and Passion

What is my Purpose? What is my Passion?

(I hope you are asking yourself these questions as you read.)

~

Rick Warren's[1] blockbuster book, *Purpose Driven Life*, inspired me. I learned from it – but was already living a purpose driven life before reading the book. Why? Because my purpose driven Master already gave me His purpose driven Book on how to live a purpose driven life. The Master Himself said, *"Behold, I have come to do Your will, O God." Hebrews 10:9.* That is my desire – to please Him. To help me fulfill this desire I have adopted and memorized the purpose statement of our Lord Jesus' most zealous apostle, Paul. He wrote:

"To them God willed to make known what are the riches of the glory of this mystery among the Gentiles: which is Christ in you, the hope of glory. Him we preach, warning every man and teaching

---

1   *During my mission trip to Ukraine in the spring of 2013, I heard from John Murphy, a fellow missionary, that Rick Warren's son committed suicide and now many atheists are scoffing and accosting Rick as a bad father in their blogs and websites. How sad. How insensitive. How cruel. I implore you to join me in earnest prayer for Rick and Kay Warren and family in their deep grief. Let's also pray for God to touch multitudes of tender hearts with triumphant truth in the midst of terrible tragedy. How very thankful I am for the powerful comfort of Romans 8:28-29: "And we know that all things work together for good to those who love God, to those who are the called according to His purpose. 29 For whom He foreknew, He also predestined to be conformed to the image of His Son, that He might be the firstborn among many brethren."*

By the way, I do recognize that many atheists are not as cruel and insensitive as those who are blatantly expressing their opinions and scoffing. In fact, some express genuine kindness – and there are some Christians who are unkind, cruel and insensitive. However, I also recognize that when Christians are cruel and unkind, they are sinfully violating the teachings of Christ and His apostles – and when atheists respond in kindness it is because they have borrowed the Biblical standard of kindness. Atheism has no absolute moral standard for anything! There is more about this later in the book.

every man in all wisdom, that we may present every man perfect in Christ Jesus. To this end I also labor, striving according to His working which works in me mightily." Colossians 1:27-29 (NKJV)

My purpose in writing this book is to speak the truth in love to those surrounded by and saturated with our increasingly corrupt cultural constructs. I write not only to my fellow believers in Jesus Christ who accept Him as The Way, The Truth and The Life and believe the Bible to be the infallible Word of Truth, but also to those who believe the Bible is an outdated book filled with irrelevant rules and monstrous myths. I will attempt to speak the truth in love while clearly, concisely, and conclusively dismantling any objectives supported by corrupt concepts and in some cases undergirded by outright lies. I realize that this is a huge task and very difficult to balance. I feel like a tightrope walker because it's easy to fall over by getting unbalanced on either side. If I lean too hard on stressing truth I can come across to you as harsh and uncaring, but if I lean too far toward being so "polite and gentle" that I never offend you with hard truth, then I end up becoming a compromising coward who doesn't do you any good. In fact, I may do you a great deal of harm by sharing and spreading a false security. Would you rather have a doctor who is straightforward enough to tell you the truth as kindly as possible even when it hurts, or a doctor who lets you die of cancer or heart disease because he is too "kind" to tell you the truth that could save your life? Do you want a postmodern doctor who has a postmodern view of truth? What is that? That would be, "Well, my truth is that all my tests show that you have a serious, life threatening blood clot that must be dealt with immediately – but your 'truth' is that you feel fine and aren't experiencing pain (yet), so therefore, you are fine. No problem! So I won't bother you with my hard truth because you are so comfortable with your 'soft truth'!" If you find a doctor like that, I hope you have sense enough to run. *Postmodernism's "your truth and my truth are both true" is a huge lie!* Unfortunately, Joseph Goebbels was right when he said that if you tell a lie big enough and often enough, most people will believe it. Hitler adopted this philosophy and used it effectively in his propaganda campaign to take control of Germany. That is the best explanation I know for why so many people believe the lies of the evolutionist, the abortionist, and the con-artist ventriloquist who puts his words into other peoples' mouths. Unfortunately many of these "ventriloquists" are paid to be journalists in major media outlets.

WHY DID JESUS COME INTO THE WORLD?

*"Pilate therefore said to Him, 'Are You a king then?' Jesus answered, 'You say rightly that I am a king. **For this cause I was born, and for this cause I have come into the world, that I should bear witness to the truth.** Everyone who is of the truth hears My voice.'"* John 18:37

*"Then Jesus said to those Jews who believed Him, '**If you abide in My word, you are My disciples indeed. And you shall know the truth, and the truth shall make you free.**'"* John 8:31-32

*"**Sanctify them by Your truth. Your word is truth.**"* John 17:17

*"We are of God. **He who knows God hears us;** he who is not of God does not hear us. By this we know the spirit of truth and the spirit of error."* 1 John 4:6

I do need to confess that in my writings I tend to lean hard on sharing truth and don't come across as kind as I do when speaking person to person. I am praying for God to help me genuinely "speak the truth in love", but please realize that if I do come across to you as harsh or uncaring, my motive is because I truly do care and desire that all who hear God's truth will discover the grace and mercy and love to be found in God. A healthy, spiritual relationship with God can only be realized when based upon the truth.

To demonstrate to you that I actually am serious about being balanced in my manner of presentation, I want to share with you a letter I wrote to some leaders seeking their input and reviews:

"I am in the process of writing another book and I wonder if you will consider helping me. I recognize the need to keep a balance between expressing truth and expressing love (kindness/affection) in my writing. Paul was accused by his opponents in Corinth of being a different man in his writing than he was in physical presence. For me that is not only an accusation - it is a reality. I realize that when I am writing and feeling a zeal for truth and righteousness I can come across too strong and harsh - but when I'm sitting across from a sobbing sinner or an angry individual who has been deeply hurt by unfeeling or inconsistent Christians, I'm tempted to cushion the truth with overt kindness which may soften the truth too much. I need balance. I do want to speak the truth in love and recognize that sometimes love must be tough - but not unkind. Paul by inspiration wrote to Timothy both these passages:

1. "I charge you therefore before God and the Lord Jesus Christ, who will judge the living and the dead at His appearing and His kingdom: Preach the word! Be ready in season and out of season. Convince, rebuke, exhort, with all longsuffering and teaching." 2 Timothy 4:1-2 (NKJV)

2. "But avoid foolish and ignorant disputes, knowing that they generate strife. And a servant of the Lord must not quarrel but be gentle to all, able to teach, patient, in humility correcting those who are in opposition, if God perhaps will grant them repentance, so that they may know the truth, and that they may come to their senses and escape the snare of the devil, having been taken captive by him to do his will." 2 Timothy 2:23-26 (NKJV)

It is my desire to fulfill these mandates with balance as I write "More than Conquerors in Cultural Clashes". I'm asking if you will review chapter by chapter what I've written and point out from your perspective any points you believe need to be refined and better balanced. I do not promise to make every change you suggest, but I do promise to give every suggestion careful consideration and earnest prayer. We are living in extremely crucial and volatile times and I definitely want to be both clear and balanced - neither too polite nor too harsh. My deep desire is to win the unconverted to Christ and strengthen believers to be bold witnesses for Jesus. Will you help me? I have tried to get a balance in those I'm asking to review.

Here is my wish for each of you: "Now may the God of hope fill you with great peace and joy as you trust in Him so that you may overflow with hope by the power of the Holy Spirit." Romans 15:13

Yours & His,
Rick"

Now here are my purposes for this book:

1. **My first purpose for this book is to give some practical answers to the question David posed for us in Psalm 11:3: "If the foundations are destroyed, what can the righteous do?"** It is obvious to committed Christians that the foundations of our nation (and all of Western civilization that was based on Christian principles) are destroyed, or are being destroyed. What shall the righteous do? Shall we throw up our hands and give up in despair? In a recent broadcast by Ravi Zacharias he identified the four foundations he sees being destroyed: 1. Belief in eternity 2. Belief in morality 3. Belief in accountability 4. Belief in charity (courtesy). This book is designed to give both encouragement and practical ideas of what we can do.

Target Audiences

a. My first target audience – the bull's eye of the target – is committed Christians, especially Christian leaders, who are disheartened and discouraged. Don't give up the battle for truth and righteousness! God is not done with you yet! We have not yet begun to fight! It's time to get into the battle. Do you want the wimpy, weak-willed, give-it-up attitude of Saul and his soldiers – or the conquering confidence of David? The wimpy "warriors" were comparing themselves with Goliath. David was comparing Goliath with GOD – Awesome, Almighty Jehovah – King of Kings and Lord of Lords! Where is your focus??? *"Therefore do not cast away your confidence, which has great reward." Hebrews 10:35.*

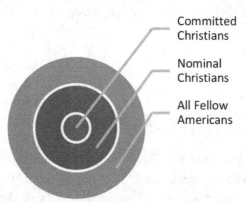

Committed Christians

Nominal Christians

All Fellow Americans

"Now the just shall live by faith; but if anyone draws back, My soul has no pleasure in him." Hebrews 10:38. "Therefore strengthen the hands which hang down and the feeble knees..." Hebrews 12:12.

b. The circle around the bull's eye is my *second target audience* – the multiplied millions of Americans who profess to be "born again Christians" – yet are living careless, frivolous, flippant lives with lifestyles no different than their pagan neighbors. My target is their overinflated apathy and abysmal ignorance of our extreme danger as a nation. My purpose is to kick them hard enough in the back side of the lap so as to wake them up to reality and shock them into positive action! *"As many as I love, I rebuke and chasten. Therefore be zealous and repent. Behold, I stand at the door and knock. If anyone hears My voice and opens the door, I will come in to him and dine with him, and he with Me. To him who overcomes I will grant to sit with Me on My throne, as I also overcame and sat down with My Father on His throne. He who has an ear, let him hear what the Spirit says to the churches."* Revelation 3:19-22. I truly believe you are being called by the Spirit of God to march in our Lord's army and stand on His promise rather than sitting on the premises!

c. The second circle around the bull's eye is my *third target audience* – all my fellow Americans. My purpose for those of you who have never made a commitment to the Lord Jesus Christ is to wake you up to your desperate need for the Savior and persuade you to commit to Him your "lives, your fortunes, and your sacred honor"!

Yes, Jesus is the answer for changing our corrupt culture! Satan can **never** destroy Christ's church, for "*the gates of hell shall not prevail against it*" – but he is doing an effective job of destroying the foundations of our nation. The only hope for America as a constitutional republic based on Christian principles is another Great Awakening. **It's happened before – it can happen again if there is genuine repentance and revival in our churches and widespread spiritual awakening in the United States of America!**

2. **My second purpose for this book is to persuade you to choose the will of God and please Him to be the highest priority of your life.** That is, I hope to share in a motivating manner to persuade you to surrender your will to the will of God, to avoid the judgment of God's wrath upon you for sin, and for you to find peace and joy in forgiveness through Jesus Christ that you cannot receive anywhere else. Paul wrote: "*Therefore we make it our aim, whether present or absent, to be well pleasing to Him. For we must all appear before the judgment seat of Christ, that each one may receive the things done in the body, according to what he has*

done, whether good or bad. Knowing, therefore, the terror of the Lord, we persuade men..."

3. **My third purpose for this book is to expose error and demolish foolish and evil arguments.** I am well aware that many people now expect Christians to be so "nice" – so "polite" that they would never argue. FALSE! Jesus ripped the masks off both the Sadducees (liberals) and the Pharisees (legalists), exposing their wicked schemes and hypocrisies. Also, He took a whip and drove the crooked money grabbers out of the temple. If your perception of Jesus is that He is only the meek and mild people pleaser, your view is not yet balanced. **May I introduce you to Jesus Christ, Lion of the Tribe of Judah and King of Kings, Lord of Lords!**

I believe that every committed Christian needs to "contend earnestly for the faith." Here is the Word of God to us through Jude: *"Beloved, while I was very diligent to write to you concerning our common salvation, I found it necessary to write to you exhorting you to contend earnestly for the faith which was once for all delivered to the saints. For certain men have crept in unnoticed, who long ago were marked out for this condemnation, ungodly men, who turn the grace of our God into lewdness and deny the only Lord God and our Lord Jesus Christ." Jude 3-4.* Have ungodly men crept into churches, perverting the grace of God? Absolutely! It was happening in the first century and it is happening in the twenty-first century – at an accelerated speed. True gratitude for grace produces purity – not perversion!!! Paul wrote to Titus about this very issue: *"For the grace of God that brings salvation has appeared to all men, teaching us that, denying ungodliness and worldly lusts, we should live soberly, righteously, and godly in the present age, looking for the blessed hope and glorious appearing of our great God and Savior Jesus Christ, who gave Himself for us, that He might redeem us from every lawless deed and purify for Himself His own special people, zealous for good works. Speak these things, exhort, and rebuke with all authority. Let no one despise you." Titus 2:11-15.*

Wonderful Promises

As we earnestly contend for the faith we can also revel in the wonderful promises and truths Jude gives us at the conclusion of his short epistle. *"But you, beloved, building yourselves up on your most holy faith, praying in the Holy Spirit, keep yourselves in the love of God, looking for the mercy of our Lord Jesus Christ unto eternal life. And on some have compassion, making a distinction; but others save with fear, pulling them out of the fire, hating even the garment defiled by the flesh. Now to Him who is able to keep you from stumbling, And to present you faultless before the presence of His glory with exceeding joy, To God our Savior, Who alone is wise, Be glory and majesty, Dominion and power, Both now and forever. Amen." Jude 20-25.*

Valid Communication

Presenting truth, contending for truth and exposing error - in a debated format, open discussion, or in written form is a valid means of communication - if it is done right. When it gets twisted to become self-seeking, mean-spirited and intent on victory at any cost is when debate is bad. I often participated in the "Man and the Christian Worldview Symposiums" in Yalta and Simferopol, Ukraine (on the Crimean peninsula) where we had open discussions, lively debates, and clarifying disagreements. The founder, Georges Carillet, moderated and reminded us often to speak with kindness and respect to the other person, no matter how much we disagreed on viewpoint. Only about one third of the participants were committed Christians. Many were Marxist atheists with strong, evolutionistic perspectives, some came from New Age perspectives, and some came from traditional Orthodox backgrounds with theistic evolutionist pre-suppositions. At times the debates became heated, yet through it all in the few days we spent together each year, we became friends through honest sharing in our presentations and debates (plus laughter at mealtimes). One medical doctor/professor, who claimed to be an atheist, and a philosophy professor, who at first came with the purpose of convincing us to believe atheistic Marxism, (but his worldview radically changed from the symposiums and the books I gave him, including "The Case for Christ"), would greet me with open arms and a hug when they saw me again. I pray for them and many others.

4. **My fourth purpose for this book is to help prepare believers to be bold witnesses for Jesus Christ and to be ready to give clear answers to tough questions.** The apostle Peter wrote, *"But sanctify the Lord God in your hearts, and always be ready to give a defense to everyone who asks you a reason for the hope that is in you, with meekness and fear; having a good conscience, that when they defame you as evildoers, those who revile your good conduct in Christ may be ashamed. For it is better, if it is the will of God, to suffer for doing good than for doing evil." 1 Peter 3:15-17 (NKJV)* For a fuller treatment of this purpose, please see my book, *Ready to Give An Answer*, or Jeff Vines' excellent book, *Dinner with Skeptics*. As we pursue this purpose we need to remember three powerful principles:

   a. **We only get one performance on the stage of this life, so perform well for the audience of One. We are not here to please men, but to please Almighty God.** Peter ended up denying Christ when by fear he conformed to peer pressure. I have too – how about you? Peter repented. I repented. Have you?

   b. *"Only one life, twill soon be past – only what's done for Christ will last." - Missionary C.T. Studd.* A practical application of this principal is found in an outline I heard from Adrian Rogers:

Jesus:

Desire Him Pre-eminently!

Seek Him passionately!

Trust Him perpetually!

    c.   *"He is no fool who gives what he cannot keep to gain what he cannot lose."* *Missionary martyr Jim Elliot*

Seek to be Discerning

To you who are fellow Christians, please take note that everyone who asks you a question, especially a tough question, is not necessarily looking for an answer. It is important to seek to discern the motive of the questioner. Why? Because it's easy to waste hours trying to answer questions for people who aren't looking for answers. I know from experience with those who were looking for excuses or looking for money, etc.

How do you know if the inquirer is serious? If he listens to your answer, if he asks more questions about the same subject, if he is willing to do some "homework" (like reading an article or book, listening to a CD, or watching a video on that topic) he probably is truly seeking answers. However, if you start to answer his question and he suddenly asks you a question on a different subject before you even have the chance to answer his first question, he isn't looking for answers. He is probably looking for excuses for his rebellion. When you start to answer his "tough question", you are taking away his excuse, so he throws you another "tough question" to try to stump you. It may be a game to him. It would be a good idea to switch to asking him some questions. Jesus was a master at questions and stories. Ray Comfort and Kirk Cameron have excellent input in "The Way of the Master" DVD series. Here is a list of questions that I have used to engage people both in private conversations and in classroom settings.

REFLECTION & RELATIONSHIP QUESTIONS

1. Would you like to be able to build strong, true, lasting relationships in your life?

        a. Good relationships in your family

        b. Good friendships

        c. Good romance leading to a good marriage

        d. Good relationship with Almighty God

2. Which of the above-mentioned relationships do you believe is the most important? Why?

3. To build good relationships, shouldn't you first be concerned with building good character?

4. If you want to have good friends, shouldn't you become a good friend?

5. Do you consider yourself a good person? Why or why not?

6. By what standard do you measure what is good and what is bad?

7. If you died today and stood before Almighty God,

what would you say if He asks you, "Why should I let you into my heaven?

8. What standard does Jesus hold up as good? (Jesus said: *"Be perfect – as My Father in heaven is perfect!"* and *"There is none good but one!" – God!*)

9. Have you ever violated any of God's commands? Lied? Cheated? Stolen? Lusted? Envied? Used God's name in vain? If so, and you are not forgiven, did you know that your destiny is hell – not heaven?

10. Would you like to know how you can be forgiven and be given the power to live an abundant life? Explain the gospel – (I Corinthians 15:1-8) Death for our sins – burial – resurrection!

How we respond:

Acts 16:31 – *"Believe on the Lord Jesus Christ, and you will be saved..." (NIV)*

In the above scripture there is one command and one promise. What is the command?

What is the promise?

Acts 2:38: "...Repent, and let every one of you be baptized in the name of Jesus Christ for the remission of sins; and you shall receive the gift of the Holy Spirit." (NIV)

In the above scripture there are two commands and two promises.

What are the two commands?

What are the two promises?

What are the necessary conclusions?

CONFRONTING THE BASIC QUESTIONS
(Don't Run From the Essential Issues!)

There are at least six basic questions which every human being asks himself (or herself). This is part of what distinguishes us as human beings---animals do not ask such questions. Here are the questions:

1. Where did I come from?	Origin
2. Why am I here?	Purpose
3. Who am I really?	Identity
4. Is there meaning to life?	Reality
5. Where am I going?	Destiny
6. How do I know how I ought to live?	Morality

Chapter 1: Purpose and Passion

If a student goes through educational training for many years, even including graduate studies after college or university, yet never has any serious examination of the basic questions of life, is he truly educated? If educational institutions only provide naturalistic/evolutionary answers to these basic issues of life, while not even considering the evidence for a Designer outside of life, have they truly educated their students?

There is only one book which has adequate and valid answers to all of these fundamental questions, yet it is ignored, spurned, and mocked in many institutions of learning. The Bible is consistently the best-selling book in the world (without even a close second) – and for good reason. It is the Book that not only answers the questions of the mind, but also touches the heart and reaches to the deepest yearnings of the soul, longing for forgiveness, peace and joy.

I heard a story on "Love Worth Finding" that went something like this:

A college professor asked his students how many of them read the Bible. Several responded that they did. Then he asked, "How many of you understand what you read in the Bible?" Only one young man responded that "Yes", he was understanding what he read. The professor, in a condescending way, replied that he read the Bible himself – but didn't understand it. Then he asked the student, "How is it that you understand the Bible even though I can't understand it?" The student responded, "Sir, with all due respect. I want to point out to you that the Bible contains God's love letters to His family members. The reason you don't understand is because you are reading someone else's mail."

The Word of God is sharper than a two-edged sword, and the Spirit of God uses it like a scalpel to cut out sin before he uses it as a healing balm. Those who are not willing to deal with their sin **will not** understand His deep truths until they are willing to accept the simple truth that they are sinners in desperate need of a Savior. For those who refuse to admit that their own pet sins are a serious and deadly cancer - despicable in the eyes of God – much of the Bible will remain a monumental mystery – incomprehensible nonsense.

The Bible

This Book Contains:

"The mind of God, the state of man, the way of salvation, doom of sinners, and happiness of believers. Its doctrines are holy, its precepts are binding, its histories are true, and its decisions are immutable. Read it to be wise, believe it to be safe, and practice it to be holy. It contains light to direct you, food to support you and comfort to cheer you. It is the traveler's map, the pilgrim's staff, the pilot's compass, the soldier's sword and the Christian's charter. Here Paradise is restored, Heaven opened, and the gates of hell disclosed. Christ is its Grand Subject, our good its design, and the glory of God its end. It should fill the memory, rule the heart, and guide the feet. Read it slowly, frequently, prayerfully. It is a mine of wealth, a paradise of glory, and a river of pleasure. It is given you in life, will be open at the Judgment and be remembered forever. It involves the highest responsibility, rewards the greatest labor, and condemns all who trifle with its holy contents." – Author Unknown

Is this book what its writers claimed - the inspired Word of Almighty God? After all, He created us for a reason. Doesn't it make sense that He would want to communicate with us? Or is the Bible just a book of myths, fables, and lies? If the writers were not recording God's Word to them, they were lying. Herbert Spencer[2] spent

---

2   *What is especially impressive about the amazing way that Herbert Spencer's research corresponds with Genesis 1:1 is that he was not doing his research to confirm the truth of the Bible. Herbert Spencer was a strongly committed evolutionist. Here is a brief overview about him from Wikipedia: "Herbert Spencer (27 April 1820 - 8 December 1903) was an English philosopher, biologist, anthropologist, sociologist, and prominent classical liberal political theorist of the Victorian era.*
Spencer developed an all-embracing conception of evolution as the progressive development of the physical world, biological organisms, the human mind, and

years as a research scientist, analyzing the universe before concluding that the universe has five basic components:

1. Time   2. Force   3. Energy   4. Space   5. Matter

Is it only by pure coincidence that the very first verse of the Bible contains all five of these components? Consider that Moses penned these words nearly 3,500 years before Herbert Spencer did his research and took up his pen to write his conclusions. Take note and consider carefully:

1. In the beginning	time
2. God	force
3. created	energy
4. the heavens	space
5. and the earth	matter

Did Almighty God inspire Moses to write these amazing words---or is this just luck? Coincidence?

Was it also pure coincidence that Moses wrote down that God commanded His people to wash their hands thoroughly in running water after touching a dead body – and that he told them that if they obeyed His commands they would not have the diseases

---

human culture and societies. He was 'an enthusiastic exponent of evolution' and even 'wrote about evolution before Darwin did'. As a polymath, he contributed to a wide range of subjects, including ethics, religion, anthropology, economics, political theory, philosophy, biology, sociology, and psychology. During his lifetime he achieved tremendous authority, mainly in English-speaking academia. 'The only other English philosopher to have achieved anything like such widespread popularity was Bertrand Russell, and that was in the 20th century.' Spencer was 'the single most famous European intellectual in the closing decades of the nineteenth century' but his influence declined sharply after 1900…

Spencer is best known for coining the expression 'survival of the fittest', which he did in Principles of Biology (1864), after reading Charles Darwin's On the Origin of Species. This term strongly suggests natural selection, yet as Spencer extended evolution into realms of sociology and ethics, he also made use of Lamarckism…"

that plagued the heathen nations around them? It took medical science nearly 3,400 years to catch up to the wisdom recorded in God's Word. Even in 1848 in Vienna, when Dr. Semmelweis had proven that doctors could reduce postpartum fever and death by just washing their hands between patients, he was laughed at with scorn! For many more years thousands of patients continued to die from diseases that were spread by doctors examining patients with unwashed hands after conducting autopsies on corpses. Finally the truth could be ignored no longer and the rule became firmly established and accepted that doctors must wash thoroughly in running water after autopsies--resulting in a drastic drop in death and disease rates in hospitals. **As always, the truth which was clearly articulated in God's Word was spurned and mocked by the world - to its own detriment.**

Is There Truth – Truly?

I've been writing repeatedly about my concern that I "speak the truth in love", so does this mean that I am so naïve that I believe in truth – actual, real, solid TRUTH? Yes, I do! Truly! Certainly! Absolutely! For those of you who respect the Bible, consider these two powerful passages. *"For what if some did not believe? Will their unbelief make the faithfulness of God without effect? Certainly not! Indeed, let God be true but every man a liar. As it is written: 'That You may be justified in Your words, and may overcome when You are judged.'" Romans 3:3-4. "For this reason we also thank God without ceasing, because when you received the word of God which you heard from us, you welcomed it not as the word of men, but as it is in truth, the word of God, which also effectively works in you who believe." 1 Thessalonians 2:13.*

The Relevance of Relativity

You may be wondering how it is possible to persuade people with truth or expose error when the post-modern concept that "all truth is relative" is so prevalent. It seems to be everywhere, especially in academia. Allan Bloom's book, *The Closing of the American Mind*, begins with the statement that practically every student who enters college or university already believes that all truth is relative. Of course the flip side of "all truth is relative" is "there is no absolute truth!" If someone states that all truth is relative, you just may want to ask if his statement is actually true or relatively true. The statement is a self defeating contradiction! **How can he positively state that all truth is relative when he is asserting that his own statement is absolutely true?** If he says, "There is no absolute truth," he has just asserted an absolute statement about what he perceives to be true. **Just ask, "Are you absolutely sure?"** If he has a sense of humor, he may laugh. If he doesn't, he may look horrified or embarrassed. His erroneous stronghold has just been demolished. Postmodernism is still parading arguments that have deceived millions even though they were dead on arrival because they committed suicide!!

How Ironic!!!

The naturalist (atheist) argues for absolutes when it comes to God's laws of nature, but argues against absolutes when it comes to God's laws of ethics. He denies the possibility of miracles because they are exceptions to the laws of nature, but he denies absolutes in moral matters because of the possibility that there may be exceptions. So the "liberal" naturalist promotes "situational ethics" while at the same time rigidly affirming that "laws of nature" are absolute. Isn't this revealing to his true motives???

My friend, if you still want to cling to the concept that "all truth is relative and there is no absolute truth", try using that idea in court. Imagine what you would do if you are innocent, but being charged with a serious crime. Now you are called to the witness stand and asked, "Do you swear to tell the truth, the whole truth, and nothing but the truth, so help you God?" Are you going to reply to the bailiff, the judge, and the jury, "No, sir, I cannot do that because there is no such thing as absolute truth"? **The bottom line**

is - do you actually believe what you claim to believe when it comes down to the nitty-gritty, real life situations?

This issue is critical because in spiritual warfare Satan and his emissaries desperately want to destroy truth. Why? Jesus said, *"I am the Way, the TRUTH, and the Life"! John 14:6.* He also prayed, *"Sanctify them by Your truth. Your word is truth." John 17:17 (NKJV).* It is satanic to seek to destroy absolute truth. **God's Word is absolute truth! Jesus Himself is absolute truth**.

Do you find it surprising that Pilate asked Jesus, 'What is truth', then walked away without waiting for an answer? Pilate didn't recognize TRUTH when he was staring Him in the face. Pilate wasn't looking for an answer; he was looking for an excuse. Oh, yes, he was looking for an answer to his dilemma – a way out of his bad situation – but he wasn't looking for transforming TRUTH that demands repentance but gives wonderful grace and refreshing, life changing forgiveness. To Pilate's credit he did tell the religious leaders that he found no fault in Jesus.

Friend, what are you looking for – answers or excuses? Either way you will find what you are looking for! *"Seek and you shall find." Matthew 7:7.* Are you looking for a way to hang onto your pet sin and still slip into Heaven's gate, or transforming TRUTH that demands repentance?

The Crucial Factor of the Will

Even as God Himself is three in one, and every human being is three in one (spirit, soul, and body), even so the human mind (heart) is also three in one – intellect, emotion, and will. Are you sometimes perplexed – even confused – by the fact that highly intelligent people can believe opposite and conflicting ideas about the same subject; for example, the existence of God. Please remember – and **never** forget - that every decision any human being makes is more than an intellectual choice! Consider how advertisers entice you to buy products. Do they appeal only to your intellect? If it is a new car, the ad may say, "See the elegance! Feel the power! Smell the leather!" Are they appealing to your intellect? Often we decide to buy when our **emotion** overpowers our **intellect** to bring us to be **willing** to part with the money – then we justify the purchase with intellectual sounding reasons (excuses). What makes us think that our faith choices are pure intellect?

Can We Know Truth?

So is it really possible to know truth? Yes, it is! We have the Word of the Genius Himself Who created every one of us. Jesus said, "*If anyone wills to do His will, he shall know concerning the doctrine, whether it is from God or whether I speak on My own authority.*" John 7:17. The translation of this verse in the NIV reads, "*Anyone who chooses to do the will of God will find out whether my teaching comes from God or whether I speak on my own.*" Now consider the NLT, "*Anyone who wants to do the will of God will know whether my teaching is from God or is merely my own.*" This is the most crucial test of truth – being **willing** to do the will of God!!

The Crucial Test

Adrian Rogers told on a broadcast, how he confronted an atheist with this test. First he asked the atheist, "Do you know that God does not exist?" to which the atheist replied, "yes". Then Adrian asked him if he knew everything there is to know in the entire universe. To this question the atheist quickly replied, "No, of course not." Then Adrian asked him if there is the possibility that God does exist in the vast area of knowledge that he doesn't know. This question motivated the atheist to renounce his atheist position and switch to being an agnostic. Adrian resisted the temptation to clarify to him that the word "agnostic" is transliterated from the Greek language into English, and literally means "not know", but if you take the same meaning from the Latin language, the word would be "ignoramus". However, Adrian did ask him if he would be willing to find out if God is real if there were a method by which he could actually find out for sure. The agnostic agreed that he would. Adrian asked if he would be willing to sign a statement agreeing to this test – then he showed him John 7:17 and pointed out that if he is willing to **do** the will of God he will truly **know** that the teaching of Jesus does come from God. That, my friend, is the crucial test! When I was willing to submit my stubborn will to the will of God, then I learned that God is real. God is good, and Jesus' Word is true. I **know** that Jesus is The Way! Jesus is The Truth! Jesus is The Life!

I don't know if the agnostic actually signed the agreement, but he apparently did agree to the test. Adrian said the man called him later and thanked him profusely. By the way, the man originally contacted Adrian Rogers asking him if he would counsel his wife because she was threatening to commit suicide. It turned out that she was contemplating suicide because her husband was being abusive to her. **Praise God for the transforming power of Jesus! Adrian Rogers also made the astute comment that an atheist/humanist/agnostic cannot find enough evidence to believe in God for the same reason that a thief can't find a policeman!**

WHAT FOUNDATIONS ARE BEING DE-STROYED?

BELIEF IN ETERNITY

BELIEF IN MORALITY

BELIEF IN ACCOUNTABILITY

BELIEF IN CHARITY

Chapter 1: Purpose and Passion

The Problem of Evolutionism

Of all the pernicious problems we face in the cultural clashes of the twenty-first century in the United States – and worldwide – probably the most pervasive, persuasive, and pernicious of all is the coarse, crude curse of evolutionism. This subtle lie of Satan has been effectively exposed and demolished in Bruce Malone's books and DVDs, as well as in the early chapters of *Ready to Give an Answer* and many of the references we give in the back of this book. I will not go into great detail here about this evil deception because it is so thoroughly demolished in those other works, yet I believe it deserves mention as the foundation for almost every one of the other issues and cultural clashes. Why should I make such a bold accusation against such a "harmless" theory? Don't I realize that Charles Darwin is highly honored in Great Britain, the United States, and much of the rest of the world? Following his death, clergymen in England exalted his status by burying his body in Westminster Chapel – the same place where David Livingston and other great men were buried. *Why would any church or Christian organization of any stripe honor the memory of a man who rejected and renounced Biblical truth and Christianity, became an agnostic (polite terminology for atheist), and popularized the anti-Christ doctrine of his paternal grandfather, Erasmus Darwin?* Appalling! Yet it's true! And it is still happening. There are multiplied hundreds of churches and so-called "Christian" leaders who celebrate Darwin Day on February 9. Beware! As with the Trojan Horse and the conquest of Babylon by the Medes and Persians, **the enemy is far more dangerous when he is already inside your supposed walls of protection. Beware of any church or "Christian" institution that honors Darwin and promotes any shade of evolutionism.**

Could it be that the decision of some English clergy to honor Charles Darwin by burying his body in Westminster Chapel was incredibly naïve and foolish? When most Englanders listened to Neville Chamberlain's compromising advice about Hitler instead of

Winston Churchill's strong warnings, they were acting ridiculously foolish, but not as foolish as exalting Charles Darwin's' memory to equality with David Livingston! David Livingston brought light and life and truth to multitudes through medicine, ministry and the Master. Charles Darwin brought doom, death and destruction to millions with his abominable false religion of evolutionism. (See Chapter 3 of *Ready to Give an Answer,* entitled "Catastrophic Consequences of Darwinism". If you do not have a printed copy of *Ready to Give an Answer,* you can read it on our website at www.overseasoutreach.com, or on the website for White Fields Overseas Evangelism at www.white-fields.org.) Hitler, Stalin, and Mao Tse-tung could **never** have murdered millions as they did without the pernicious lie of evolutionism! If we teach kids they are nothing but animals, why are we surprised when they act like animals??? To their great credit, Englanders did wake up to Winston Churchill's earnest pleas and strong warnings about the very real threat of Hitler and his Nazi forces in time to change the course of history. Will enough Americans be that wise concerning Darwin and evolutionism? Friend, if you are feeling defensive about my labeling of evolutionism as a lie, please skip now to the last appendix to this chapter and read the quotations of admissions by various evolutionists.

In the early 1800's and even in the 1850's Christianity was a thriving, vital force in England – and all of Great Britain. Spiritually, socially, politically, psychologically, financially – in every conceivable way the Bible and vibrant Christian faith was a vital force. Today in England, Great Britain, and all of Europe the evidences of vibrant Christian faith as a potent influence in the culture are nearly extinct. Great Britain was once the greatest missionary producer in the world – now it is a spiritual wasteland. In Darwin's time, multiple thousands crowded into London Tabernacle to hear Charles H. Spurgeon preach God's Word, and there were other large congregations as well. Now multitudes of former church buildings have been turned into mosques, museums, and market places. You will have to search to find the few vibrant congregations of committed Christians. Do you suppose that it is mere coincidence that Charles Darwin's most famous book, "The Origin of Species" was published in 1859 and passionately promoted by Thomas Huxley and other evolutionists who rejected the Biblical account of origins and the Flood? Then in 1872 his second most famous science fiction book, "The Descent of Man" was published, which promoted the idea more directly that mankind descended from apes (or a common ancestor to the apes). Do you know that Darwin's ideas were most strongly opposed by scientists who knew the scientific laws of biogenesis proven conclusively by Louis Pasteur? They knew that "life comes only from life", "every creature reproduces after its own kind" (with a great deal of variety within kinds), and "every effect must have an adequate cause". These are laws of science that the fantasy of evolutionism blatantly violates – yet the voices of reason and fact were gradually overwhelmed by the voices of rebels against Almighty God – men who wanted a "scientific" excuse to justify their immoral lifestyles. Now the more our crazy culture promotes evolutionism, the more we find ourselves swimming in the cesspools of sinful degradation. The clergymen who honored Darwin will hang their heads in shame on the day of Judgment. *"When we compromise, we become part of the problem we once sought to solve." - Kenneth Beckman.*

Please realize that when I refer to compromise with this quotation I am referring to compromise on clearly stated Biblical doctrines – not on incidentals. There is a summary of Biblical principles, which someone traced back to the 1300's, which reads as follows:

In essentials – unity

In incidentals (opinions) – liberty

In all things - charity

Evolutionism

Perhaps you are wondering why I use the term evolutionism. It's because the "ism" on the end of a word identifies it as a religion (or belief system). Humanism has been recognized and accepted as a religion by the government of the United States of America. Belief in evolutionism is one of the basic doctrines of the religion of humanism. Actually and logically the expelling of Christmas programs and Christian symbols from public schools isn't because religion is now restricted **from** schools, it's because the religion of humanism is now deeply entrenched **in** our public schools. It is Christ and Christianity the humanists want expelled. This is nothing new. The entrenched religion of corrupted Judaism expelled Jesus and his apostles from their synagogues. Jesus said, 'If they hated Me, they will hate you." Sometimes the humanist religion will tolerate Islam, occultism, shamanism and witchcraft in the school systems without a fight because they all see Jesus and Biblical Christianity as their common enemy.

Evolutionism is a worldview religion that its proponents love to parade as objective science. Therefore, in their writings they may refer to "evolution versus creationism" and equate it with science versus religion. The fact is that **both** evolutionism and creationism are religions! They are worldviews! They are philosophies. They deal with many scientific subjects, but at the core they are both belief systems. The difference is that we who are Christians freely acknowledge that we have a belief system, for *"without faith it is impossible to please Him." Hebrews 11:6.* The proponents of evolutionism are often so adamant in their belief system that they refuse to look at contrary evidence, yet they are also often blind to their own condition in believing evolutionism to be pure science, not a religion. Evolution is "science falsely so-called".

Friend, if you are tempted to try to reconcile evolutionism with creationism through theistic evolutionism, please consider this phrase in its context of strong warning. Since the word "science" literally means knowledge, here it is in the NKJV: *"O Timothy! Guard what was committed to your trust, avoiding the profane and idle babblings and contradictions of what is falsely called knowledge— by professing it some have strayed concerning the faith. Grace be with you. Amen." 1 Timothy 6:20-21.* I tried to reconcile creationism with evolutionism. It is futility!

One example comes to my mind immediately. In one of Don Patton's seminars (where I was physically present) he told about an experience he had while doing research on dinosaur tracks and human tracks together at the Paluxy River near Glen Rose, Texas. They had a couple of curiosity seeker guests with them who were not part of the research team. There was a young man in his late teens who was not a Christian, but very interested in the creationism vs. evolutionism controversy. He was well aware of the reports of fossilized human footprints being found in the same strata of rock as fossilized dinosaur footprints, and the monumental implications of those reports.[3]

---

3   *Evolutionists were (and are) adamant about their commitment to a philosophically manufactured geological timetable (supported by circular reasoning – the rocks are dated by the fossils in them and the fossils are dated by the rocks in which they are found)! They confidently assert that it is impossible for human beings and dinosaurs to have lived together on earth at the same time. Why not? Because the dinosaurs died out sixty-five million years before man "evolved". Even though they may espouse relativism in morals and social issues, they proclaim this dogma as absolute truth. It is part of their evolutionistic faith! They cannot and will not compromise on their old age doctrine for the age of the earth (and universe) because they realize that their evolutionistic fantasy hinges on long ages. (Evolutionism technically does not deserve the term theory. It is not even a good hypothesis. Fantasy is a more accurate term.) On the other hand, the Bible declares that all land animals and man were created by Almighty God on the sixth day. Did you get that? Dinosaurs and human beings were created the same day! (See Genesis 1:24-31)*
I am well aware of the controversy about the human footprints in stone at the Paluxy River being genuine footprints, but I believe the evidence that they are actually human footprints is rock solid. I'm very disappointed that many creationists have backed off and if you want to know more about it you are welcome to write to me at overseasoutreach@earthlink.net or P.O. Box 1224, Nampa, ID 83653.
As a final note, my friend and co-worker for Northwest Science Museum, Stan Lutz, is a paleontologist who made molds (casts) of the footprints. He is absolutely 100% convinced that the human tracks are genuine. So are other creation scientists

The other guest with them was an older man who professed to be an honest seeker after truth, but in reality was a committed, dogmatic evolutionist who was not open to the real truth. The evidence of his unwillingness to see the actual, factual truth came out when Don Patton and his team **did** discover another human footprint fossilized in the same strata of the rock where the dinosaur footprints were found. Don pointed out the track to the younger man, who promptly put his own bare foot into the impression and said, "It's the same size as my foot (9D if I remember correctly)!" Don also invited the older man to come observe the human track, but that man turned the other way and refused to even look at the track! Why would anyone refuse to look at what he professed to be seeking? Because it would blow the lid off his assumptions, his biases and his chosen lifestyle. It would destroy his worldview. The bottom line is that he didn't want to repent. Besides, by refusing to look he could go back to his buddies and say, "I didn't see any human footprints." In contrast, the young man was convinced by the evidence, repented, and became a believer.

Another issue that Don Patton clarified in his seminar was the false claim by some evolutionists that the human footprints were deceptions carved by creationists. Don said the human tracks in question were fossilized in the riverbed (the flow of the river had been diverted), so the creationist team dug back the bank where the tracks ended – underneath they found the trail of tracks continuing!

Dr. Don Patton is a geologist, archaeologist and paleontologist with many and varied accomplishments to his record. You can check his website at www.bible.ca. If you want to write to him to verify my report of his experience, his email address is dpatton693@aol.com.

---

who examined the footprints before erosion blurred them.

What about Theistic Evolutionism?

Theistic evolutionism is the concept that God used evolution to create everything. Wrong! **God did not use evolution to create anything! Here are my reasons:**

1. God inspired the writers of the Bible to tell us what He did, when He did it, and how He did it. He spoke – and it was done! When? In the beginning! Please, please do not twist the Word of God to try to make it fit into a biased, compromising position in order to try to please the evolutionists. They will probably laugh at you anyway. *Psalm 33:6 says, "By the word of the LORD the heavens were made, and all the host of them by the breath of His mouth."* What is it that is so hard to understand? It isn't the wording – that is plain enough. It is only hard to understand if you do not want to accept such an awesome, powerful God as your Creator and Ruler! *Psalm 33:8-9 says, "Let all the earth fear the LORD; let all the inhabitants of the world stand in awe of Him. For He spoke, and it was done; He commanded, and it stood fast."*

2. Creation is not evolution! Evolution is not creation. They are opposite and opposing worldviews which do not mix logically or realistically.

    If you tell me that your son was playing basketball without a basketball it would be more logical and reasonable than saying that God created by evolution. I can picture a boy pretending to dribble and shoot a basketball, even though he doesn't have a basketball. It is his fantasy. Theistic evolutionism, like atheistic evolutionism, is fantasy, not reality. You can as easily drink a huge boulder as you can logically reconcile the chasm between evolutionism and creationism. (For further confirmation see Without Excuse, The Collapse of Evolution, Why do Men Believe Evolution against All Odds? and other references in the back of this book.)

3. There are some things God cannot do because they are a violation of His own character. God cannot lie. Therefore, God did not use evolution. He told us what He did – He spoke and it was done! That is the power of His Word. He does not violate His own Word.

When Jesus spoke to the wind and the waves "Peace – be still", they obeyed His voice. Instantly! What if it had taken two days? Two hours? Would His disciples have been awestruck? NO! That could have happened naturally. The wind and waves recognized the voice of their Creator – and obeyed, instantly! When authority speaks, things happen. He is not some "progressive creator" who takes millions of years to get anything done by trial and error.

By the way, how is your OQ (Obedience Quotient)? When He speaks, do you obey? Instantly?

Totally Incompatible

Famous British evolutionist, Sir Arthur Keith, wrote the fore-word to the 100th anniversary edition of Charles Darwin's infamous book, *The Origin of Species by Means of Natural Selection or the Preservation of Favored Races in the Struggle for Life.* (Yes, that is the actual title! It's no wonder evolutionists don't like to use the full title.) **Keith wrote, "I have come to the conclusion that the law of Christ is incompatible with the law of evolution. Nay, the two laws are at war with one another."** In this point I am in full agree-ment with Sir Arthur Keith – and I am saddened by the fact that this evolutionist had more perception than many Christians. For very good reasons I am adamantly opposed to the compromising concept of theistic evolutionism and its side-kick called "progres-sive creationism". (In fact, I'm very leery of anything labeled "pro-gressive" in our corrupted culture. It is far more likely to be regres-sive and suppressive of any hard truth from the Word of God!) *"He spoke, and it was done; He commanded, and it stood fast"* was an instantaneous, supernatural, miraculous demonstration of the power of Almighty God – not the millions (or billions) of years of trial and error and death plus suffering proposed by "progressive creationists". What is progressive about believing that God was too dumb to get it right the first time? Could this be a subtle (or not so subtle) form of idolatry for those who want to make a god in their own image rather than accepting the majestic God revealed in Scripture and humbly bowing in awe and reverence before Him?

Yes, I do speak and write strongly against the stronghold of evolutionism for many reasons. Historically, the proponents of Darwinism saw it as their intellectual smokescreen to escape from having to answer to God for their sin. If evolutionism is true, there is no sin! (Animals do not sin – they just act on their impulses.) If evolution is true, there is no God (in spite of the feeble, futile efforts of theistic evolutionists). Charles Darwin himself began with a theistic evolutionist preface in his books, but became an agnostic (which was more acceptable to him than proclaiming himself to be an atheist).

Julian Huxley, grandson of Thomas Huxley (Darwin's "bull-dog"), was the speaker for the 100th anniversary celebration of the publication of *The Origin of Species*. In 1959 Julian was perhaps the most prominent evolutionist alive. His answer to an interview question upon that occasion may shock you. He was asked why Charles Darwin's most famous book was so quickly and widely accepted. He did **not** say that it was because the scientific evidence was so convincing or overpowering. In fact, the scientists in Darwin's time were his most adamant critics and opponents. **What Julian Huxley did say was that they "leapt" for "The Origin" because the idea of God interfered with their sexual preferences. I thank God that he gave an honest answer! The motivation behind the acceptance of evolutionism is sex, not science!!!** They didn't want God telling them what to do! It is exactly what the apostle Paul described in the first chapter of Romans.[4] R.C.

4   *In Romans 1:16-32, Paul shows clearly that perverted spirituality leads to perverted worship, which leads to perverted sexuality. Please read it carefully for yourself. There are now many in America and Europe who like to say, "I am*

Sproul candidly pointed out that when Bertrand Russell wrote his infamous book, *Why I am Not a Christian*, he conveniently left out the bottom line reason – his many adulteries. R.C. also noted that the flimsy excuses he did write down are easy to refute. Likewise, the flimsy excuses of today's blatant, aggressive atheists are easy to refute for those open to truth.

Evolutionism promotes doubt about God, denial of Truth, and deification of man. It inspires the arrogance of a haughty man to write "I am the Master of my fate. I am the Captain of my soul." (Poor soul – he has a sinful wretch for his master and captain!)

Evolutionists strongly reject "intelligent design" proponents as well as Biblical creationists because they easily recognize that where there is design there must be a Designer. Richard Dawkins says that intelligent people must recognize that apparent design is not really design (no matter how apparent)! Why? Because he "knows" that there is no Designer! Richard Dawkins is perhaps the most fla-grant and best known atheist in the world. He wrote that Darwin's theory of evolution makes it possible to be an intellectually fulfilled atheist. But how intellectually fulfilled can an honest man be when it is necessary to constantly twist the facts to fit with his presuppo-sitions? Francis Crick, co-discoverer of DNA, is also an evolution-ist. He did not write that the evidence for evolutionism is blatantly obvious to those who study science but rather that biologists must constantly remind themselves that what they are observing evolved – it was not designed. If it is obvious – why should they need to keep reminding themselves that it was not designed??? **Truly** every design points to a Designer.

The intricate design of a flower, an eye, or a symbiotic rela-
tionship between the bee and the flower point to a Genius who
a spiritual person" even though their spirituality may be Satan worship, pagan practices, Wicca (witchcraft), New Age distortions (I am god ... I am god!!!), etc. Isaiah 8:19-20 says, "And when they say to you, 'Seek those who are mediums and wizards, who whisper and mutter,' should not a people seek their God? Should they seek the dead on behalf of the living? To the law and to the testimony! If they do not speak according to this word, it is because there is no light in them."

designed us and everything in this vast universe for His purpose. Isn't it logical that such an intelligent Designer would give us an owner's manual to explain to us His purpose for designing us? He did! We call it The Bible (literally "The Book").

The Existence of God

Do you realize that it is impossible to prove that God doesn't exist? Why? Because it is a logical impossibility to prove a universal negative. Carl Sagan was smart enough to avoid the universal negative – but still made a blatant, impossible-to-prove statement when he boldly asserted at the opening of each program, "The cosmos is all there is – or ever will be". Do you recognize the fact is that he was stating his philosophical/religious creed before spinning his fantastic tale of evolutionism on his program "Cosmos"? Unfortunately he persuaded many gullible, receptive followers to his atheistic worldview. However they, and he, are without excuse. (Of course, he now knows better. He is dead. He is now a creationist.) I hope and pray you become not only a creationist, but also a committed Christian creationist before it is too late. The apostle Paul wrote, *"For the wrath of God is revealed from heaven against all ungodliness and unrighteousness of men, who suppress the truth in unrighteousness, because what may be known of God is manifest in them, for God has shown it to them. For since the creation of the world His invisible attributes are clearly seen, being understood by the things that are made, even His eternal power and Godhead, so that they are without excuse," Romans 1:18-20 (NKJV)* Paul also wrote, *"Therefore God also has highly exalted Him and given Him the name which is above every name, that at the name of Jesus every knee should bow, of those in heaven, and of those on earth, and of those under the earth, and that every tongue should confess that Jesus Christ is Lord, to the glory of God the Father." Philippians 2:9-11 (NKJV)* Do you want to confess Him as Creator and Lord **now** while you have the chance to accept Him as Savior and receive forgiveness – **or then, when He will be your final Judge and it is too late?** You may be wondering, "What should I do?" Those who heard the Apostle Peter's powerful message also asked that question. Please carefully and prayerfully consider his reply. *"'Therefore let all the house of Israel know assuredly that God has made this Jesus, whom you crucified, both Lord and Christ.' Now when they heard this, they were cut to the heart, and said to Peter and the rest of the apostles, 'Men and brethren, what shall we do?' Then Peter said to them, 'Repent, and let every one of you be baptized in the name of Jesus Christ for the remission of sins; and you shall receive the gift of the Holy Spirit.'" Acts 2:36-38 (NKJV)*

Do you understand **why** it is logically impossible to prove that God doesn't exist? **Because you would have to become God to prove He doesn't exist** – a logical impossibility. You would have to be everywhere in the universe simultaneously (that is omnipresent), and you would have to be able to function in every dimension simultaneously, plus you would have to be all knowing to know that God was not present in a different dimension than where you were presently searching. We function in a three dimension world. But God is Spirit and invisible to us unless He chooses to manifest Himself to us tangibly in some way. How many dimensions are there? God knows! We don't!

Atheists, agnostics and skeptics of various stripes often like to parade their skepticism toward God and the Bible as a badge of honor and intellectual superiority – yet the infallible Word of God says: *"The fool has said in his heart, 'There is no God." They are corrupt, they have done abominable works, there is none who does good. The LORD looks down from heaven upon the children of men, to see if there are any who understand, who seek God. They have all turned aside, they have together become corrupt; There is none who does good, no, not one. Have all the workers of iniquity no knowledge, who eat up my people as they eat bread, and do not call on the LORD? There they are in great fear, for God is with the generation of the righteous. You shame the counsel of the poor, but the LORD is his refuge." Psalm 14:1-6.*

MORAL OR AMORAL?

If this world – and the entire universe – is the result of an amoral, naturalistic process called evolution, then there is no logical basis to ask any moral question. You cannot logically reason from an amoral universe to a moral explanation for the existence of evil. Therefore, the question often asked by atheist philosophers (evolutionist/naturalist) is totally invalid. What question? "How can you Christians believe in a loving God when there is so much evil and suffering in this world?" Doesn't that question assume that there is reality to the concepts of "good" and "evil"? Definitely! Sorry – that is a moral question! An amoral universe has no room for moral questions!!!

Are You Following Where The Evidence Leads?

When the famous British atheist, Anthony Flew, turned away from his long-held and widely acclaimed allegiance to atheism, he was questioned why he would do such a thing. His reply was that he was compelled to follow where the evidence led. That is a very good reply! Are you following where the evidence leads??

I recently heard an interview with the now famous, converted atheist and popular author, Lee Strobel. Lee said that Anthony Flew was the most notorious philosophical atheist of the twentieth century (Richard Dawkins may now occupy that infamous role). When Lee heard the report that Anthony Flew had renounced his atheism and had become a believer in God, he found it very hard to believe, so he searched for the opportunity to interview Anthony Flew for himself, and asked him the question, "Why?" Anthony Flew told him that it was because of the biological complexity that could not happen by chance. Anthony Flew even wrote a book entitled, *There Is a God*.

It is also significant that Anthony Flew had debated the well known apologist for Biblical Christianity and specialist on the evidences for the resurrection of Jesus Christ, Gary Habbermas. Obviously, Gary's winsome manner and Christian courtesy, coupled with absolutely overwhelming and powerful evidence that the "historical Christ" is actually Jesus Christ revealed in the Scriptures, had a profound impact on Anthony Flew. Gary Habbermas became a friend to Anthony Flew and carried on quite a correspondence with him. Debate, when carried out in a proper manner with love and respect in the power of the Holy Spirit, is a valid means of communication.

Did Anthony Flew ever move beyond intellectual acceptance of the existence of God to genuine, deep repentance and commitment to the Lord Jesus before he died? I don't know. Have you?

Logic

It is not illogical to believe in one, true Almighty God, who is infinite, all wise and all knowing – and who is the ultimate first cause of all things. Many of the greatest intellectuals of all time believed and **do** believe in Him. (I give many examples in the second chapter of *Ready to Give an Answer*. You can access it on our website at www.overseasoutreach.com.) Why is it logical and absolutely scientific to believe He is the ultimate first cause even though we cannot see Him? Because it is a basic scientific law that every effect must have an adequate cause. To be an adequate cause for this vast universe with its delicate balance and intricate designs for life on earth, He has to be the all-powerful, all-wise, all-knowing genius who is also infinite and eternal. He has to be a thinker – because we can think! He has to be moral – because we have moral consciences. He has to be a person – because we have personality.

Adequate Cause

Let's focus for just a few moments on one aspect - the statement, "He has to be the all-powerful, all-wise, all-knowing genius Who is also infinite and eternal. He has to be a thinker – because we can think." Contemplate the amazing capacity of the human brain for a moment – then compare that with the incomprehensible genius of God. Memory is one example. Of the billions and billions of words, thoughts, and visual images which have passed through your brain the past year, 10 years, 20 – even 50 years or more – your memory is capable of recalling vividly and in precise detail some significant events or words from past years –even in your childhood – which you will never forget. Do you remember where you were and what you were doing when you first heard or saw the news about the 9/11/01 attacks on America? What about the attempted assassination of Ronald Reagan, or the actual assassination of John F. Kennedy? There is no invention of man – no computer anywhere that can match the capacity of the human brain. **That human brain has to have an adequate cause.** God Almighty is beyond awesome! His mind designed the billions of stars, galaxies, planets, comets, moons – and our solar system, and His spoken Word called them into existence. He said, "Let there be light – and there was light." Genesis 1:3. Instantly – on the first day of Creation! Scientists cannot number the vastness of the galaxies, let alone the individual stars –yet He calls them all by name. He knows your name too – and He is calling you Home. He knows your every thought, hope, dream, longing, hurt, frustration – and your every sin and rebellion. But He loves you infinitely and took a human form so He could shed His blood to pay the penalty for your sin. Think of the capacity of His mind to know your every thought simultaneously with every thought of billions of other human beings, both living and dead! Think of the capacity of His heart to hurt for your hurts and care for your concerns simultaneously with caring for every other human being - and every creature in His vast creation.

Josh McDowell's, Evidence that Demands a Verdict, masterfully shows the intricate design of God in His infallible Word and amazing fulfilled prophecies. Bruce Malone, Richard and Tina Kleiss, and Julie Von Vett masterfully show the scientific genius of God in biology, botany, astronomy, geology, chemistry, etc. in their intriguing books, A Closer Look at the Evidence and Inspired Evidence.

Each of the last two books has a devotional thought for each day of the year, which demonstrates the power, wisdom, and genius of our Mastermind Creator. (You can contact me – or Bruce Malone – for copies at Search for the Truth Ministries -www.searchforthetruth. net.)

Schizophrenic Aeronautic Engineering

Have you read or heard that aeronautic engineers are carefully studying the amazing flight designs of hummingbirds and dragon flies in order to improve the designs and capabilities of helicopters? The mobility and flight flexibility of these creatures is astounding. Does it seem schizophrenic for the evolutionistic scientists to be studying the intricate designs of creatures which they believe evolved by random chance with **no intelligent design**???

Yearning with No Satisfaction on this Earth

Do you experience a strange nostalgia when you hear the haunting lyrics of the song, "Memories," which Andy Williams popularized with his captivating voice? "Memories ... memories – etched upon the pages of my mind." Do you sense an other-world ache and yearning when you sit in a funeral service or stand beside the casket – or grave side - of a friend or loved one? Why is that? Where does that longing come from? It did not slither from the slime! It did not climb up the ladder of evolutionism by the "law of tooth and claw"!! It came from the heart of Almighty God Who created you for Himself and is your Father, calling you Home by His Spirit. "He has made everything beautiful in its time. Also He has put eternity in their hearts..." Ecclesiastes 3:11.

BLOODY AND CRAZY!!

The infamous German Philosopher, Friedrich Nietzsche, who was the renegade son of a pastor, originated and promoted the "God is Dead" philosophy. Before his tragic death in 1900, he made two astounding predictions about the twentieth century (based upon the acceptance of his godless philosophy):

1. That the twentieth century would be the bloodiest in history. Not only was he accurate, it turned out that there was more bloodshed in the twentieth century than in all nineteen before.

2. He also predicted that the death of God mentality would send shock waves of insanity around the world. (Please consider that Nietzsche built his philosophy upon the distorted drivel of Darwinism.) How accurate was this prediction? Friedrich himself spent the last thirteen years of his life in an insane asylum. Also please consider this question as you read chapters 2, 3, and 4 in this book you hold.

We are now plagued with a growing band of aggressive atheists like Richard Dawkins. Does it seem ironic – even crazy – that Richard Dawkins is a professor at Oxford University, where their motto for many years has been, "The Lord is My Light"?

A few years ago Dawkins spoke at an atheist rally and gave them this advice about how to deal with religious people: "Mock them." Ravi Zacharias candidly asks the question why Dawkins doesn't go practice his own advice in Saudi Arabia. Could it be that he does recognize that he may have a much more negative reaction from Muslim fundamentalists than from Christian fundamentalists??? Perhaps the only positive for Dr. Dawkins in this scenario would be that he would only need to buy a one-way ticket!!!

Who Created God?

When a child asks, "Who created God?' he is asking that question out of immature ignorance, because if someone created God, He wouldn't be God! Then the child could ask, "Who created the god who created God?" This irrational questioning could go on infinitely. There has to be an ultimate first cause of all things! **That is logical and scientific.** Sometimes even adults ask the same immature question, but it is only because they do not understand the definition of who God actually is. Besides this, there is the fact that the law of cause and effect does not apply to God. Do you remember why? **Because God is not an effect. He is the cause – the First Cause of all things!**

Think about it! Do you know of any invention that did not first exist as an intangible idea in the mind of the inventor, **before** it existed in tangible, material form as the material expression of the inventor's idea? **Whether the invention is as simple as a pen or as complex as a robot or computer, the same principle prevails. It existed first as an idea in the inventor's mind. This amazing universe with all its astounding beauty, mystery, and complexity existed first in the mind of the Master Inventor! He is the original Scientist!!!**

Nothing

When Aristotle was asked the question, "What is nothing?" he replied, "That which rocks dream about." Today an evolutionist may reply, "That which everything came from." Here is another foolish, logical impossibility proposed by some who scoff at a miraculous creation by our eternal, omnipotent God. **Julie Andrews had it right when she sang, "Nothing comes from nothing. Nothing ever could." That is logic. Truth.**

Why do they accept the premise, "In the beginning there was nothing – then it condensed, exploded, and became everything"? Because they have come to realize the impossibility of the universe being eternal as Fred Hoyle, Carl Sagan and some Greek philosophers postulated. How do we know that the universe is not eternal? Because heat dissipates. What happens if you take a pan of boiling water off the burner? Will it still be hot an hour later? Not unless you put it on another hot object. Are there any hot objects in the universe? Absolutely! Our sun, for example. If the universe were eternal we wouldn't even be here. Why not? Because all the heat in the stars, including our sun, would have dissipated into the cold, dark expanses of the universe. Everything would be stone cold dead! There would be no life **at all** on planet earth without the warmth of the sun.

Wrong Feet???

Did you hear the story of the mother who told her three-year-old son that he had his shoes on the wrong feet? With a puzzled look on his face he stared at his feet for a moment, then looked up and said: "Ah, Mom – you're spoofing me! These are the only feet I have!!"

I really wonder how many kids who have been inundated, indoctrinated, and infused with evolutionism (especially billions and billions of years) simply look up at us (Biblical creationists) and think, "Ah, you're spoofing me!" They have **never** seen creation scientist's writings or DVDs concerning the powerful evidence for God's amazing creation, but from toddlerhood they have seen "Land Before Time" plus textbooks and movies "declaring evolution is a fact" and distorted displays in "Natural Science Museums." Let's pray for God to open their eyes to the genuine evidence of true science!

I was one of those kids who had been indoctrinated with evolutionism and I struggled with it – but I praise God for drawing me out of the darkness into the light!

I want to share the review I wrote for *Intermountain Christian News* about the lecture presented by Dr. Thomas Kindell.

Evolutionism Kaput!

(Dead on Arrival)

This is the title I would choose to describe the compelling and convincing lesson presented Thursday evening, February 28, 2013, in Boise, for Foundations in Genesis by Dr. Thomas Kindell. The actual title was "Fallacies of Evolutionary Geology and Radio-isotope Dating." Dr. Kindell is an able apologist and outstandingly keen in "casting down strongholds."

In his introduction Thomas showed that evolutionism has already struck out by documenting "Three Strikes against Evolution" through quotations from prominent evolutionists themselves:

1. *"Macro-evolution is impossible to observe." - Quotation from T. Dobzhansky. This fact removes evolutionism from the realm of applied science. Originally science was defined to be knowledge obtained by tests that are observable, demonstrable, and repeatable. This is applied science used for inventions. Evolutionism can be categorized as origin science or forensic science. Applied science deals with facts. Forensic science deals with speculations about what happened in the past. Macro-evolution is not a fact.*

2. *"Mutation selection mechanism effectually dead" – S. J. Gould, 1980. Steven Gould said that they (evolutionists) need to find a better mechanism. They haven't!*

3. *"Not a single 'watertight' transitional fossil known" – Collin Patterson, leading paleontologist at the British Museum (which has the greatest fossil collection in the world).*

After effectually showing the "Three strikes – you're out!" record of evolutionism, Dr. Kindell then pointed out that evolutionists don't play according to the rules. Why?

1. *They insist on having another chance because <u>they</u> make the rules and they now dominate academia and the sciences.*

2. *They changed the definition of science to fit their materialist/ naturalistic worldview. They have defined the possibility of God (and supernatural intervention) out of the equation by demanding that every scientific question can only be answered from all natural causes. Since they now control the colleges, universities, the science journals, and the peer review standards, any creationist or intelligent design scientist who seeks to introduce a supernatural Creator into an equation is black-balled and expelled. Ben Stein's blockbuster documentary, "Expelled", very definitely and dramatically documents this fact. Evolutionists conveniently changed their definition of science to become their philosophy of naturalism.*

The remainder of Thomas' lecture exposed the multiple fallacies of their fourth strikeout – the standardized and honored so-called geology chart*, which does not exist in reality anywhere on earth except in the minds of evolutionists. For it to exist in reality as pictured, it would need to be nearly 100 miles deep. Grand Canyon is only about one mile deep.

* (The chart is actually a philosophical portrayal of naturalistic dogma from the fantasy of a lawyer named Charles Lyell, with the help of James Hutton and a few others. Charles Lyell strongly influenced Charles Darwin with his "Principles of Geology" three volume set. Now his philosophy has been enshrined in the halls of "science" classrooms and "science" textbooks, where it doesn't belong. In reality, it belongs only in philosophy and fantasy books.)

* The last paragraph (above) in parentheses is my own footnote to Dr. Kindell's comments.

Exposing the Fraud of Macro-Evolution

"Evolution is a fairytale for grown-ups. It has helped nothing to the progress of science." Statement by Dr. Louis Bouroune, Australian Publication, March 8, 1984, p. 17. Dr. Bouroune, formerly president of the Biological Society of Straussburg, is the director of the Zoological Museum and director of Research at the Natural Center of Scientific Research in France.

Questions for Chapter 1 – First Half

1. Who is the first target audience for this book? Second? Third?

2. I listed four purposes for this book. What are they?

1.

2.

3.

4.

3. I listed six basic questions that every rational human being sometimes asks. What are they?

1.   4.

2.   5.

3.   6.

4. What is so scientifically accurate and amazing about Genesis 1:1?

5. If someone tells you, "There are **no** absolutes; everything is relative!", how will you respond?

6. Can we know Truth? If so, how do you know and how can you test that knowledge?

7. What is evolutionism and what do you see as the two most serious problems with it?

8. Does theistic evolutionism solve the scientific and theological problem with evolutionism? Please explain your reply.

9. What very significant statement did the evolutionist Sir Arthur Keith make about the law of Christ? Do you agree with him? Why or why not?

10. Is it possible for anyone to prove that God does not exist? Please explain your answer.

Bonus question: If someone asks, "Who created God?" – how will you reply?

What is Creationism?

(Honoring our Awesome God, Who Is Our Creator and Sustainer)

Creationism is nothing new – it is simply the Biblical theology about origins. Creationism is simply emphasizing what the Bible says about who God is as Creator and what the Bible teaches about creation without any compromise with the devious doctrines of macro-evolutionism that have developed in the past two hundred years, since before Charles Darwin's book, *The Origin of Species*, was published in 1859 and popularized after that. So in essence, creationism is the restoration of Biblical doctrine about God as Creator and sustainer of the entire universe! The doctrine of creation needs to be restored to its prominent place in Biblical theology because some well intentioned, but misguided Christian leaders – including theologians and scientists - have accepted the propaganda of evolutionists who teach that the earth is billions of years old and evolutionism is a fact. Whether the compromised position is called theistic evolution, progressive creation, the gap theory, or anything else, if they try to shove millions or billions of years into the text of Genesis, it is **not** Biblical theology. **Any compromise with evolutionism is destructive to Biblical theology and devastating to Biblical faith.**

The primary problem with evolutionists and compromisers is **not** that they are stupid – most are highly intelligent. The problem is that they firmly believe they "know" so many things that are not Biblically or scientifically sound!

Monstrous Problems – Awesome God!

That is the title of one of my favorite lessons, which is an overview of the book of Job and which shows how God used dinosaurs to demonstrate His awesome power and majesty to Job. What was the result? Consider the first six verses of Job chapter 42 (NKJV).

"Then Job answered the LORD and said: 'I know that You can do everything, And that no purpose of Yours can be withheld from You. You asked, "Who is this who hides counsel without knowledge?" Therefore I have uttered what I did not understand, Things too wonderful for me, which I did not know. Listen, please, and let me speak; You said, 'I will question you, and you shall answer Me.' I have heard of You by the hearing of the ear, But now my eye sees You. Therefore I abhor myself, And repent in dust and ashes."

Isn't it a tragic shame that Biblical skeptics have hijacked dinosaurs to very effectively use them for their evolutionary propaganda? We need to recapture dinosaurs to proclaim the majestic glory of God as He did for Job! Also we need to demonstrate the truth that our Awesome God was/is/always will be the original Scientist. Do you realize that Genesis 1:1 is an amazing statement of scientific reality? Cosmologist Herbert Spencer did research for years to determine the basic components of the universe. As a result he found there are five essential components – if any of them were missing, the universe would not exist. These components are:

1. Time   2. Force   3. Energy   4. Space   5.Matter

Is it mere coincidence that all five basic components are given in Genesis 1:1?

1. In the beginning = Time.

2. God = who is force (and much more).

3. Created – here is the energy.

4. The heavens = space.

5. The earth = matter.

Amazing! Simply amazing! Could this be mere coincidence? You can believe it was mere coincidence if you wish, but I believe Almighty God did it that way on purpose to demonstrate His glory and to confound the skeptics! **Our God is an Awesome God!!!** Many skeptics like to declare that they believe in science – not miracles. However, the actual truth is that every rational human being **does** believe in at least one huge miracle! What miracle? The existence of this universe and everything in it. Sir Isaac Newton (honored by many as the greatest scientist) said, "This universe exists, and by that one impossible fact declares itself a miracle." No matter how you choose to believe this universe got here – if you believe it exists – you do believe in miracles! If you do not believe that this universe and everything in it exists – remember that I said every **rational** human being does believe....

Also the potent portion of the Word of God found in Isaiah 40:21-31 is more impressive and powerful to me the oftener I read and ponder its implications.

"*Have you not known? Have you not heard? Has it not been told you from the beginning? Have you not understood from the foundations of the earth?* **It is He who sits above the circle of the earth**, *And its inhabitants are like grasshoppers,* **Who stretches out the heavens like a curtain**, *And spreads them out like a tent to dwell in. He brings the princes to nothing; He makes the judges of the earth useless. Scarcely shall they be planted, Scarcely shall they be sown, Scarcely shall their stock take root in the earth, When He will also blow on them, And they will wither, And the whirlwind will* *take them away like stubble. "To whom then will you liken Me, Or to whom shall I be equal?" says the Holy One.* **Lift up your eyes on high, And see who has created these things, Who brings out their host by number; He calls them all by name, By the greatness of His might And the strength of His power;** *Not one is missing. Why do you say, O Jacob, And speak, O Israel: "My way is hidden from the LORD, And my just claim is passed over by my God"? Have you not known? Have you not heard? The everlasting God, the LORD, The Creator of the ends of the earth, neither faints nor is weary. His understanding is unsearchable. He gives power to the weak, And to those who have no might He increases strength. Even the youths shall faint and be weary, And the young men shall utterly fall, But those who wait on the LORD shall renew their strength; They shall mount up with wings like eagles, They shall run and not be weary, They shall walk and not faint."*

Cosmologists do not yet know how many galaxies there are because they cannot find the ends of the universe, but Almighty God knows every star and calls it by name. (Isaiah 40:26). **Not only does He know trillions of stars by name – He knows <u>you</u> by name.** He knows your concerns, your sorrows, your sins – and He wants to call you to Himself, forgive your sin, calm your fears, hold you in His forgiving heart, fill you with abundant joy and commission you to spiritual service in His conquering Kingdom. **Are you ready to enlist? How exciting! How challenging to be enlisted in the service of the King – and walk with Him!**

Sergei Golovin and several others who read Hebrew have pointed out that the word translated "circle" in verse 22 could more accurately be translated "**sphere**". **Those who misinterpreted the phrase "four corners of the earth" to mean that the earth is flat missed the fact that God revealed through His prophet Isaiah over 700 years B.C. that the earth is a sphere.** (I have read that there are actually "four corners" – bumps – on the surface of the earth, but the phrase probably refers to north, south, east, and west.)

Also in verse 22 the phrase "**Who stretches out the heavens like a curtain**" is a good description of another scientific fact –

that **the universe is expanding**. The discovery of strong evidence for an expanding universe clarified to scientists years ago that **the universe had to have a beginning**, so in their evolutionary mind-set, some proposed and accepted the "Big Bang Theory". They did not choose to believe God's record found in Genesis 1:1 and many other Scriptures.

I realize that some theologians and old universe advocates fawn over the Big Bang Theory, but there are massive contradictions between that theory and the Biblical account of God's creation. As Kenneth Beckman emphasized, "When we compromise, we become part of the problem we once sought to solve!"

David Darling in 1996 wrote an intriguing description of the superstitious speculations of scientists supporting the Big Bang Theory. Here is a quotable quote on "The Origin of the Universe".

"What is a big deal – the biggest deal of all – is how you get something out of nothing. Don't let the cosmologists try to kid you on this one. They have not got a clue either – despite the fact that they are doing a pretty good job of convincing themselves and others that this is really not a problem. 'In the beginning,' they will say, 'there was nothing – no time, space, matter or energy. Then there was a quantum fluctuation from which...' Whoa! Stop right there. You see what I mean? First there is nothing, then there is something. And the cosmologists try to bridge the two with a quantum flutter, a tremor of uncertainty that sparks it all off. Then they are away and before you know it, they have pulled a hundred billion galaxies out of their quantum hats."

I choose to believe the Word of God!

By the word of the LORD the heavens were made, And all the host of them by the breath of His mouth. Let all the earth fear the LORD; Let all the inhabitants of the world stand in awe of Him. For He spoke, and it was *done;* **He commanded, and it stood fast.** Psalm 33:6,8-9 (NKJV).

What you have just read is a taste of what I have had opportunity to share both in secular classrooms and Christian settings in Estonia, Latvia, Russia, Ukraine and the Republic of Georgia since the summer of 1998.

The Origin of Evolutionism

The basic issue is not complex. The philosophy of evolutionism traces back to the Greek philosophers 300 – 400 B.C., with possible roots in Hinduism, so it is definitely a pagan philosophy with some religious similarities to Hinduism. (Hindu's believe in Karma which is the evolution of the soul through many lifetimes in order to become better and better). The doctrine of long ages of time (now billions of years) is essential to evolutionism and on this issue they will not compromise because, as stated by evolutionist George Wald, "*Time is in fact the hero of the plot…given so much time the 'impossible' becomes possible, the possible probable and the probable virtually certain. One has only to wait: time itself performs miracles.*" (George Wald, "The Origin of Life', Physics and Chemistry of Life, 1955, p. 12) Later, Carl Sagan wrote: "*The secrets of evolution are death and time – the deaths of enormous numbers of life forms that were imperfectly adapted to the environment; and time for a long succession of small mutations that were by accident adaptive, time for the slow accumulation of patterns of favorable mutations.*" (Carl Sagan, "Cosmos", 1980, p. 30)

As you can plainly see from these quotations, deep time plus chance plus death are the gods of evolutionism. Theistic compromisers with evolutionism say "no" to chance and materialism but "yes" to deep time and death, so they reject two of the gods of evolutionism but accept two others. It is the same fatal fallacy the Israelites fell into when they compromised with the pagan religions around them. "They worshiped Jehovah and served other gods." Kenneth Beckman said, "When you compromise you become part of the problem you once sought to solve." How true! Compromised positions that accept evolutionism's time table of billions of years are **not** Creationism! They are not Biblical theology! Why not? Because our almighty, awesome Creator is not some bumbling idiot who takes millions or billions of years of trial and error to do a job! When Authority speaks, things happen – instantly! Consider these pertinent, potent passages from the Word of God:

"*In the beginning God created the heavens and the earth. The earth was without form, and void; and darkness was on the face of the deep. And the Spirit of God was hovering over the face of the waters. Then God said, "Let there be light"; and there was light."* Genesis 1:1-3

"For in six days the LORD made the heavens and the earth, the sea, and all that is in them, and rested the seventh day. Therefore the LORD blessed the Sabbath day and hallowed it." Exodus 20:8-11

"By the word of the LORD the heavens were made, And all the host of them by the breath of His mouth. He gathers the waters of the sea together as a heap; He lays up the deep in storehouses. Let all the earth fear the LORD; Let all the inhabitants of the world stand in awe of Him. For He spoke, and it was done; He commanded, and it stood fast." Psalm 33:6-9

*"God, who at various times and in various ways spoke in time past to the fathers by the prophets, has in these last days spoken to us by His Son, whom He has appointed heir of all things, through whom also He made the worlds; who being the brightness of His glory and the express image of His person, and **upholding all things by the word of His power**, when He had by Himself purged our sins, sat down at the right hand of the Majesty on high, having become so much better than the angels, as He has by inheritance obtained a more excellent name than they."* Hebrews 1:1-4

"By faith we understand that the worlds were framed by the word of God, so that the things which are seen were not made of things which are visible...But without faith it is impossible to please Him, for he who comes to God must believe that He is, and that He is a rewarder of those who diligently seek Him." Hebrews 11:3, 6

The Problem of Distant Starlight

I have been asked several times how it is possible for the earth and universe to be only about 6,000 years old when the universe is so vast that it takes billions of light years for starlight to reach the earth from far off galaxies. Many astronomers claim that starlight is just reaching the earth now from some galaxies that are 15 to 20 billion years old. One friend of mine boldly and brazenly asserted that God would be deceptive if the universe is not 15 to 17 billion years old. I told him that God is **not** deceptive! He cannot lie. He told us what He did, when He did it, and how He did it. He **spoke** the universe into existence **in** the beginning!!! **He created everything full grown and fully functioning!** He created Adam and Eve as a **man** and **woman** – not babies. Adam and Eve saw the sun, moon, and stars on the sixth day of Creation. How do we know that? The record says: "*Then God said, 'Let there be lights in the firmament of the heavens to divide the day from the night; and let them be for signs and seasons, and for days and years; and let them be for lights in the firmament of the heavens* **to give light on the earth**'*; and it was so. Then God made two great lights: the greater light to rule the day, and the lesser light to rule the night. He made the stars also. God set them in the firmament of the heavens* **to give light on the earth***, and to rule over the day and over the night, and to divide the light from the darkness. And God saw that it was good. So the evening and the morning were the fourth day.*" Genesis 1:14-19. For further clarification please Google *Fourth Day Alliance*. By the way, if you can't believe it unless you understand it, please explain to me exactly what electricity is! (Our electricians have learned how to work with and use electricity, but they can't explain it either.) Beyond that – try explaining the intricate workings of <u>a woman's mind!!!</u>

Russell Humphries, in his little book, Starlight and Time, mentions the fact that time on earth is measured by earth's position in the solar system and the speed that the earth rotates. For example: one day of twenty-four hours is one revolution of the earth on its axis. One year is one revolution of the earth around the sun. How would time be measured out in the vast regions of space? Of course, God Himself is not limited by our time constraints, but in His revelation to us, the Bible, He speaks to us in our own environment of time.

Context

"*Lord, You have been our dwelling place in all generations.* ***Before the mountains were brought forth, or ever You had formed the earth and the world, even from everlasting to everlasting, You are God****. You turn man to destruction, and say, 'Return, O children of men.' For a thousand years in Your sight are like yesterday when it is past, and like a watch in the night.*" Psalm 90:1-4. The context of this passage is about the majesty of our awesome God, who is above and outside of our limitations of time, space, energy, etc. This is not telling us about how much time God took to create everything. He inspired Moses to tell us that information in Genesis 1 and Exodus 20:8-11. In these passages God reveals to us what He did and how long He took to do it. Unfortunately, those with the preconceived philosophy of deep time for the origin of the universe will often pluck this passage of Scripture out of context to attempt to reinterpret the revelation of God in Genesis 1 and Exodus 20:11. This is called eisegesis – reading into the text your own preconceived notions rather than reading the text to understand what it actually says. It is unwise and dangerous to distort the Word of God to promote an agenda!!!

To understand the application of Psalm 90, please notice verse 12 and verse 17: *"So teach us to number our days, that we may gain a heart of wisdom… And let the beauty of the LORD our God be upon us, and establish the work of our hands for us; yes, establish the work of our hands."*

*"**The LORD reigns, He is clothed with majesty; the LORD is clothed, He has girded Himself with strength.** Surely the world is established, so that it cannot be moved. Your throne is established from of old; You are from everlasting. The floods have lifted up, O LORD, the floods have lifted up their voice; the floods lift up their waves. The LORD on high is mightier than the noise of many waters, than the mighty waves of the sea."* Psalm 93:1-4

These powerful passages teach us that Almighty God spoke and it was done! The meaning of the words is no mystery – **the issue is whether or not we choose to believe Him.** I have been asked the question, "Couldn't God use evolution to create?" The answer is **No**! Why not? There are several very good reasons. Here are three:

1. There are some things that God cannot do! One of them is that He cannot violate His own nature. He is by nature perfect and all powerful, so therefore He cannot be an incompetent semi-god who uses trial and error and death over millions of years to evolve something from something

else. That is **not** creation!

2. God cannot lie! He told us what He did and how He did it. As He spoke light into existence, so He spoke all things into existence. He spoke and it was done!

   Jesus demonstrated His power as God when the storm was raging on the Sea of Galilee and His disciples were terrified. They thought their boat would sink. The record says: *"Then He arose and rebuked the wind, and said to the sea, 'Peace, be still!' And the wind ceased and there was a great calm. But He said to them, 'Why are you so fearful? How is it that you have no faith?' And they feared exceedingly, and said to one another, 'Who can this be, that even the wind and the sea obey Him!'"* Mark 4:39-41. Would Jesus' disciples have been awestruck if the wind and waves died down two days after Jesus spoke the words? Two hours? NO! **They were awestruck because the wind and waves obeyed Him instantly! They were awestruck because God spoke and it was done! They recognized Jesus was indeed God in flesh – and He was in their boat!**

3. **Creation is not evolution! Evolution is not creation. They are opposite and opposing worldviews that cannot be reconciled.** Trying to harmonize evolutionism with creationism is like trying to ride two horses simultaneously - even though they are going different directions! It is vain to try – yet whole groups of semi-believers, like those in "Biologos" and "Reasons to Believe", are wasting time and energy, plus confusing believers by trying to harmonize and reconcile what cannot be harmonized. I refer to them as semi-believers because they choose to believe the portions of Scripture they like, yet reject the clear statements in the Word of God about when and how God created. This is an extremely serious rejection of God's foundational truths.

It is a sad fact that some unbelievers are more perceptive than these compromising believers in recognizing the logical inconsistencies between creationism and evolutionism. Sir Arthur

Keith, one of the leading evolutionists of the 20th century wrote: "Evolution is unproven and unprovable. We believe it because the only alternative is special creation, and that is unthinkable." Why was special creation "unthinkable" to him? Because he was committed to the philosophy of naturalism, which rules God out of the equation concerning the origin of all things. Richard Lewontin, another leading evolutionist, wrote that he recognized that evolutionists believe some things that are absurd, but they choose to believe them because they have a prior commitment to naturalism and they "cannot allow a Divine foot in the door".

Friends, you cannot win such unbelievers to God's truth by compromising God's truth!

"For what if some did not believe? Will their unbelief make the faithfulness of God without effect? Certainly not! Indeed, let God be true but every man a liar. As it is written: 'That You may be justified in Your words, and may overcome when You are judged.'" Romans 3:3, 4

Who Is a Creationist?

A creationist is a Christian believer who accepts God's revealed truth about creation and refuses to compromise with the lies, distortions and propaganda of evolutionism.

Are Creationists Divisive?

Have you heard the false accusations by compromising believers that creationists are dividing the Body of Christ? The truth is that those who reject the revealed Word of God are the ones guilty of dividing the Body of Christ. From the first verse of Genesis through the book of Revelation, the Word of God teaches that our awesome, miracle working, almighty God created all things "by the Word of His power".

When I, as a creationist, am accused of dividing the Body of Christ, I am reminded of the time when Ahab accused Elijah of troubling Israel. The record says that Elijah responded by saying, "I have not troubled Israel, but you and your fathers' house have in that you have forsaken the commandments of the Lord, and you have followed the Baals." I Kings 18:18

Those of us who warn the people of God about the compromises of human doctrine are attempting to restore the truth of God as revealed in Scripture. However, we are often called trouble makers and divisive. We need to recall that Ahab did it with Elijah. The leaders of Israel did it with Jesus and the apostles. Jesus prepared us when He said, "If they hate me, they will hate you." I do believe and teach, "In essentials, unity; in opinion, liberty; in all things, love." Is the Biblical doctrine of creation an essential truth? If not, why not? It is foundational. Revelation 14:6-7 shows it to be the foundation of worship and an essential truth in the everlasting gospel!!! "Then I saw another angel flying in the midst of heaven, having *the everlasting gospel* to preach to those who dwell on the earth—to every nation, tribe, tongue, and people— *saying with a loud voice, 'Fear God and give glory to Him,* for the hour of His judgment has come; *and worship Him who made heaven and earth, the sea and springs of water.'"*

Not only does the everlasting gospel teach us to worship God because he created all things, but also the everlasting gospel is the revelation of Who the Creator is. He is by His own nature One God with plurality engrained within Himself – the Hebrew word for God "Elohim" is both singular and plural in its nature. Please pay careful attention to these pertinent passages:

"In the beginning God created the heavens and the earth. The earth was without form, and void; and darkness was on the face of the deep. And the **Spirit of God** *was hovering over the face of the waters. Then God said, "Let there be light"; and there was light." Genesis 1:1-3.*

"Then God said, 'Let **Us** *make* **man** *in* **Our** *image, according to Our likeness; let* **them** *have dominion over the fish of the sea, over the birds of the air, and over the cattle, over all the earth and over every creeping thing that creeps on the earth.' So God created man in His own image; in the image of God He created him; male and female He created them. Then God blessed them, and God said to them, 'Be fruitful and multiply; fill the earth and subdue it; have*

dominion over the fish of the sea, over the birds of the air, and over every living thing that moves on the earth." Genesis 1:26-28.

"'Hear, O Israel: The LORD *our God, the* LORD *is* one! *You shall love the* LORD *your God with all your heart, with all your soul, and with all your strength."'* Deuteronomy 6:4-5.

"For unto us a **Child** *is born, unto us a* **Son** *is given; and the government will be upon His shoulder.* And His name will be called *Wonderful, Counselor,* **Mighty God, Everlasting Father,** *Prince of Peace."* Isaiah 9:6.

"'You are My witnesses,' says the LORD, *'And My servant whom I have chosen, that you may know and believe Me, and understand that I am He. Before Me there was no God formed, nor shall there be after Me.* I, even I, am the LORD, *and besides Me there is no sav-ior."'* Isaiah 43:10-11.

"...looking for the blessed hope and glorious appearing of our great God and Savior Jesus Christ," *Titus 2:13.*

"Thus says the LORD, *the King of Israel, and his Redeemer, the* LORD *of hosts: 'I am the First and I am the Last; Besides Me there is no God."'* Isaiah 44:6.

"I am the LORD, *and there is no other; there is no God besides Me. I will gird you, though you have not known Me, that they may know from the rising of the sun to its setting that there is none be-sides Me. I am the* LORD, *and there is no other; I form the light and create darkness, I make peace and create calamity; I, the* LORD, *do all these things."* Isaiah 45:5-7.

"In the beginning was the Word, and the Word was with God, and the Word was God. *He was in the beginning with God. All things were made through Him, and without Him nothing was made that was made...And the Word became flesh and dwelt among us, and we beheld His glory, the glory as of the only begotten of the Father, full of grace and truth."* John 1:1-3, 14.

"He has delivered us from the power of darkness and conveyed us into the kingdom of the Son of His love, in whom we have re-demption through His blood the forgiveness of sins. He is the image of the invisible God, the firstborn over all creation. For by Him all things were created *that are in heaven and that are on earth, vis-*

ible and invisible, whether thrones or dominions or principalities or powers. All things were created through Him and for Him. And He is before all things, and in Him all things consist. And He is the head of the body, the church, who is the beginning, the firstborn from the dead, that in all things He may have the preeminence." Colossian 1:13-18.

"To them God willed to make known what are the riches of the glory of this mystery among the Gentiles: which is **Christ in you, the hope of glory.** *Him we preach, warning every man and teaching every man in all wisdom, that we may present every man perfect in Christ Jesus. To this end I also labor, striving according to His working which works in me mightily." Colossians 1:27-29.*

"As you therefore have received Christ Jesus the Lord, so walk in Him, rooted and built up in Him and established in the faith, as you have been taught, abounding in it with thanksgiving. **Beware lest anyone cheat you through philosophy and empty deceit,** *according to the tradition of men, according to the basic principles of the world, and not according to Christ.* **For in Him dwells all the fullness of the Godhead bodily; and you are complete in Him, who is the head of all principality and power."** *Colossians 2:6-10.*

"God, *who at various times and in various ways spoke in time past to the fathers by the prophets,* **has in these last days spoken to us by His Son,** *whom He has appointed heir of all things, through whom also He made the worlds;* **who being the brightness of His glory and the express image of His person,** *and upholding all things by the word of His power, when He had by Himself purged our sins, sat down at the right hand of the Majesty on high, having become so much better than the angels, as He has by inheritance obtained a more excellent name than they." Hebrews 1:1-4.*

"And without controversy great is the mystery of godliness: **God was manifested in the flesh,** *Justified in the Spirit, Seen by angels, Preached among the Gentiles, Believed on in the world, Received up in glory." 1 Timothy 3:16.*

What Should Be Our Ministry?

In view of all theses potent passages about the nature of God, what then should be our ministry? Consider also these powerful passages:

"And Jesus came and spoke to them, saying, 'All authority has been given to Me in heaven and on earth. **Go therefore and make disciples of all the nations,** *baptizing them in the name of the Father and of the Son and of the Holy Spirit, teaching them to observe all things that I have commanded you; and lo, I am with you always, even to the end of the age.' Amen." Matthew 28:18-20.*

"Therefore, since we have this ministry, as we have received mercy, we do not lose heart. *But we have renounced the hidden things of shame, not walking in craftiness nor handling the word of God deceitfully, but by manifestation of the truth commending ourselves to every man's conscience in the sight of God. But even if our gospel is veiled, it is veiled to those who are perishing, whose minds the god of this age has blinded, who do not believe, lest the light of the gospel of the glory of Christ, who is the image of God, should shine on them.* **For we do not preach ourselves, but Christ Jesus the Lord,** *and ourselves your bondservants for Jesus' sake. For it is the God who commanded light to shine out of darkness, who has shone in our hearts to give the light of the knowledge of the glory of God in the face of Jesus Christ. But we have this treasure in earthen vessels, that the excellence of the power may be of God and not of us."* 2 Corinthians 4:1-7.

How Relevant is the Gospel?

What is the treasure we have in our "earthen vessels" (bodies)? What is the mystery of the gospel? **"Christ in you – the hope of glory!!!"** We have the "light of the knowledge of the glory of God in the face of Jesus Christ". **Is this treasure relevant to every culture on earth?** Consider the fact that the apostle Paul was a Jew with Roman citizenship who was born and raised in the Greek culture of the city of Tarsus. He ministered powerfully in all of these cultures. To the **Jews, light** was supremely important; to the **Greeks,**

knowledge was supremely important; to the **Romans, glory** was supremely important. Now please read verses 6-7 again. *"For it is the God who commanded light to shine out of darkness, who has shone in our hearts to give the* **light** *of the* **knowledge** *of the* **glory** *of God in the face of Jesus Christ. But we have this treasure in earthen vessels, that the excellence of the power may be of God and not of us."* Amazing! Simply amazing!!!

From Atheism to the Almighty

By the time I was 10 or 11 years old I declared myself to be an atheist by saying, "I don't believe in God—I've never seen Him." It would have been so easy for me to remain and harden in this rejection of the truth of the Bible and the Almighty because I wanted to be "a real man". My distorted view of masculinity probably stemmed from the fact that most of the men in my family were Biblical skeptics and unbelievers, especially on my father's side of the family. In retrospect, I realize that my motives for declaring my unbelief were really emotional, not intellectual. The problem wasn't and isn't that God has not left clear evidence of Himself and His Word. The major problem was that I knew I was a sinner, and I didn't want to repent. If I admitted the reality of God and the truth of His Word, I would need to face my sin problem and change. Instead, I denied His existence. Jesus had already accurately described the situation when He said, "**men loved darkness rather than light, because their deeds were evil**." John 3:19

I am so thankful to God that He drew me out of that web of unbelief. He used Mom (who sent me to Sunday School, VBS and Christian Service Camp), loving, yet strict teachers, and a powerful and faithful preacher of the Word, Talmage Pace. Through them and a dramatic answer to my first fervent prayer, the Holy Spirit convicted me of my sin and drew me to Christ's love and forgiveness. I was twelve years old in January of 1956 when my Dad lost his left arm in a horrible tractor accident. He was working far from town and lost so much blood before arriving at the hospital that the doctors thought they were working on a corpse at first. When I overheard the whispers in my family (since they were trying to shield me from the stark reality that Dad wasn't expected to live through the night), I prayed earnestly that God would save Dad's life. Almighty God was there and heard me. Dad's recovery amazed the doctors. One of them told Mom later that initially he wouldn't have bet a plugged nickel on Dad's chances to recover. **God answers prayer! The God I worship is not only the Almighty Creator, but He is also the gracious Heavenly Father, who loved me in spite of my sin, heard my prayer and answered "yes" to my request, even though I was a foul-mouthed unbeliever who said that I didn't believe in Him.** He demonstrated Himself to me and drew me to Himself. The way God drew me to Himself was to motivate me by His love and grace to come to Bible classes and church services on my own consistently to hear and believe the Good News that Jesus died for my sin and arose from the dead to save me. I accepted His grace and responded to the command in Acts 2:38. *"…Repent, and be baptized every one of you in the name of Jesus Christ, for the remission of sins, and ye shall receive the gift of the Holy Spirit."* (KJV)

Several years ago during a communion service I wrote this note to Jesus:

Dear Jesus,

I appreciate You because You took me as a lonely, confused, frustrated, heartsick, sinful kid, saved me by Your precious blood and gave me a purpose in life. All that I am, all that I have accomplished, and all that I ever will accomplish—I owe it all to You!

I love you!
Rick

Powerful Passages

Please consider these powerful passages:

"For God so loved the world that He gave His only begotten Son, that whoever believes in Him should not perish but have everlasting life. For God did not send His Son into the world to condemn the world, but that the world through Him might be saved. "He who believes in Him is not condemned; but he who does not believe is condemned already, because he has not believed in the name of the

only begotten Son of God. And this is the condemnation, that the light has come into the world, and men loved darkness rather than light, because their deeds were evil. For everyone practicing evil hates the light and does not come to the light, lest his deeds should be exposed. But he who does the truth comes to the light, that his deeds may be clearly seen, that they have been done in God." John 3:16-21;

"***Nor is there salvation in any other, for there is no other name under heaven given among men by which we must be saved.***" Acts 4:12

WHAT IS MY PASSION?

I don't know about you, but I can't afford to have a bad day. When I'm tempted to sink into the "bad day" syndrome because of prevailing evil, outrageous politicians, time pressures, and the encroachment on our freedom of speech by unbelievers who want to eliminate "under God" from our pledge of allegiance and eliminate "In God We Trust" as our national motto, etc., then it's time to remember that our God calls us to "number our days that we may apply our hearts to wisdom." In view of eternity I have only a few days on earth, so I want to revel in each one of them and make it count to the glory of God. Glorious spring days of lavish sunshine, cool breezes, brilliant blossoms, and singing birds make it easier for me to love life, but at a deeper level I am committed to living my life with a passion even when the rain is horizontal and the raging wind tries to rip my coat off my back.

Not only do I love life with a passion, but I also love my wife with a passion, for both are glorious gifts from God. I am committed to seeking out creative new ways to show Della that I cherish her. Although my love for Della is richer and deeper than the day I said, "I do" years ago, yet I'm stretching for the mark of showing to both Christians and non-Christians how much Jesus loves His Bride by how I treat Della.

I also have a passion for sharing solid evidence for Christian faith and for proclaiming the Word of Truth with clarity and conviction. Those of us who have experienced the exhilaration of sharing God's Word with responsive listeners, whether in personal evangelism, a small group, or an audience know there is hardly a more thrilling experience in life. However, I must evaluate constantly if my passion for preaching is for a sense of self-importance or truly for the glory of God and the edification of the Body of Christ.

I have a passion for life, for my wife, and for sharing truth, but all of this is insignificant if I do not first and foremost have a passion for God Himself. Often we sing, "As the deer panteth for the water, so my soul longeth after Thee." **Is this truly my deepest longing, or am I only mouthing the words?** Asaph, in Psalm 73:25 wrote, "*Whom have I in heaven but you? And being with you, I desire nothing on earth.*" Wow! That's powerful! Can I say that? Augustine wrote, "Thou has made us for Thyself, O God, and our hearts are restless until we find our rest in Thee." Yes! I agree. **My rest is in Him. My hope is in Him. My joy is in Him. I do have a passion for God Himself, but I want that passion to intensify until it burns out all the dross in my life.**

What about you? What is your P. Q.? (That's Passion Quotient.) In His presence is fullness of joy. **Here's wishing you a passionate, joy-filled life as you share the evidences you have learned, and especially the truths you've observed directly from the Word of God.** "*But sanctify the Lord God in your hearts: and be ready <u>always</u> to give an answer to <u>every</u> <u>man</u> that asketh you a <u>reason</u> of the <u>hope</u> that is in you, with meekness and fear.*" 1 Peter 3:15 (KJV)

When someone asks you, "What do you know for sure?" why not say, "I know that Jesus Christ is Lord and that the evidences for His resurrection are overwhelming?" You may be amazed and thrilled as you see how God opens doors of opportunity for you when you are ready and willing to be a bold witness for Him.

"Walk in wisdom toward those who are outside, redeeming the time. Let your speech always be with grace, seasoned with salt, that you may know how you ought to answer each one." Colossians 4:5-6 (NKJV)

What is Your Passion?

John Maxwell advises us to ask three questions to evaluate what our true passion is:

1. What do you sing about?

2. What do you cry about?

3. What do you dream about?

When you answer these questions you will probably know what your passion is, but then you must also evaluate another vital question – Is this a godly passion or a selfish passion? If it is a godly passion, then pursue it with all your heart. If it is a selfish passion, ask God to cleanse your heart and give you a new passion.

The Wisdom of Men vs. the Wisdom of God

If you want to understand more clearly the vast contrast between the wisdom of men and the wisdom of God, please give careful and prayerful consideration to the following Scripture passages: *"**For the message of the cross is foolishness to those who are perishing, but to us who are being saved it is the power of God**. For it is written: 'I will destroy the wisdom of the wise, and bring to nothing the understanding of the prudent.' Where is the wise? Where is the scribe? Where is the disputer of this age? **Has not God made foolish the wisdom of this world?** For since, in the wisdom of God, the world through wisdom did not know God, it pleased God through the foolishness of the message preached to save those who believe. For Jews request a sign, and Greeks seek after wisdom; but we preach Christ crucified, to the Jews a stumbling block and to the Greeks foolishness, but to those who are called, both Jews and Greeks, **Christ the power of God and the wisdom of God. Because the foolishness of***

Chapter 1: Purpose and Passion

God is wiser than men, and the weakness of God is stronger than men. *For you see your calling, brethren, that not many wise according to the flesh, not many mighty, not many noble, are called.* **But God has chosen the foolish things of the world to put to shame the wise, and God has chosen the weak things of the world to put to shame the things which are mighty;** *and the base things of the world and the things which are despised God has chosen, and the things which are not, to bring to nothing the things that are,* **that no flesh should glory in His presence. But of Him you are in Christ Jesus, who became for us wisdom from God—and righteousness and sanctification and redemption— that, as it is written, 'He who glories, let him glory in the LORD.'"** 1 Corinthians 1:18-31. The main point here is that you **will** be considered a fool by someone! **Would you rather be considered a fool by the foolish, rebellious, ungodly crowd – or considered a fool by Almighty God?** Who will be your Judge on that final Judgment Day? So, whose fool do you choose to be today?

Remember, you do not know the day – the time – when you will be called to meet your Maker!

"Who is wise and understanding among you? Let him show by good conduct that his works are done in the meekness of wisdom. But if you have bitter envy and self-seeking in your hearts, do not boast and lie against the truth. This wisdom does not descend from above, but is earthly, sensual, demonic. For where envy and self-seeking exist, confusion and every evil thing are there. But the wisdom that is from above is first pure, then peaceable, gentle, willing to yield, full of mercy and good fruits, without partiality and without hypocrisy. Now the fruit of righteousness is sown in peace by those who make peace." James 3:13-18

"But even if our gospel is veiled, it is veiled to those who are perishing, whose minds the god of this age has blinded, who do not believe, lest the light of the gospel of the glory of Christ, who is the image of God, should shine on them. For we do not preach ourselves, but Christ Jesus the Lord, and ourselves your bondservants for Jesus' sake. **For it is the God who commanded light to shine out of darkness, who has shone in our hearts to give the light of the knowledge**

of the glory of God in the face of Jesus Christ." 2 Corinthians 4:3-6

We should never doubt in the dark what God has shown us in the light! Whenever we are tempted to doubt God and His Word, we can turn our eyes to Jesus and focus on His light – the light that will turn our doubts toward the humanistic philosophy of evolutionism. Become a dedicated Darwin doubter! Charles Darwin doubted his own ridiculous fantasy about life coming from dead matter and mankind evolving from primates, but he expressed those doubts in private letters or kept them to himself rather than truly repenting and publically denouncing his devious doctrine. Consider this quotation: **"But then with me the horrid doubt always arises whether the convictions of man's mind, which has been developed from the mind of the lower animals, are of any value or at all trustworthy. Would any one trust in the convictions of a monkey's mind, if there are any convictions in such a mind?"** Charles Darwin, from letter to William Graham, 1881.

Darwin did openly admit in *The Origin of Species*, that his macro-evolutionism seems absurd when considering the intricacies of the eye – but he chose to believe his fantasy in spite of the facts. An eye is irreducibly complex – everything has to work simultaneously and instantly or you cannot see. How do you function for millions of years while your eyes are evolving? **The reason his fantasy seems absurd is because it *is* absurd!**

More than Conquerors

In accord with the theme of this book, I want to share with you the outline of a message I prepared for the annual banquet of Lifeline Pregnancy Resource Center in Nampa, Idaho (our home).

<u>Introduction:</u> Why I am passionate about the sanctity of life.

1. Because God is passionate about the sanctity of life. Is God pro-choice or pro-life? <u>Both!</u> He tells us what choice to make! *"I call heaven and earth as witnesses today against you, that I have set before you life and death, blessing and cursing; therefore choose life, that both you and your*

descendants may live;" Deut. 30:19

2. Because I believe in the sovereignty of God. God is the author or life and He has placed us here on earth for His purpose. We do not have the right to play God by murdering innocent human beings in their mothers' wombs. What should be the most protected place on earth (a mother's womb) has become for millions of babies the most dangerous place to be.

3. Because of the lives of my daughter and granddaughter.

Text: *"And we know that all things work together for good to those who love God, to those who are the called according to His purpose. For whom He foreknew, He also predestined to be conformed to the image of His Son, that He might be the firstborn among many brethren. Moreover whom He predestined, these He also called; whom He called, these He also justified; and whom He justified, these He also glorified. What then shall we say to these things? If God is for us, who can be against us? He who did not spare His own Son, but delivered Him up for us all, how shall He not with Him also freely give us all things? Who shall bring a charge against God's elect? It is God who justifies. Who is he who condemns? It is Christ who died, and furthermore is also risen, who is even at the right hand of God, who also makes intercession for us. Who shall separate us from the love of Christ? Shall tribulation, or distress, or persecution, or famine, or nakedness, or peril, or sword? As it is written: "For Your sake we are killed all day long; We are accounted as sheep for the slaughter."* **Yet in all these things we are more than conquerors through Him who loved us.** *For I am persuaded that neither death nor life, nor angels nor principalities nor powers, nor things present nor things to come, nor height nor depth, nor any other created thing, shall be able to separate us from the love of God which is in Christ Jesus our Lord."* Romans 8:28-39

Purpose Statement:

The purpose of this message is to emphasize how to implement in our spiritual battle the truth that **in Christ** we are "**More than Conquerors**".

I. **We must understand that we cannot win in human strength or wisdom because this is spiritual warfare.**

1. **Examine yourself whether you are in the faith.**

2. **We are "More than Conquerors" through Him who loves us. Without Him we can do nothing!**

3. **Be filled with the Spirit.** *For you were once darkness, but now you are light in the Lord. Walk as children of light…**And do not be drunk with wine, in which is dissipation; but be filled with the Spirit**,*" Ephesians 5:8, 18; "*So he answered and said to me: 'This is the word of the* Lord *to Zerubbabel:* '**Not by might nor by power, but by My Spirit,**' *Says the* Lord *of hosts.*'" Zechariah 4:6

   1. Eyes on Jesus

   2. Heart filled with the Spirit

   3. Feet on the straight and narrow

4. Use the right weapons – "*For though we walk in the flesh, we do not war according to the flesh. For the weapons of our warfare are not carnal but mighty in God for pulling down strongholds, casting down arguments and every high thing that exalts itself against the knowledge of God, bringing every thought into captivity to the obedience of Christ,*" 2 Corinthians 10:3-5

   Remember that Jesus calls us salt and light. Salt heals and preserves – also burns. Light illuminates and heals – it also exposes dirt!

II. **Understand the immensity of Satan's lies and don't expect a fair fight.**

    A. Abortion lies

    B. Evolutionism lies

III. **Understand the intensity of the battle.**

    A. The intensity of the battle demands intensity of training, trials and discipline.

        1. Marines – Navy Seals – rigorous.

        2. My experience

    B. How is God working in your life? Think of Job, Apostle Paul, Joni Earekson Tada.

Conclusion *"Molding a Man"*

*"When God wants to drill a man,
and thrill a man, and skill a man,
When God wants to mold a man
to play the noblest part;
When He yearns with all His heart,
to create so great and bold a man
that all the world will be amazed,
Watch His methods, watch His ways;*

*How He relentlessly perfects
whom He royally elects;
How He hammers us and hurts us
and with mighty blows converts us
into trial shapes of clay*

*which Only God can understand,
While our tortured heart is crying
and we lift beseeching hands.*

*How God bends, but never breaks
when His good He undertakes;
How He uses whom He chooses,
and with every purpose fuses us;
By every act induces us
to try His splendor out –
God knows what He's about!"*

~ Dale Martin Stone

Adrian Rogers said, "The grace of God can turn your scars into stars!"

"Those who are wise shall shine like the brightness of the firmament, and those who turn many to righteousness like the stars forever and ever." Daniel 12:3 (NKJV)

My prayer for each of you is that you would be wise, turn many to righteousness and shine like the brightness of the firmament forever and ever.

Fellow Christians - Do You Get the Point?

Already in Christ we are "more than conquerors". That is our identity on the authority of the Word of God! In America there are millions of Christians (at least those who claim to be born again believers). **If only a fraction of these professed Christians will believe we are more than conquerors and act upon that fact, then we can transform our corrupt culture this year!** Be who you are! Conquerors! More than conquerors! Do not be intimidated by our corrupted culture. Remember: *"Fear not, for I am with you; be not dismayed, for I am your God. I will strengthen you, yes, I will help you, I will uphold you with My righteous right hand."* Isaiah 41:10; *'For God has not given us a spirit of fear, but of power and of love and of a sound mind"* 2 Timothy 1:7. Share your testimony! Adopt an orphan! Rescue an addict! Love your neighbor! Use your God-given spiritual gift (or gifts) to the glory of God! Use your own creativity to find ways to touch other lives with the love of Christ. Pray every day, "Lord, fill me with your Spirit and put me in the right place at the right time with the right words to honor you" – then watch with anticipation how He gives you glimpses of His amazing power and grace. Become an active soldier in the Lord's army of grace and glory! **Come help us transform America and change the world – one soul at a time!**

Touching Lives

*My life shall touch a dozen lives
before this day is done,
Leave countless marks for good
or ill
ere sets the evening sun,*

*This is the wish I always wish,
the prayer I always pray;
Lord, may my life help other lives
it touches by the way.*

Supreme Importance!

   "To convert one sinner from the error of his way is of more importance than to deliver an entire kingdom from temporary danger." But remember to be persistent, for it is often a long process. We need to be persistent in caring, persistent in sharing, persistent in praying. Let's remember our privilege to *"have this treasure in earthen vessels"* and be diligent to use our freedom of speech in America effectively while we still have it. Remember:

   "But even if our gospel is veiled, it is veiled to those who are perishing, whose minds the god of this age has blinded, who do not believe, lest the light of the gospel of the glory of Christ, who is the image of God, should shine on them. For we do not preach ourselves, but Christ Jesus the Lord, and ourselves your bondservants for Jesus' sake. For it is the God who commanded light to shine out of darkness, who has shone in our hearts to give the light of the knowledge of the glory of God in the face of Jesus Christ. But we have this treasure in earthen vessels, that the excellence of the power may be of God and not of us." 2 Corinthians 4:3-7;

   "Therefore we make it our aim, whether present or absent, to be well pleasing to Him. For we must all appear before the judgment seat of Christ, that each one may receive the things done in the body, according to what he has done, whether good or bad. **Knowing, therefore, the terror of the Lord, we persuade men;** *but we are well known to God, and I also trust are well known in your consciences. For we do not commend ourselves again to you, but give you opportunity to boast on our behalf, that you may*

have an answer for those who boast in appearance and not in heart. For if we are beside ourselves, it is for God; or if we are of sound mind, it is for you. For the love of Christ compels us, because we judge thus: that if One died for all, then all died; and He died for all, that those who live should live no longer for themselves, but for Him who died for them and rose again. Therefore, from now on, we regard no one according to the flesh. Even though we have known Christ according to the flesh, yet now we know Him thus no longer. Therefore, if anyone is in Christ, he is a new creation; old things have passed away; behold, all things have become new. Now all things are of God, who has reconciled us to Himself through Jesus Christ, and has given us the ministry of reconciliation, that is, that God was in Christ reconciling the world to Himself, not imputing their trespasses to them, and has committed to us the word of reconciliation. **Now then, we are ambassadors for Christ**, *as though God were pleading through us: we implore you on Christ's behalf, be reconciled to God. For He made Him who knew no sin to be sin for us, that we might become the righteousness of God in Him.*" 2 Corinthians 5:9-21

Supreme Relevance!

Paul shared the everlasting gospel of God's amazing grace through Jesus Christ to the corrupt cultures of the Israelites, the Greeks, and the Romans – and it was pertinent and relevant to all of them. For the Israelites **light** was the supreme essence they valued; to the Greeks, **knowledge** was the supreme essence of their value system; but for the Romans it was **glory** that reigned supreme. Paul brilliantly summarized it to all of them by his spirit-inspired words. "*For it is the God who commanded light to shine out of darkness, who has shone in our hearts to give the light of the knowledge of the glory of God in the face of Jesus Christ.*" 2 Corinthians 4:6. Again, remember we have the very same treasure to share that Paul had, and it is just as relevant and urgent to our corrupt culture. *"But we have this treasure in earthen vessels, that the excellence of the power may be of God and not of us."* 2 Corinthians 4:7

The Bottom Line

Courage is not the absence of fear – it is conquering of fear! **"For God has not given us the spirit of fear, but of love and of power and of a sound mind."** 2 Timothy 1:7.

WE ARE MORE THAN CONQUERORS.

WE WILL BE CIVIL - BUT

WE WILL NOT BE SILENT!!

Note: The radio broadcast "Love Worth Finding" continues to replay the stirring messages of the late Adrian Rogers and they also offer his thought provoking booklet "Evolution - Fact or Fiction?"

Supplement #1 to Chapter 1

Personal Passion for Pro-Life

In the message outline "More than Conquerors", I listed #3 "Because of my family Sandy and Rachel". Sandy is our adopted daughter, who is now office manager for our business and ministry, and Rachel was our handicapped granddaughter. Rachel was our first granddaughter and our son and daughter-in-law did not realize she was handicapped until after she was born. The doctor callously told Randy that his newborn daughter had Trisomy 18 and probably wouldn't live more than two to six months – then walked out of the room leaving him with the burden of telling his wife the devastating news. Rachel actually lived for ten years, and although she could not walk or talk, she could receive and give love. She was a powerful influence in all of our lives in expanding our compassion for handicapped children and their families. Just writing this chokes me up and brings tears to my eyes. Who has the right to say that her life was worthless and that she should have been killed before birth? About 80 percent of Down's syndrome children are aborted before birth (according to the latest statistic I heard), yet Down's syndrome children are often the most loving kids on earth. Love is the greatest gift! (See 1 Corinthians 13.) The humanistic (atheistic) evolutionary viewpoint is that such children are worthless. "She is a burden –so kill her before she sees the light of day" is their attitude. Now this viewpoint extends to most unborn children "because the earth is already overpopulated". Isn't that playing God?

On a recording of one of Ravi Zacharias' presentations, he told that his mother was a teacher for a class of Down's syndrome children, and when she died they sobbed and sobbed. Why? They so loved their teacher! They are often the most loving human beings – it seems God endows them with an extra measure of His greatest gift – unselfish love. Yet the corrupt culture of so-called political correctness says kill them in the womb – they don't deserve to live. How foolish! How evil! This is the despicable state of our once great nation. Please pray! Earnestly pray!

Chapter 1: Purpose and Passion

Now I want to share Sandy's story:

Sandy's Story

In October 1969, a tiny newborn girl was left at the door of Holt Adoption Agency in Seoul, Korea. The co-workers guessed her birth date as October 20, and gave her the name Jong In Lee. Della and I had the opportunity and privilege to adopt this bundle of joy and renamed her Sandra Joy (which goes well with her older brother's name, Randal Troy, right? He is two years and one day older than she is). Sandy has truly been a joy to us through the years and is now also our office manager for our business (Deighton Lighting) and our ministry (Overseas Outreach). She has given birth to three beautiful daughters who also would not exist if she had been aborted.

When Sandy was a ninth grader at South Jr. High in Nampa, there was a classroom discussion about abortion. Most of the students were in favor of abortion, but an alert and perceptive teacher noticed that Sandy was feeling very disturbed by the pro-abortion perspectives. We are so thankful for this sensitive and compassionate teacher who gave Sandy a platform to express her viewpoint. She said, "I think Sandy has something she would like to say." Normally Sandy is very shy and doesn't speak out in a group, but when given this opportunity, she did speak up by saying, "I'm glad my Mother didn't kill me. She gave me life, birth and the opportunity to be adopted by parents who love me." A hush filled the room as those young teens suddenly realized they were talking about killing real people – and one of them was their own classmate. We felt so proud of Sandy when she told us of this incident – and we are even more proud of her today. She is a deeply committed Christian who exudes integrity and has been to us a model of how to forgive someone who has deeply wounded her (and all of us). It's hard to imagine how depleted our lives would be without Sandy. (Besides, she typed this up for me, so your life would be depleted without her too!)

We recognize that both Sandy and Rachel would have been prime targets for the abortion industry's death mentality, and our hearts ache for over fifty million children in America whose lives have been destroyed since the Roe vs. Wade decision in 1973 – plus the multiple millions of women (and men who pressured them into abortion) whose lives have been depleted, depressed, and devastated by sorrow, guilt, despair and anguish through abortion. To you the Savior's arms are open. His blood paid the penalty. Forgiveness is real. Accept Him in deep repentance and be buried with Him in baptism to walk in newness of life. (Romans 6:3-11) Then you can sing from your heart, "Jesus paid it all – all to Him I owe! Sin had left a crimson stain, but He washed it white as snow!" Amen! Praise God. What wonderful peace!

Here is a copy of a recent note from our friend and my former student, Steve Bragg, who for a long time turned away from our Lord and delved deeply in to a rebellious lifestyle, then truly repented and is serving as a missionary church planter in the Philippines:

"Thanks Rick for your kind thoughts. I have prayed for you, Della and family just now. We are happy here. We are all well. The Lord's Church is progressing and I'm in awe that He would continue to use such a one as me. Forgiveness, mercy and grace must be eternal with no beginning and end. The depth, height, width of them would appear to be without end or measure as well. Eternity is without end and measure. Like our eternal God, His attributes are eternal. Thank you Lord!

Living by forgiveness, mercy, and grace,
Steve"

SUPPLEMENT #2 TO CHAPTER 1

Frustration Confession

Since confession is good for the soul, I want to confess that sometimes I feel strong frustration with what I see and hear in Christendom – and even among true Christians. Have you also observed a lot of inconsistent thinking – compromise positions – double standards (especially the practice of adopting another standard of "truth" which conflicts with the Bible, while professing to truly believe the Bible)? It could be the Bible plus horoscope – or – plus "Watchtower" – or – plus Vatican – or – plus a "Living Prophet" – or – plus evolutionist assumptions and assertions.

This last one is especially prevalent within churches and Bible Colleges, which claim to be conservative and Bible believing. They often assert on one hand that the Bible is the inerrant Word of God, yet on the other hand ignore or reject what the Word of God plainly teaches in the early chapters of Genesis. Why? Because they have adopted another plumb line – another standard – "science". (Perhaps they have missed what Paul wrote to Timothy about "oppositions of science falsely so called". 1 Timothy 6:20 KJV). Because they assume that "science" has proven the universe to be 17 billion years old and the age of the earth to be 4 1/2 billion, they often adopt some compromise position such as the gap theory or the day – age theory and try to read it into the Bible. Every compromise theory ends up teaching that suffering and death existed in the world before Adam sinned – which is a blatant contradiction of God's Word. This is a cursed earth <u>because</u> of the rebellion of our original parents.

Exposition is drawing out from the Bible what it actually says – not reading into it what you want it to say in order to fit in with some pre-conceived notion. Many Christians have bought into believing in millions of years without considering the implications Biblically, historically, or factually. Why? Because they have heard so often that the earth is millions of years old, and they assume it has been proven scientifically. Therefore they feel they must harmonize this so-called "science" with Scripture. Let's examine this assumption Biblically, historically and factually.

1. Biblically. Does the Bible teach that God created the universe in six days and rested on the seventh? Absolutely! Just read it in Genesis 1! Were they literal days? Why would we think otherwise unless trying to compromise with evolutionism (and not look foolish in the eyes of the world)? Yes, I know that God didn't create the sun until the fourth day, but on the first day He created light. The sun is simply a light-holder. Are you aware that **every** place in the Old Testament where God puts a number with the word "yom" (Hebrew word for "day"), He was speaking of a literal day? So in Genesis 1 He had Moses write 1st day, 2nd day, etc. And to punctuate what He was saying, He had Moses write "and the evening and the morning were the first day", etc. Very clear. Do we get it?

Years ago when we were missionaries in Germany, a theologian at a conference began expounding his theory that the early chapters of Genesis were merely allegory, adopted from other ancient writings. One astute missionary wife asked him, "When you begin cutting, where do you stop?" He didn't give her a direct answer, but I do remember him saying, "Perhaps if you had read what I have read, you would believe what I believe." I remember thinking, "I hope not!" and "If I ever come to believe what he now believes, I hope I will have the integrity to resign and get a different line of work!" If I didn't believe the Word of God, why would I continue as a teacher or preacher? Did God intend for us to write off the early chapters of Genesis as mere allegory, or does He take those chapters seriously as true history? What type of writings are the first five books of the Bible? Law! History! How do you read law and history? Literally-unless dealing with an obvious figure of speech. Consider this weekly news from *Answers in Genesis*, February 18, 2006.

"Genesis is quoted from or referred to in the rest of the Bible more than any other book of the Bible.

"In the New Testament alone, there are at least 200 quotations from-or references to-Genesis. In fact, there are over 100 citations or direct references in the New Testament to the first eleven chapters of Genesis. And every one of those eleven chapters is referred to somewhere in the New Testament.

"Not only that, but each New Testament author refers somewhere in his writings to Genesis, chapters one to eleven in particular. And Jesus Himself quoted or referred to the first chapters of Genesis on six different occasions.

"If Genesis isn't true, then Jesus Christ would have been lying. Also, the rest of the Bible collapses, since every biblical doctrine of theology-directly or indirectly-is founded on the book of Genesis. That's why Genesis is referred to so often throughout the Bible.

"Believing Genesis is the key to fully understanding God's Word."

(Copied by permission of Answers in Genesis. For further information about AiG, see their website: www.answersingenesis. org).

If the plain, strongly emphasized statements about the days of creation are not literal, what logical basis do we have to believe that Adam and Eve were literal? (Please carefully and prayerfully re-read Romans 5:12-21.) If the first Adam was not literal, what about the second Adam, who came to take away the curse? If the days of creation in chapter one of Genesis were not literal, how did they get literal by Exodus 20:11? (Or are we to understand that God was telling the Israelites that they were to work six long geological ages before they were to rest for one long geological age?) If we cannot take the early chapters of Genesis as literal history, what logical basis do we have for believing that the later chapters are literal history? And if Genesis 2:29-31 doesn't mean that there were no carnivorous beasts before the curse, what does it mean? Can we take the Bible seriously or not? If not, should we just regard it as another piece of ancient literature with legends like the Gilgamesh epic or Greek and Roman mythology? Liberal churches have done that for years, and now they often refuse to take seriously what the Bible says about homosexuality, etc.

Consider this quote from an article in "the American Atheist":

"Christianity has fought, and still fights science, and will fight science to the desperate end over evolution, because evolution destroys utterly and finally the very reason Jesus' earthly life was supposedly made necessary.

"Destroy Adam and Eve and the original sin, and in the rubble you will find the sorry remains of the Son of God. Take away the meaning of His death; if Jesus was not the Redeemer who died for our sins, and this is what evolution means-then Christianity is nothing." ~ G. Richard Bozarth

Although I strongly disagree with G. Richard Bozarth on his idea that evolutionism is scientific, yet I do believe that he has a much clearer perception than many Christians concerning the vital nature of understanding Genesis as true and literal history. How sad that some Bible colleges and seminaries are so spineless about upholding a literal Genesis because they don't want to appear "unscientific"!

2. Historically. Are you aware that historically the estimated age of the earth has doubled every 20 years for the past 80 years or so, according to the speculations of evolutionists? Why? Do you know where the geology chart used by evolutionists came from? Terry Mortinson did his Ph.D. research on this subject and has a very enlightening DVD available from Answers in Genesis. I will summarize simply by saying that the geology chart is **not** based on scientific research, but on philosophical assumptions.

3. Factually. If you assume that the evolutionists have strong evidence for their assertions that it takes millions of years for fossils to form or for objects to become petrified, please open your mind and reconsider. Are you aware that there are fossils of one fish swallowing another fish and an ichthyosaur in the process of giving birth to its young? Such fossils had to have formed instantly in a catastrophe (such as a worldwide flood). If petrification takes millions of years, how do you explain a petrified hat, a petrified ham,

a petrified clock and a petrified pair of cowboy boots? If dinosaurs died out millions of year ago, how do you explain dinosaur bones discovered in both Alaska and Montana with red blood cells still in the marrow?

Have you heard over and over that it took millions of years for the Grand Canyon to form? Are you aware that a miniature Grand Canyon was formed in a few hours near Mount St. Helens from an aftershock of the May 18, 1980, explosion? Logically, there is no way the little bit of water in the Colorado River could form the Grand Canyon no matter how much time was involved, but a massive flood could have done so in a short time.

Please Pray for Purpose & Passion

If you look back to pages 30-34 you can review my purposes for writing this book. All of these purposes are pertinent and power-ful, and I feel passionate about these purposes. Purpose #3 is "to expose error and demolish foolish and evil arguments." Perhaps you have noticed that I'm passionate about this purpose to exposing the foolish and evil arguments for both evolutionism and abortion. What I've noticed, however, is that many Americans, even Chris-tians, do not see the fact that the lies about evolution are the foun-dation for the lies promoting abortion. Friend, please wake up! Realize that the foundational truth for the sanctity of human life is the fact that we are created in the image of God. NO animal is created in the image of God!!! Every human being is created in the image of God! The most destructive lie of evolutionism is that we are animals – just animals – which are continuing to evolve. Ernst Haeckel's destructive lie that every human baby goes through a re-capitulation of all the stages of evolution in his mother's womb was exposed as a fraud in 1874, yet it is still found in so-called "science" textbooks. Haeckel intentionally falsified his pictures of the stages of a baby's development. Isn't that outrageous? Are you outraged? I pray that you become passionate for both creationism and pro-life causes, and I pray for a stronger convergence of the creation movement and the pro-life movement. Both have had tremendous growth in recent years – may that growth become exponential as they converge into one interlocked, potent movement for truth and righteousness! Will you pray with me for this???

Haeckel called his theory "Ontogeny recapitulates Phylogeny." The fact is "Ontogeny decapitulates phylogeny"! Interpreted, this means "Reality cuts the head off evolutionism"!!!

When I teach on "Worldview" in college and university class-rooms in Ukraine, I tell the students, "God has given you the freedom of choice, so you have the privilege to believe that in the beginning there was nothing – then it exploded and became every-thing – with no plan, no design, no purpose, no meaning – and no hope. It is not science; it is a naturalist belief system. It is a bleak, hopeless philosophy which produces terrible consequences, but you have the freedom to choose to believe it if you wish. I once believed that doctrine, but I don't have enough faith to believe that nothing produces everything with no intelligent purpose or design. I choose to believe – and the weight of evidence demands this: 'In the beginning God created the heavens and the earth.' Genesis 1:1. Furthermore, I believe that you are not an accident. Every one of you is a unique individual created by Almighty God for a purpose. No one who ever lived or ever will live is exactly like you. He loves you and designed you with unique abilities to perform the work He created you to do. Searching out your designed gifting, finding the purpose for which God has put you here on earth, and fulfill-ing that purpose will be your greatest joy and your most fulfilling reason to be alive!!!"

It is dying to sin and selfishness in order to live my life to the glory of God by functioning the way He has wired me that I experi-ence indescribable joy! He will do that for you also if you choose to submit to the Lord Jesus Christ and accept His grace and forgive-ness of your sin. He paid the penalty for your sin – and mine – on the cross. Take a good look at Jesus on the cross agonizing and dying for you. Will you accept Him as your Savior, or reject Him in order to live life in your own self-centered way? If you choose to turn away from His outstretched arms (perhaps because you fear what others will think, say, or do) consider the consequences! *"But the cowardly, unbelieving, abominable, murderers, sexually immoral, sorcerers, idolaters, and all liars shall have their part in the lake which burns with fire and brimstone, which is the second death."* Revelation 21:8

Please, please carefully, seriously, prayerfully reconsider your choice! Consider these powerful words of Moses to the children of Israel:

"I call heaven and earth as witnesses today against you, that I have set before you life and death, blessing and cursing; therefore choose life, that both you and your descendants may live; that you may love the LORD your God, that you may obey His voice, and that you may cling to Him," Deuteronomy 30:19-20

SUPPLEMENT #3

The Meaning of Evolutionism

In another excellent broadcast for "Love Worth Finding", Adrian Rogers pointed out the inevitable consequences of believing the fantasy of evolutionism:

"People who believe they are animals will live like animals!
People who believe they are animals will treat others like animals!"

Does this open your eyes to why our country has sunk so deeply into violence, pornography, immorality, and degradation of every sort?

God, Christ, and Creation are banned from most of America's schools, colleges, and universities, while Darwin, death, Nietzsche, and Freud feed the roots of our innate carnal nature, so why should we be surprised to see the fruits of violence and perversion flourishing in our corrupt culture?

For verification of these and other fascinating discoveries contact one or all of the following:

1) Creation Resource Publications:
   (503)626-4447
   (866)225-5229
   mail@creationresource.com
   www.unlockingthemysteries.com

2) Answers in Genesis
   1-800-778-3390
   www.answersingenesis.org

3) Institute for Creation Research

1-800-628-7640
www.icr.org

4) "It's a Young World After All"
   www.creationism.org/ackerman/

5) Creation Today
   www.creationtoday.org

6) Creation Ministries International
   www.creation.com

7) Creation Evidence Museum
   www.creationevidence.org

8) Creation Research Society
   www.crsbooks.org

9) *Search for the Truth Ministries
   www.searchforthetruth.net

* This is the one I most highly recommend!

Another Stirring Story

There is another stirring story I highly recommend that you acquire and read – "**Witness for Life**", by Stacy Long. The subtitle is "**Rape victim gives child life**" and it was published in the June 2013 issue of *AFA Journal*, P.O. Drawer 2440, Tupelo, MS 38803. Their website is www.afajournal.org.

Closing Thought

Aspire to inspire before you expire!!!

QUESTIONS FOR CHAPTER 1 – SECOND HALF

1. I make the strong assertion, "Any compromise with evolutionism is destructive to Biblical theology and devastating to Biblical faith." Do you personally believe that this is a true and accurate statement? Why or why not? Explain your answer.

2.   Please carefully read Isaiah 40:21-31 before you reply. What scientific facts do you find in this passage of Scripture? Also, what most impacts you personally about this potent portion of the Word of God?

3.   Briefly explain the origin of evolutionism and who are the personified "heroes of the plot" in the evolutionists' make-believe story?

4.   If someone asks you to explain the problem of distant starlight from a Biblical creationist viewpoint, how will you reply?

5.   Who is a creationist, and do you personally believe that creationists are divisive?

6.   Is there a connection between creationism and "the everlasting gospel?" Please explain.

7.   I have shared my testimony in the section "From Atheism to the Almighty", so you can better understand my passion and purpose in this chapter. Will you please briefly write down your testimony so you can more confidently and fluently share it with others? You will touch lives I will never touch, and some people will relate better to you than anyone else. You are a unique creation of God, and you are here on this earth to fulfill His purpose for your life.

8.   What is your passion? What are you doing about it? Is it a godly passion?

9.   How would you summarize the contrast between the wisdom of men and the wisdom of God?

10. In Darwin's own writings, especially in private letters, he expressed his inner struggles and doubts about his "theory" of evolutionism. One of the most revealing statements he ever made is actually published in *The Origins of Species,* when he was discussing the intricacies of the eye. What did he say about it?

Bonus question: How is God molding you to be in reality and practical application more than a conqueror?

Thought question: The atheist astronomer, Carl Sagan, had a mantra which he repeated in each program: "The Cosmos is all that is, or ever was, or ever will be!" (Notice that Cosmos is capitalized.) Please analyze what kind of statement this is. Is this:

    1. A scientific statement? If so, how could he prove it? Do you think he was simply trying to avoid saying "God does not exist!" (a negative statement)?

    2. A philosophical statement? (That is – was this mantra of his simply a statement of what he wanted to believe?)

    3. Do you think when Carl Sagan stands at the judgment bar of our Awesome God, he will say, "The Cosmos is all there is, or ever was, or ever will be!"?

    4. Do you think Carl Sagan has already changed his mind since his death?

CHAPTER 2:
PERILOUS TIMES AND
POLITICAL TROUBLES

Patriotism

Another very strong purpose of mine for writing this book is patriotism. My heart aches as I witness the demise before my eyes of this once great nation. The following quotation has been attributed to a Scottish judge, author and historian, Alexander Tyler (or Tytler), but no one could document it in his writings. Therefore, the following words are simply a wise observation from an unknown source:

"The average age of the world's greatest civilizations from the beginning of history, has been about 200 years. During those 200 years, these nations always progressed through the following sequence:

From bondage to spiritual faith;
From spiritual faith to great courage;
From courage to liberty;
From liberty to abundance;
From abundance to complacency;
From complacency to apathy;
From apathy to dependence;
From dependence back into bondage."

A Resounding, Ringing Reminder that Freedom is not Free from 100 years after 1776!!

"In 1876, President James A. Garfield, in speaking to the Congress, issued a warning.

Listen to what he said:

'Now more than ever before the people are responsible for the character of their Congress. If that body [referring to elected politicians] be ignorant, reckless, and corrupt it is because the people tolerate ignorance, recklessness, and corruption. If it be intelligent, brave, pure it is because people demanded these high qualities to represent them.'

Then he added:

'If the next centennial [100 years from now] does not find us a great nation, it will be because those who represented the enterprise, the culture, the morality of the nation, did not aid in controlling the political forces.'"

"Our Constitution was made only for a moral and religious people. It is wholly inadequate for the government of any other."

- John Adams, coauthor of the Declaration of Independence and second president of the U.S. (1797-1801)

The Price of Freedom

On the 4th of July, 2013 I heard a stimulating and challenging message by Michael Youssef on the radio, which sparked this prayer in my heart:

"O Lord, Our founding fathers who signed the Declaration of Independence on July 4, 1776, pledged their lives, their fortunes, and their sacred honor. Some of them did pay with their lives, some of them saw their sons slaughtered on the battlefields of the Revolutionary War, and most of them did lose their fortunes and their property because they would not sacrifice their sacred honor. Many witnessed their houses and property burned by the enemy in spite for the stand they took – but stand they did! They stood for truth and liberty. Since that fearful time and those fateful battles, multitudes of American bodies lie buried, often on foreign fields – bodies of those who also paid the ultimate price to protect the liberty we now enjoy. Remind us often, Lord, of the price they paid that we might be free. Remind us that freedom is not free. Remind us that the price of freedom is vigilance and responsibility as we face the enemies of our freedom – both those on the outside of our borders and those, who like termites, are eating away our freedoms from inside our government, educational, scientific, and media institutions. O Lord, give us courage to stand against the enemies of truth, righteousness, and liberty with the strength and courage of our forefathers. And please protect us from another bloody revolutionary war or civil war! (What is civil about war, anyway?)

Most of all, O Lord, remind us of the ultimate price Jesus paid for our freedom from sin – its penalty, its power, and finally, its presence. Thank You! Thank You! Thank You!

In the Name above all names, Jesus our Lord, Amen." Rick

Should Christians be "Dabbling" in Politics?

Some readers may already be offended with me because they cling strongly to the opinion that Christians should not get involved in politics – and certainly a Christian leader should not mention political issues from the pulpit nor write about these issues in a book. It is my purpose in this section of the book to refute this lie that has kept millions of Christians silent while our nation is sinking in sin, succumbing to sexual lies and pandering to political propaganda. The fact is that we are mandated by Almighty God to be political and speak truth to our decadent, depraved culture about politics and all other realms. Those of us who speak out on political issues are not the ones being unfaithful to our calling as Christians, but those keeping silent are. These are my reasons for making such a blatant statement:

1. The word "politic" is simply using the English letters for the Greek word for citizen. Please consider these two powerful passages from Paul's prison epistle to the Philippians:

   > "Brethren, join in following my example, and note those who so walk, as you have us for a pattern. For many walk, of whom I have told you often, and now tell you even weeping, that they are the enemies of the cross of Christ: whose end is destruction, whose god is their belly, and whose glory is in their shame—who

set their mind on earthly things. **For our citizenship is in heaven**, *from which we also eagerly wait for the Savior, the Lord Jesus Christ, who will transform our lowly body that it may be conformed to His glorious body, according to the working by which He is able even to subdue all things to Himself.*" Philippians 3:17-21 (NKJV) **Please note that our "citizenship is in heaven" – but it is to influence how we act on earth.** In an earlier passage to the Philippians Paul wrote: "*Only let your* **conduct** *be worthy of the gospel of Christ, so that whether I come and see you or am absent, I may hear of your affairs, that you stand fast in one spirit, with one mind striving together for the faith of the gospel, and not in any way terrified by your adversaries, which is to them a proof of perdition, but to you of salvation, and that from God.*" Philippians 1:27-28 (NKJV)

In this passage the word translated "**conduct**" comes from the same Greek root as "**citizenship**" in Philippians 3:20, so it **could be translated, "Only let your politics be worthy of the gospel of Christ…and not in any way terrified by your adversaries…"** Powerful! **If you are a Christian, you are a <u>citizen</u> (<u>politic</u>) of heaven and are to <u>conduct</u> your <u>politics</u> in a godly manner to bring glory to God!** In other words, as a citizen of the Kingdom of Heaven, you are to conduct yourself in a godly manner in all things – including politics and fulfilling your responsibilities as an American citizen.

2. If you are an American citizen, you do have responsibilities as a citizen to uphold. Are you voting? Are you encouraging those who are standing up for our constitutional freedoms that others gave their lives for us to have and hold? Are you speaking out against the enemies who are working like termites to destroy our house from within? If not, I hope you bow your head in shame – then truly and deeply repent (change your course of action)! As I write this, I'm listening to Dr. James Dobson's "Family

Talk" program with Elaine Donnely about the Obama administration's huge push to put military women on the front lines of combat. Have you expressed your disgust and opposition to this radical feminist agenda issue to your representatives in Congress (both House and Senate)? If not – why not? It will destroy our military strength and destroy the lives of women who, on the front lines would be sleeping in the same tents with men, have no privacy, and be subjected to rape and torture if captured by an enemy. (Perhaps our most dangerous enemies are now inhabiting Washington, D.C. and promoting this outrageous, ungodly agenda!)

3. Many of the greatest leaders in the Bible were both spiritual and political leaders – Moses, Joshua, and David, for example.

4. The Old Testament prophets clearly and boldly spoke out on social and political issues.

5. John the Baptist, Jesus, and the apostles spoke directly and powerfully to political leaders about truth and righteousness. Are we following their example?

6. Remember that when a moral issue becomes a political issue it doesn't stop being a moral issue. **You wouldn't blurt out that Christians should not be speaking up on moral issues, would you? I hope not!**

For clarification, I wish to express that my commitment to "speak the truth in love" does not mean that I will compromise Biblical truth in order to come across more friendly than the stark reality of the glaring truth of the Word of God. In other words, I want to be your friend, but I will not pamper you nor coddle you to gain your friendship. If you choose to become my enemy, I wish to ask you two questions:

1. Do I become your enemy because I tell you the truth?

2. Are you looking for truth – Biblical answers – or are you looking for excuses?

"So Heavenly Minded He Is of No Earthly Use?"

Have you also heard the oft-repeated accusation that some believer may be "so heavenly minded that he is of no earthly use"? On rare occasions I have met someone who may, by stretching the definition of "heavenly minded," fit this description. However, my general observation is that most of our churches are struggling to survive with lukewarm, half-hearted members who are so worldly minded they are of no heavenly use! How else do we explain the fact that Barna polls show little or no difference in lifestyle between the so-called "born again Christians" and the rest of our worldly society? Whether the subject is abortion, pornography, drug and alcohol abuse, co-habitation, violent and immoral movies and video games, there is practically no measurable difference in poll after poll. Why not? Because most of those professing to be Christians are not living like Christians. Perhaps most of them are self deceived – and on Judgment Day will hear the saddest words in the Bible – "*I never knew you; depart from me, you who practice lawlessness!*" Matthew 7:23.

When a Christian is truly heavenly minded, he or she will be of maximum earthly use! Missionaries like the apostles, Patrick (who went back to Ireland with the Gospel after being taken there as a slave), William Carey, Adoniram Judson, Amy Carmichael and many others, transformed whole cultures by being truly heavenly minded: "*If then you were raised with Christ, seek those things which are above, where Christ is, sitting at the right hand of God. Set your mind on things above, not on things on the earth. For you died, and your life is hidden with Christ in God. When Christ who is our life appears, then you also will appear with Him in glory. Therefore put to death your members which are on the earth: fornication, uncleanness, passion, evil desire, and covetousness, which is idolatry. Because of these things the wrath of God is coming upon the sons of disobedience, in which you yourselves once walked when you lived in them. But now you yourselves are to put off all these: anger, wrath, malice, blasphemy, filthy language out of your mouth. Do not lie to one another, since you have put off the old man with his deeds, and have put on the new man who is renewed in knowledge according to the image of Him who created him, where there is neither Greek nor Jew, circumcised nor uncircumcised, barbarian, Scythian, slave nor free, but Christ is all and in all. Therefore, as the elect of God, holy and beloved, put on tender mercies, kindness, humility, meekness, longsuffering; bearing with one another, and forgiving one another, if anyone has a complaint against another; even as Christ forgave you, so you also must do. But above all these things put on love, which is the bond of perfection. And let the peace of God rule in your hearts, to which also you were called in one body; and be thankful. Let the word of Christ dwell in you richly in all wisdom, teaching and admonishing one another in psalms and hymns and spiritual songs, singing with grace in your hearts to the Lord. And whatever you do in word or deed, do all in the name of the Lord Jesus, giving thanks to God the Father through Him."* Colossians 3:1-17. *"Oh, the depth of the riches both of the wisdom and knowledge of God! How unsearchable are His judgments and His ways past finding out! 'For who has known the mind of the* Lord? *Or who has become His counselor? Or who has first given to Him and it shall be repaid to him?' For of Him and through Him and to Him are all things, to whom be glory forever. Amen. I beseech you therefore, brethren, by the mercies of God, that you present your bodies a living sacrifice, holy, acceptable to God, which is your reasonable service. And do not be conformed to this world, but be transformed by the renewing of your mind, that you may prove what is that good and acceptable and perfect will of God."* Romans 11:33-12:2.

Perilous Times

"But know this, that in the last days perilous times will come: For men will be lovers of themselves, lovers of money, boasters, proud, blasphemers, disobedient to parents, unthankful, unholy, unloving, unforgiving, slanderers, without self-control, brutal, despisers of good, traitors, headstrong, haughty, lovers of pleasure rather than lovers of God, having a form of godliness but denying its power. And from such people turn away!" 2 Timothy 3:1-5 (NKJV)

In Matt Proctor's penetrating presentation "Getting the Most from Revelation," he quotes another preacher who said, "*The church must be prophetic or it will be pathetic.*" How true! In the section entitled, "I See Evil More Clearly (chapters 12-18)" Matt wrote:

"Looming over these chapters, John shows us evil personified as a violent dragon, two grotesque beasts, and a prostitute. We need these shocking images because we don't always see evil as plainly as that. The world teaches us to call un-nice things by nicer names. Instead of cheating, it's creative accounting. Instead of lying, it's massaging the truth. Instead of homosexuality, it's an alternative lifestyle. Instead of profanity, it's freedom of expression. It's not gossip; it's concern. *Satan is a deceiver, and his most effective strategy is dressing up ugly realities in beautiful words.*

So in these chapters, John exposes the evil that seeks to deceive his readers. False religion and godless government are not simply well-meaning but misguided institutions. They are evil beasts that belong to the dragon. Follow the strings, and you will find they are marionettes of Satan, puppets of the prince of this world. The fallen culture around you may at first appear attractive, and it will seem she is offering you the beginning of a beautiful relationship. But in Revelation 17, John unmasks her as a cheap, diseased streetwalker. She will be destroyed and all those with her, so don't be seduced.

John is teaching us to call sin by its true name. What looks harmless is hellish. This world is not a playground but a battleground, and the battle rages in the things I buy, movies I see, activities I pursue, conversations I have, priorities I set, and beliefs I live by. In all of these, Satan will tempt me to make subtle compromises, and I must keep my eyes wide open. When I read Revelation, I see evil more clearly." ("Getting the Most from Revelation" by Matt Proctor, *One Body*, Spring 2013 Issue)

The message of Revelation about wickedness is more graphic, but it is not different from the message of Psalm 9:17. "*The wicked shall be turned into hell, and all the nations that forget God.*"

"Righteousness exalts a nation, but sin is a reproach to any people."
Proverbs 14:34

"In Times Like These"
by Victor Knowles

"Among the apostle Paul's last words were these: '*But mark this: There will be terrible times in the last days*' (2 Tim 3:1). Other translations say 'perilous times,' 'difficult times,' and even 'violent times.' We are certainly living in times like these today. Christians are being persecuted and killed the world over at a frightening rate. The 'Arab Spring' has sprung and it is anything but a pretty picture. But the blood of the martyrs is still the seed of the church!

We need to remember that God's people have always been in the crosshairs of the devil and his angels. The Philistines were determined to wipe out Israel. Haman plotted to exterminate the Jews. King Herod thirsted for the blood of the Christ child. Saul of Tarsus went about breathing out threats and slaughter against the church. (Isn't it 'amazing grace' that God turned the worst persecutor of the church into the greatest preacher of the truth?)

I've been reading the book of Daniel as of late. Talk about 'perilous times' for the people of God! Four young men from Judah were now prisoners of war in Babylon (modern day Iraq). They were far from home, but not far from God! 'But Daniel resolved not to defile himself with the royal food and wine, and he asked the chief official for permission not to defile himself in this way' (Dan 1:8). Daniel's courageous resolve led to God pouring out His blessing on the four POWs (Dan 1:17). Incredibly, they were found to be ten times better than their rivals (Dan 1:20).

John Wayne said, 'Courage is being scared to death, but saddling up anyway.' In chapter 3 we find Shadrach, Meshach and Abednego saddling up. They spoke as one: 'O Nebuchadnezzar, we do not need to defend ourselves before you in this matter. If we are thrown into the blazing furnace, the God we serve is able to save us from it, and he will rescue us from your hand, O king. But even if he does not, we want you to know, O king, that we will not serve your gods or worship the image of gold you have set up' (Dan 3:;16-18). Here were men of character, conviction, and courage. They wouldn't bend, they wouldn't bow, they wouldn't burn! God delivered them and caused the law of the land to be changed!

Courage is not the absence of fear; it is a firm resistance to fear. King Darius issued a decree banning all prayers except to him. 'Now when Daniel learned that the decree had been published, he went home to his upstairs room where [t]he windows opened to Jerusalem. Three times a day he got down on his knees and prayed, giving thanks to his God, just as he had done before' (Dan 6:10). Talk about open courage! Daniel was delivered from the lion's den and once again the law of the land was changed. The pagan king even exclaimed, 'His kingdom will not be destroyed, his dominion will never end' (Dan 6:26). This passage is cited in Revelation 11:15, 'The kingdom of the world has become the kingdom of our Lord and of his Christ, and he will reign forever and ever.' We win, we win!

In 1944, during some of the darkest days of WWII, an American housewife named Ruth Caye Jones wrote a timeless hymn, 'In Times Like These.' In times like these, she wrote, you need a Savior, you need an anchor, and you need the Bible. 'Be very sure your anchor holds and grips the Solid Rock.' And now it is 2012. We are living in times that are perilous, difficult, and even violent. WE still need a Savior, and we have Him in Jesus Christ. We still need an anchor, and that anchor is courageous faith. We still need the Bible, and thank God we still have the Word of God that assures us that no matter what happens . . . We win! We win!

Courage, brother, do not stumble, Though thy path be dark as night; There's a star to guide the humble: Trust in God and do the right." (Victor Knowles, "Knowlesletter", October 2012)

What on earth are you doing for Heaven's sake?

"NEVER HAPPEN HERE?" *by Ray Hawk*

"Did you know the church has been at war since it was established on that first Pentecost after Jesus' resurrection? The apostle Peter wrote, "Be self-controlled and alert. Your enemy the devil prowls around like a roaring lion looking for someone to devour. Resist him, standing firm in the faith, because you know that YOUR BROTHERS THROUGHOUT THE WORLD ARE UNDERGOING THE SAME KIND OF SUFFERINGS." (1 Peter 5:8-9).

In Africa, the East, Australia, Europe, Russia, India, and England, Islam makes its goal of world conquest no secret with street marches, warning placards, riots, bombings, church burnings, destruction of Christian businesses, home invasions, beatings, imprisonment, and murder.

Ideologies such as humanism, skepticism, agnosticism, and atheism are also negative forces against Christianity. In China and North Korea, Christians are arrested and public assemblies are outlawed. So, they meet in secret. This is just the hem of the garment of what is happening in our world. Yet, some refuse to believe this conflict has reached our shores. Have there been any indications of Christianity being ridiculed, or threats leveled against our faith?

1. Do you remember when prayer in public schools was common? Is it now?

2. Do you remember when Christmas carols were sung in classrooms? Are they now?

3. Do you remember when Christmas plays were performed in public schools?

4. Do you remember when the Ten Commandments were displayed in schools, courthouses, and other local and State buildings? Are they now?

5. Do you remember when prayers were common at graduations and football games?

6. Do you remember when "one nation under God" in the pledge wasn't challenged?

7. Are school employees reprimanded or fired if they pray on school property or hand out religious material?

8. Do you remember when abortion was considered illegal?

9. Do you remember when abortion after the first trimester was unlawful?

10. Do you remember when abortion after the second trimester was unlawful?

11. Do you remember when abortion of a living baby being born was unlawful?

12. Do you remember when our government considered homosexuality unlawful?

13. Do you remember when our government considered cross dressing unlawful?

14. Did boys show up at school dressed like girls and expect to be treated as girls?

15. Did you know homosexuals are producing their own Bible called "The Queen James Bible" so they can justify their sexual preferences?

16. Did you know that an amendment was attached to a defense bill by one of our political parties in 2009 that makes it a felony to publicly criticize the homosexual lifestyle, including sermons teaching that it is a sin?

17. Did you know there are nine states so far that offer a marriage license to homosexual couples as well as the District of Columbia?

18. Did you know that two men may marry or two women and the government will grant them the same legal considerations of a husband and wife?

19. Did you know the 2009 law caused a Christian, who runs a marriage chapel, to be sued by a homosexual couple whom he refused to marry, based on his religious convictions, and he lost and paid them a hefty sum? Regardless of religious convictions he either has to marry such couples or close his business.

20. Did you know that businesses, run by Christians, must pay for "health" items for employees that the owners have biblical objections to? If they refuse they must pay outrageous fines, even on a daily basis until they comply.

21. Did you know our government attempted to force hospitals, operated by churches, to pay for those "health" items which their faith objected to?

22. Did you know homosexual couples have some privileges offered by our government that married couples who are male and female don't enjoy?

23. Did you know "political correctness" is demanding that your faith be expressed only in private and not publicly?

24. Did you know that the public, in the past fifty years, has been desensitized to sin, and acclimated to accept it? Think of the things we accept today that we would have been horrified about just twenty years ago. We are seeing a tolerance for sin and intolerance for faith.

These are but a single drop in the vast ocean of ridicule, intimidation, and force being used against Christianity.

WHO BELIEVES THAT "IT" CAN'T HAPPEN HERE? IT ALREADY HAS!

'There is a way that seems right to a man, but in the end it leads to death' Proverbs 16:25" (Ray Hawk, March 10, 2013. Used by permission.)

THE REALITY

The reality is that the so-called mainstream news media outlets are not objective news reporters. They have been infiltrated by the philosophy of Marxism and have been pro- paganda machines for many years for the Democrats – who are their fellow comrades propagating Marxist philosophy. Do you know that all the way back in 1944, the candidate for president who had run at least twice on the Communist Party USA decided not to run again? Why? Because the Democratic Party had adopted the Communist platform.

(See a brief comment on the Republican Party on page 158)

Battlefronts in the Cultural Conflicts

I want to share two brief news items from the February 17, 2013 issue of *The Times and the Scriptures*:

"Muslims File federal Complaint, T&S Classic reprinted from 2/14/10 Officials Narrowly Escape "Hate Crime" Charges

Two Lancaster, CA officials seem to have narrowly escaped criminal charges after the mayor made a statement supporting Christianity and a councilwoman briefly posted a Facebook com- ment criticizing a Muslim honor killing. The Council on Amer- ican-Islamic Relations (CAIR) complained to the local Human Relations Task Force which investigated and then cleared the pair after requiring apologies. Now CAIR has filed federal complaints.

Last month Mayor R. Rex Parris said, "We are growing a Christian community and we should never shy away from that." When CAIR objected, Parris said they should understand that he is a Christian "not ashamed of the gospel," and he refused at first to apologize. Councilwoman Sherry Marquez removed her comment about honor killings from her Facebook page after 90 minutes, but the Task Force packaged the two cases and heard them together. Both Parris and Marquez apologized before the public hearings. That "helped" according to the committee, but they nevertheless ruled that the words were "divisive, exclusive, and inflammatory." In both cases, they said, people had been "harmed," and both could have been ruled hate crimes.

Christian attorneys say the cases show that hate-crimes laws can "chill free speech."

For discussion: Review articles on hate crime laws in our 5-17-09 and 11-1-09 Bulletins. Could Mayor Parris have meant "Christian community" in the same sense that the U.S. Supreme Court has recognized America as a "Christian nation"? On the subject of honor killings, see our 1-31-10 "Hot Topic Roundup." Why should anyone in America have to apologize for criticizing such a practice? Review Backgrounder $45, Free Speech vs. intolerance, with its thorough biblical study on religious freedom of expression. Read about the persecution of Paul for his implied criticism of a non-Christian religion (Acts 19:23 ff.)

School board votes to keep Jesus

An Ohio school district voted unanimously Tuesday night to keep a portrait of Jesus hanging in the middle school where it's been for 65 years, denying a federal lawsuit's claim the portrait's display unconstitutionally promotes religion in a public school.

The board said the portrait belongs to the student group that put it up, the Hi-Y club. The portrait's frame is inscribed with the club's name and the Christian-based service group is the portrait's owner, not the school. Superintendent Phil Howard said after the meeting. "We can't make that kind of endorsement (of religion) as a government entity. But we also can't infringe upon the rights of our student groups and our students."

For discussion: Will the war on God in our schools ever end? Who do you suppose will win? See the first paragraph on the second page of Backgrounder #24, Normal Christian Education.
Copyright 2013, *The Times and the Scriptures*, 948 Darlene Ave, Springfield, OR 97477, www.timesandscriptures.com"

Even from these few brief articles it is easy to discern that the tone of our corrupt culture in twenty first century America is much closer to "God in the hands of angry sinners" than it is to "Sinners in the Hands of an Angry God" (the title of Jonathan Edwards' most famous sermon). Now in America, you are likely to hear very often the statement, "You can't legislate morality." This declaration is not only false, it is absolutely ridiculous! Every law legislates somebody's morality (or immorality)!!! Instead of godly morality being legislated by our government, now outrageous, ungodly immorality is often being promoted and enforced in the form of legislation favoring the practices of fornication, abortion, and homosexuality. The welfare system rewards fornication by paying unwed mothers more for each child she has out of wedlock – but if she gets married – no funds. This system encourages the wrong behavior with monetary rewards.

What "Wall of Separation"?

Does the 1st Amendment of our Constitution erect a "wall of separation" between God and our government? God and our schools? God and our city council meetings? God and our graduation ceremonies? The brief answer is NO! Absolutely not! Weren't our founding fathers concerned about keeping God's nose out of their newly formed government? Certainly not! They sought His guidance on their knees for days after futilely wrangling with each other for weeks. In fact, it was Ben Franklin, a man who honored God even though he was not a Christian, who rose and called to his fellow framers of our Constitution to prayer.

"Benjamin Franklin's Request for Prayers at the Constitutional Convention"

"Benjamin Franklin

July 28, 1787

Mr. President. . .

In this situation of this Assembly, groping as it were in the dark to find political truth, and scarce able to distinguish it when presented to us, how has it happened, Sir, that we have not hitherto once thought of humbly applying to the Father of lights to illuminate our understanding? In the beginning of the Contest with G. Britain, when we were sensible of danger we had daily prayer in this room for the divine protection. – Our prayers, Sir were heard, & they were graciously answered. All of us who were engaged in the struggle must have observed frequent instances of a superintending providence in our favor.

To that kind providence we owe this happy opportunity of consulting in peace on the means of establishing our future national felicity. **And have we now forgotten that powerful friend? Or do we imagine that we no longer need his assistance? I have lived, Sir, a long time, and the longer I live, the more convincing proofs I see of this truth – that God Governs in the affairs of men. And if a sparrow cannot fall to the ground without his notice, is it probable that an empire can rise without his aid? We have been assured, Sir, in the sacred writings, that "except the Lord build the House they labour in vain that build it."** *I firmly believe this; and I also* *believe that without his concurring aid we shall succeed in this political building no better, than the Builders of Babel: We shall be divided by our little partial local interests; our project will be confounded, and we ourselves shall become a reproach and bye word down to future ages. And what is worse, mankind may hereafter from this unfortunate instance, despair of establishing Governments by Human wisdom and leave it to chance, war and conquest.*

I therefore beg leave to move – that henceforth prayers imploring the assistance of Heaven, and its blessing on our deliberations, be held in this Assembly every morning before we proceed to business, and that one or more of the Clergy of this City be requested to officiate in that Service- . . ."

So what about that "Wall of Separation" we so often hear about? Isn't there a wall of separation in our Constitution? No! There is not! Such a wall of separation of God from government was written into the constitution of the former Soviet Union – but not into our constitution. Thomas Jefferson did refer to a wall of separation in a personal letter to the Danbury Baptist Association – but the wall he referred to was a wall around the government to keep it from infringing on their freedom of religion – not a wall to keep God out of government or out of schools or out of court rooms or out of graduation ceremonies, etc. We have been lied to over and over so many times that most American citizens now believe the lie about a "wall of separation" to keep God and His Word out. Do you realize what the First Amendment actually says? Here it is:

"Congress shall make no law respecting an establishment of religion, or prohibiting the free exercise thereof; or abridging the freedom of speech, or of the press; or the right of the people peaceably to assemble, and to petition the Government for a redress of grievances."

Who is being restricted? God? NO! Christians? NO! Congress? YES! **Our founding fathers were concerned about re-**

stricting the encroachment of government on the free exercise of religion!!!

The Pilgrims came to America "for the glory of God and the advancement of the Christian faith"!

(See the documentation in the powerful DVD documentary, *Monumental: In Search of America's National Treasure*, by Mark Craig Productions)

"God cannot be separated from government because He carries government on His shoulders!" *"For unto us a Child is born, unto us a Son is given; and the government will be upon His shoulder. And His name will be called Wonderful, Counselor, Mighty God, Everlasting Father, Prince of Peace." Isaiah 9:6*

"Did You Know?"

"DID YOU KNOW?

As you walk up the steps to the building which houses the U.S. Supreme Court you can see near the top of the building a row of the world's law givers and each one is facing one in the middle who is facing forward with a full frontal view ... it is Moses and he is holding the Ten Commandments!

DID YOU KNOW?

As you enter the Supreme Court courtroom, the two huge oak doors have the Ten Commandments engraved on each lower portion of each door.

DID YOU KNOW?

As you sit inside the courtroom, you can see the wall, right above where the Supreme Court judges sit, a display of the Ten

Commandments!

DID YOU KNOW?

There are Bible verses etched in stone all over the Federal Buildings and Monuments in Washington, D.C.

DID YOU KNOW?

James Madison, the fourth president, known as 'The Father of Our Constitution' made the following statement:

'We have staked the whole of all our political institutions upon the capacity of mankind for self-government, upon the capacity of each and all of us to govern ourselves, to control ourselves, to sustain ourselves according to the Ten Commandments of God.'

DID YOU KNOW?

Every session of Congress begins with a prayer by a paid preacher, whose salary has been paid by the taxpayer since 1777.

DID YOU KNOW?

Fifty-two of the 55 founders of the Constitution were members of the established orthodox churches in the colonies.

DID YOU KNOW?

Thomas Jefferson worried that the Courts would overstep their authority and instead of interpreting the law would begin making law an oligarchy the rule of few over many.

How then, have we gotten to the point that everything we have done for 232 years in this country is now suddenly wrong and unconstitutional? . . ."

Also, did you know that the phrase "wall of separation between church and state" is **not** to be found anywhere in the Constitution or in the Amendments? It actually comes from a private letter written to the Danbury Baptist Association to assure them that the government would **not** infringe on their freedom of religion.

Do you know what the 1st Amendment does actually say? *"Congress shall make no law respecting an establishment of religion, or prohibiting the free exercise thereof; or abridging the freedom of speech, or of the press; or the right of the people peaceably to assemble, and to petition the government for a redress of grievances."* The restrictions were put on **Congress**!!!

Did you know that all these lawsuits by the ACLU and Freedom From Religion are bogus? They are based on lies! Twisted concepts. How sad! How deplorable!

By the way, the communist governments of the former Soviet Union nations did erect a "wall of separation' between God and government. Whose leadership is America now following? It's **not** too late to turn back to the Godly examples of our founding fathers!

GOD'S WISDOM ON HOW TO HANDLE A FOOL

"Every prudent man acts with knowledge, but a fool lays open his folly. . . He who walks with wise men will be wise, but the companion of fools will be destroyed." Proverbs 13:16, 20. *"Excellent speech is not becoming to a fool, much less lying lips to a prince. . . Rebuke is more effective for a wise man than a hundred blows on a fool."* Proverbs 17:7, 10. *"Do not speak in the hearing of a fool, for he will despise the wisdom of your words."* Proverbs 23:9. *"As snow in summer and rain in harvest, **so honor is not fitting for a fool**. . . **Do not answer a fool according to his folly, lest you also be like***

him. Answer a fool according to his folly, lest he be wise in his own eyes. . . Like one who binds a stone in a sling is he who gives honor to a fool." Proverbs 26:1, 4-5, 8

Verses 4 and 5 may be used by a fool to prove that the Bible contradicts itself. Instead of listening to a fool, read these verses again and again to understand the depth of wisdom given about how to handle a fool. Verse 4 warns us not to allow ourselves to degenerate into the same level of foolishness so we "become like him." Verse 5 clarifies to us that there is proper time, place, and manner to use satire. Some questions are so saturated with foolish philosophy that they do not deserve a serious reply. **Satire may be the most appropriate response.** Elijah, Isaiah, and Jesus all used satire effectively. If someone asks you, "How do I even know that I exist?" you can wisely respond by asking the question, "Who is asking???" Yes, it is satire – but entirely appropriate satire for such a foolish question.

John Wesley has given us an ideal illustration of both humility and quick wit in handling a fool.

On one occasion, John came face to face with a liberal preacher on the opposite side of a one-way walking bridge (perhaps just a log over the stream). The liberal threw down a challenge, "I never give way to a fool!!" John replied, "But I do!" and stepped aside.

Weapons of our Warfare

I'm thankful for the Christian legal organizations that are battling for our constitutional freedoms in the courts of America, but Christians cannot delegate all responsibility for winning victories in the cultural clashes to these Christian legal groups. Why not? Because this is spiritual warfare. We **are** at war! Yes, I'm talking to **you** – and to me! We can make a difference – one heart and one soul at a time, one phone call or one letter at a time – to a friend, to a representative, to your mayor, etc. Remember, however, how we are to approach this. Consider these passages of Scripture:

"*Walk in wisdom toward those who are outside, re-deeming the time. Let your speech always be with grace, seasoned with salt*, that you may know how you ought to answer each one." Colossians 4:5-6. "*For though we walk in the flesh, we do not war according to the flesh. For the weapons of our warfare are not carnal but mighty in God for pulling down strongholds, casting down arguments and every high thing that exalts itself against the knowledge of God, **bringing every thought into captivity to the obedi-ence of Christ**,*" 2 Corinthians 10:3-5. "*Finally, my brethren, **be strong in the Lord and in the power of His might**. Put on the whole armor of God, that you may be able to stand against the wiles of the devil. For we do not wrestle against flesh and blood, but against principalities, against powers, against the rulers of the darkness of this age, against spiritual hosts of wickedness in the heavenly places. **Therefore take up the whole armor of God, that you may be able to withstand in the evil day, and having done all, to stand.** Stand there-fore, having girded your waist with truth, having put on the breastplate of righteousness, and having shod your feet with the preparation of the gospel of peace; above all, taking the shield of faith with which you will be able to quench all the fi-ery darts of the wicked one. And take the helmet of salvation, and the sword of the Spirit, which is the word of God; **pray-ing always with all prayer and supplication in the Spirit**, being watchful to this end with all perseverance and suppli-cation for all the saints— and for me, **that utterance may be given to me, that I may open my mouth boldly to make known the mystery of the gospel**, for which I am an ambas-sador in chains; that in it **I may speak boldly, as I ought to speak**.*" Ephesians 6:10-20.

Let's boldly face the issues with truth and righteousness from God's Word in the power of the Holy Spirit. Let's move forward in faith – not shrink back in fear! *"For God has not given us a spirit of fear, but of power and of love and of a sound mind."* 2 Timothy 1:7. "For though He was crucified in weakness, yet He lives by the power of God. For we also are weak in Him, *but we shall live with Him by the power of God toward you.* . . . . All the saints greet you." 2 Corinthians 13:4, 13.

Solomon's wisdom became widely known and praised throughout the ancient world nearly 1,000 years before Christ, and he remained the wisest man on earth until "the Word became flesh and dwelt among us" John 1:14. Consider these wise words of Solomon: "A wise man's heart inclines him to the right, but a fool's heart to the left." Ecclesiastes 10:2 (ESV)

Could these words be prophetic??? Just wondering. ~ Rick Deighton

Their Finest Hour

We have a choice – we can wilt, wither, and whimper in fear before the giants as did the cowardly Israelites at the border of Canaan – or boldly take them on as Joshua and Caleb challenged them to do. Recognize that no matter how big and powerful the opponents – they are no match for Almighty God! **In God's presence we have the power!**

Let's consider and be encouraged by Winston Churchill's famous speech as Great Britain faced the gruesome onslaught of the invading Nazi forces.

Delivered to the House of Commons, 18 June 1940, following the collapse of France. Many thought Britain would follow.

'What General Weygand called the Battle of France is over. I expect that the battle of Britain is about to begin. Upon this battle depends the survival of Christian civilisation. Upon it depends our own British life, and the long continuity of our institutions and our Empire. The whole fury and might of the enemy must very soon be turned on us. Hitler knows that he will have to break us in this island or lose the war. If we can stand up to him, all Europe may be free and the life of the world may move forward into broad, sunlit uplands. **But if we fail, then the whole world, including the United States, including all that we have known and cared for, will sink into the abyss of a new Dark Age made more sinister, and perhaps more protracted, by the lights of perverted science. Let us therefore brace ourselves to our duties, and so bear ourselves that if the British Empire and its Commonwealth last for a thousand years, men will still say, 'This was their Finest Hour.'"**

If the Brits had withered and whimpered in fear instead of rising to the challenge they would have gone under. **We have a choice. Which way, America??? Is our finest hour yet ahead of us? Not if we continue down the polluted path of political correctness!**

What is Wrong with Being Politically Correct?

Do you know what is wrong with "politically correct'? It isn't! It is politically, morally and spiritually corrupt. Do you know where the politically correct doctrine originated? Probably not – I didn't either until very recently, but I did have enough Biblical and historical and philosophical information to identify politically correct doctrine as raw, unvarnished Marxism. **An acquaintance in a local business told me that political correctness comes directly out of the little red book entitled, "Quotations from Chairman Mao Tsetung"!** He also told me the book is still available on Amazon, and I should look on page 147. I ordered my own copy. Here are a couple of sentences from page 147: *"Without the style of hard* *struggle, it is impossible to maintain a firm **and correct political orientation**." ..... "What really counts in the world is conscientiousness, and the Communist Party is most particular about being conscientious."* Page 1 of this little book says, "***The force at the core leading our cause forward is the Chinese Communist Party. The theoretical basis guiding our thinking is Marxism-Leninism.***"

Do you realize that Mao was the worst mass murderer in history? Yes, he orchestrated the murder of far more people than Hitler and Stalin! Why should we want to compromise God's inspired Word to comply with "political correctness"?

"***Beware lest anyone cheat you through philosophy and empty deceit, according to the tradition of men, according to the basic principles of the world, and not according to Christ. For in Him dwells all the fullness of the Godhead bodily; and you are complete in Him, who is the head of all principality and power.***" Colossians 1:8-10

"POLITICAL CORRECTNESS"

Insanity or Intentional Strategy by the Enemy Within our Own Gates???

"[We have] rules of engagement that predominantly favor the enemy's protection over our own… this is insanity." ~ Karen Vaughn, mother of slain SEAL Team Six hero, Aaron Vaughn

"The rules of engagement created a restrictive environment for our special operations people that literally don't allow them to win, that don't allow them to protect themselves adequately." ~ ~ General Jerry Boykin

"With bounties on their heads and targets on their back… they were shot down by the Taliban who were positioned in the tower of a building in the perfect place, at the exact time to launch an attack." ~ Doug Hamburger, father of slain SEAL Team Six hero, Patrick Hamburger

"Rules of engagement... How about my heart? How about my mind? I cry every day, and my kids cry. To win the hearts and minds of those people? They hate us... They know the rules of engagement." Charles Strange, father of slain SEAL Team Six hero, Michael Strange

"Political correctness... has infected every level of leadership command in our military today. It manifested itself in our counter insurgency strategy with its restricted rules of engagement which unnecessarily put the lives of our military forces at risk. It cost numerous lives and thousands with horrendous, permanent injuries. All in the failed hope of winning the hearts and minds of a tribal society. This makes no sense." ~ Admiral James Lyons

"We've got to get the word out. We've got to do something to take back this country. We have to stand up." ~ General Paul Vallely

A Perceptive Prediction from the Past

William and Katherine Booth faced the monumental issues of their day with faith rather than fear. What was the result? They started the Salvation Army, which now ministers to multiplied multitudes of downtrodden people in many nations.

As the nineteenth century was drawing to a close, William Booth had the foresight to write that the greatest dangers of the coming twentieth century were likely to be:

1. Christianity without the Holy Spirit
2. Religion without Christ
3. Government without God
4. Forgiveness without Repentance
5. Redemption without Regeneration
6. Heaven without Hell

Do I mean to imply that William Booth was a Holy Spirit

inspired prophet? No! Do I mean that he was an astute observer of social and religious trends? Yes, definitely! It is almost uncanny how accurately his predictions have continued playing out through the twentieth century and into the twenty-first.

"Isn't it ironic that after 70 years of shutting God out, Russia wanted Him back, yet we in America are shutting Him out?" (Approximate quote from Ravi Zacharias)

Spectator or Participant?

As you observe these dangerous trends being played out in our American churches and general culture, I hope you don't content yourself with being a spectator in these momentous times of radical change. Get involved! Become a positive participant! You may wonder, "What can I do?" Speak up for God's truth – Biblical principles! Witness to friends, relatives, neighbors, acquaintances, co-workers, etc. Write letters to editors, senators, representatives, mayors, etc. If you cannot speak- you can still pray!

I want to share with you some examples of letters and articles I've written. The first one is copy of a letter I wrote to US Senator from Idaho, Mike Crapo on May 8, 2010:

"Dear Mike, (Mike Crapo – U.S. Senator from Idaho)

I really appreciate that you answer my letters. Thank you for clearly pointing out to me that according to the Constitution, the impeachment of a president must begin with the House of Representatives – not the Senate. It has been a long time since I've read our Constitution – and I do believe that as Americans we are duty bound to follow our Constitution. Apparently you also believe this. For this reason I believe that we must push with all our might for the impeachment of Barack Obama – which should also include his unconstitutional government of radical anti-American czars, answerable only to him. He has established the pattern of a tyrant – not the pattern of honoring our Constitution.

- What do you call it when a "president" trashes our Constitution, while following the Communist playbook, "Rules for Radicals" by Saul Alenski, to the letter?

- What do you call it when our "president" bows to the king of Saudi Arabia and apologizes to the world for American "aggression" and intentionally alienates America's closest ally by humiliating Israeli Prime Minister Netanyahu?

- What do you call it when a "president" seizes control of one private enterprise after another?

- What do you call it when a "president" continues aggressively pushing to bankrupt our nation, so that we implode and fall to foreign powers?

- Why has Obama spent thousands – perhaps hundreds of thousands of dollars to fight lawsuits, instead of producing a legitimate birth certificate? But since Hawaii accepted his "certificate of live birth", it looks like we are stuck with it.

Barack Obama's actions are far more serious than naïve stupidity. These are the actions of a man intent on destroying the American Republic founded by our forefathers. Who dares call it treason? I do!!! Will you? Will you aggressively recruit friends of the Constitution in the House of Representatives to impeach Barack Obama? This is not just partisan politics. This is the survival of our nation! I've seen first hand the disastrous results of socialism/communism in many of the eastern European nations. I don't want to see them here! But America is now like a socialist train on the downhill slope, with out-of-control spending and continuing government takeovers. Can we survive another three years of this treason?

When I was a senior in high school, I read J. Edgar Hoover's powerful expose´ of communistic tactics entitled, "Masters of Deceit". Have you read it? Obama is a master of deceit.

Who is more dangerous to our national security – Osama or

Obama? I believe it is Obama! He and his radical czars are like a malignant cancer, which needs to be cut out. It's urgent!

When I was a graduate student, I read "None Dare Call It Treason" by John Stormer. Have you read it?

This undermining of our Constitution has been going on for many years. It's time to stop it – now! Will you move into action by pointing these things out to our friends in the House?

You are facing a monumental task – impossible in human strength and wisdom. I am praying for you.'

"Now to Him who is able to keep you from stumbling, and to present you faultless before the presence of His glory with exceeding joy, to God our Savior, Who alone is wise, be glory and majesty, dominion and power both now and forever. Amen." Jude 24-25

Hopefully,
Yours & His,
Rick Deighton"[1]

Now I choose to share with you a recent entry in our Overseas Outreach prayer letter – March 2013:

"Believe It or Not….

If you doubt my assertion in a former prayer letter that I believe Barack Obama to be the most dangerous hypocrite in the world, please carefully read the **"Quote of the Decade"** below and notice the date.

~ Rick D.

---

1   *I did not realize when I wrote this letter that there is a much better and more logical way to indict Barack Obama for his fraud, crimes and treason - to expose him as an imposter who does not - and cannot legally be called Mr. President. He should be tried and convicted as guilty of fraud, perjury and treason. See Appendix 2 in Chapter 6.*

"The fact that we are here today to debate raising America's debt limit is a sign of leadership failure. It is a sign that the US Government cannot pay its own bills. It is a sign that we now depend on ongoing financial assistance from foreign countries to finance our Government's reckless fiscal policies. Increasing America's debt weakens us domestically and internationally. Leadership means that, 'the buck stops here.' Instead, Washington is shifting the burden of bad choices today onto the backs of our children and grandchildren. America has a debt problem and a failure of leadership. Americans deserve better."   ~ Senator Barack H. Obama, March 2006

God has brought down emperors (and those who pretend to be) like Nebuchadnezzar and Napoleon – He can do it again. Napoleon Bonaparte wrote: *"I know men and I tell you everything about Him (Christ) amazes me. His spirit overawes me, and his will confounds me. There is no possible comparison between him and any other being in the world. He is truly a being by himself. His birth, history of his life, the profoundness of his doctrine, his gospel, his march across the ages – all these are to me a wonder, an insoluble mystery."*

Here is another quote from Napoleon Bonaparte: *".....Alexander, Caesar, Charlemagne, and I have founded empires. But on what did we rest the creation of our genius? Upon force. Jesus Christ founded His Empire upon love; and at this hour millions of men would die for Him."*

Please pray with us for Barack Obama – and his liberal colleagues – to be truly converted. Not only them, but also many strong conservatives, like David Horowitz, Michael Savage, and Glenn Beck, who understand our political situation as a nation, but don't yet understand Who Jesus is. Pray that they all bow in humble repentance before the King of kings and Lord of lords! Jesus is the one – and only – hope for America – and for the world.

DEALING WITH DISCOURAGEMENT

Are you one of the discouraged conservatives who feels like it's too late for America? You may feel, "It's no use – it's over! There is no hope. America is a lost cause."

Remember Who is really in charge! Honestly evaluate our situation as a nation, pray earnestly, pay close attention to the ending of this chapter (and every chapter), watch for what God is doing, and wait expectantly for the appearance of our Blessed Hope!

Humor Based on Truth

"If you don't read the newspaper, you are uninformed. If you do read the newspaper, you are misinformed." ~ Mark Twain

"I contend that for a nation to try to tax itself into prosperity is like a man standing in a bucket and trying to lift himself up by the handle." ~ Winston Churchill

"If you think health care is expensive now, wait until you see what it costs when it's free!"

~ P. J. O'Rourke"

DO YOU ALSO SEE HYPOCRISY?

"Fathom the hypocrisy of a government that requires every citizen to prove they are insured ….. but not everyone must prove they are a citizen."

"And now, any of those who refuse, or are unable, to prove they are citizens will receive free insurance paid for by those who are forced to buy insurance because they are citizens."

~ Ben Stein

Now I choose to share our September 2011 issue, entitled:

"Cultural and Political Warfare Are Actually Symptoms of Spiritual Warfare

Dear Friends & Prayer Partners,

I want to share with you a copy of a letter I wrote to a personal friend after the November 2008 election. He was elated that Barack Obama won the election and was disappointed and frustrated with me because I did not share his joy and enthusiasm over the results. In fact, I was grieving. The results of the November 2010 elections and the actions of the Tea Party movement are greatly encouraging – but we recognize that the "cultural warfare" and "political warfare" are only the outward symptoms of the deep reality of spiritual warfare raging in our nation, in our churches, in our communities, and most of all in our own hearts. Therefore, I want to share with you a copy of this letter to my friend dated November 17, 2008, but first I want to share with you a copy of a response I sent to a young lady who wrote to us about our February -March letter, which requested urgent prayer for America.

* *

March 18, 2011

Dear Friend,

Thank you for taking the time and effort to write to us about our last prayer letter and the *Agenda* DVD. We are sending you the DVD as a gift. Please be sure to watch it all and share it with as many as you possibly can.

About your concern that "*it is very close to gossiping*" (what I wrote about Barack Obama) – then your "*Oops, so sorry. I am a hypocrite! I just did….*" Don't worry! What you wrote is a fact – not gossiping. You wrote: "*I also believe that our world (US) is falling apart. I believe it is because of Obama's taxes. He is making the economy bad.*" Jesus said, "By their fruits you shall know them."

That is, we will know the difference between true believers and hypocrites by their deeds!!! Exposing and refuting the teachings and actions of false teachers is not gossip! God commands us to do so. Their teachings and deeds are public record – not whispered secrets. Barack Obama is the blatant hypocrite! He professes to be a Christian, but his deeds are anti Christ. If exposing false teachers and calling the workers of iniquity hypocrites is wrong, then Jesus and His apostles were guilty because they did that. But Jesus never sinned! He (and they) are not guilty! Please read carefully Matthew 23, 2 Peter 2, and the epistle of Jude with this in mind. In fact, the apostle Paul said to expose and rebuke evil. We will send you more documentation to prove that Barack Obama is in fact a false teacher whose deeds need to be exposed.

Now concerning your observations about homosexuals. You wrote: "*Homosexuals. I am against it, although I do not protest against it. They are mostly nice people. I have met gay guys before, like at a store. They are weird, but they are not bad people.*" By whose standard do you declare, "*they are not bad people*"? By yours – or God's? Yes, it is true that all people are sinners, but it also true that some sins are far more dangerous and harmful than others. All diseases are diseases, but some diseases are much more dangerous than others. Wouldn't you agree that cancer of the brain is more dangerous than chicken pox? God also categorizes some sins as more toxic and dangerous than others. Homosexual practices are categorized in God's Word as "abomination." Please read Lev. 18:22; Romans 1:16-32; and 1 Cor. 6:9-11.

By the way, the average age for death of most Americans is 74 – but the average age of death for homosexuals who don't repent is 42. (Or even for some who do repent and stop practicing their perversion, but have already contracted AIDS or other deadly diseases.) Dangerous? Absolutely! Also, I refuse to call them "gay" because this is the word homosexual leaders chose to redefine their behavior to make it sound good. The word "gay" means carefree and happy. Those who practice homosexuality are not carefree and happy because they are practicing corruption and perversion in the eyes of Almighty God. We have three relatives in this perversion – one of them already died of AIDS. Their lifestyle is not "gay" (carefree and happy). We are mandated to love them, pray for them, and seek to rescue them from the pit. Please carefully read Jude verses 17-25.

You wrote: "*Is the president not a person?*" Yes, Obama is of course a person! I pray often for him to repent and be baptized in the name of Jesus Christ for the forgiveness of sin. That would be the greatest blessing he could ever have – and a tremendous blessing to our country. I pray for him, but I do not respect him. He has already been exposed in too many lies and his evil deeds are on record. Is that gossip? No! It's public record of his deeds. He has adopted an evil philosophy – this is not just "mistakes". He needs to deeply and thoroughly repent.

Yes, we will also pray for you! Will you pray for us? For America? For Ukraine?

In the grace and love of our Lord Jesus,
Rick

November 17, 2008

Dear Brother,

You told me that you doubt that Harry [his preacher] has ever been converted, that he is a liar and a con-man. Why? Because his actions don't fit with his words. That is exactly what I believe about Barack Obama and why I pray for him to be converted. Please carefully and prayerfully read his voting record and the documented record of his lies. Don't just believe his rhetoric – look at his record!

His very first appointment is a man named Rahm Emanuel, who was involved with the scandal of Fanny Mae and Freddy Mac – and yet walked away with $18 million severance pay. Ridiculous!

Obama's voting record shows him to be 100% pro-abortion and 100% pro-homosexual. The sanctity of life and the sanctity of marriage are the most vital issues of our times, as slavery was the issue of the times in the 1800's, but Obama is dead wrong on both of these vital issues. **We need to pray for his conversion.** As I said to you on the phone, "If I wanted a socialist nation run by homosexuals and abortionists, I would have voted for Obama."

Especially when seeking to woo evangelicals into his camp, Obama talks the talk about his faith in Christ. He does not walk the walk. His record rebukes his rhetoric and exposes his hypocrisy.

I don't care that John McCain called Barack Obama an honorable man in his defeat speech – it was the politically polite thing to say. It proves nothing to me because his record speaks for itself. McCain's record is better than Obama's, but I'm not thrilled with him either. So do I believe McCain was lying about that? Yes, of course! *"Let God be found true, though every man a liar."* Romans 3:4.

I realize that Obama gets multitudes of glowing reports (that ignore his lies, blunders, and distortions). Why? Because most journalists listened to their professors who told them "socialism is good." Obama is <u>not</u> our savior, nor is he the messiah as some are claiming!

You said socialism is not bad – it's godless socialism that is bad. I strongly disagree. Socialism is bad – evil to the core – because it is godless in its very nature. It is based on the godless, anti-Christian philosophies of Karl Marx, Charles Darwin, and Sigmund Freud. Socialism is not a Christian (Biblical) worldview for the following reasons:

1. The goal of socialism is the destruction of private property. Ideally, everyone equally owns everything (but in practice everyone becomes equally poor except the ruling elite). It was Karl Marx who wrote "To each according to his need – from each according to his ability." Sounds good on the surface, doesn't it? But who determines the need and who takes from those who have ability? The government (ruling elite)! So this violates the Biblical teachings as follows:

    a. It creates a wrong focus of dependency. "The Government is my shepherd" instead of "The Lord is my Shepherd." It is idolatry.

    b. It violates the Biblical principle of ownership. The command, "*Thou shalt not steal*" has no meaning if there is no ownership of private property. Under socialism, the government steals all private property from its citizens and gives it to whomever they will (usually themselves). Poor people remain poor, wealthy and middle class citizens are reduced to poverty.

2. Socialism undermines the Biblical principle of responsibility. I am responsible for my actions; I should bear the responsibility of my foolish actions, but on the other hand I should reap the rewards of wise decisions and hard work. The Book of Proverbs is full of such wisdom. If you believe in socialism you may as well tear up and throw away the book of Proverbs. You cannot believe both! It's schizophrenic to believe you can combine these two contrary belief systems. Socialism is now falsely called progressivism; more accurately it should be called regressivism!!!

    Socialism shifts the responsibility and the blame from the individual to "society". This is devastating. Socialism means that whenever I foul up, IT'S NOT MY FAULT! Society bears the blame! Also, what is everybody's responsibility becomes nobody's responsibility! Perhaps this is why so much trash and garbage is tossed on the ground in the cities, forests, and countryside of former Soviet Union nations. It takes time for people to recover from socialism and take responsibility! In contrast, the Bible teaches individual responsibility. *"Let him that stole steal no more: but rather let him labor, working with his hands the thing which is good, that he may have to give to him that needs."* Ephesians 4:28. This is God's way! On the other hand, the liberal left (socialists) love to be liberal (generous) with other people's money. If John Kerry cares so much about the poor, when is he going to sell any of his seven mansions and distribute the funds to starving people in America, Africa, or Haiti?

Socialism destroys the incentive of the ambitious, hard working individual by taking from him what he earned and giving it to the lazy and immoral slouch. Our own welfare system is a socialistic disaster that rewards immorality by giving more and more money to unwed mothers who keep having more children. It punishes those who get married or who work hard to produce a garden, etc.

3. Socialism teaches that human nature is basically good and the problem is with the environment and the economy. "Take these nice people out of their bad environment and give them a good education and they will become productive citizens." One astute observer wrote that if you take a thief out of his bad environment and give him a good education, he will steal the whole railroad instead of stealing scrap metal from the railroad. (Basically this is what has happened with Fanny Mae and Freddy Mac – but the thieves were officers in the company. They are walking away with millions of dollars in severance pay in spite of their bad decisions, while all of us tax payers are left to foot the bill because Congress decided to bail them out. This is socialism in practice! It stinks!)

The Bible teaches that human nature is basically evil. It is corrupt because it is the fruit of a corrupt tree. We inherit the corrupted, selfish nature of Adam; we need to repent, be converted and transformed into the new nature of the second Adam. If any man is in Christ he is a new creation. *"By their fruits you shall know them,"* Jesus said. (I do not see the fruit of a new nature in Barack Obama.)

Jeremiah wrote by Inspiration *"The heart is deceitful above all things, and desperately wicked; who can know it?"* Jeremiah 17:9. Freud didn't know it! Darwin didn't know it! Marx didn't know it! But God does! He is the One – the only One who knows the human heart. He says we each need a new heart. A radical heart transplant! Yes, America needs change, but not a change of economy to total socialism. America needs a change of heart – one heart at a time.

I have traveled extensively in Eastern Europe and have seen repeatedly the poverty and devastation of socialism; however, in each of those nations, I've seen the beauty of transformed lives – changed hearts by the power of the Holy Spirit – lives reflecting the glory of God in the face of our Lord Jesus Christ. True Christianity can survive, and even thrive in spite of oppression, opposition, ridicule, and persecution.

4. So what is the difference between socialism and communism? Very little! They are the same basic philosophy. Usually socialism is viewed as the soft form and communism the hard form of the philosophy. Actually, I think socialism is simply the polite name for communism.

I see the election of Barack Obama as a judgment of God upon America. We are getting what we, as a nation, deserve. One of the seven things that God hates is the shedding of innocent blood. What blood is more innocent than that of a baby, born or unborn? With the blood of over 48,000,000 innocent babies on our hands since 1973, when the Supreme Court judicially "legalized" the murder of the innocents, we have far more blood on our hands as a nation than Nazi Germany. Was the election of Obama the will of God? Obviously yes – His permissive will – as it was when rebellious Israel clamored for a king like the other nations. Was Samuel disappointed? Definitely! But God told him *"They have not rejected you – they have rejected Me!"* Do I see this as the death of our nation? Yes, I do, and I am seriously disappointed. I am grieving. Some are saying to grieving Christians like me, "Come on. Get over it!" Would you be so cold and heartless with a widower who just lost his wife? Yes, I am hurt and I am grieving, but I will recover. I thank God for the good that His sovereignty will bring from this election, even though I can't see it now. We sorrow not as others who have no hope – but we do sorrow. I sorrow that millions more babies will die under an Obama administration while Planned Parenthood flourishes with their godless slaughter houses falsely called "health clinics." I sorrow that the free enterprise nation I once knew, that was built on godly principles and slogans like "In God we trust" and "Under God" may soon be thrown on the scrap heap of history under the nebulous banner of "Change." I grieve that Obama will appoint hundreds more radically liberal activist judges and Supreme Court Justices who will promote abortion, homosexuality (under the "gay rights" banner), and pornography (under the "free speech" banner). They will glory over their arrogant power thrust over the legislative branch and gloat over the oppression of those "right wing fanatics" (meaning Christians who truly uphold Biblical standards of morality and marriage). It has already been happening, but it is about to speed up dramatically. So please, cut me some slack and give me some time to grieve. I still say with Job, *"The Lord has given, the Lord has taken away, blessed be the name of the Lord."*

For many years we, as a country, have been sliding down the socialist slope, but now in electing Obama I'm afraid we've gone over the edge. We have become a socialist nation and will reap the bitter consequences that Russia and all the former Soviet Union nations are reaping. The country I grew up in had many positive role models, even in Hollywood, like Roy Rogers and Dale Evans. Instead of family bashing sitcoms and cartoons (like The Simpsons), we even had positive TV programs that honored father and families; Father Knows Best, Leave It to Beaver, Ozzie and Harriet. We had wholesome humor from Lucille Ball and Red Skelton. A man's word was his bond, we rarely locked our doors, a man and woman got married first, and then lived together, we kids could roam the neighborhood after dark playing hide and go seek, and "gay" meant carefree and happy. Why? Because our nation had a foundation built upon a Biblical worldview with Christian principles. That has been undermined by Darwinism and socialism. If I sound nostalgic... you're right. I miss it and I grieve over what we have lost and where we, as a nation, are heading. We are very far down the road of rebellion, but it still isn't too late for repentance and a turn around. There are some very positive signs; prayer and fasting movements, purity conferences, etc. Earnest prayer is what we need yet more and more. With God all things are possible. His grace is our only hope for ourselves, and for our country.

So do I see Barack Obama as our enemy? Yes, definitely! I believe he is severely lacking in moral integrity and that he is an enemy of truth and righteousness. Any man with a heart so cold he will vote repeatedly to let the living baby die in a soiled linen closet or on a cold surgical table after he survived a botched abortion, and then lie to the public in spite of his record, is an enemy of truth and righteousness. This same heartless man voted repeatedly to protect the inhumane practice of partial birth abortion. Yes, I see him as an enemy! But Jesus said, "*Love your enemies*", so I pray for God to fill me with His Holy Spirit and pour out His love into my heart for this man. I am determined to love him and pray for him in spite of the fact that I view his policies and practices as ungodly and despicable. (Also behind Obama are George Soros, Tom Gill, and other liberal billionaires. Pray for them to repent too.)

My feelings toward Barack Obama's election have absolutely nothing to do with racism. Skin color is no issue with me – it's his heart that matters. Actually, there is only one race – the human race! We all come from Adam and Eve through Noah. I have very high regard for Alan Keyes, a black American statesman who carries himself with dignity, speaks with integrity, and has a passionate fervor for protecting the sanctity of life, the sanctity of marriage, and the sanctity of the Biblical work ethic. He knows better than to lead us down the primrose path of socialism. Alan Keyes often quotes our Bill of Rights, pointing out that we are **endowed by our Creator with certain inalienable rights – life, liberty, and the pursuit of happiness.** I may have some serious theological differences with Alan Keyes on some important issues, but on these foundational basics for good government, we are in complete agreement. If Alan Keyes were our president elect, I would be elated, clicking my heels, and finding it much easier to be hopeful about the future of our nation. (By the way, Jeremiah knew and believed in the sovereignty of Almighty God, yet he grieved deeply over his decadent, rebellious nation and the resulting judgment from God. He is known as the "weeping prophet.")

To understand more clearly my grief at the direction our nation has chosen in following Obama, please read thoughtfully the enclosed article "From a Vision of a Socialist Utopia: A Report From Auschwitz". Did you know the Nazis were the "National Socialist Party"? Two very powerful sentences from this article say, "The German people found the Nazi party compelling because they were bitter about economic hardship and wanted immediate change. They cried out for it in trance-inducing rallies led by an appealing, gifted orator who possessed an almost magical self-assurance." This is almost eerie! Obama's rallying cry throughout his campaign has been change – change – change! But the changes he wants look ominous to me. The change America needs is not socialism, but a change of heart! We need a deep, true spiritual awakening wherein millions come to their knees in genuine repentance and surrender of their lives to the Lord Jesus Christ. (By the way, concerning socialism, you aren't forgetting that the former Soviet Union's official name was "Union of Soviet Socialist Republics", are you?)

I am disappointed and saddened that a majority of Americans voted for Obama. But I believe that God will bring good from this, and I will continue to love Him, thank Him, and praise Him."

What about Civil Disobedience?

Is it ever right and justified for Christians to be involved in civil disobedience? To word this another way, should Christians ever disobey a higher authority? The answer is YES! Definitely! However, that answer needs to be qualified and clarified. Christians are not to be characterized by a rebellious attitude toward authorities – but if a higher authority demands that you obey him rather than the HIGHEST AUTHORITY – then it is our godly duty to obey the highest authority. That is what the apostles did. *"And when they had brought them, they set them before the council. And the high priest asked them, saying, 'Did we not strictly command you not to teach in this name? And look, you have filled Jerusalem with your doctrine, and intend to bring this Man's blood on us!' But Peter and the other apostles answered and said:* **'We ought to obey God rather than men.** *The God of our fathers raised up Jesus whom you murdered by hanging on a tree. Him God has exalted to His right hand to be Prince and Savior, to give repentance to Israel and forgiveness of sins.* **And we are His witnesses to these things, and so also is the Holy Spirit whom God has given to those who obey Him."'** Acts 5:27-32

Generally our attitude toward authorities should be respect, submission, and obedience (see Romans 13:1-4). However, whenever an authority demands that we violate our own consciences and/or disobey a command of God, then we are to be submissive to Almighty God first and foremost.

For example:

1. If parents demand that their children lie or steal for them should they do it? No! Absolutely not!

2. If a husband demands that his wife watch pornography with him, should she do it? No! Absolutely not!

3. If an authority in a hospital demands that a nurse participate in an abortion, should she do it? No! Absolutely not.

4. If a government demands that you participate in or celebrate a pseudo-wedding of homosexuals, should you do it?

Now it's your turn to answer. Our corrupt culture is moving fast and you are going to have to draw the line. Are you ready to say as Martin Luther did, **"Unless I am persuaded by Scripture … I can do no other. Here I stand, so help me God!!!"**

Do you have the guts to stand with brave men and women who wouldn't bow, they wouldn't bend – but many of them did burn? Are you willing to say with the apostles, **"We must obey God rather than men!"**?

Resort to Violence?

When the persecution against Christians in America increases to even more intense violence, let's remember that God tells us in His Word, "*Vengeance is Mine – I will repay says the Lord.*" Deuteronomy 32:35. Here is the context in Romans 12:19 where this passage is quoted: "*Beloved, do not avenge yourselves, but rather give place to wrath; for it is written, 'Vengeance is Mine, I will repay,' says the Lord.*"

Another fact to remember is that if the early Christians had retaliated violently to their persecutors, they may have killed Saul of Tarsus. You know – the one who was dramatically converted after our Conquering Christ appeared to him in His resurrection power on the road to Damascus? You know – he was the one God called to become the apostle Paul – the most effective missionary in history except for Jesus Himself. You remember, don't you – he was the one God used to write nearly half of the books in the New Testament Scriptures? What a tragic loss it would have been if the early Christians had resorted to violence in reaction to persecution. Is there a lesson here for us? Several lessons?

Conclusion

In conclusion to this chapter, I want to share this pertinent, potent, poignant prayer by Bob Russell, then quotes from Victor Knowles and Adrian Rogers.

"THE PRAYER"

"Heavenly Father, we come before you today to ask Your forgiveness and to seek Your direction and guidance. We know Your Word says, "Woe to those who call evil good," but that's exactly what we have done. We have lost our spiritual equilibrium and reversed our values.

We confess that:
We have ridiculed the absolute truth of Your Word and called it pluralism.
We have worshipped other gods and called it multi-culturalism.
We have endorsed perversion and called it an alternative lifestyle.
We have exploited the poor and called it the lottery.
We have neglected the needy and called it self-preservation.
We have rewarded laziness and called it welfare.
We have killed our unborn children and called it a choice.
We have shot abortionists and called it justifiable.
We have neglected to discipline our children and called it building self-esteem.
We have abused power and called it political savvy.
We have coveted our neighbor's possessions and called it ambition.
We have polluted the air with profanity and pornography and called it freedom of expression.
We have ridiculed the time-honored values of our forefathers and

called it enlightenment.

Search us, O God, and know our hearts today; cleanse us from every sin and set us free.

Guide and bless these men and women who have been sent to direct us to

The center of Your will. I ask it in the name of Your Son, the living Savior, Jesus Christ. Amen. [2]

The Blasphemy and the Victory

"…Following the reelection of President Obama, entertainer Jaime Foxx praised the president at the 2012 BET Soul Train Awards, saying, "It's like church in here. First of all, give an honor to God and our Lord and Savior Barack Obama." To this day the White House has not denounced this outright blasphemy. It is one thing to be narcissistic; it is quite another to have a Messianic complex. Earlier, the May 14, 2012 cover of *Newsweek* magazine declared 'the first gay president,' placing a rainbow halo over his head. Are the times we live in merely disgusting … or are they extremely dangerous?

But no matter the resident in the White House, John saw a Rider on a white horse (Rev 19:11)! The armies of heaven followed Him on white horses (19:14), the beast and the false prophet were captured and cast into hell (19:20), and Satan himself was hurled into hell (20:10). God shall dwell with us and wipe away every tear (211:4), Jesus is coming quickly (22:7, 12), and we shall have the right to the tree of life and enter through the gates into the beautiful city (22:14). Beyond the terror of man is the glory of God." ("One Body", Spring 2013, "Caesar or Christ?" By Victor Knowles)

---

2   *This prayer was originally written by Bob Russell and published in "The Lookout." Joe Wright decided it was the ideal prayer to use for the Kansas Senate. I honor him for his candid honesty and bold courage to speak out in using this prayer. Let's follow his shining example!*

The Commitment

Finally, I want to share this concise, clear, crisp quotation from the late Adrian Rogers:

"The church is not the servant of the state!
The church is not the master of the state!
The church is the conscience of the state!
We will be civil – but WE WILL NOT BE SILENT!!!"

The Bottom Line

Courage is not the absence of fear – it is conquering of fear! "For God has not given us the spirit of fear, but of love and of power and of a sound mind." 2 Timothy 1:7.

WE ARE MORE THAN CONQUERORS.

WE WILL BE CIVIL - BUT

WE WILL NOT BE SILENT!!

SUPPLEMENT TO CHAPTER 2

Amazingly Insightful and Instructive Quotations from Thomas Jefferson

"The democracy will cease to exist when you take away from those who are willing to work and give to those who would not."

"It is incumbent on every generation to pay its own debts as it goes. A principle which if acted on would save one-half the wars of the world."

"My reading of history convinces me that most bad government results from too much government."

"No free man shall ever be debarred the use of arms."

"The strongest reason for the people to retain the right to keep and bear arms is, as a last resort, to protect themselves against tyranny in government."

"To compel a man to subsidize with his taxes the propagation of ideas which he disbelieves and abhors is sinful and tyrannical."

Observations on the Republican Party

Many people do not realize that the Republican Party was organized to represent freedom and justice for all, including slaves, and that Abraham Lincoln was the first Republican President. Currently the platform for the Republican Party is excellent, but sadly, the practice is less than honorable for the elite leadership of incumbent compromisers who are intent on marginalizing and eliminating the tea party patriots. I am now a member of the Constitution Party, but I vote for a candidate based on his or her stand for Biblical principles. It is way past time for Republicans to tear down the "Big Tent" policy which shelters rank liberals like John McCain! Republicans, it's high time for you to muster the courage to stand strong for your own pro-life, pro-family platform!!

QUESTIONS FOR CHAPTER 2

1. Should Christians be dabbling in politics? Why or why not?

2. Is there a real danger of Christians becoming "so heavenly minded they are of no earthly use"? Explain your answer.

3. Do you believe that tyranny can never happen here? Why or why not?

4. What are three battlefronts in the cultural clashes?

5. Is there a "wall of separation" between church and state written into our Constitution? What has been twisted and convoluted about this concept?

6. What did the Pilgrims state were their two purposes for coming to the new world (which became America)?

7. What is wrong with being "politically correct" according to our corrupt culture? Where did "politically correct" originate?

8. Are you content with being a spectator – or are you going to become a participant in "fundamentally transforming America" back to the purpose of our founders? If so, how?

9. Is socialism a good and Biblically solid form of government? Why or why not?

10. Is civil disobedience ever right or necessary for a Christian? Please explain.

Bonus question: What is the blasphemy and what is the victory I reported near the end of the chapter?

Chapter 3:
How Truly Tolerant is the Tolerant Troop?

"Tolerance in our society has come to mean 'give up your way immediately and accept mine or you are a prejudiced bigot' and considered intolerant for not letting the other be intolerant!"
~ D. Lloyd Thomas

The question I've used as the title for this chapter is pertinent and relevant because the meaning of the word "tolerance" has changed. If we personify "tolerance" as a woman, she has not only changed a few items in her wardrobe, she has had a complete make-over. Both Josh McDowell and Randy Alcorn have clearly documented and illustrated this radical change of meaning. I want to use portions of an insightful article by Randy Alcorn to clarify this transformation in meaning:

"Same Words – Different Meaning"

"Defining Truth in Postmodern Christianity"
By Randy Alcorn

"...Of course, evangelicalism as a subculture is riddled with any number of failings, and tends to be geared toward a certain audience that can unintentionally exclude postmoderns. These criticisms we should welcome and take seriously and make changes where appropriate. But we dare not throw out the baby of Christian truth with the bathwater of evangelical failings. What's at stake in this issue is not merely different ideas on how we relate to culture or live out and share the faith – what is at stake is the faith itself, historic Christianity.

When it comes to the issue of objective truth, this is where some churches seem to me to be stepping over the line. Truth is an issue of seismic proportions, and if we have eyes to see, it is everywhere around us. Often we don't see it, though, because we can have nice conversations at church in which we assume that those we've talked with meant the same thing we did when they used certain words. But in fact, they didn't.

161

For instance, a teenager comes home from school. Her Christian parent asks, "What did you learn today"?

After an obligatory mumble, she says, "In social science we talked about the importance of being tolerant."

"That's nice," the parent says. Daughter talks, and you nod, because you know Jesus loved people and extended them grace, and we should too. A few minutes later the conversation is over, and you walk away having affirmed what she learned in class, without understanding the context and meaning of her culture – and the fact that what you actually affirmed was anti-Christian.

Why? Because *tolerant* means two radically different things to you and to her. To you it means being kind and loving to people who think and act in ways you know to be wrong, according to Scripture. To the students and their teacher – and by assimilation even to your Christian teenager unless she is exceptionally well-grounded in Scripture – tolerant means believing that all ways of thinking and acting are equally valid, and NOT wrong.

By believing Jesus is the only way for people to enter Heaven, you are by definition intolerant. By embracing tolerance, in the sense it is most widely used in this culture, our young people (whether or not they state it and regardless of what their church believes) are rejecting the idea that Jesus is the only way.

There are significantly different meanings out there for the old words *truth, tolerance, love, grace, redemption, salvation* and even *Christ*. Postmodern evangelicalism does not simply invent new words, which would be far better for purposes of clarity – it uses the same old words and attaches to them new meanings, often meanings contradictory to the original.

…The notion that there is no such thing as objective truth – and therefore no objective meaning for words such as the *resurrection* and *grace* – is a natural extension of both our culture's self-preoccupation and mental laziness. It is self-flattery to imagine truth is merely whatever I decide, think, and make of life. It is also laziness. Once people sought truth by going to philosophers and historic religions, now they sit and watch television and simply absorb worldviews without consciously evaluating them.

Everyone has a worldview, but few really seek to find the right one. The myth that there is no right worldview, that all are equally valid, becomes moral justification for believing whatever we wish, and keeps us from seeking further. No one needs to go to the trouble of searching for truth if no objective truth exists. If truth is merely whatever I think, at the end of the day – or the end of my life – I will have truth even though I've never expended any effort to find it. (Let's face it, as Christians we can be just as lazy when it comes to recognizing heresy and passing it off as merely a different way of saying – or a fresh way of perceiving – the same old truths).

The bane of fundamentalism is truth without grace. The bane of much postmodern evangelicalism (or post-evangelicalism, if you prefer) is grace without truth. This is tolerance, something much cheaper than grace, and which – unlike grace – doesn't require Christ to empower it.

Tolerance is the world's self-righteous substitute for grace. True grace recognizes truth and sin and deals with it in the most radical and painful way – Christ's redemption. Tolerance recognizes neither truth nor sin, and says "Everything's fine," negating or trivializing incarnation, redemption, and the need for regeneration. Christ came precisely because people are not fine without him.

Francis Schaeffer profoundly affected me and countless other young seeking minds in the '70s. We need to hear voices like his today. And we need to listen carefully as we talk with each other and especially with the young not only just in our culture, but also in our own homes and churches. We need to not simply hear the words they say, but also ask them, "What do you mean?" Then we need to say words back to them, words steeped in Scripture, and explain to them what we mean – which is hopefully what God means – by those revealed words. (Randy Alcorn, "Eternal Perspectives" Spring 2010, www.epm.org)

Social and political liberals love to tout tolerance. In fact, they spout and tout tolerance as though it is their badge of honor.

It appears that there is no subject where they are more adamant about tolerance than the subject of homosexuality. Of course, they don't like us to use such an "abrasive" term – rather, they also tout the terminology of "being gay". At the outset I want to clarify that in my writing and speaking, I refuse to bow to the prevailing pressure to use their terminology to soften the more abrasive word homosexual. Why not? Because using the word "gay" is part of the calculated and planned strategy of the radical homosexual activists to change the perception of all Americans (all humans, actually) concerning their immoral practices. They not only want acceptance, they want dominance! They want us to comply with their terminology and bow to their demands. I refuse to comply. **I do want to "speak the truth in love" as the Bible teaches, but true love is often tough love that does not compromise with evil. It does not comply with the enemies of truth by agreeing to their playing field or their distorted terminology**. Therefore, the only time you will see the term "gay" in this book in reference to homosexuality, is when you read it in a quote from someone else.

The Danger of Compromise

Kenneth Beckman, retired professor at Boise Bible College, reminded us often, "When you compromise you become part of the problem you once sought to solve!" His resounding words ring true – and nowhere is it more evident than in the clash of worldviews with Biblical truth and morality on one side, crashing against evolutionism and homosexual immorality on the other side. Jesus was both the Master teacher and the Master Lover of all humanity, yet when He boldly confronted and exposed false teachers, He used some of the toughest language you will ever find in all literature. Consider these few verses from Matthew 23: *"Woe to you, scribes and Pharisees, hypocrites! For you travel land and sea to win one proselyte, and when he is won, you make him twice as* *much a son of hell as yourselves. Woe to you, blind guides, who say, 'Whoever swears by the temple, it is nothing; but whoever swears by the gold of the temple, he is obliged to perform it.' Fools and blind! For which is greater, the gold or the temple that sanctifies the gold?"* Matthew 23:15-17.

False Teachers

There are many, many religious leaders who are false teachers promoting the homosexual agenda and proclaiming that people can come to Jesus "just as you are" – without change, without repentance. This is an abominable lie! While their pagan or professed Christian colleagues are pompously parading their "Pride" in the streets, stripping off clothing, shocking innocent children with perverse practices, and glorying in their shame, the false teachers are lying to them by saying "I'm okay – you're okay. Jesus loves you just as you are. He made you that way and He doesn't require you to change your sexual orientation or practices." That kind of teaching is not love – it's lies! Yes, Jesus loves you just as you are, but He loves you too much to let you stay that way. The Gospel of Mark begins, *"The beginning of the gospel of Jesus Christ, the Son of God."* (Mark 1:1) and the first recorded words of Jesus in Mark's gospel are "...*"The time is fulfilled, and the kingdom of God is at hand. Repent, and believe in the gospel."* (Mark 1:15). **Repentance** = turn around (about face)! **It is essential to believing the gospel and accepting Jesus as Savior and Lord.**

What do you think Jesus will say to these false teachers? If you have been teaching this heresy, consider these verses: *"Therefore we make it our aim, whether present or absent, to be well pleasing to Him. For we must all appear before the judgment seat of Christ, that each one may receive the things done in the body, according to what he has done, whether good or bad. Knowing, therefore, the terror of the Lord, we persuade men; but we are well known to God, and I also trust are well known in your consciences... Therefore, if anyone is in Christ, he is a new creation;*

old things have passed away; behold, all things have become new. ... Now then, we are ambassadors for Christ, as though God were pleading through us: we implore you on Christ's behalf, be reconciled to God. For He made Him who knew no sin to be sin for us, that we might become the righteousness of God in Him." 2 Corinthians 5:9-11, 17, 20-21. "But the cowardly, unbelieving, abominable, murderers, sexually immoral, sorcerers, idolaters, and all liars shall have their part in the lake which burns with fire and brimstone, which is the second death." Revelation 21:8. I implore you with Peter's words: "Repent therefore and be converted, that your sins may be blotted out, so that times of refreshing may come from the presence of the Lord," Acts 3:19.

Secularization – The Spirit of the Age

What is the meaning of the word "secularization," and why do I call it the spirit of the age? Secularization is the mood, the mindset, the paradigm of those who have been brainwashed by evolutionism and Marxism. Briefly, secularization signifies the attitude not only that evolutionism is science, and Christianity (which they prefer to call religion) is faith - blind faith, but also that someone with a secular viewpoint is objective. Those of us who have faith in Jesus Christ as Lord are often considered prejudiced, biased, or ignorant. This is in spite of overwhelming objective proofs for the resurrection of Jesus and the historical and archeological accuracy of the Bible. Strangely, they are very open to people being "spiritual" – as long as that term means Wicca (witchcraft), Islam, Paganism, New Age Hinduism, or almost anything except Biblical Christianity. Why? Could it be because those religious (spiritual) systems come from the dark side (Satan), and do not require repentance and life change? I see a very strong bias – even prejudice and ignorance - concerning Biblical Christianity. Do you see it? Is that position objective??? Who refuses to look at the evidence? Who is pre-judging? What do you think?

I've spent a lot of time around academia, especially in the past 12 to 15 years, and I notice the secularization mindset is especially strong on most campuses. So if you go there expecting objectivity – don't be surprised if you are shocked by the level of bias you encounter!

THE WAY OF SALVATION

Salvation is not easy believism. In our own strength, stamina, or self-righteousness it is impossible. But with God all things are possible. Salvation in Christ is a miracle of His grace. *"Therefore, if anyone is in Christ, he is a new creation; old things have passed away; behold, all things have become new." 2 Corinthians 5:17.*

"God does not give us truth for consideration – He gives us truth for obedience." ~ *Charles Stanley*

Salvation by Grace Through Faith

The Word of God makes it clear that God not only gives us truth to believe, but also to obey. Of course, if you do not believe Him, you will not obey Him. We are saved by grace through faith. *"But God, who is rich in mercy, because of His great love with which He loved us, even when we were dead in trespasses, made us alive together with Christ (by grace you have been saved), and raised us up together, and made us sit together in the heavenly places in Christ Jesus, that in the ages to come He might show the exceeding riches of His grace in His kindness toward us in Christ Jesus. For by grace you have been saved through faith, and that not of yourselves; it is the gift of God, not of works, lest anyone should boast. For we are His workmanship, created in Christ Jesus for good works, which God prepared beforehand that we should walk in them." Ephesians 2:4-10; "For we ourselves were also once foolish, disobedient, deceived, serving various lusts and pleasures, living in malice and envy, hateful and hating one another. But when the kindness and the love of God our Savior toward man appeared, not by works of righteousness which we have done, but according to His mercy He saved us, through the washing of regeneration and renewing of the Holy Spirit, whom He poured out on us abundantly through Jesus Christ our Savior, that having been justified by His grace we should become heirs according to the hope of eternal life." Titus 3:3-7*

What is Saving Faith?

Faith, (trust in Christ as the object of our faith) is essential to our salvation. Hebrews 11 is well known as the faith chapter. Please carefully note these verses near the beginning of the chapter: *"By faith we understand that the worlds were framed by the word of God, so that the things which are seen were not made of things which are visible. . . But without faith it is impossible to please Him, for he who comes to God must believe that He is, and that He is a rewarder of those who diligently seek Him." Hebrews 11:3, 6*

It is also important to note that true faith is obedient faith. Professed faith that does not obey God is not trust, it is not saving faith.

Please notice Jesus' own statement as to why He came into the world: *"Pilate therefore said to Him, 'Are You a king then?' Jesus answered, 'You say rightly that I am a king. For this cause I was born, and for this cause I have come into the world, that I should bear witness to the truth. Everyone who is of the truth hears My voice.'" John 18:37.* Did you also notice what he expects from us? Read that last sentence again! And what does he expect when we hear His voice? Consider what he bluntly told Nicodemus, the high ranking Pharisee who came to Him by night. *"Jesus answered and said to him, 'Most assuredly, I say to you, unless one is born again, he cannot see the kingdom of God.' Nicodemus said to Him, 'How can a man be born when he is old? Can he enter a second time into his mother's womb and be born?' Jesus answered, 'Most assuredly, I say to you, unless one is born of water and the Spirit, he cannot enter the kingdom of God'. . . For God so loved the world that He gave His only begotten Son, that whoever believes in Him should not perish but have everlasting life. For God did not send His Son into the world to condemn the world, but that the world through Him might be saved. 'He who believes in Him is not condemned; but he who does not believe is condemned already, because he has not believed in the name of the only begotten Son of God. And this is the condemnation, that the light has come into the world, and men loved darkness rather than light, because their deeds were evil. For everyone practicing evil hates the light and does not come to the light, lest his deeds should be exposed. But he who does the truth comes to the light, that his deeds may be clearly seen, that they have been done in God.'" John 3:3-5, 16-21.* Did you catch that phrase in verse 21 where Jesus said, "**he who does the truth**"? Do you remember the quote from Charles Stanley? Here it is again: *"God does not give us truth for consideration, He gives us truth for obedience."* Charles did not just makeup this idea, he got it from Jesus. The apostle John tells us in the last verse of John 3: *"Whoever believes in the Son has eternal life; whoever does not obey the Son shall not see life, but the wrath of God remains on him." John 3:36* (ESV) Consider the apostle Paul's word to the Thessalonians: *"since it is a righteous thing with God to repay with tribulation those who trouble you, and to give you who are troubled rest with us when the Lord Jesus is revealed from heaven with His mighty angels, in flaming fire taking vengeance on those who do not know God, and on those who do not obey the gospel of our Lord Jesus Christ. These shall be punished with everlasting destruction from the presence of the Lord and from the glory of His power, when He comes, in that Day, to be glorified in His saints and to be admired among all those who believe, because our testimony among you was believed." 2 Thessalonians 1:6-10*

What is the Way of Salvation?

Jesus Himself is the Way of Salvation!!! He said, *"I am the Way, the Truth, and the Life. No one comes to the Father except through Me." John 14:6.* Wouldn't you be wise to hear Him? To believe Him? To obey Him? *"Then Peter said to them, 'Repent, and let every one of you be baptized in the name of Jesus Christ for the remission of sins; and you shall receive the gift of the Holy Spirit.'" Acts 2:38*

What is the Connection Between Repentance and Baptism?

The word "baptize" literally means immerse, and is translated "be immersed" in some versions of the Bible. **This makes perfect sense when we understand that in surrendering to the Lordship of Jesus Christ, a believer is proclaiming the gospel to the eyes of those who witness this monumental event, and at the same time declaring his or her willingness to die to sin and self, be buried, and rise again.** Consider Paul's question to believers in Rome: *"Or do you not know that as many of us as were baptized into Christ Jesus were baptized into His death? Therefore we were buried with Him through baptism into death, that just as Christ was raised from the dead by the glory of the Father, even so we also should walk in newness of life. For if we have been united together in the likeness of His death, certainly we also shall be in the likeness of His resurrection, knowing this, that our old man was crucified with Him, that the body of sin might be done away with, that we should no longer be slaves of sin. For he who has died has been freed from sin. Now if we died with Christ, we believe that we shall also live with Him, knowing that Christ, having been raised from the dead, dies no more. Death no longer has dominion over Him. For the death that He died, He died to sin once for all; but the life that He lives, He lives to God. Likewise you also, reckon yourselves to be dead indeed to sin, but alive to God in Christ Jesus our Lord." Romans 6:3-11*

Now consider his description of the essence of the gospel to the believers in Corinth: *"Moreover, brethren, I declare to you the gospel which I preached to you, which also you received and in which you stand, by which also you are saved, if you hold fast that word which I preached to you—unless you believed in vain. For I delivered to you first of all that which I also received: that Christ died for our sins according to the Scriptures, and that He was buried, and that He rose again the third day according to the Scriptures,"* *1 Corinthians 15:1-4.* Now look again at *Acts 2:38: "Then Peter said to them, "Repent, and let every one of you be baptized in the name of Jesus Christ for the remission of sins; and you shall receive the gift of the Holy Spirit."* What two commands are contained in this powerful verse? What two promises are there to be received? Now do you understand how the gospel is not only a message to be received and believed, but also to be obeyed? **It is not in any way earning our salvation – it is submitting by faith to the Lordship of Jesus!** Do you also understand why there is no command to baptize babies in the New Testament Scriptures? Baptism is for believers, not babies! Can babies hear and understand the gospel? Can babies believe the gospel? Can babies obey the gospel? Can babies repent? Babies are already covered by the grace of God. Jesus said, *"But Jesus said, "Let the little children come to Me, and do not forbid them; for of such is the kingdom of heaven." Matthew 19:14*

Jesus often told his followers to count the cost. What cost? Currently in America most people would not be threatened with bloodshed for believing, receiving, and obeying the gospel. That may change sooner than we think to become like fifty-five or fifty-six other nations where obeying the gospel could cost you your life. Americans now are likely to face some scorn and ridicule. So what? Consider these heavy words of Jesus: *"... Whoever desires to come after Me, let him deny himself, and take up his cross, and follow Me. For whoever desires to save his life will lose it, but whoever loses his life for My sake and the gospel's will save it. For what will it profit a man if he gains the whole world, and loses his own*

soul? Or what will a man give in exchange for his soul? For whoever is ashamed of Me and My words in this adulterous and sinful
generation, of him the Son of Man also will be ashamed when He
comes in the glory of His Father with the holy angels." Mark 8:34-
38

Ananias warned Saul (later named Paul) what he would face,
but also told him how God would powerfully use him to spread the
gospel. Then he said: "And now why are you waiting? Arise and
be baptized, and wash away your sins, calling on the name of the
Lord." Isn't that a potent question for you to consider? Where is
your faith? Where is your courage? "For whatever is born of God
overcomes the world. And this is the victory that has overcome
the world—our faith. Who is he who overcomes the world, but he
who believes that Jesus is the Son of God? This is He who came by
water and blood—Jesus Christ; not only by water, but by water and
blood. And it is the Spirit who bears witness, because the Spirit is
truth. For there are three that bear witness in heaven: the Father,
the Word, and the Holy Spirit; and these three are one. And there
are three that bear witness on earth: the Spirit, the water, and the
blood; and these three agree as one." 1 John 5:4-8. Isn't it baptism
where all of these converge?

Amazing Faith and Commitment

I've read that once, when Patrick was baptizing a convert in
Ireland, he jammed a spear with a Christian banner on it into the
sand of the sea just before he dipped the man under the water. To
his surprise, he noticed some red in the water as he raised the man
up – and discovered that he had inadvertently jammed the spear
through the man's foot. After apologizing to him sincerely, Patrick
asked, "Why didn't you cry out?" The man replied, "I thought it
was part of the commitment ceremony." What a clear perspective!
Jesus shed His blood for you – are you willing to shed your blood
for Him?

Paul wrote to the Colossians: "I now rejoice in my sufferings
for you, and fill up in my flesh what is lacking in the afflictions of
Christ, for the sake of His body, which is the church," Colossians

1:24. Please realize that when Jesus cried out, "It is finished!" there was nothing lacking in His sacrifice of blood for our salvation; however, the commitment to take that marvelous message of salvation to the ends of the earth has been costing the blood of the martyrs for nearly 2,000 years. Consider this challenging article from Jim Dau, the president of Voice of the Martyrs, November 2013:

"Christians in Syria today are caught in the crossfire between a ruthless authoritarian regime and jihadist warriors who have swarmed to the region to fight what they consider a holy war to reclaim land. And the jihadists believe every bit of land they control is sacred Islamic territory.

Many Christians have fled the violence, but many others have remained in Syria for a variety of reasons. Some have stayed in the country because they have nowhere else to go, while others have stayed behind to answer a higher calling – a godly calling to reach the lost in Syria, even at the risk of their lives. Just last week, our staff met with one couple who are working to answer God's call in Syria. "Samer" and "Liena" are leaders in a boldly evangelical church that has continued to meet during the civil war; the church is growing rapidly even as the violence escalates.

Staying in Syria was not an easy decision for Samer and Liena. A church offered to sponsor their relocation to Europe and to provide housing, all living essentials and even private schooling for their two children. But after much prayer and fasting, they decided to continue their ministry at home.

'It was so hard living in a place where terrorists were coming from other countries,' Liena said. 'These men were saying, 'We will kill everyone who does not believe what we believe as Salafis and strict Muslims.' The couple knows, as do all Christians in Syria, that if their country falls into the hands of the radicals, Christians will be given three choices: convert to Islam, leave the country or die.

Samer and Liena threw themselves before God. They prayed, 'God, as Christians, what do you want us to do?'

'We were crying and praying,' Liena said. 'We fasted for many

days. *We put ourselves on the altar.' They prayed and fasted until they had made a decision. They would stay in Syria, no matter the cost.*

One night as their neighborhood was heavily shelled by mortars, the family huddled together in the front room of their home. Liena pointed to the front door and said to her children, 'Look at this door. One day, God may allow someone from those terrorist people … to come in this door. They will have a big beard and very threatening faces, maybe they will have swords. They will put their swords on our necks, and you may see some blood. They will hurt us.

'We will have pain, but don't' worry about this pain. We will close our eyes, and we will pen them again in heaven, and we will be with Jesus, singing with the angels.

'Just tell these people, 'I forgive you, and Jesus loves you.' God did not call the family home to him that night. Instead, they continue to be lights for Christ in Syria. While they still have the option of leaving the country at any time, they feel strongly that God has them there for a purpose. One of those purposes is bringing attention to how Christians are suffering because of the war.

This month's newsletter focuses on the persecuted church in the historically rich nation of Syria, where brutal acts of war have drawn the attention of the world. The Voice of the Martyrs continues to stand with our brothers and sisters in Syria who boldly proclaim the love of Christ." (Material provided by The Voice of the Martyrs, PO Box 443, Bartlesville, OK 74003, 1-918-337-8015, www.persecution.com, thevoice@vom-usa.org)

I believe "Samer" and "Liena" are taking seriously the commission the apostle Paul gave to Timothy, his son in the faith. Are you??? Here is the commission: "*You therefore, my son, be strong in the grace that is in Christ Jesus. And the things that you have heard from me among many witnesses, commit these to faithful men who will be able to teach others also. You therefore must endure hardship as a good soldier of Jesus Christ. No one engaged in warfare entangles himself with the affairs of this life, that he may please him who enlisted him as a soldier." 2 Timothy 2:1-4*

Can you say as Paul did: *"I have been crucified with Christ; it is no longer I who live, but Christ lives in me; and the life which I now live in the flesh I live by faith in the Son of God, who loved me and gave Himself for me." Galatians 2:20?*

The Testimony of a <u>Former</u> Homosexual

Recently I heard the testimony of a former homosexual who spoke up during the open question and comment time following one of Ravi Zacharias' apologetic messages. He testified about how he repented and left behind the addiction to homosexual behavior, and stressed that although it was not easy, God gave him the victory. He no longer yields to the temptations and does not practice his sinful inclinations. I believe he said that it has been twenty years now that he is free from homosexual practices. He said that he was slandered and attacked not only by the secular crowd, but was also mocked and called a liar by professing Christians who told him he couldn't change – that it was impossible because he was "born that way." Like the blind man who was slandered and attacked by the religious leaders in Jesus' day, this man was slandered and attacked by "religious leaders" in our day. But like the blind man who said, "This I know – once I was blind, but now I can see", this ex-homosexual can say, "This I know – once I was a homosexual, but now I am free!"

If you are still adamantly convinced that homosexuals can't change – please don't persecute those who have changed and are being changed by the power and grace of God. **"With God all things are possible!"**

Dangerous Fundamentalists

It is my observation that atheists, humanists, and various types of left wing liberals tend to lump Islamic fundamentalists and Christian fundamentalists together as dangerous fundamentalists. This is evidence that those who do so are either woefully ignorant of the facts or are intentionally distorting the facts to promote their own agenda, worldview, and prejudice. The basic fact is that Islam and Biblical Christianity are fundamentally different and polar opposites in many ways in spite of a few surface similarities. One of the most basic differences in the fundamental nature of these two faith systems was made crystal clear by a concise statement by former Attorney General John Ashcroft: He said that **Islam is a religion in which Allah rewards you for sending your son to die for him. Christianity is a faith in which God sent His Son to die for you.** Remember that fundamentals are the basics. With just a little study you can easily see that Islam and Christianity are only superficially similar – yet basically **very** different!

Another popular lie promoted by atheist (humanist) groups is that religion is the cause of most of the wars and bloodshed in all of human history. I want to point out three glaring flaws in this monumental lie: 1. They exclude their own religion of Humanism (a euphemism for atheism) from this broad sweeping incrimination. 2. They refuse to distinguish between the fundamental differences in religions. They do not acknowledge the possibility of true religion and false religion because they make the broad sweeping claim that all religions are false (theirs excluded, of course)! 3. They ignore the fact that the worst mass murderers in all of history – Stalin and Mao Tse-tung – were Marxist atheists. Together these two atheists orchestrated the deaths of over eighty million people. Hitler was a committed Darwinist who added a deadly mixture of occultism with Nietzsche's atheistic, anti-Christ philosophy. He was also responsible for the murder of millions of people, whom he considered sub-human scum. He and his Nazi henchmen were proud of speeding up the evolution processes by wiping out and eliminating the "culls" of humanity (and sub-humanity). **They gloried in their shame!**

Friend, if you are being tempted by atheism, please take a closer look at your philosophy. Isn't it leading you down a dead end street of meaninglessness despair and destruction? I have been there. Atheism is a hopeless philosophy. Without God there is no design, no meaning, no purpose, and no hope. Dostoyevsky also accurately nailed down the fact that **atheism has no**

morality. Although some atheists borrow their moral principles from Biblical theology, they actually have no logical basis for such morality. Dostoyevsky wrote that if there were no God, anything would be permissible. The truth of his statement is validated in Adolph Hitler. His near success in his massive effort to exterminate the Jews (and others he considered sub-human, enemies of the state, or worthless eaters) was undergirded by his philosophy – a potent mixture of atheistic Darwinism and Nietzscheism seasoned with deadly occultism. Like mixing drugs and alcohol – this powerful mixture of false philosophy and religion sparked the murder of millions and set off World War II. (Please see a more complete documentation of this in my book, *Ready to Give an Answer*, chapter 3, "Catastrophic Consequences of Darwinism".) Actually, Hitler was also a Marxist. Nazi means national socialist.

A Muslim man once told me that Hitler was a Christian. Whether he believed this lie because Hitler was born in Austria, which was once considered a Christian nation where Roman Catholicism was the dominant religion, believed it because Hitler was a master con-artist who manipulated both Catholic and Lutheran church leaders to cooperate with his diabolical agenda, or if he merely told me this lie because it fit his own agenda, I do not know. What I do know is that Adolf Hitler was **not** a Christian by Biblical standards, or by any stretch of an honest man's evaluation. There is a plaque still on display at the Auschwitz death camp which says, "*I want to train up a generation of young people without conscience. Impervious, relentless, cruel*", with Hitler's name on it as the author. Does that saying fit with Jesus' commands to turn the other cheek, forgive those who hurt you and to love your enemy? Ravi Zacharias candidly pointed out that it is never valid to portray any religion or philosophy by its distortions or aberrations. God does teach us in His Word to debate fairly and honestly according to truth and righteousness. "*For though we walk in the flesh, we are not waging war according to the flesh. For the weapons of our warfare are not of the flesh but have divine power to destroy strongholds. We destroy arguments and every lofty opinion raised against the knowledge of God, and take every thought captive to obey Christ,*" 2 Corinthians 10:3-5

(ESV). Those who build up straw men to knock down, then pound their chests and yell over their triumphs only parade their own foolish immaturity. Most of the blatant atheist/humanist books and blogs fit in this category – right along with a Muslim's portrayal of Hitler as a Christian. Twice God tells us in His Word, "The fool has said in his heart 'there is no God.'" See Psalm 14:1 and Psalm 53:1, then notice the rest of the verse: *"The fool says in his heart, "There is no God. They are corrupt, doing abominable iniquity; there is none who does good."*

It is true that there are some shameful blots on the pages of church history – and recent history. There are many who claimed the name of Christ who have sunk into gross corruption and committed atrocities. However, Ravi's concise, practical wisdom is **"Never judge a philosophy by its abuses."**

When Christians (or professing Christians) choose to yield to the flesh instead of the Spirit, they are capable of doing terrible evil and causing trouble and trauma for generations – even centuries. David, the prominent Psalmist of Israel, who was known as a man after God's own heart, became an adulterer, liar, and murderer when he yielded to the lust of the flesh. When Almighty God sent the prophet, Nathan, to tell David a captivating story and expose his corruption, David humbled himself and truly repented instead of proudly reacting in wrath by ordering Nathan to be executed or banished. In his humble repentance, powerfully expressed in Psalm 32 and 51, David once again became a man after God's own heart. Yet in spite of his deep repentance, David and his entire family (as well as the nation) suffered severe consequences for his sin.

When a Christian (or professing Christian) commits sin – even a terrible crime – what does it actually demonstrate? **It does not demonstrate that Christianity is false**!!! It does demonstrate that human nature is not basically good with a few superficial flaws (as humanism/atheism teaches). And it does demonstrate the truth and accuracy of God's Word concerning human nature. Consider this evaluation of human nature which the Holy Spirit inspired Paul to write to the Romans: *"What then? Are we better than they? Not at all. For we have previously charged both Jews and Greeks* *that they are all under sin. As it is written: "There is none righteous, no, not one; There is none who understands; There is none who seeks after God. They have all turned aside; They have together become unprofitable; There is none who does good, no, not one." "Their throat is an open tomb; With their tongues they have practiced deceit"; "The poison of asps is under their lips"; "Whose mouth is full of cursing and bitterness." "Their feet are swift to shed blood; Destruction and misery are in their ways; And the way of peace they have not known.""There is no fear of God before their eyes." Now we know that whatever the law says, it says to those who are under the law, that every mouth may be stopped, and all the world may become guilty before God. Therefore by the deeds of the law no flesh will be justified in His sight, for by the law is the knowledge of sin." Romans 3:9-20.* The law of God and the daily news reports confirm the depravity of man (often those their neighbors thought were good), and our desperate need for the Savior. That is why Jesus came!

"God Sent Us a Saviour"

"If our greatest need had been information,
God would have sent us an educator.
If our greatest need had been technology,
God would have sent us a scientist.
If our greatest need had been money,
God would have sent us an economist.
If our greatest need had been pleasure,
God would have sent us an entertainer.
But our greatest need was forgiveness,
So God sent us a Saviour."

~ Roy Lessin

In Christ Alone

Verse 1
In Christ alone my hope is found
He is my light my strength my song
This Cornerstone this solid Ground
Firm through the fiercest drought and storm
What heights of love what depths of peace
When fears are stilled when strivings cease
My Comforter my All in All
Here in the love of Christ I stand

Verse 2
In Christ alone who took on flesh
Fulness of God in helpless babe
This gift of love and righteous-ness
Scorned by the ones He came to save
Till on that cross as Jesus died
The wrath of God was satisfied
For every sin on Him was laid
Here in the death of Christ I live

Verse 3
There in the ground His body lay
Light of the world by darkness slain
Then bursting forth in glorious Day
Up from the grave He rose again
And as He stands in victory
Sin's curse has lost its grip on me
For I am His and He is mine
Bought with the precious blood of Christ

Verse 4
No guilt in life no fear in death
This is the power of Christ in me
From life's first cry to final breath
Jesus commands my destiny
No power of hell no scheme of man
Can ever pluck me from His hand
Till He returns or calls me home
Here in the power of Christ I'll stand

CCLI Song # 3350395

Keith Getty | Stuart Townend

ALL SPOILED AND BLOTTED

Ravi Zacharias shares a story given to him by an elementary teacher. As I recall, it goes something like this:

"He came to me with a quivering lip, and handed me his paper all spoiled and blotted. I'm sorry, teacher, may I have another chance? I'm so sorry I spoiled this one!

I smiled understandingly as I replied, 'Here is a new one for you - do better now, my child.'

I went to the throne with a trembling heart and handed God my day all spoiled and blotted. 'I'm sorry, Father – may I have another chance? I am so sorry I've ruined this one.'

His gracious eyes sparkled with love as He replied, 'I forgive you. You have another chance – do better now, my child.'"

"For I know the thoughts that I think toward you, says the LORD, thoughts of peace and not of evil, to give you a future and a hope. Then you will call upon Me and go and pray to Me, and I will listen to you. And you will seek Me and find Me, when you search for Me with all your heart. . . 'Call to Me, and I will answer you, and show you great and mighty things, which you do not know.'" Jeremiah 29:11-13; 33:3

"Seek the LORD while He may be found, call upon Him while He is near. Let the wicked forsake his way, and the unrighteous man his thoughts; let him return to the LORD, and He will have mercy on him; and to our God, for He will abundantly pardon. 'For My thoughts are not your thoughts, nor are your ways My ways,' says the LORD. 'For as the heavens are higher than the earth, so are My ways higher than your ways, and My thoughts than your thoughts. For as the rain comes down, and the snow from heaven, and do not return there, but water the earth, and make it bring forth and bud,

that it may give seed to the sower and bread to the eater, so shall My word be that goes forth from My mouth; it shall not return to Me void, but it shall accomplish what I please, and it shall prosper in the thing for which I sent it." Isaiah 55:6-11

The Heart of the Problem is the Problem of the Heart!

Why was David a man after God's own heart? I believe the Word of God indicates it was because of his humility. Even after Samuel anointed him to be the next king of Israel while Saul was still on the throne, David humbly waited for God's timing to ascend to the throne. He still saw Saul as "God's anointed" and would not strike him down when he had opportunity after opportunity to do so – and in spite of the fact that Saul was trying to kill him. After David's terrible sins of adultery, murder and hypocrisy, God sent Nathan the prophet to expose him and confront him. If David were an arrogant man he would likely have said to Nathan, "How dare you accuse me?" He had the power to order Nathan to be exiled or executed – yet he did not react in arrogance and anger. David humbly confessed his sins and truly repented. The word of God teaches *"God resists the proud, but gives grace to the humble." "Humble yourselves in the sight of the Lord, and He will lift you up."* James 4:6, 8

\The Deepest Rooted Sin

Pride is probably the deepest rooted sin in the human heart – and the hardest for us to detect in ourselves. Arrogance is like bad breath – it stinks to others when we don't even notice we have it. A good test to tell if you have a proud heart is this – how do you deal with correction? If someone who cares for you points out a sin you need to repent of, do you react in anger or do you humbly consider the Word of God, repent, confess your sin, and ask forgiveness? *"If we confess our sins He is faithful and just to forgive us our sins, and to cleanse us from all unrighteousness."* 1 John 1:9. Are you humble enough to repent? Are you humble enough to thank the person who cared enough to confront you? Paul wrote to the Corinthians: *"Examine yourselves to see whether you are in the faith; test yourselves. Do you not realize that Christ Jesus is in you—unless, of course, you fail the test?"* 2 Corinthians 13:5.

Here is another test of whether you have a humble spirit or an arrogant heart, whether you are truly converted – do you abhor (intensely hate) what is evil? Do you cling to what is good? *"Let love be without hypocrisy. Abhor what is evil. Cling to what is good. . . Do not be overcome by evil, but overcome evil with good."* Romans 12:9, 21.

> *"I expect to pass through this world but once;*
> *Any good things, therefore that I can do, or any*
> *Kindness that I can show to any fellow creature,*
> *Let me do it now; let me not defer or neglect it,*
> *For I shall not pass this way again."*
>
> *~ Attributed to Etienne De Grellet*

The issue of a humble spirit before God is so crucial that the Holy Spirit inspired Paul to put it immediately after his strong exhortation to present our bodies as a living sacrifice to God, to refuse to be conformed to this world, and to be **transformed** by the renewing of our minds. Notice, *"I beseech you therefore, brethren, by the mercies of God, that you present your bodies a living sacrifice, holy, acceptable to God, which is your reasonable service. And do not be conformed to this world, but be transformed by the renewing of your mind, that you may prove what is that good and acceptable and perfect will of God. For I say, through the grace given to me, to everyone who is among you, not to think of himself more highly than he ought to think, but to think soberly, as God has dealt to each one a measure of faith."* Romans 12:1-3

It is also highly significant that he does not say that low self-esteem is the root cause of our bad behavior (nor does any other Biblical writer). Could it be that that teaching does not come from the Holy Spirit? **Self control – not self-esteem is listed as fruit of the Spirit!!!**

Are All Religions Fundamentally the Same?

Ravi Zacharias has also clearly analyzed the false statement many people parrot that "all religions are fundamentally the same even though they have superficial differences". Ravi accurately says that the religions have a few superficial similarities even though they have huge fundamental differences. These differences include opposite teachings about our origin, destiny, purpose, meaning, morals and theology, as well as heaven, hell and salvation. Check it out! He's right!

The Word of God says: *"Test all things; hold fast what is good. Abstain from every form of evil."* 1 Thessalonians 5:21-22 (NKJV), and *"Beloved, do not believe every spirit, but test the spirits to see whether they are from God, for many false prophets have gone out into the world. By this you know the Spirit of God: every spirit that confesses that Jesus Christ has come in the flesh is from God, and every spirit that does not confess Jesus is not from God.* This is the spirit of the antichrist, which you heard was coming and now is in the world already. Little children, you are from God and have overcome them, for he who is in you is greater than he who is in the world. They are from the world; therefore they speak from the world, and the world listens to them. We are from God. Whoever knows God listens to us; whoever is not from God does not listen to us. *By this we know the Spirit of truth and the spirit of error. Beloved, let us love one another, for love is from God, and whoever loves has been born of God and knows God. Anyone who does not love does not know God, because God is love.* In this the love of God was made manifest among us, that God sent his only Son into the world, so that we might live through him. In this is love, not that we have loved God but that he loved us and sent his Son to be the propitiation for our sins. Beloved, if God so loved us, we also ought to love one another. No one has ever seen God; if we love one another, God abides in us and his love is perfected in us. By this we know that we abide in him and he in us, because he has given us of his Spirit. And we have seen and testify that the Father has sent his Son to be the Savior of the world. Whoever confesses that Jesus is the Son *of God, God abides in him, and he in God. So we have come to know and to believe the love that God has for us. God is love, and whoever abides in love abides in God, and God abides in him. **By this is love perfected with us, so that we may have confidence for the day of judgment, because as he is so also are we in this world. There is no fear in love, but perfect love casts out fear.** For fear has to do with punishment, and whoever fears has not been perfected in love. We love because he first loved us. If anyone says, "I love God," and hates his brother, he is a liar; for he who does not love his brother whom he has seen cannot love God whom he has not seen. And this commandment we have from him: whoever loves God must also love his brother."* 1 John 4:1-21 (ESV).

Now here is that same passage from the NLT: *"Dear friends, do not believe everyone who claims to speak by the Spirit. You must test them to see if the spirit they have comes from God. For there are many false prophets in the world. This is how we know if they have the Spirit of God: If a person claiming to be a prophet acknowledges that Jesus Christ came in a real body, that person has the Spirit of God. But if someone claims to be a prophet and does not acknowledge the truth about Jesus, that person is not from God. Such a person has the spirit of the Antichrist, which you heard is coming into the world and indeed is already here. But you belong to God, my dear children. You have already won a victory over those people, because the Spirit who lives in you is greater than the spirit who lives in the world. Those people belong to this world, so they speak from the world's viewpoint, and the world listens to them. But we belong to God, and those who know God listen to us. If they do not belong to God, they do not listen to us. That is how we know if someone has the Spirit of truth or the spirit of deception. Dear friends, let us continue to love one another, for love comes from God. Anyone who loves is a child of God and knows God. But anyone who does not love does not know God, for God is love. God showed how much he loved us by sending his one and only Son into the world so that we might have eternal life through him. This is real love—not that we loved God, but that he loved us and sent his Son as a sacrifice to take away our sins. Dear friends, since God loved us that much, we surely ought to love each other. No one has ever seen God. But if we love each other, God lives in us, and his love is brought to full expression in us. And God has given us his Spirit as proof that we live in him and he in us. Furthermore, we have seen with our own eyes and now testify that the Father sent his Son to be the Savior of the world. All who confess that Jesus is the Son of God have God living in them, and they live in God. We know how much God loves us, and we have put our trust in his love. God is love, and all who live in love live in God, and God lives in them. And as we live in God, our love grows more perfect. So we will not be afraid on the day of judgment, but we can face him with confidence because we live like Jesus here in this world. Such love has no fear, because perfect love expels all fear. If we are afraid, it is for fear of punishment, and this shows that we have not fully experienced his perfect love. We love each other because he loved us first. If someone says, 'I love God,' but hates a Christian brother or sister, that person is a liar; for if we don't love people we can see, how can we love God, whom we cannot see? And he has given us this command: Those who love God must also love their Christian brothers and sisters."*

I choose to believe God! How about you? Who do you choose to believe?'

True vs. False Religion

As a clear example of the difference between true and false religion, plus powerful testimony to the true meaning of love and joy in the midst of rejection and persecution, I want to share with you this VOM article by Todd Nettleton. (Published by Voice of the Martyrs, February 2013)

"It was a long, hot drive to the tin-roofed house in southern Nepal where our VOM team met Danmaya. The air conditioner in our taxi couldn't quite keep up with the sultry afternoon heat, and when we ducked into the brick house where Danmaya lives, it was even hotter.

The house belongs to Danmaya's pastor. He and his family invited Danmaya to stay with them in their one-room house after her husband kicked her out because of her Christian faith.

When a Christian friend shared the gospel with Danmaya six years ago, she received it willingly. She was weary of trying to please thousands of Hindu gods, and she felt in her heart the truth of God's love through Jesus Christ.

When she told her husband about her Christian faith, he didn't think it would last. At first, he simply told her to keep it to herself so she wouldn't bring shame on their high-caste family. But Danmaya's faith did last, and it also began to grow. About a year after she first heard the gospel, Danmaya asked to be baptized. Then her husband knew it wasn't just a fad or phase his wife was going through. She was a Christian.

'This is not our custom,' he told her. 'Give up your faith. Otherwise, I will leave you.' After Danmaya was baptized, her Hindu husband threw her belongings out of the house, kicked her out and married another woman. Even Danmaya's parents turned her away when she refused to renounce her faith. But when her earthly family kicked her out, her spiritual family opened their doors and welcomed her into their small brick house.

Hearing Danmaya's story, you may picture a downtrodden, angry woman living in homeless desperation after being abandoned by her husband. But this childless, deserted woman couldn't stop smiling. She told us that she has forgiven her husband and even prays for his new wife. 'In the beginning I had a kind of bitterness in my heart [toward him],' she said. 'But later I came to know that unless I forgive him I cannot go the right way to God. So I have forgiven.

'I used to think that whatever persecution comes – even if I die – I will be alive with Christ in heaven,' she told our team. 'That hope kept me strong.'

Before we left that little brick house and got back into our taxi, we gave the pastor a small gift to help with Danmaya's expenses. She and the pastor thanked us repeatedly for coming, as if we'd done something special.

We drove almost two hours to meet Danmaya. But after hearing her story and seeing the radiant joy of the Lord on her face, I knew that I'd happily drive eight hours to spend one hour with such a Godly saint."

So, my friend, who were the intolerant ones in this story? Was it the fundamental Christians – or was it the fundamental Hindus? Will the left wing, liberal propaganda change if they even read multiple stories like this published by VOM and other mission organizations? Most of the persecution of Christians is coming from Muslim nations or Marxist nations. Where are the news reports about this in the major media sources?

Two Types of Fear

1. Unholy Fear = fearing what people think of you, what may happen to you, and everything else except God. "*The fear of man brings a snare, but whoever trusts in the LORD SHALL BE SAFE.*" Proverbs 29:25

2. Holy Fear = fearing God Himself, which gives us a holy boldness, spiritual knowledge, and godly wisdom. "Fear not, for I am with you!"

"*And now, Israel, what does the LORD YOUR GOD REQUIRE OF YOU, BUT TO FEAR*

THE LORD YOUR GOD, TO WALK IN ALL HIS WAYS AND TO LOVE HIM, TO SERVE THE

LORD YOUR GOD WITH ALL YOUR HEART AND WITH ALL YOUR SOUL, AND TO KEEP THE COMMANDMENTS OF THE LORD AND HIS STATUTES WHICH I COMMAND YOU TODAY FOR YOUR GOOD?" Deuteronomy 10:12-13

"*Have I not commanded you? Be strong and of good courage; do not be afraid, nor be dismayed, for the LORD YOUR GOD IS WITH YOU WHEREVER YOU GO.*"

Joshua 1:9

"The fear of the LORD IS THE BEGINNING OF KNOWL-EDGE, but fools despise wisdom and instruction." Proverbs 1:7

"And to man He said, 'Behold, the fear of the Lord, that is wisdom, and to depart from evil is understanding.'" Job 28:28

"Let us hear the conclusion of the whole matter: Fear God and keep His commandments, for this is man's all." Ecclesiastes 12:13

You won't often find wisdom in the halls of intellectualism, but you will find the epitome of human pride, arrogance, and foolishness. You will find both knowledge (science) and wisdom in a loving and surrendered relationship with our Father and Creator – Almighty God.

The Intolerant Tolerant Troop on Parade

Now to further illustrate the intolerance of the tolerant troop, I want to share with you a few brief articles from Christian news sources that are nearly completely ignored by the major media sources. Are they ignoring what is truly happening if it doesn't fit their leftist agenda?

"Want To Be Popular? Do Not Do This...

Want to be popular? Or want to avoid controversy?

Don't become a Christ-follower. If you take a clear stand for Jesus, or even for traditional biblical values, intimidation and criticism will likely come your way.

That seems evident in two stories in this issue of *Christian News Northwest*.

One is the news that New York quarterback Tim Tebow,

widely known for his strong Christian faith, has backed out of a scheduled appearance at First Baptist Church in Dallas, Texas, later this spring.

That church has come under fire in the past year not only because of Pastor Robert Jeffress's unwavering view that the homosexual lifestyle is a sin, but also because of his belief that religions other than Christianity are heretical. Jeffress counters that his teachings are consistent with historic Christian beliefs and that his church is wrongly being characterized as hateful.

Like Jeffress himself, we were surprised and disappointed by Tebow's decision. It is obvious he was not prepared for the criticism he faced initially in accepting the church's invitation to speak. But we also feel some measure of sympathy for Tebow, because he simply may not have been aware of the extent of the controversy surrounding the Dallas church.

The other story, based here in Oregon but getting national attention, is Page 1 of this issue. Gresham business owners Aaron and Melissa Klein are being charged with discrimination because, as Christians, they didn't believe they should provide a wedding cake for a same-sex couple.

In this day and age, Christians such as Tebow, Jeffress or the Kleins are labeled as bigoted or hateful because of their Bible-based beliefs. This kind of attack isn't new – Christ-followers have been mischaracterized since the days of the early Church. But it sure is sad to see it happening in modern-day America." (John Fortmeyer, Publisher/Editor, "Christian News Northwest", March 2013, Portland area)

"Pastor Giglio No Longer Welcome On Inaugural Platform"

"In a sudden reversal with stunning implications for religious tolerance in America, aggressive and obviously influential homosexual activists pressured Pastor Louis Giglio to withdraw from offering the benediction at this month's presidential inauguration a few days after he accepted the invitation.

Giglio holds strong biblical views on homosexuality but has

avoided the subject in his popular public ministry. A homosexual organization had to dig deep to find a 1990's sermon he preached which identified the practice as a sin based on standard Old and New Testament scriptures. The group used the sermon to threaten a media-driven scandal, prompting Giglio to withdraw as quietly as possible.

News media started reporting the incident Thursday as simply a withdrawal on the pastor's part, but if he had done otherwise the presidential inauguration Committee would clearly have ousted him. As it was, the committee apologized for inviting him and promised to replace him with a "pro-gay pastor."

For discussion: This is a very public government rejection of a pastor simply for having once preached a Bible-based sermon on homosexuality. What could this precedent turn into long-term? We will have more information and analysis on this late-breaking development next week."

"New – And Only – Black Senator Gets 'F' From NAACP"

"A black U.S. Senator has been a rarity lately. Neither party has had one for years, that is, until SC Gov. Nikki Haley (a rare Native American Republican woman!) appointed Rep. Tim Scott to replace the recently resigned Sen. Jim DeMint.

Sen. Scott is a pro-life, pro-traditional marriage Christian who favors repealing ObamaCare and cutting federal taxes, spending, and borrowing. That resume is probably enough to account for the fact that the National Association for the Advancement of Colored People is not celebrating this historic appointment of the first black Senator ever from South Carolina.

NAACP President Ben Jealous says Scott "opposes civil rights" because he favors a smaller government and that would work against "real issues of concern" to his organization's constituents. "We have some Republicans who believe in civil rights – unfortunately he is not one of them," Jealous said. The NAACP has given Scott an "F" rating because they rate "what's in people's hearts."

The newly-seated Senator, asked for a response on a television interview, said that speaking as a black man raised by a low-income single mother, it is "ridiculous and baseless" to claim he is opposed to civil rights. "Mr. Jealous thinks bigger government means more freedom. I just totally disagree."

For discussion: Notice how moral/biblical issues such as some of those that distinguish Sen. Scott supersede other considerations that supposedly bind interest groups together. (Examples: a black organization that does not want to "advance" a black Senator, or women's organizations that will not support a pro-life woman.) Is that a good thing or not? How about a "gay rights" organization that opposes a homosexual's right to seek sexual orientation counseling? (See last week's lead article.) Does this just show that the most important defining classifications of people are the two described in Matt. 12:30?"

("The Times and the Scriptures," January 13, 2013. Used by permission.)

"The Limits of 'Diversity'"

"Angela McCaskill is many things. She's the first black woman to earn a doctorate at Gallaudet University, a school for deaf people like herself. She's worked there for 23 years and is now the school's chief diversity officer.

Oh, and she's also suspended - technically, "on administrative leave"-because she's just a little too diverse for their taste.

McCaskill, you see, goes to church. And one day, after her pastor preached against same-sex marriage, she signed a petition at her church to let Maryland voters decide the issue. Seems she was under the impression that American citizens have the right to do such things.

Not any more, apparently. After a homosexual publication, the *Washington Blade*, got a hold of the signatures and posted them on line, a gay activist at the school noticed, complained to the higher-ups, and –bam!-McCaskill was suspended.

It may not last. She's got a lawyer, and the PR is terrible for

Gallaudet, which-about 10 seconds after the story went national-announced it wants to work things out with her. Then again, it's been well over a month since then, so we'll see.

However this story turns out, it's clear what "diversity" really means to some people: Christians need not apply." (Originally appeared in the January/February 2013 issue of Focus on the Family's Citizen magazine. Copyright © 2013 Focus on the Family. All rights reserved. International copyright secured. Used by permission.)

"California Bans Gay Change Therapy"

"In a stunning power grab orchestrated by homosexual activists, California has passed a law banning mental health professionals from offering minors any therapies meant to change sexual orientation.

The bill, passed by the state legislature and signed by Gov. Jerry Brown, was sponsored by state senator Ted Lieu, who is heterosexual. Gay activists have claimed for years that attempts to get kids to change sexual orientations are harmful and they have pushed for a law banning the practice.

"No one should stand idly by while children are being psychologically abused, and anyone who forces a child to try to change their sexual orientation must understand this is unacceptable," Lieu said.

But the law is extremely controversial because it allows the government to decide what types of therapies mental health professionals can use and, perhaps even more alarming, how parents raise their children.

The conservative Pacific Justice Institute said it will challenge the law in court.

"The privacy concerns are fairly significant," PJI staff attorney Matthew B. McReynolds told the Los Angeles Times. "In our view, it's an intrusting beyond what the government has done before."

Journalist Stephen Beale said liberals always seem to demand the freedom to choose for individuals – until the choice runs contrary to their worldview.

"Apparently, the possibility that a teenager may want to change his or her sexual orientation of their own accord – not due to the firm prodding of overbearing parents – never crossed their minds," Beale said." (AFA Journal, January 2013, p. 7. Used by permission.)

My Personal Experience with the Tolerant Troop

When will the "tolerant troop" become indignant and intolerant of gender and racial slurs like "male chauvinist pig," "homophobic bigot" and "old, fat white man"? When are they going to get outraged by death threats and obscene names called and sent to promoters of Proposition 8 for California and other Biblical marriage proponents? When are those who rail against hypocritical Christians going to rail against hypocritical tolerant troopers?

In August 1992 we moved to Gresham, Oregon, to help serve a local congregation there and I learned firsthand the intense bias of the homosexual activists against those who take a stand for Biblical morality and morals. I saw newspaper articles and cartoons blasting and mocking Lon Maybon – a conservative Christian man who dared take a public stand against the homosexual agenda. Since I had already experienced the slanted power of the press directed at me, I decided he couldn't be all bad if the liberal press hated him this much, so I went to see and hear him myself. What I experienced was not a wild-eyed radical as portrayed by left-wing media sources, but rather a soft spoken, Christian man with a backbone of steel. In his brief testimonial he described becoming increasingly disturbed by the encroaching and aggressive agenda of the homosexual activists while wondering, "Why doesn't someone do something to stop this?" He got the strong impression that God was calling him to do something to stop it, so he started a petition to block homosexual activists from promoting their agenda in the public schools. I doubt if he realized what a firestorm of protest, criticism, mocking, ridicule and slander he would unleash on himself by exercising his right and duty as a concerned American citizen. The longer I listened, the more I realized he was simply and straightforwardly articulating clear, Biblical morality in contrast with cultural corruption. The epitomy of cultural clashes converge and culminate on the issues of sexuality and morality concerning contraception, abortion, sex education, and marriage. Lon Maybon touched a raw nerve and the liberal elite were determined to never let him forget it.

Some months later when I volunteered to help gather signatures, I experienced the most hate-filled glares I have ever seen. Was the tolerant troop tolerant of us – concerned American citizens? Hardly!!! Fortunately there were many petition signers who commended us and urged us on – but not many were willing to commit to gathering petition signatures.

"I Have a Dream!"

September 15, 2013 was the 50th anniversary of Martin Luther King's famous speech. There has been great progress in racial relationships since that day – but much still needs to be accomplished. I also have a dream. I **dream of seeing another great awakening in America**, with genuine revival in our churches and millions of souls bowing to the Lord Jesus Christ and unreservedly giving their hearts to Him. **I earnestly desire spiritual awakening and pray daily for this. Will you join me?**

What can we do About It?

Again, I want to return to this question so that these news reports are not just an exercise in futility. So, what shall we do?

1. Pray! Fervently pray! Every great awakening begins with prayer. Remember – it's always darkest before the dawn,

and "with God all things are possible". *"If My people who are called by My name will humble themselves, and pray and seek My face, and turn from their wicked ways, then I will hear from heaven, and will forgive their sin and heal their land." 2 Chronicles 7:14*

2.   We need to take seriously the Biblical responsibility of training our children – and grandchildren if possible - in truth and righteousness. Parents are **the** primary educators commissioned by Almighty God to instill a Biblical and Godly worldview in their children. Bible teachers, Christian school teachers, youth leaders, and pastors/teachers are crucial and helpful as supplemental influences, but God commissioned parents with the task of training their children. Consider these Scriptures: *"Hear, O Israel: The LORD OUR GOD, THE LORD IS ONE! You shall love the LORD YOUR GOD WITH ALL YOUR HEART, WITH ALL YOUR SOUL, AND WITH ALL YOUR STRENGTH. And these words which I command you today shall be in your heart. You shall teach them diligently to your children, and shall talk of them when you sit in your house, when you walk by the way, when you lie down, and when you rise up. You shall bind them as a sign on your hand, and they shall be as frontlets between your eyes. You shall write them on the doorposts of your house and on your gates."* Deuteronomy 6:4-9. Note: This same principle carries over to us as grafted in to Israel. Proverbs 22:6 says, *"Train up a child in the way he should go, And when he is old he will not depart from it."* Ephesians 5:33 says, *"Nevertheless let each one of you in particular so love his own wife as himself, and let the wife see that she respects her husband."* Note: The best way for children to learn how a man is to treat his wife and how a wife is to respect her husband is to see it modeled by their parents. Ephesians 6:1-4 says, *"Children, obey your parents in the Lord, for this is right. 'Honor your father and mother,' which is the first commandment with promise: 'that it may be well with you and you may live long on the earth.' And you, fathers, do not provoke your children to wrath, but bring them up in the*

training and admonition of the Lord."

The best way for children to learn to develop the courage to stand for truth, righteousness, and against peer pressure is to see that courage of conviction modeled by their parents. Here is a great example from the April 2013 issue of *Citizen Magazine*, p. 9 in the section, "Overheard": "I'd rather have my kids see their dad stand up for   what he believes in than to see him bow down because one person complained."   Gresham, Ore., baker Aaron Klein, who is facing a state investigation because he wouldn't bake a wedding cake for a lesbian couple. KGW-TV, Feb. 2, 2013.

Speak up for truth and righteousness while we still can, in every way we can. Be strong! Be bold! Be active! Get involved! That is so much better than whimpering about what you should have done after it is too late.

"Do not boast about tomorrow, for you do not know what a day may bring forth."

Proverbs 27:1

As an example of what we can do, here is a copy of a letter I wrote February 1, 2013 to the Leadership Team of the Boy Scouts:

"To the Leadership Team of Boy Scouts,

Please, please do not severely disappoint us by compromising with the homosexual agenda. I realize the homosexual activists are putting powerful pressure on you to comply with their agenda. We have admired you for standing strong for truth and righteousness – please don't abandon us now. I hope you stand against tyranny like Patrick Henry rather than compromising your integrity and committing treason like Benedict Arnold.

When facing overwhelming odds, Joshua needed reassurance. God spoke to him saying: *"Be strong and courageous, for you shall cause this people to inherit the land that I swore to their fathers to give them. Only be strong and very courageous, being careful to do according to all the law that Moses my servant commanded you. Do not turn from it to the right hand or to the left, that you may have good success wherever you go. This Book of the Law shall not depart from your mouth, but you shall meditate on it day and night, so that you may be careful to do according to all that is written in it. For then you will make your way prosperous, and then you will have good success. Have I not commanded you? Be strong and courageous. Do not be frightened, and do not be dismayed, for the* LORD YOUR GOD IS WITH YOU WHEREVER YOU GO." *Joshua 1:6-9 (ESV)*

Yours & His,
Rick Deighton"

Unfortunately, the majority of Boy Scout leaders voted to allow practicing homosexuals to become scouts. However, this cowardly compromise did not satisfy the voracious appetite of the homosexual activists for power, control and total affirmation because the Boy Scout decision makers excluded homosexuals from leadership positions. (It was like trying to work out a compromise with a wild-eyed hungry tiger!)

RIGHT WING RADICAL?

Am I afraid that someone will call me a right wing radical? Not on your life! Why not?

1. Who is it who is being radical?

2. Satan is the father of lies – so why should I care if he inspires someone to call me radical? I would rather be right than wrong! Jesus Himself is seated at the right hand of the Father!

3. I would rather be considered a "right wing radical" than a fellow traveler with the left-wing liberals pretending to be loving.

Friend, if you have been traveling with the wrong crowd, please consider:

"Fools mock at sin, but among the upright there is favor. The heart knows its own bitterness, and a stranger does not share its joy. The house of the wicked will be overthrown, but the tent of the upright will flourish. There is a way that seems right to a man, but its end is the way of death. Even in laughter the heart may sorrow, and the end of mirth may be grief. The backslider in heart will be filled with his own ways, but a good man will be satisfied from above. The simple believes every word, but the prudent considers well his steps. A wise man fears and departs from evil, but a fool rages and is self-confident." Proverbs 14:9-16

"Do not be deceived: 'Evil company corrupts good habits.' Awake to righteousness, and do not sin; for some do not have the knowledge of God. I speak this to your shame."

1 Corinthians 15:33-34

It's time – past time to repent and come home to the Father. His heart aches for you and His arms are open wide. Now is the time! **"Do not boast about tomorrow, for you do not know what a day may bring forth."** Proverbs 27:1

The Holy Spirit commissions us to overcome evil with good. *"Let love be without hypocrisy. Abhor what is evil. Cling to what is good. . . Do not be overcome by evil, but overcome evil with good."* Romans 12:9, 21. Consider this powerful example from *Breakpoint (A Christian Perspective on Today's news and Culture)*:

"The Sewer and the Dropbox"

"Overcome evil with good -- that was Chuck Colson's mantra. And nowhere is it more applicable than in the fight against abortion, as one loving Korean pastor is proving.

The images and video broadcast around the world triggered shock and disgust: a team of Chinese firefighters sawed open a narrow sewage pipe and removed a screaming newborn baby. The tiny boy, whose only name was "59," after the number of his hospital incubator, miraculously survived after being flushed or dropped—we're still not sure—into a public sewer, where he became lodged.

Realizing what she says was a mistake, the baby's mother notified authorities, who rushed to the scene and dismantled the pipe piece by piece until the exhausted and frightened baby appeared. The young single mother says she meant to abort the baby when she found out she was pregnant—but couldn't afford the procedure.

Well, the good news is that Baby 59 is doing well and has since been taken home by his mother's family. And more good news is that the incident has brought China's abominable One Child Policy back to the fore of the world's attention, and highlighted the fact that—whatever the details of baby 59's case—countless infants are abandoned by their mothers in China every year because of this terrible, terrible law.

That's to say nothing of forced abortions and infanticide under the policy, another gruesome example of which emerged just days ago when a six-month pregnant woman died of hemorrhaging following a forced abortion.

But China isn't the only Asian country where being born alive is no guarantee of safe conduct. In South Korea, hundreds of infants are abandoned on the streets every year. The problem is so severe that one Korean pastor decided to take unprecedented action.

His story is the subject of an award-winning documentary by 22-year-old American film student, Brian Ivie.

Stirred by a report in the LA Times about Pastor Lee Jong-rak and his unique solution to infant abandonment, Ivie raised enough money to lead a team to Seoul, South Korea to capture this tiny but inspirational ministry.

Pastor Lee Jong-rak calls it his "Drop Box." The concept is simple. Instead of aborting or abandoning their infants, mothers who either can't keep or don't want their babies bring them to the wooden box affixed to Pastor Lee's house. They say goodbye, and shut the door. The box, which is equipped with lights and a heater, reads in Korean, "Please don't throw away unwanted or disabled babies, or babies of single mothers. Please bring them here instead."

When the box opens, a bell rings, and Pastor Lee, his wife, or a volunteer comes and takes the child inside. Since Pastor Lee installed the Drop Box in 2009, as many as 18 babies a month have arrived, and the same number of children currently live in his home, which doubles as an orphanage. He and his wife have even adopted ten of their own—the maximum number local authorities will allow.

Sometimes he speaks to the mothers face-to-face. One told him she intended to poison herself and her newborn before hearing about the Drop Box. Another simply left a note, which read:

"My baby! Mom is so sorry. I am so sorry to make this decision...I hope you meet great parents...I don't deserve to say a word. Mom loves you more than anything else. I leave you here because I don't know who your father is. I used to think about something bad, but I guess this box is safer for you...Please forgive me."

Brian Ivie's award-winning film of this incredible story is set for public release this fall. Come to BreakPoint.org to learn more about it.

The fight for life is more than just political. In so many ways, it's decided in the cultural imagination—and heroes like this provide the inspiration we need to replace cultures that spawned Kermit Gosnell, sewer pipes, child abandonment and forced abortions with a culture that looks more like the home of Pastor Lee Jong-rak.

That, my friends, is overcoming evil with good.

Next Steps

As John pointed out, Lee Jong-rak is a great example of what one person can do to overcome evil with good. Pastor Lee's ministry transcends politics and reaches to our imagination."

("Reprinted with permission of Prison Fellowship, P.O. Box 1550, Merrifield, VA 22116, www.colsoncenter.org.")

"GOD, GIVE US MEN..."

"God give us men...ribbed with the steel of Your Holy Spirit...men who will not flinch when the battle's fiercest... men who won't acquiesce, or compromise, or fade when the enemy rages. God give us men who can't be bought, bartered, or badgered by the enemy, men who will pay the price, make the sacrifice, stand the ground, and hold the torch high. God give us men obsessed with the principles true to your word, men stripped of self-seeking and a yen for security...men who will pay any price for freedom and go any lengths for truth. God give us men delivered from mediocrity, men with vision high, pride low, faith wide, love deep, and patience long...men who will dare to march to the drumbeat of a distant drummer, men who will not surrender principles of truth in order to accommodate their peers. God give us men more interested in scars than medals. More committed to conviction than convenience, men who will give their life for the eternal, instead of indulging their lives for a moment in time. Give us men who are fearless in the face of danger, calm in the midst of pressure, bold in the midst of opposition. God give us men who will pray earnestly, work long, preach clearly, and wait patiently. Give us men whose walk is by faith, behaviour is by principle, whose dreams are in heaven, and whose book is the Bible. God give us men who are equal to the task. Those are the men the church needs today."

~ The Growth Factor, Bob Moorehead

The Commitment

Finally, I want to share this concise, clear, crisp quotation from the late Adrian Rogers:

"The church is not the servant of the state!
The church is not the master of the state!
The church is the conscience of the state!
We will be civil – but WE WILL NOT BE SILENT!!!"

The Bottom Line

Courage is not the absence of fear – it is conquering of fear! "For God has not given us the spirit of fear, but of love and of power and of a sound mind." 2 Timothy 1:7.

WE ARE MORE THAN CONQUERORS.

WE WILL BE CIVIL - BUT

WE WILL NOT BE SILENT!!

Supplement

I highly recommend these two articles by Tim Wildmon: "**White House, Media put American Lives at Risk by soft-pedaling Jihad**" (June 2013 afaJournal) and "**The Irony of Intolerance**" (September 2013 afaJournal). Contact information for afaJournal: P.O. Drawer 2440, Tupelo, MS 38803, www.afajournal.org. Also, the AFA has an excellent, pertinent article by Teddy James entitled "Faith and the Military - Can They Coexist?" in the AFA journal for January 2014.

Questions for Chapter 3: How Truly Tolerant is the Tolerant Troop?

1. What is the difference between the dictionary definition of "tolerance" and the current post-modern usage of the word?

2. Is the new meaning of this word accurate or twisted? Explain your answer.

3. Sometimes in friendships or in family relationships it is necessary to compromise our opinions and preferences for the sake of peace; however, what happens if we compromise on matters of truth and righteousness?

4. The Biblical teaching about salvation is **not** easy believism. What very important truth is often deleted and avoided in many (if not most) churches attempting to be seeker sensitive (or seeker driven)?

5. If homosexuals can't change, how do you explain former homosexuals who have changed?

6. Who are the dangerous fundamentalists?

7. What is the heart of the problem?

8. Are all religions fundamentally the same? Explain your answer.

9. Can you name two examples of intolerance among those who profess to promote tolerance?

10. How can we promote positive change?

CHAPTER 4:

PHONY MATRIMONY VS. MERRY MARRIAGE

(Con-artists are still Selling Genuine Imitations)

To begin this chapter, I want to share with you two brief articles from our February 2013 prayer letter for Overseas Outreach:

The Sanctity of Marriage and Life

Dear Friends & Prayer Partners,

The sanctity of marriage and the sanctity of life are intricately interwoven and founded in Scripture all the way back to Genesis, the Book of Beginnings. It was God Himself who said: *"Let Us make man in Our image, according to Our likeness; let them have dominion over the fish of the sea, over the birds of the air, and over the cattle, over all the earth and over every creeping thing that creeps on the earth.' So God created man in His own image; in the image of God He created him; male and female He created them. Then God blessed them, and God said to them, 'Be fruitful and multiply; fill the earth and subdue it; have dominion over the fish of the sea, over the birds of the air, and over every living thing that moves on the earth."' Genesis 1:26-28 (NKJV).*

Note that God Himself created them male and female. He is the Originator of marriage, and He told them to reproduce (sanctity of marriage and family). *Hebrews 13:4 reads, "Let marriage be held in honor among all, and let the marriage bed be undefiled, for God will judge the sexually immoral and adulterous." (ESV).*

By inspiration of the Holy Spirit the apostle Paul labeled "forbidding to marry" as a "doctrine of demons" (1 Timothy 4:1-3). Why? Because demons know that forced celibacy backfires into misuse and perversions of sexual desire. (It is now costing the Roman Catholic Church not only much shame and scoffing, but also millions of dollars). Demons promote perversions, inflame passions and invite promiscuity, whereas God promotes the commitment of one man and one woman to each other for life in monogamous marriage. The children born into such a loving committed union are far more likely to grow up to be happy, healthy, helpful and holy than those from broken homes. Joe Garman, founder of American Rehabilitation Ministries, told me that prisoners send out millions of Mother's Day cards, but rarely request Father's Day cards. You don't suppose that the absence of a loving father's guidance contributed to their criminal activity, do you? What a shocking thought for those with a "politically correct" mindset. Our government not only undermines marriage with its welfare rules, but our courts have even sanctioned the production of pornography and sadistically violent video games as "freedom of speech" under our Constitution. Our founding fathers would be horrified at such perversions – but demons rejoice. By the way, you don't suppose that the "doctrine of demons" has any influence in Hollywood, do you?

This month we celebrate Valentine's Day, which can also be easily distorted and perverted, but let's truly celebrate the joy and wonder of romantic love in committed marriages. Valentine was a courageous pastor and Christian leader in the third century, who honored the sanctity of matrimony as God's institution by continuing to perform wedding ceremonies for young couples even after Caesar's decree "forbidding to marry" was announced. Caesar wanted more men to enlist in his military and feared that marriage would be a deterrent to his conquests. Valentine paid for his commitment to marriage with his life and is honored as a Christian martyr. Are you committed to truth and courageous enough to speak up for Biblical marriage in a world gone mad?

To honor the sanctity of marriage I want to share with you copies of the letters Della and I wrote to each other and displayed at our 50th Wedding Anniversary celebration. We hope and pray that many of you also grow in your love and commitment to your spouse through the years and that your relationship with God grows "sweeter as the years go by".

Dear Rick,

❖ *I love the fact that you are sold out – heart and soul – to God.*

❖ *I love your diligence and love for the study of God's Word. Your Bible knowledge amazes and inspires me.*

❖ *I love your tenderness with me when I'm hurting or not feeling well.*

❖ *I love your sense of humor.*

❖ *I appreciate your love for our children and grandchildren.*

❖ *I love to see your eyes light up and your big smile when Trinity does something cute.*

❖ *I love to see you dance around the house when music fills the air.*

❖ *I love you for being quick to forgive me when I've been irritable and "hard to live with".*

❖ *I love you because I know I can trust you to be faithful to me – even when you are far away in Ukraine or somewhere else.*

❖ *I love you for being persistent in business, even when there is one frustrating thing after another to deal with.*

❖ *I love you for your honesty and integrity in business, in ministry, in personal relationships.*

❖ *When you've been misunderstood and your ministry has been undermined, you have simply committed it to God and continued to serve Him. I love you for that humble spirit, Rick.*

Some of our friends will also remember the song "Peggy Sue" that was popular when we were teenagers, but may never have thought of the fact that the name Della Lu fits just as well in the poetic rhythm of the song. Here is my altered version of a few words from the song:

I love you, Della Lu, with a love so rare and true – Oh Della – Oh Della Lu (ooo – ooo – ooo - ooo)!

Why do I love you, Della Lu? Here are seven reasons – isn't seven the perfect number?

1. *I love you because your beautiful smile (which says, "I love you") lights up my life like a glorious sun break on a winter day in western Oregon – and it sets my heart to fluttering all over again.*

2. *I love you because your integrity is deep and strong (as when you quit a very good paying job rather than to buckle under the pressure to lie for the company).*

3. *I love you for your deep loyalty to your commitments, your friends, and to me.*

4. *I love you for your devotion to Christ, to His church, to His mission, and to your family.*

5. *I love you for being a frugal, diligent, hard-working, productive wife – as described in Proverbs 31.*

6. *I love you for your careful attention to details – which makes you a superb bookkeeper and treasurer for our business, our mission, and our personal finances.*

7. *I love you for your service as my volunteer secretary who turns my hand-written scribbles into legible letters, emails, articles, reports, booklets and books. Back in our Bible College days at BBC, Kenny Beckman once wrote on my report: "A – thanks to*

a devoted wife". Some glorious Day I may hear from our Lord, 'Well done, good and faithful servant – thanks to a devoted wife!'

How to Handle Conflict

Because of our innate differences, any two people (or more) who live together will sometimes irritate each other, and because we all inherit a selfish nature, sometimes our wills will clash. There will be conflict. **The key to having good relationships is learning how to handle conflict.** Some conflicts will be mild; some may be explosive. Since not one of us is always right, there are four phrases that make a marriage work:

I was wrong

I am sorry

Please forgive me

I love you

These four phrases are based on the Biblical principles of love, acceptance, and forgiveness. In fact, these same principles and phrases build beautiful relationships – not only in marriage but also in family and friendships. However, don't try using these phrases as a gimmick. No one loves and appreciates a hypocritical con-artist. Honesty is the best policy!

"Distorted Diversity Produces Profane Perversity"

Should we be so open-minded that we cave in to the "politically correct" crowd who wants us to believe that so-called "gay marriage" is the wave of the future (and the present), and that we should accept their warped mantra that the loving thing to do is accept it? Those who oppose "gay marriage" (according to their agenda) are guilty of "hate speech." One of Ronald Reagan's witty sayings is especially appropriate here: "*Some people are so open-minded their brains fall out!*"

Has it ever occurred to you how much our corrupt culture has distorted diversity because of the convoluted concepts of 'political correctness'? Almighty God created true diversity when He Himself created human beings male and female and He Himself ordained the marriage of one man to one woman. Why?

1. **It takes the unique characteristics of both male and female to reflect the image of God!** Consider the record: 'Then God said, 'Let Us make man in Our image, according to Our likeness; let them have dominion over the fish of the sea, over the birds of the air, and over the cattle, over all the earth and over every creeping thing that creeps on the earth.' So God created man in His *own* image; in the image of God He created him; male and female He created them.' Genesis 1:26-27 (NKJV).

   Notice that God by His very nature is unity in diversity! He said, 'Let **Us** make man in **Our** image'! The concept of one God existing as unity in plurality from the very beginning is expressed here in the first chapter of Genesis. Colossians chapter one tells us that Jesus created all things, and Colossians 2:9 tells us, 'in Him dwells all the fullness of the Godhead bodily'. Genesis 1:1 says, 'In the beginning God created the heavens and the earth.' Genesis 1:2 says 'And the Spirit of God was hovering over the face of the waters.' The concept of one Almighty God with the plurality of his nature is to be reflected in **man** (human beings) existing as male and female. Although God is **always** referred to in Scripture as He, some of His characteristics are best reflected by the female side of humanity. For example, God's love is portrayed as even greater than that of a nursing mother for her own child. Therefore God chose to create humans as male and female to reflect His image. However, men learn how to be the courageous and bold protector of their children (tough) balanced with the playful moments holding them or tousling their hair (tenderly) by being imitators of God.

2. **He ordained marriage and told Adam and Eve to be fruitful and multiply. It was God Himself who created humans as sexual beings able to reproduce children.** God ordained marriage both for companionship and for the union of a man with his wife to produce godly offspring! God inspired Malachi to expose the treachery of profaning the marriage covenant. 'Have we not all one Father? Has not one God created us? Why do we deal treacherously with one another by profaning the covenant of the fathers? … Yet you say, 'For what reason?' Because the Lord has been witness between you and the wife of your youth, with whom you have dealt treacherously; yet she is your companion and your wife by covenant. But did He not make them one, having a remnant of the Spirit? And why one? **He seeks godly offspring. Therefore take heed to your spirit, and let none deal treacherously with the wife of his youth.'** Malachi 2:10, 14-15 (NKJV). "Husbands, likewise, dwell with *them* with understanding, giving honor to the wife, as to the weaker vessel, and as *being* heirs together of the grace of life, that your prayers may not be hindered." 1 Peter 3:7.

The so-called 'marriage' of a man with a man or a woman with a woman is perversity – not diversity. It distorts the purposes of marriage and profanes 'the Lord's holy institution which He loves' (Malachi 2:11). Basic Biblical theology and basic human anatomy expose the basic human depravity of those distorting diversity by promoting 'same sex marriage'. Homosexuality is still called an abomination in God's Holy Word. (See Leviticus 18:22 and 1 Corinthians 6:9-11.) **Politically correct concepts convolute and corrupt God's holy institution of marriage and every other subject** they touch.** Remember, 'Beware lest anyone cheat you through philosophy and empty deceit, according to the tradition of men, according to the basic principles of the world, and not according to Christ. For in Him dwells all the fullness of the Godhead bodily;'** Colossians 2:8-9 (NKJV)"

Now I want to share an excellent article by Bob Russell, which Victor Knowles printed for Viewpoint June/July 2012 of the *Knowlesletter*:

"President Obama vs. Biblical Truth on the Issue of Gay Marriage"

"President Barack Obama came out in favor of same sex marriage last week, the first President of the United States to do so. As expected, liberals in the media are praising the President's stand as 'courageous' and 'aligning himself with the entire world in standing for civil rights.'

An increasing number of liberal church leaders are also endorsing the gay life style; even ordaining homosexual ministers and performing gay marriages. Liberal churches rationalize their stance by pointing out that while the Old Testament condemns same-sex relationships, Jesus said nothing about it, so it must be okay.

Granted, there is no recorded statement from Jesus on the subject of homosexuality. However, we have no direct quote from Jesus about slavery or rape either. So, obviously, the absence of a statement from Jesus doesn't qualify as an endorsement.

Furthermore, it isn't just the recorded words of Jesus that followers of Christ consider to be God's Word. The entire New Testament is regarded as God-breathed (2 Timothy 3:16) and the standard of absolute truth. Right and wrong are not determined for us by personal emotion, majority opinion, current trends, or influential experts, but the Bible. Jesus prayed, 'Sanctify them in the truth, your word is truth.'

The New Testament book of Romans states: 'Because of this, God gave them over to shameful lusts. Even their women exchanged natural relations for unnatural ones. In the same way the men also abandoned natural relations with women and were inflamed with lust for one another. Men committed indecent acts with other men, and received in themselves the due penalty for their perversion.' (Romans 1:26-27)

Clearly, both the Old and New Testaments forbid same sex relationships. Although each individual has innate strengths and weaknesses and we are vulnerable to different temptations, none of us is given a license to yield to our base, carnal desires. We're told, 'deny self' and, 'abstain from the evil desires that war against your soul.' To endorse gay marriage is to disregard the plain teaching of Scripture.

The question is not whether the Bible condones same sex marriage – it clearly does not. The question is whether Christian leaders will be courageous enough to take a Biblical stand and accept the inevitable persecution that will follow or will we just say what itching ears want to hear? Will we stand for God's truth or embrace the spirit of the age?

Folks, this is not a political issue. It's a spiritual issue that goes to the very core of our belief system. God ordained marriage in the Garden of Eden as sacred. If believers don't have the courage to stand up for marriage, then we are not worthy to be called followers of Christ.

Kudos to the Roman Catholic Church. The pope and many local bishops are speaking out fearlessly on this issue. It's time for evangelical leaders to stand up and be counted as well. I've observed that many Bible-believing preachers are weary of the battle and are growing strangely silent on the subject. They're apprehensive of being accused of being homophobic and lacking compassion. Many are dodging the issue in hopes their church will not be branded with a negative image in the community.

Martin Luther once said, '**If I be valiant all along the battle line except at the point where Satan presses his attack, I am not valiant for Christ.**' Satan is directly attacking the sanctity of life, the sacredness of marriage and religious liberties. This is no time for us to grow weary in doing good. **Now more than ever we need Christian leaders to be strong and courageous.** Admittedly, you're going to be labeled homophobic and intolerant. The bullies in the gay and lesbian community will hurl insults at your church, accuse you of hate speech and being out of step with where the culture is heading.

I beg you to remember that Jesus said, 'If you're ashamed of me AND MY WORDS then I will be ashamed of you when you stand before my Father who is in heaven.' And 'Blessed are you when people insult you, persecute you and falsely say all kinds of evil against you because of me. Rejoice and be glad, because great is your reward in heaven.' (Matthew 5:11-12)" (Bob Russell, "The Knowlesletter", June/July 2012, "Viewpoint")

As backup information to the articles shared so far in this chapter, I now quote from the February 27, 2011 issue of *The Times and the Scriptures Weekly Bulletin*:

"Obama Declares Marriage Defense Unconstitutional"

He's Decided Homosexuality is "Immutable"

"In a stunning move that must have the Supreme Court wondering whether it still has any role in government, President Obama Wednesday declared the Defense of Marriage Act (DOMA) unconstitutional and instructed the Justice Department to stop defending it in court. Attorney General Eric Holder, only too happy to comply, has already notified courts that the federal government is pulling out of all related cases, even those already in progress.

Holder announced, 'The president and I have concluded that Section 3 of DOMA is not constitutional,' and that 'sexual orientation is an immutable characteristic.' That notion, of course, is disputed by professionals who can find no genetic cause for the behavior, and certainly by former homosexuals, but it was foundational to this executive declaration of unconstitutionality.

The executive proclamation was a step toward fulfilling

predictions that the repeal of 'Don't Ask Don't Tell' by the lame duck Congress would hasten the onset of nation-wide 'gay marriage.' (Review 1-2-11 *Bulletin*) Holder's statement cited that repeal as evidence that 'the legal landscape has changed' since 1996 when DOMA was passed and signed by President Clinton.

Some experts see a silver lining in the presidential power grab. Congress can intervene in defending duly-passed laws, and the House might step in to defend DOMA despite the Obama-Holder surrender. Heritage Foundation's Chuck Donovan says the law may now get better defense than the 'half-hearted farce of a representation [by] the Obama Justice Department.' Christian legal organizations might now be welcome to help defend DOMA. Matt Staver of Liberty Counsel says, 'This law has been attacked before and upheld as constitutional.'" ("The Times and the Scriptures", Weekly Bulletin for February 27, 2011. Used by permission.)

Answers Magazine for October-December 2012 carried this brief article:

"Homosexual Marriage – Golden Rule for Marriage?"

"ACCORDING TO PRESIDENT OBAMA, his view of marriage has "evolved" since his election. He now supports homosexual marriage. While this may not surprise those who have followed his metamorphosis his reasoning may:

[Michelle and I are] both practicing Christians. . . .But, you know, when we think about our faith, the thing at root that we think about is not only Christ sacrificing himself on our behalf, but it's also the Golden Rule, you know? Treat others the way you would want to be treated.

In 2008, President Obama said, 'God's in the mix' for defining marriage, which at that time he asserted was strictly between a man and a woman. But he now says the Golden Rule (the concept Christ taught in Matthew 7:12) compels him to endorse so-called gay marriage.

However, that sort of thinking twists Scripture. When Jesus

gave the Golden Rule, He said it sums up the old Testament's teachings. That would include both the creation of marriage between
a man and a woman in Genesis 2:18-25 (which Jesus affirmed in
Mark 10) and God's decree against homosexual behavior in Leviticus 18:22.

When given a chance to weigh in on the issue, American
voters continue to affirm a position consistent with God's Word. In
all 32 states where same-sex marriage has been put to the voters,
they have rejected it. Most recently, North Carolina voted 60%-
40% to affirm biblical marriage in the state constitution. Every state
that has allowed same-sex marriage has ignored voters and gone
through the courts or legislatures.

While treating others as we want to be treated is at the
foundation of Christianity, it does not allow us to rewrite Scripture. Jesus guaranteed that Scripture would never change (Matthew
24:35) – even if politicians' views do." ("Answers Magazine", October-December 2012, Used by permission.)

An Open Letter to My "Progressive" Friends

(Do I become your Enemy because I tell you the Truth?)

Rick Deighton

Does the fact that I believe the Word of God is true make me
outdated and bigoted? I sincerely believe that God's command to
me to "be content with such things as you have", applies not only
to my finances but also to my own body and its separate parts. I
remember that the Word of God distinctly tells us that it was God
Himself Who created human beings as male and female – equal,
but separate and distinct. Their equality is demonstrated in the fact
that He gave **them** dominion over the earth, the sea and the creatures in earth's domain. See Genesis 1:26-28.

Am I outdated because I believe that a man should walk, talk
and act like a man? That he should be the strong leader of his fam-

ily and be their primary provider and bold protector? Also that a woman should look, walk, talk and act like a woman? As a matter of fact, God has some very clear instructions about these matters in His Word!

The Ultimate Confusion

During the late 1960's, another Christian leader and I were meeting together with a student from Northwest Christian College to pray for the unity of the body of Christ. One day he shared with us a deep burden on his heart – cross dressing. Sometimes when all alone he would dress in women's clothing. He was ashamed of himself for doing this and only came to bare his soul before us because he felt we would continue to accept him and pray with him for victory over this temptation to pretend to be a woman in spite of the fact that God created him to be a man. We did.

I recognize that there is such a condition as gender confusion – and it has gotten much worse than it was when I was a kid because of the massive homosexual advertising campaign passionately promoted by Hollywood. In fact, it appears that homosexuals and Hollywood are now bonded with superglue! All kids are confused about some things, but with godly training, experience and maturity, most of them outgrow even sexual identity confusion. Little girls who wanted to act like tomboys and little boys who liked dolls usually grew up just fine before the campaign to solidify their confusion, warp their maturing process, and push them like pawns for promoting homosexual agendas. The Bible says, "foolishness is bound up in the heart of a child", but warped wisdom and twisted tenderness teaches us **not** to try to change their confusion with the cold hard facts. A male is a male down to every last cell in his body! A female is a female down to every last cell in her body. (This is a scientifically verifiable fact. Check it out if you doubt – and be sure to check reliable sources.) **No amount of twisted tenderness or sharp scalpels performing "sex change surgeries" will ever change the fact of who God created you to be.**

Sexual Molestation Causes Confusion and Leaves Deep Scars!

There is very strong evidence that many, if not most, gender confused individuals were sexually molested as children. If you are one of those individuals, my heart aches for you. You very likely have deep fear and anger issues to work through. However, remember that you are responsible for your actions and attitudes **now** – as an adult. **You are not guilty for the actions of the pedophile who molested you, but if you who were molested follow in the same wicked path and become a molester, you are guilty!** God can and will break your bondage and set you free. He will forgive you and transform your life by the blood of Jesus and the power of the Holy Spirit if you surrender your will to Him and accept His forgiveness, His grace, His power. Then He can use you as His tool to help rescue others from their bondage. *"'Come now, and let us reason together,' Says the Lord, 'Though your sins are like scarlet, they shall be as white as snow; though they are red like crimson, they shall be as wool.'"* Isaiah 1:18. *"And you will seek Me and find Me, when you search for Me with all your heart."* Jeremiah 29:13. Can you pray as Isaiah did? *"Yes, in the way of Your judgments, O Lord, we have waited for You; the desire of our soul is for Your name and for the remembrance of You. With my soul I have desired You in the night, yes, by my spirit within me I will seek You early; for when Your judgments are in the earth, the inhabitants of the world will learn righteousness."* Isaiah 26:8-9

Self-Centered Pride is the Core of Rebellion Against God

I remember in my teens going through a "rebel without a cause" stage. The basic problem was that I simply didn't want **anyone** – not even **God** – telling me what to do (or not to do)! I needed to repent, for the Word of God teaches that rebellion is as the sin of witchcraft (1 Samuel 15:23). Are you a grown man or woman (or a teen) still nursing and coddling an adolescent attitude of rebellion? Pride and self-centeredness are at the core of all sinful rebellion. "I want what I want when I want it and how I want it," is the manifestation of that sinful attitude. I implore you to wake up to reality! Your family and friends, the whole world, and God Himself, do not revolve around you!!! Jesus loves **you** more than you can possibly realize! Yes, with all your hang-ups, confusion and rebellion, He still loves you. **Sometimes His love is tough love. He is not an enabler. He loves you too much to leave you as you are.** You may fight and struggle and reject Him with His austere commands, but I hope you at least come to recognize and realize that **all** of His commands are for our own good – whether we like them or not. If you were taking care of a two-year-old child who wants to play with a sharp knife – would you let him have it? If he gets upset, screams, and throws a tantrum, would you give it to him? I hope not! Why not? Because you care for him. You know better than he does what is good for him and what will harm him.

Almighty God wants to Give you Victory!

God Almighty wants you to have victory over your pet sins and hang ups – not defeat! Don't you think it's time to repent and submit to His wisdom and His authority? Don't you realize that He knows better than you how you should be living your life? He created you for a purpose. He gave you your talents, abilities, and a unique blend of personality traits. Don't you think He knows best how to use those gifts to His glory and your eternal good? Isn't it time for you to take a hard look at the big picture? Won't you consider eternal values and consequences instead of your short-sighted pleasure and desires? Please consider these potent passages:

"*Do not be deceived, God is not mocked; for whatever a man sows, that he will also reap. For he who sows to his flesh will of the flesh reap corruption, but he who sows to the Spirit will of the Spirit reap everlasting life.*" Galatians 6:7-8

"*Beloved, I beg you as sojourners and pilgrims, abstain from fleshly lusts which war against the soul, having your conduct honorable among the Gentiles, that when they speak against you as evildoers, they may, by your good works which they observe, glorify God in the day of visitation."* 1 Peter 2:11-12

*"Likewise you younger people, submit yourselves to your elders. Yes, all of you be submissive to one another, and **be clothed with humility**, for '**God resists the proud, but gives grace to the humble**.' Therefore humble yourselves under the mighty hand of God, that He may exalt you in due time, casting all your care upon Him, for He cares for you. Be sober, be vigilant; because your adversary the devil walks about like a roaring lion, seeking whom he may devour. Resist him, steadfast in the faith, knowing that the same sufferings are experienced by your brotherhood in the world."* 1 Peter 5:5-9

"You Shall Not Covet"

Has it ever occurred to you that the command of God, "You shall not covet," applies directly to the issues of cross-dressing and attempts to switch gender??? Why? Because if you are dissatisfied with the gender God created you, then you end up coveting the type of body God did not give you.

Do you realize that coveting is idolatry? This is serious – very serious! *"Therefore put to death your members which are on the earth: fornication, uncleanness, passion, evil desire, and covetousness, which is idolatry."* Colossians 3:5. *"The wicked in his pride persecutes the poor;*
*Let them be caught in the plots which they have devised. **For the wicked boasts of his heart's desire**; he blesses the greedy and renounces the Lord."* Psalm 10:2-3. Coveting is desiring – longing for – something that belongs to someone else.

GRIPING – OR GRATITUDE?

Do you realize that dissatisfaction with the sexuality God has given you is sinful discontent? If you are grumbling and complaining because you want to be a woman, but God made you a man, or that you want to be a man, yet God made you a woman, then you are guilty of ingratitude. This also is serious – very serious. God condemned the whole nation of Israel (with the only exceptions being Joshua and Caleb) to die in the wilderness because of their ingratitude, complaining, and lack of faith in Him. Paul, by inspiration, wrote: *"... because, although they knew God, they did not glorify Him as God, nor were thankful, but became futile in their thoughts, and their foolish hearts were darkened. ... Therefore God also gave them up to uncleanness, in the lusts of their hearts, to dishonor their bodies among themselves, who exchanged the truth of God for the lie, and worshiped and served the creature rather than the Creator, who is blessed forever. Amen."* Romans 1:21, 24-25

Beware of the Father of Lies!

If you are struggling with the temptations I've described, be careful! Be on your guard! Satan is the father of lies. He is subtle and persistent. If you have been yielding to the temptations, you need to deeply and truly repent. If you choose instead to harden your heart and stiffen your neck in rebellion – beware!!!

The bottom line issue is sin. **Rebellion is like the sin of witchcraft! If you are not satisfied with the gender God gave you, you need to repent!** God tells you to "be content with such things as you have" – that includes body parts. Stop envying the members of the opposite sex and stop lusting after their body parts that you don't have because God didn't give them to you. Wake up and grow up! You can throw a tantrum and parade in the street spewing venom if you so choose – but it will not change the facts. **Recog-**

nize that confusion about your gender – whether you are male or female – is the ultimate confusion, and *"God is NOT the author of confusion"*! 1 Corinthians 14:33

Who Is the Author of Confusion?

Who then is the author of confusion? Satan! Who do you choose to follow – subtle Satan or conquering Christ? Christ is the conqueror of confusion. Trust Him! Follow Him!

I'm thankful to be a man. That is who God created me to be. I don't wear earrings, frilly nightgowns, pink panties or a bra. By the way, Della is my wife and she does wear those things – for which I'm also thankful. There is enough confusion in the world without us adding to it. If what I've expressed makes me appear outdated – fine! I would much rather be outdated than rebellious. And if the fact that I don't want my tax dollars funding so-called "sex change surgeries" and I don't want some man who calls himself by a female name barging into a ladies' restroom, locker room or shower room shocking my wife, daughter, granddaughters or other flustered females makes me a bigot – so be it. Call me a bigot if you please. I can handle it. If you think I'm an outdated, uncouth, blunt bigot – that's okay. We still live in a country with the freedom of speech (in spite of those who want to steal it or squelch it). You can exercise your freedom of speech as I have mine. But please, please, while you are exercising your freedom of speech –speak to your Creator. **Ask Him, "Lord, what would You have me to do?" And please also read His Word – His wisdom. He will speak to you if you approach Him with an open heart. By His amazing grace He rescued me from my pit, and by His amazing grace He can rescue you from yours.**

Is Self Identification Valid?

Often the excuse given by proponents of homosexual behavior – including cross-dressing and homosexual "marriage" – is self-identification. If a man feels more like a female than a male – does that make him a female? Should that give him the right and privilege to enter and use women's' restrooms and shower rooms? What makes you think he is not a male predator looking for his next victim while pretending to feel more like a female than a male? **Why are city municipalities bowing to such outrageous imbecility? Politically correct? NO! Politically, socially and morally insane!**

Also, if you get the impression that such cowardice on the part of government officials makes me angry – you are absolutely right! Sometimes anger toward evil, injustice, cowardice and outright moral stupidity is the most appropriate emotion for an individual who cares about truth, justice and righteousness. **Jesus got angry!** He drove out the wicked money changers from the temple. **The Word of God says, "Be angry – and sin not!"**

Anger in itself is not sin – but we must be careful how we handle it. I am expressing my anger in words and praying for positive change in society. I am not sending death threats or attacking anyone's person. Why? *"For the weapons of our warfare are not carnal but mighty in God for pulling down strongholds, casting down arguments and every high thing that exalts itself against the knowledge of God, bringing every thought into captivity to the obedience of Christ,"* 2 Corinthians 10:4-5.

By the way, if a Caucasian man decides that he feels more like a black man, do you think our "politically correct" politicians will sign him up for affirmative action?

Also, the quote, "be content with such things as you have" is actually mentioned in the context of sexual purity versus impurity. Please notice for yourself. "Marriage is honorable among all, and the bed undefiled; but fornicators and adulterers God will judge. Let your conduct be without covetousness; *be content with such things as you have.* For He Himself has said, "I will never leave you nor forsake you." Hebrews 13:4-5.

Personal Convictions

I realize that part of what I am expressing is my own personal conviction and choice, which I do not bind on you as a doctrinal issue. I know of brothers in Christ who choose to wear long hair, earrings and tattoos, but are reaching souls for Christ. Some of them see their choice of style as a means of becoming "all things to all men that by all means I might win some". I praise God for their success in reaching souls for Christ, but still choose not to conform to the prevailing styles of our corrupt culture that complicates and confuses the distinctions between males and females. (By the way, tattoos were specifically mentioned and forbidden under the old covenant law, Leviticus 19:28, along with many other specific taboos under the law.) This is not an issue of law versus grace, but an issue of discernment and wisdom about how to relate to others in our corrupt culture, and how to wisely apply Biblical principles in our outreach. The flip side of conformity to culture in order to relate was also penned by Paul: *"I beseech you therefore, brethren, by the mercies of God, that you present your bodies a living sacrifice, holy, acceptable to God, which is your reasonable service. **And do not be conformed to this world, but be transformed by the renewing of your mind**, that you may prove what is that good and acceptable and perfect will of God."* Romans 12:1-2 (NKJV). The NLT of verse 2 reads: *"Don't copy the behavior and customs of this world, but let God transform you into a new person by changing the way you think. Then you will learn to know God's will for you, which is good and pleasing and perfect."*

I once asked a brother in Christ, "If you aren't trying to look like a woman, a pirate, or a rock singer, why wear an earring?" His reply was not too impressive, and I still believe it is a valid question. You have the right to wear long hair, earrings and pink panties if you want to, but if you choose to do so, I hope that you are a woman!

Who is Your Example?

A shining example of my major point is the Christian philosopher and evangelist, Ravi Zacharias, who speaks to multiplied thousands of college students each year on major campuses around the world. Ravi does not wear long hair, earrings, tattoos, or baggy pants to attempt to be relevant – yet there are overflowing crowds nearly every place he speaks. Why? He is a master communicator, who speaks truth in love and shows the relevance of the Word of God and the person of Jesus Christ to hurting hearts hungering for light, love, life, forgiveness, peace, truth, and joy. He dresses in a suit and does not conform to the world's wild styles, yet his message of the Master is winsome to multitudes. Let's go and do likewise!

I do also recognize the hard truth so candidly expressed by Chuck Swindoll: "God reserves the right to use people who disagree with me!" I do want to clarify that in sharing this quote from Chuck Swindoll I'm primarily referring to the disputable matters that Paul wrote about in Romans 14. These would be matters of opinion and conviction rather than matters of God's clear, distinct revelation of truth. However, it is also true that our creative Father even uses Satan and evil men to carry out His ultimate purposes – as He did at Calvary. Had they known and understood His plan they "would not have crucified the Lord of Glory." An ancient summary of Biblical convictions reads:

In essentials – unity
In opinions – liberty
In all things – charity

This is wise counsel – but often we still struggle with which things are essentials and which are opinions. That's when "in all things – charity" comes most into play.

Oh yes – I almost forgot to tell you that I **do** believe in gay marriage – if you look up the true meaning of the word "gay", before it became an intentionally warped word by those promoting the homosexual agenda. Now I prefer to call it merry marriage – one man and one woman committed to each other for life to love and serve God by loving and serving each other, their family, their church, their community, and their world. Am I still an outdated bigot?

"The greatest gift one generation can give to the next is a moral society." ~ Dietrich Bonhoeffer

"Gay Pride Parade"???

On Saturday, June 15, 2013, when I was walking, praying and distributing Christian literature along the Wilson Creek greenbelt trail near our home, a fellow believer asked me why I wasn't distributing the literature at the "Gay Pride Parade" over in Boise. The man told me that he is now divorced because his wife had rejected him to become a lesbian and that she was probably marching in that parade. Is that something to be proud of? What is it that she – and the other participants - are celebrating? He also told me about a Christian military man who was invited to speak briefly to a group of homosexuals as the representative of the "right wing" conservative Christians. He accepted their invitation. So what did he tell them? He said approximately the following: **"I'm not straight and you're not gay. We are all sinners in need of the grace of God!"** It's true! It cuts through the layers of lies, excuses, and blatant rebellion to get to the heart of the issue.

One of those deceptive lies that is perpetrated by so-called theologians who choose to practice homosexuality is that the sin of Sodom was the lack of compassion and hospitality to strangers. If you don't believe this is a blatant distortion of the Word of God, I challenge you to take a concordance and read every passage in Scripture about Sodom and sodomy. Here is one example: *"as Sodom and Gomorrah, and the cities around them in a similar manner to these, having given themselves over to sexual immorality and gone after strange flesh, are set forth as an example, suffering the vengeance of eternal fire."* Jude 7. In warning us about "ungodly men who turn the grace of God into licentiousness and deny the only Lord God and our Lord Jesus Christ", Jude further says, *"But these speak evil of whatever they do not know; and whatever they know naturally, like brute beasts, in these things they corrupt themselves. Woe to them! For they have gone in the way of Cain, have run greedily in the error of Balaam for profit, and perished in the rebellion of Korah."* Jude 10-11. What is the "way of Cain"? Cain was the one who could have sung, "I Did it My Way," when he offered to God a bloodless offering – the work of his own hands. When God confronted him with his wrongdoing and the sin lurking at his door, instead of conquering the temptation, Cain killed his brother. (Genesis 4:6-8). Beware of religious people who determine to do it their own way. Don't follow them because "I Did It My Way" could be the theme song of those on their way to hell. They may also decide to attack you if you dare to confront them. Confront them anyway. God did! Jesus did! The apostles did!

Later, on the radio, I heard a story about a "straight" Boy Scout leader who marched with the homosexuals in the Salt Lake City "Gay Pride Parade" in solidarity with their cause. **What a travesty! What a ludicrous distortion of truth and righteousness!** Why does "a married man with children and a golden retriever" want solidarity with a parade of people who glory in their shame? Did the leaders of the homosexual agenda intentionally call people to demonstrate their rebellion against God? They oppose and mock God's standards by marching under the banner of attitudes and actions that God hates. See Genesis 19 (the story of Lot and the judgment of the city of Sodom plus Gomorrah).

1. The attitudes God hates are pride and rebellion, yet rebels who glory in their shame want to parade their pride.

2. The actions God hates are all forms of sexual immorality – that is, every form of sexual activity outside the marriage bond of one man with one woman. Adultery, fornication, bi-sexuality, homosexuality, pornography, beastiality, etc.

3. The other actions God hates are the practices of lying, twisting Scriptures, and distorting scientific research in vain attempts to justify polluted practices. The homosexual agenda is fueled and promoted by lies. Consider these pertinent passages of Scripture: *"These six things the LORD HATES, Yes, seven are an **abomination** to Him: A proud look, A lying tongue, Hands that shed innocent blood, A heart that devises wicked plans, Feet that are swift in running to evil, A false witness who speaks lies, And one who sows discord among brethren."* Proverbs 6:16-19.

> *"Now the purpose of the commandment is love from a pure heart, from a good conscience, and from sincere faith, from which some, having strayed, have turned aside to idle talk, desiring to be teachers of the law, understanding neither what they say nor the things which they affirm. But we know that the law is good if one uses it lawfully, knowing this: that the law is not made for a righteous person, but for the lawless and insubordinate, for the ungodly and for sinners, for the unholy and profane, for murderers of fathers and murderers of mothers, for manslayers, for fornicators, for sodomites, for kidnappers, for liars, for perjurers, and if there is any other thing that is contrary to sound doctrine, according to the glorious gospel of the blessed God which was committed to my trust." 1 Timothy 1:5-11.*

Homosexual behavior is classified as an abomination in the Word of God. Leviticus 18:22: *"You shall not lie with a male as with a woman. It is an abomination."* As you may have noticed in the Proverbs 6 passage, **both a proud look and a lying tongue are also classified as "an abomination to Him,"** therefore God not only hates the attitude of pride that parades the shame of homosexual behavior, He hates practice of such degradation and the lies used to justify and promote it. **We are to have compassion on those trapped by any form of corruption or addiction, but how dare any Christian defy God by seeking to justify such ungodly practices?**

"They're equating their sin with my skin." (Dwight McKissic of Arlington, Texas, who is black, on efforts to compare same-sex marriage to the civil-rights movement. The Blaze, June 21, 2012)

Born that Way?

Please do not hit me with the old worn-out lie that homosexuals are "born that way and it is impossible to change their orientation". The fact is that every last one of us is born with a corrupted sinful nature which is attracted to sin like iron to a magnet. We are all by nature "children of wrath" – "without God and without hope in this world" because we are all children of our original parents, Adam and Eve. We live on a cursed earth because of their rebellion – their sin – in violating God's one restriction on their freedom. Eve chose to believe Satan's lie over God's truth, and Adam chose to sin with Eve, rather than to alone stand with God for truth and righteousness. Now, rather than wasting your time blaming them for your condition, it will be far better and more profitable (progressive, if you please) to believe the Word of God that you are yourself a sinful rebel. *"For there is no difference, for all have sinned and come short of the glory of God."* Romans 6:22-23. "There is none righteous, no not one". In fact, the prophet Jeremiah by inspiration wrote, *"The heart is deceitful above all things, and desperately wicked. Who can know it? I, the Lord, search the heart, I test the mind, even to give every man according to His ways, and according to the fruit of his doings."* Jeremiah 17:9-10. What are you going to say when you stand before the judgment bar of Almighty God and see every thought, motive and action of your entire life? *"For the word of God is living and powerful, and sharper than any two-edged sword, piercing even to the division of soul and spirit, and of joints and marrow, and is a discerner of the thoughts and intents of the heart. And there is no creature hidden from His sight, but all things are naked and open to the eyes of Him to whom we must give account."* Hebrews 4:12-13 (NKJV). I don't want justice – I want grace! What about you? I have accepted the grace of God – for my penalty was paid for by the blood of my Lord Jesus Christ. What about you?

HOW DO YOU HANDLE CRITICISM?

(Humbly Listening or Proudly Rejecting?)

Ravi Zacharias tells of a furious man he knew who came storming out of a counseling session and asked him: "Do you know what he said to me? He said that I don't handle criticism well!!!" Need I comment?

In the same broadcast, Ravi quipped, "The depravity of man is the most easily verifiable truth – but he most strongly resisted." He illustrated this with an example of a reaction he got from a woman in an academic setting. During the question session following his presentation, an irate lady with a shrill voice was strongly opposing Ravi's point about human beings having a flawed nature – as the Word of God teaches. Jeremiah 17:9 says, *"'The heart is deceitful above all things, and desperately wicked; who can know it?"* As she became more intense with her argument, her anger became more evident, her face more red and her voice more shrill, Ravi resisted the temptation to say what he felt like saying – "Sit down and be quiet – you just proved my point!"

Ravi had already presented truth, so he responded with compassion instead of logic. He could have embarrassed her before the whole crowd. I'm not sure I would have resisted that temptation, but in this case I realize that his compassion was better than logic. I want to be more like this in speaking the truth in love. There is a time to confront – a time to speak – but also a time to be silent. In this case his silence was an act of love while letting the truth already spoken sink in. After all, our purpose is to win people, not arguments.

Friend, how do you handle criticism – by humbly listening or proudly rejecting? Will you be wise enough to honestly, humbly consider these passages from God's wisdom literature?

"He who corrects a scoffer gets shame for himself, and he who rebukes a wicked man only harms himself. Do not correct a scoffer, lest he hate you; rebuke a wise man, and he will love you. Give instruction to a wise man, and he will be still wiser; teach a just man, and he will increase in learning. 'The fear of the Lord is the beginning of wisdom, and the knowledge of the Holy One is understanding'. . . Open rebuke is better than love carefully concealed. Faithful are the wounds of a friend, but the kisses of an enemy are deceitful." Proverbs 9:7-10, 27:5-6

"It is better to hear the rebuke of the wise than for a man to hear the song of fools." Ecclesiastes 7:5

Bottom line note: Some years ago when Alexander Solzhenitsyn spoke to a gathering of Harvard students, warning them of the consequences of adopting Marxism, they mocked him. Were those brilliant students demonstrating wisdom or foolishness? Remember that intelligence and wisdom are **not** the same. You can have a head full of information and a heart full of rebellion and foolishness. I remember my Dad speaking of the "educated fools" – those with a bushel of information without a thimble full of practical good sense(no wisdom of how to use it).

Good by Nature?

Just think about it! Do you really believe that we human beings are born good by nature? If so, why do parents have to diligently teach their children to share instead of being selfish; to tell the truth rather than telling lies to protect self? Indeed, "They go forth from the womb speaking lies." Psalm 58:3. The fact is that we are all by nature stubborn, selfish, sinful rebels. That's why we need to be born anew from above – to receive a new nature given to us by our gracious God, Who then uses our experiences to mold us into the image of His Son, our Lord Jesus Christ.

It is true that God created human beings good by nature – but they did not stay that way. On the sixth day, after He had created human beings "male and female", He declared his creation "very good." This is proof positive that sex and sexuality are not inheritantly evil. Sexuality is by God's creation a beautiful gift from our Creator to be handled with care and celebrated in marriage and family.

The reason human beings are no longer good by nature is that rebellion against God by our original parents changed everything, and brought a curse on earth. Their nature was corrupted by sin, and that corrupted nature has been the inheritance of every human being. Sin has consequences – terrible consequences that affect other people. It was true for Adam and Eve – it is true for us!

WARNING!!

There is a Baptist preacher who travels to homosexual events with a few followers **in order to shout denunciations and carry signs like, "God Hates Fags". This man is a renegade and a false teacher. He does not "speak the truth in love" as the Word of God teaches (commands), so he is not a representative of Biblical Christianity and does not represent Baptists. He and his followers are a shame and reproach to the cause of Christ – as are any others who choose to use his tactics. We are to "expose**

the unfruitful works of darkness" – but not with the hateful, ungodly tactics he uses. Likewise, those who claim
to be pro-life, yet take the law into their own hands by
killing abortion doctors (or attempting to do so) are not
representing Biblical Christianity. They also are distorting truth and righteousness. What if the early Christians
had murdered Saul of Tarsus in retaliation for his ungodly persecution?

They would have killed the man God planned to
transform into the apostle Paul!

Is it Possible to Change?

Is it possible for human beings to change - to deny self and sinful temptations instead of soaking in sinful self-indulgence (whether lust, greed, envy or perverted attractions toward homosexuality,
beastiality, child pornography, etc.)? Yes! Definitely! *"For the grace
of God that brings salvation has appeared to all men, teaching us
that, denying ungodliness and worldly lusts, we should live soberly,
righteously, and godly in the present age, looking for the blessed hope
and glorious appearing of our great God and Savior Jesus Christ."*
Titus 2:11-13 (NKJV). I am personally a converted liar, luster and
lover of pleasure rather than a lover of God. I personally know
many converted addicts – who were hooked on drugs, alcohol, and
pornography – **but now love God more than their sinful inclinations.** I know personally two converted homosexuals – and have
heard testimonies of many others who no longer yield to their
sinful inclinations. One of them lives here locally and is married
with a family. Don't try to convince me that homosexuality is a
genetic condition – like skin color – that cannot be changed. I have
also personally heard black people who repudiate and despise the
agenda of homosexuals who claim their "civil rights" on the basis of
the civil rights of black people. I know ex-homosexuals, but I don't
know any ex-black people! Do you? Be honest! Admit that the

claim that homosexuals "were born that way and cannot change" is planned propaganda. Thank you!

I know of a church in Colorado that cares enough for confused people to train them how to act properly. There was a man in their congregation who was **not** a homosexual, but who gave the impression of such because many of his actions and mannerisms reflected feminine traits. Why? He lacked masculine mentors in his family, so from a small child he had learned to mimic the mannerisms of his mother and sisters. That is probably a major factor with many boys growing up in single mother families where they do not have a father image to be a model for them of how to act like a man. The men in the congregation cared enough for this man to speak the truth in love to him about his feminine looking mannerisms and mentored him in how to think, walk, talk and act like a man. **Friends – this is love in action!** They did not mock him. They did not whisper about him or gossip about him. They mentored him. Let's go and do likewise!

Friends, God loves you just as you are – but He loves you too much to allow you to stay that way. That is how Christians are to love one another. It is also how we are to love our opponents – our enemies who hate who we are and what we stand for. Please consider, *"For God so loved the world that He gave His only begotten Son, that whoever believes in Him should not perish but have everlasting life."* John 3:16 – then, *"By this we know love, because He laid down His life for us. And we also ought to lay down our lives for the brethren."* 1 John 3:16.

Now look at something else John wrote in his epistle of love in action – *"Now by this we know that we know Him, if we keep His commandments. He who says, "I know Him," and does not keep His commandments, is a liar, and the truth is not in him. But whoever keeps His word, truly the love of God is perfected in him. By this we know that we are in Him. He who says he abides in Him ought himself also to walk just as He walked. Brethren, I write no new commandment to you, but an old commandment which you have had from the beginning. The old commandment is the word which you heard from the beginning. Again, a new commandment I write to you, which thing is true in Him and in you, because the darkness is passing away, and the true light is already shining. He who says he is in the light, and hates his brother, is in darkness until now. He who loves his brother abides in the light, and there is no cause for stumbling in him. But he who hates his brother is in darkness and walks in darkness, and does not know where he is going, because the darkness has blinded his eyes. . . Do not love the world or the things in the world. If anyone loves the world, the love of the Father is not in him. For all that is in the world—the lust of the flesh, the lust of the eyes, and the pride of life—is not of the Father but is of the world. And the world is passing away, and the lust of it; but he who does the will of God abides forever."* 1 John 2:3-11, 15-17. Friends, as another brother put it succinctly, "I'm not who I want to be, and I'm not who I'm going to be, but **thank God I'm not who I used to be!!!** Can you also say that?

Struggles and Temptations

Every human being struggles with temptations. In fact, the struggle increases after committing to follow Christ for two reasons:

1. Before surrendering your life to Jesus you were more inclined to surrender to temptation than to resist it.

2. There is an enemy to our souls – Satan – and spiritual warfare is real – often intense. He wants to recapture you.

However, not only is there hope – there is certain victory in Christ. **In Christ is the key factor.** Abide in Christ! Focus on Christ! Walk with Christ. "For whatever is born of God overcomes the world. And this is the victory that has overcome the world—our faith." 1 John 5:4

It is a good idea to saturate your mind with the powerful truths in Romans chapter 6, 7 and 8.

Chapter 6. My old man of sin died with Christ, was buried in baptism, and I am now a new man raised with Christ.

Chapter 7. My new man of righteousness in Christ is haunted by the old man of sin who seems to have more lives than a cat. Scat cat! Go back to the grave where you belong!

Chapter 8. I am a new man in Christ! I am inhabited, possessed, and empowered by His Holy Spirit. I have nothing to fear – not even fear itself. Why not? **Because in Christ I am more than a conqueror!** That is my identity.

Some recovery programs have the participants stand up in front each session and make a false confession – at least for those in Christ. Each one is to say, "I am an alcoholic" or "I am a sex addict", etc. NO! If you are **in Christ** that is **NOT** who you are! **Don't dwell on who you were – focus on who you are.** Isn't it much better to say, "Satan is after me"? He is persistent with temptations – but we buried my old man. **I am a new man in Christ! I am more than a conqueror!"**

I have trusted Christ for forgiveness and salvation – I can trust Him for victory over my addictions, my hang-ups and my pet sins, as well as my irritations, aggravations and frustrations. I don't need to lose my cool! I don't need to blow my stack! I don't need to try to drown my sorrows in alcohol! In my core being, my spirit, I am a child of the King. His Spirit lives inside my spirit. I AM MORE THAN A CONQUEROR!!!

What will it look like in your life if you truly believe that you are MORE THAN A CONQUEROR??? Who can thwart you? What can stop you when you are MORE THAN A CONQUEROR??!

If you are struggling with homosexual temptations or tendencies, I highly recommend that you consider reading these articles:

1. "Sodom more than a gay issue…", by Ed Vitagliano (*AFA Journal*, June 2013, pgs. 16-17, www.afajournal.org)

2. "Journey of Grace: From lesbianism to the parking lot to church. An interview with author Rosaria Butterfield", from *World Magazine*, by Marvin Olasky (Samaritan Ministries, May 2013, *Christian Health Care Newsletter*)

3. "No Truth Without Love – No Love Without Truth", by Dr. Albert Mohler (*Eternal Perspectives*, Summer Issue 2013)

Know When to Fight and When to Flee!

Being more than a conqueror in spiritual warfare involves the wisdom of knowing when to fight and when to flee. We are to confront evil and fight the good fight by exposing the works of darkness with the light.

However, when Satan's strategy involves sexual temptations, the wisdom of God mandates flight instead of fight! *"Flee sexual immorality. Every sin that a man does is outside the body, but he who commits sexual immorality sins against his own body"* 1 Corinthians 6:18. *"Flee also youthful lusts; but pursue righteousness, faith, love, peace with those who call on the Lord out of a pure heart."* 2 Timothy 2:22

"...I want you to be wise in what is good, and simple concerning evil. And the God of peace will crush Satan under your feet shortly. The grace of our Lord Jesus Christ be with you. Amen." Romans 16:19b-20. To bring balance to these exhortations (commands) to flee from sexual temptation and to be wise in waiting for Him to crush Satan under our feet, let us also never forget these powerful commands from God's inspired Word: *" Watch, stand fast in the faith, be brave, be strong. Let all that you do be done with love."* 1 Corinthians 16:13-14

God's Intelligent Design for Marriage

I.   Unity in Diversity = Male plus Female

II.   Recreation plus Procreation = Fun and Family

III.   Transformation though Conflict Resolution = Character Development

God's Intelligent Design for Child Training

I.   Father and Mother – To Demonstrate and Train Children Godly Masculinity and Femininity

II.   Tough and Tender Love

III.   Discipleship through praise, encouragement and reward for good behavior and loving correction and punishment for bad behavior.

        Appropriate Corrections, Encouragements, Rewards and Punishments

        Carefully study the Book of Proverbs for wisdom and balance in these important matters.

Homophobia

Homophobia is a made-up word that homosexual activists use to intimidate those who disagree with their agenda. Do I fear being accused of being homophobic? No! Absolutely not! Why not? First of all, I don't care what homosexual activists and their "liberal" colleagues choose to call me. Second, I freely admit that I do fear the unbridled corruption that homosexual activists are pushing off on our culture. Do you realize that historically there has never been a culture (society) that has continued to survive after labeling homosexual behavior as normal? So yes, I do fear for what is happening to our country – and especially to our youth. They are constantly being brainwashed through the public schools[1] and the media with the propaganda that homosexuality is normal, acceptable, and to be celebrated. (Never mind the disease and death it is inflicting on millions worldwide!)

Some of the recent laws promoting their propaganda deserve the label, asinine. For example, consider this item from the June 9, 2013 issue of *The Times and the Scriptures*:

---

1   [9] Please see the DVD, *Indoctrination*, by Gunn Productions and the books, *Is Public Education Necessary?* and *N.E.A.: Trojan Horse in American Education*, by Samuel L. Blumenfeld.

"State ordering girls' locker rooms open to boys"

(FROM ZIONICA, 5-14-13)

The California State Assembly passed a bill [last month] mandating that schools permit boys to play on girls' athletic teams and utilize the ladies' locker room if they "gender identify" as girls – or vice-versa for girls identifying as boys.

Read more: http://zionica.com/2013/05/14/state-ordering-girls-locker-rooms-open-to-boys/#ixzz2U4WroB6T

For discussion: Are the "shame" of **Isa. 47:1-3** and the "modestly and discreetly" of **1 Tim. 2:9** too outdated to apply to 21st century co-ed showers? Or are we really supposed to accept this new "transgender" category as legitimate and worthy of special rights?" ("The Times and the Scriptures," Summer Supplement for June 9, 2013)

Is it possible for legislators to pass a more outrageous law? My wife, Della, doesn't like for me to use the term asinine, but sometimes it is the most valid description of the insanity gripping our nation – and our world. (Asinine literally means stupid, silly, or unintelligent – but it carries a stronger punch than any of those terms.) So if you like the law passed by the legislators in California, and want to call me "homophobic" – go ahead. I might choose to wear it as a badge of honor.

By the way, are we so naïve that we don't believe that curious teen boys will now pretend to become transgender to gain access to girls' locker rooms? Do you trust those declared homosexuals who are already cross-dressers to be in the locker rooms with your daughters and granddaughters (or girls going into boys' locker rooms pretending to be gender-identity boys)?

There is a third reason why I don't fear being accused of being homophobic. It is because TRUTH WALKS UNAFRAID. What I'm sharing is the truth of God both from His infallible Word and from scientific research about the dangers of homosexuality. I do not fear cross examination.

Truth invites investigation!

Truth welcomes examination!

Truth rejects contamination!

TRUTH WALKS UNAFRAID!!!

Recently I saw a sticker that says, "Trust Your Heart." This expresses the warped wisdom of the world. God in His wisdom tells us, "GUARD YOUR HEART!" Why do I need to guard my heart? Here are three portions of the Word of God that clearly tell me why:

1. *"Keep your heart with all diligence, For out of it spring the issues of life."* Proverbs 4:23.

2. *"O Lord, I know the way of man is not in himself; It is not in man who walks to direct his own steps."* Jeremiah 10:23.

3. *"The heart is deceitful above all things, And desperately wicked; Who can know it?"* Jeremiah 17:9.

My friend, if you are feeling the temptation to submit to the powerful pressure of the homosexual propaganda and intimidation steamroller – GUARD YOUR HEART!!! Remember: *"No temptation has overtaken you except such as is common to man; but God is faithful, who will not allow you to be tempted beyond what you are able, but with the temptation will also make the way of escape, that you may be able to bear it. . . .. Therefore, whether you eat or drink, or whatever you do, do all to the glory of God."* 1 Corinthians 10:13, 31.

The Commitment

Finally, I want to share this concise, clear, crisp quotation from the late Adrian Rogers:

> *"The church is not the servant of the state!*
>
> *The church is not the master of the state!*
>
> *The church is the conscience of the state!*
>
> *We will be civil – but WE WILL NOT BE SILENT!!!"*

The Bottom Line

Courage is not the absence of fear – it is conquering of fear! *"For God has not given us the spirit of fear, but of love and of power and of a sound mind."* 2 Timothy 1:7.

WE ARE MORE THAN CONQUERORS.

WE WILL BE CIVIL - BUT

WE WILL NOT BE SILENT!!

SUPPLEMENT 1 - Highly Recommended Items

I highly recommend that you read these articles:

"Blurring the Lines": From haute couture to elementary schools, activists aren't just trying to 'push the envelope' when it comes to gender distinction – they're trying to erase the line, by Jeff Johnston. Visit CitizenLink.com: http://bit.ly/zafcj6 (*Citizen Magazine*, April 2012)

"No Truth Without Love – No Love Without Truth", by Dr. Albert Mohler. Dr. R. Albert Mohler Jr. (www.albertmohler.com) serves as president of The Southern Baptist Theological Seminary. Widely sought as a columnist and commentator, Dr. Mohler has been quoted in the nation's leading newspapers. (*Eternal Perspectives*, Summer 2013)

"Piercing the Gay Paradigm", by Ed Vitagliano (*afaJournal*, September 2013) www.afajournal.org

"Sodom", by Ed Vitaliano (*afaJournal*, June 2013) www.afajournal.org

ATTENTION!

The primary reason for the conflict over homosexuality among those who claim to be Christians is that those pusing perversion have forsaken the infallible Word of God as their standard. They are putting their faith in their feelings, rather than in the Truth of what God says. Unbelief is not weakness - it is wickedness!

SUPPLEMENT 2

"It's gotten so bad we have to

(try to) pass a law that says this?"

Reprinted from Breaking Christian news, 9-25-13

"A bill sponsored in the U.S. House of Representatives strives to guarantee that tax exempt status would not be threatened by beliefs contrary to the recently mandated redefinition of marriage.

Noting the reasons for the Marriage and Religious bill, Rep. Raul Labrador (R-ID) said: "Regardless of your ideology, we can all agree about the importance of religious liberty. Our bill will protect freedom of conscience for those who believe marriage is the union of one man and one woman...'

Rep. Steve Scalise (R-LA) said, 'Recent legal challenges to Christians who refuse to provide services for homosexual weddings have caused alarm around the country. Furthermore, the Supreme Court's ruling on marriage may embolden those in government who want to impose their views of marriage on faith-based organizations. We need this legislation to protect freedom of conscience for those who believe marriage is the union of one man and one woman.'"

"First annual 'Ex-Gay Awareness Month'

awards are announced"

Reprinted from Family Research Council 10-2-13

"Monday night, the Washington, D.C. area was the site of the First Annual Ex-Gay Awareness Month Dinner and Reception. Threats to the civil rights of those who have abandoned a 'gay' identity and left the homosexual lifestyle, as well as those who have unwanted same-sex attractions and seek help to overcome them, have never been greater than they are now. Two states, California and New Jersey, have passed laws unprecedented in the history of psychology, to actually outlaw sexual orientation therapy with minors by licensed counselors.

Mat Staver of Liberty Counsel received the 'Ex-Gay Freedom Award' for his lawsuits challenging both statutes -- in fact, he left directly from the dinner for Trenton, New Jersey, to argue the case against the New Jersey law in federal district court yesterday morning. A pincer movement is underway in New Jersey – in addition to the new law restricting therapy with minors, a lawsuit by the Southern Poverty Law Center (SPLC) has charged both licensed and unlicensed counselors with 'consumer fraud.' Jews Offering New Alternatives for Healing (JONAH) is being defended by the Freedom of Conscience Defense Fund (FCDF), but the pro-homosexual activists are pursuing legal tactics that could bankrupt both organizations.

Dennis Jernigan, an ex-gay who is a renowned Christian musician (he wrote 'You Are My All in All' and other popular praise songs), provided music, while Trace McNutt, a former satanic drag queen, was winner of the 'Courage Award' for former homosexuals. The event was inspiring evidence that for homosexuals, change *is* possible – a message they have a right to hear. To help these courageous allies, go to Jonahweb.org for JONAH and ActRight.com for FCDF. (Copyright 2013, **The Times and the Scriptures**, 948 Darlene Ave, Springfield, OR 97477, www.timesandscriptures.org. Weekly Bulletin for October 6, 2013. Used by permission.)

"If I speak the truth without love – that is brutality!
If I attempt to speak in love without truth – that is hypocrisy!"
~Adrian Rogers

QUESTIONS FOR CHAPTER 4

1. What is the basis – the foundational truth – which supports both the sanctity of life and the sanctity of marriage?

2. What does distorted diversity produce?

3. Why is so-called "gay marriage" not gay and not diversity?

4. How do we know that homosexuality is not "immutable" (unchangeable)?

5. What is the ultimate confusion? Why?

6. What is at the core of rebellion against God?

7. What does the command, "You shall **not** covet," have to do with the issue of homosexuality?

8. Can you name Biblical principles that are flagrantly violated in so-called "Gay Pride Parades?"

9. Are human beings basically good by nature? Why or why not?

10. Can we actually have victory over our own struggles and temptations? How?

CHAPTER 5:
PASSIONATE FOR PURITY

Chapter 5: Passionate for Purity

Why Compromise the Purity Principal by Complying with Corrupt Culture?

~

I want to begin this chapter by sharing with you a copy of a letter I wrote to Shawn McMullen, editor of *The Lookout* magazine dated February 27, 2012.

Dear Shawn,

I'm writing in response to your February 19 issue, *Christians and Culture.* Your Secret Service Saturday is a great idea! I believe the articles "First Century Culture Shapers" and "Hold It Out" both have excellent input, but the article in between them, "Listening with Open Ears" I believe is dangerously flawed in its advice. Will you pass on my letter to Nicole R. Pramik? Will you consider publishing it as an open letter to her and the editor?

Dear Nicole,

As I consider your article "Listening with Open Ears", I want to express full agreement with your first sentence: "While Christians are called to be different from the world, we have to be familiar with the culture we live in if we want to make an impact for Christ." However, your second sentence I believe is problematic. You wrote: "We should strive to be as aware of our culture as we are of Scripture so we can communicate Christ's truth in a way people can understand." Are you sure this advice is true and accurate according to the Word of God – especially in the specific way you are recommending to become "aware of our culture"? **The Word of God says, "*Test everything. Hold on to the good.*" 1 Thessalonians 5:21. Are you willing to test your advice?**

1. **What about the test of target audience?** Were you intending this advice for seasoned veterans of cultural warfare whose minds are saturated with Scripture – or to every Christian, including the wobbly-legged new believer who is saturated already with this ungodly culture but almost totally ignorant of

Scripture? Since you make no distinction in your article, it must be intended for all Christians. I believe this shows a severe lack of discernment. A fire chief doesn't send an untrained recruit into a highly dangerous situation without strong guidance and along with a seasoned veteran. Teenage readers in Christian families may already be seeking ways to convince their parents to let them compromise with their culture by watching MTV – so they can "relate" to their peers. Now they can listen to Madonna, "Lady" Gaga and Eminem and tell their parents they are doing "research" while saturating their minds and hearts with the filth of this world.

I am now a seasoned veteran – from engaging the hippy culture and the university students in Eugene, Oregon, from 1966-70, when I was a young preacher, to speaking at "Man and the Christian Worldview" symposiums and conferences in Ukraine where the minority of us as Christians were facing Marxist/atheist scientists and professors, plus some postmodern and new age practitioners. We were able to engage them by speaking truth in love and building bridges of friendship. Although some got angry, others made significant changes. However, even as a seasoned veteran, I do not intend to follow your advice. Why not? Because I know my own weakness and vulnerability. I did not grow up in a Christian home and I learned to swear by the time I could walk and talk. My biggest battle when I gave my life to Jesus at age 12 was to allow the Holy Spirit to purify my filthy mind and foul mouth. It is still an ongoing process after all of these years and sometimes I still have mental flashbacks. Why should I pay our corrupt culture to reprogram my mind and mouth with filth under the guise of "research"? A few years ago, after Dan Brown's book, *The DaVinci Code* had been made into a movie, I scanned the book as an apologetics research project. His concepts are so perverted and vile that I felt like I had just gone swimming in a sewer. I never intend to read another Dan Brown book unless he is truly converted. I can testify that it is possible (and necessary) to engage our wicked culture without swimming in their sewer.

2. **What about the test of considering the downward pull of human nature?** In light of this, I do believe your advice is naïve and ignores the Biblical teaching about how corrupt our human nature really is. Jeremiah wrote by inspiration, "*The heart of man is deceitful above all other things and desperately wicked.*" Jeremiah

17:9. Paul by inspiration describes the battle with the old nature vividly in Romans chapter 7 – after describing radical conversion in chapter 6 and before describing triumphant victory in chapter 8. Here is his description in verses 13-20: *"Did that which is good, then, become death to me? By no means! But in order that sin might be recognized as sin, it produced death in me through what was good, so that through the commandment sin might become utterly sinful. We know that the law is spiritual; but I am unspiritual, sold as a slave to sin. I do not understand what I do. For what I want to do I do not do, but what I hate I do. And if I do what I do not want to do, I agree that the law is good. As it is, it is no longer I myself who do it, but it is sin living in me. I know that nothing good lives in me, that is, in my sinful nature. For I have the desire to do what is good, but I cannot carry it out. For what I do is not the good I want to do; no the evil I do not want to do - this I keep on doing. Now if I do what I do not want to do, it is no longer I who do it, but it is sin living in me that does it."*

WHICH NATURE ARE YOU FEEDING???

Two natures beat within my breast,

The one is foul, the other blessed.

The one I love, the other I hate;

The one I feed will dominate.

~ *Author Unknown*

3.   **What about the test of considering many strong warnings in Scripture to be very, very cautious?** I believe that your article not only ignores the severe battle between the flesh and the spirit, but also the strong warnings given to us in the Word of God. Most modern movies contain pornography and often graphic, excessive violence. Do I need to dive into the sewer to know that it stinks, or to find some delicious morsel that accidently got flushed down the toilet? Here are some of the warnings and admonitions of Scripture: *"I made a covenant with my eyes not to look lustfully at a girl"* Job 31:1. *"For these commands are a lamp, this teaching is a light, and the corrections of discipline are the way to life, keeping you*

from the immoral woman, from the smooth tongue of the wayward wife. Do not lust in your heart after her beauty or let her captivate you with her eyes, for the prostitute reduces you to a loaf of bread, and the adulteress preys upon your very life. Can a man scoop fire into his lap without his clothes being burned?" Proverbs 6:23-27. *"Do not be misled. Bad company corrupts good character."* 1 Corinthians 15:33. Lady Gaga? Eminem? *"Blessed are the pure in heart, for they shall see God"* Matthew 5:8. *"See to it that no one takes you captive through hollow and deceptive philosophy, which depends on human tradition and the basic principles of this world rather than on Christ."* Colossians 2:8. *"Therefore, dear friends, since you already know this, be on your guard so that you may not be carried away by the error of lawless men and fall from your secure position."* 2 Peter 3:17. *"Finally, brothers, whatever is true, whatever is noble, whatever is right, whatever is pure, whatever is lovely, whatever is admirable – if anything is excellent or praiseworthy – think about such things."* Philippians 4:8.

Can I watch the pornography in most movies and listen to the verbal filth in many of the popular songs and remain pure in heart? Can I concentrate on what is pure and lovely while listening to Eminem or Madonna - even if I'm searching for what is good? Here is another pertinent warning: *"Therefore let him who thinks he stands take heed lest he fall."* 1 Corinthians 10:12.

I heard a story (on Family Life Today, I believe) about a father whose teenagers were pressing him to allow them to go see a movie their friends told them was great. They admitted to him that it had a few bad parts but told him how great was the theme and other redeeming characteristics they had heard about. He told them he would think it over and pray about it.

Soon he presented them with a plate of chocolate chip cookies he had made for them and told them of the high quality ingredients he used – "However, along with the chocolate chips I also sprinkled in a few rabbit droppings," he told them. Their smiles changed to shocked expressions and they refused to eat the cookies. "If you won't eat my cookies – you don't go to the movie," he told them. I believe he was one wise father – don't you? Are we as concerned about moral and spiritual filth as we are about physical filth?

Randy Alcorn wrote a pertinent article entitled "The Radical Path to Purity" which was adapted from his powerful little book, *The Purity Principle*. Here is how he began the article.

"Suppose I said, 'There's a great-looking girl down the street. Let's go look through her window and watch her undress, then pose for us naked, from the waist up. Then this girl and her boyfriend will get in a car and have sex – let's listen and watch the windows steam up!'

You'd be shocked. You'd think, *What a pervert!*

But suppose instead I said, 'Hey, come on over. Let's watch **Titanic.'**

Christians recommend this movie, church youth groups view it together, and many have shown it in their homes. Yet the movie contains precisely the scenes I described.

So, as our young men lust after bare breasts on the screen, our young women are trained in how to get a man's attention.

How does something shocking and shameful somehow become acceptable because we watch it through a television instead of a window?

In terms of the lasting effects on our minds and morals, what's the difference?

Yet many think, **Titanic?** Wonderful! It wasn't even rated R!

Every day Christians across the country, including many church leaders, watch people undress through the window of television. We peek on people committing fornication and adultery, which our God calls an abomination.

We've become voyeurs, Peeping Toms, entertained by sin.

Normalizing evil

The enemy's strategy is to normalize evil. Consider young people struggling with homosexual temptation. How does it affect them when they watch popular television dramas where homosexual partners live together in apparent normality?

Parents who wouldn't dream of letting a dirty-minded adult baby-sit their children do it every time they let their kids surf the channels. Not only we, but our children become desensitized to immorality. Why are we surprised when our son gets a girl pregnant if we've allowed him to watch hundreds of immoral acts and hear thousands of jokes with sexual innuendos?

...

But it's just one little sex scene.

Suppose I offered you a cookie, saying, "A few mouse droppings fell in the batter, but for the most part it's a great cookie – you won't even notice."

'To fear the LORD is to hate evil' (Proverbs 8:13). When we're being entertained by evil, how can we hate it? How can we be pure when we amuse ourselves with impurity?"

As I see it, giving the advice to "Listen with Open Ears" to music with foul lyrics and watch movies with filthy pornography to someone with my background is like telling a former alcoholic to listen for good messages in beer commercials and concentrate his witnessing in the liquor stores and bars. He may reach someone, but he is putting himself on very shaky ground. If you are wearing white gloves to work in the garden, are you more likely to see muddy gloves or glovey mud?

For years I've heard the cliché about someone being "too heavenly minded to be of any earthly use", but strangely enough I've rarely met anyone like that. However, I've met, seen and read about hundreds of Christians who were too worldly minded to be of any heavenly use. If you want to rescue someone from the quicksand – throw him a rope. Don't jump into it with him to try to lift him out.

It is a known fact that pornography addiction is epidemic, and good sources of information like Family Life Today and Focus on the Family have documented that a very high percentage of church leaders are secretly pornography addicts. Yet you recommend listening with open ears and watching with open eyes to pornography laced music and movies!!! Is that going to help spread "the aroma of Christ" in our sick world? Already, about 80% of teens drop out of youth groups and church. Many never return. How do you think your advice is going to affect a group that is already so vulnerable?

Dear Nicole, please reconsider and rewrite your article. As it now stands, I believe it is a dangerous delusion that can produce perilous consequences.

"May the God of hope fill you with all joy and peace as you trust in Him, so that you may overflow with hope by the power of the Holy Spirit." Romans 15:13

Yours & His,
Rick Deighton

Pornography is Pervasive and Progressive – Perverted and Pernicious

What is the attraction of pornography? It is appealing to our baser nature. All of us are born with that perverted nature from our fallen parents (all the way back to Eden), which is attracted to evil, like iron to a magnet. The combination of the natural, God-given attraction of male to female and female to male coupled with the innate curiosity of childhood, produces an instant attraction to images of nude humans, especially of the opposite sex. Discipline is essential to discipleship! We must learn to resist, overcome, and control our natural inclinations by the power of the Word and the Spirit, or we will be sucked into all manner of pernicious perversions. Pornography is probably the most pervasive. The problem of pornography addiction, even among Christian leaders, is pitiful and pathetic. The power of Jesus can break this – and is giving victory. You can get help through many ministries including Family Life Today, Family Talk, Focus on the Family, and AFA. Every one of these can help you get a filter for your computer. Satan is out to get you, and you are allowing him to play you for a fool if you don't get a filter. Pornography is like quicksand – it's a lot easier to get into it than to get out!

My earliest exposure to pornography that I remember was a pinup picture prominently portrayed in a mechanic shop. The problem now is that I can see such pinup pictures prominently portrayed on magazine racks in grocery stores near checkout stands, which are practically as pornographic as the Playboy centerfolds of the 1950s.

My next exposure that I remember was in the 6th grade when another boy and I found a portion of a pornographic magazine on or near the playground. When our teacher found us behind the building ogling at the pictures, she threw a fit! I distinctly remember that she was not pleased with our covert activity. Good! I needed that! It's possible that she could have handled the problem better, but the fact is, she made her point in a way that we didn't forget! Why are more women not outraged now? Female flesh is being flagrantly flaunted before our male eyes, often by those females themselves. I realize that "modest apparel" is no longer easy to find for females, but conscientious Christians will not capitulate to corrupt culture! Where there is a will, there is a way.

By the way, when the two of us 6th graders got caught red handed, we did not even come up with a clever excuse like, "We want to become doctors, so we are doing scientific research in human anatomy." I doubt if she would have swallowed that lie anyway. We stood there as flat-footed, foolish, silent sinners before her righteous wrath. I thank God for her now.

What about Classic Art?

When Michelangelo was a young artist and began painting nude pictures, his teacher asked him why he was doing that. He replied that he wanted to paint people as God sees us. His teacher wisely replied, "Michelangelo, you are not God!"

Passion for Perversity

Richard Dawkins, one of the most blatant and brazen atheists in the world, promotes the idea, "There is no God –so go ahead and have fun!" Isn't this revealing of his true motive? Could it be that his concept of fun is warped and perverted? Paul spoke of false teachers as "*men of corrupt minds*" 2 Timothy 3:8, and also pointed out "*To the pure all things are pure, but to those who are defiled and unbelieving nothing is pure; but even their mind and conscience are defiled*" Titus 1:15.

Julian Huxley was perhaps even more brazen in his reply as to why Darwin's book, *The Origin of Species*, was so readily accepted and quickly became so widely popular. He answered the interviewer, "I suppose the reason we leapt at 'The Origin' is that we didn't like the idea of God interfering with our sexual mores." **How revealing!** How honest that he did not say, "because evolution is a fact!" as he asserted in the introduction he wrote for the centennial edition of The *Origin of Species*. R.C. Sproul has candidly observed and pointed out that when Bertrand Russell penned his infamous book, *Why I Am Not a Christian*, he neglected to mention his most basic reason – his adulterous escapades. R.C. also quipped that Russell's printed reasons are so easy to answer and refute. Bertrand Russell lived in a different era and was not so flippant and blatant about his true motives. **The underlying motive for adopting evolutionism is sex – not science!!!**

In considering this sub-heading of "Passion for Perversity" I don't want to pass up the perverse plans, program, and purpose of Planned Parenthood. As is true with other propaganda, such as the twisted use of the formerly good, joyous word "gay" as a synonym for homosexuality, likewise the term "Planned Parenthood" is a propaganda term for planned pushing of immoral sex as a means of harvesting multiple millions of dollars in abortions – both from the victims of their slaughter houses and from all of us as American taxpayers. The Planned Parenthood abortion mills are the most unregulated clinics in America – and more evidence keeps stacking up that they are also the most unsanitary. The "back alley" abortions are now gone, but the unsanitary, filthy butcher shop conditions prevail. I pray that the current lawsuits against Planned Parenthood will prevail and bring down this gigantic perpetrator of filth and murder. I want to share with you a brief article from *Citizen Magazine* that may shock you. However, if you know a little bit about Margaret Sanger, the founder (root) of Planned Parenthood, then you won't be surprised with the fruit of her efforts. "Jezebel" would be too polite of a label for the real Margaret Sanger. Now consider this brief look at . . .

"The Real Planned Parenthood"

"Planned Parenthood thinks there's something wrong with the sexual morals of young people: These kids today are just too darned ... conservative.

You read that right. On PP's Facebook page for teens, they've linked to an MTV video calling on kids to quit being judgmental toward promiscuity – or, as the video puts it, to 'stop the slut-shaming.'

'A lot of people define 'slut' as someone who has too much sex or too many partners,' says the speaker, a purported 'sexpert' named Francisco. 'But according to who? The slut fairy?'

Francisco doesn't want to banish the offending term, however. Just the opposite. He tells the kids that 'slut' should be used 'in a positive way' to describe 'a woman who is confident in her sexuality.' He says 'there's a little bit of slut in all of us ... So embrace it! 'Slut' should only be used for good.'

Well now. When PP talks to parents, they swear they're not encouraging teen sex, merely trying to control its consequences. When they talk to kids, they talk ... well, like this.

Next time someone asks you why Planned Parenthood shouldn't be talking to our kids in school, just tell 'em about Francisco. That should be all they'll need to hear." ("Citizen Magazine", December 2012. Used by permission.)

The real Planned Parenthood is planned perversity!!!

SAMSON

A He Man with a She Problem!

Was Samson the strongest man who ever lived, or the weakest? That depends on whether we are considering his muscles or his morals. He had a wholesome home and healthy heritage. God granted him supernatural, superior strength to serve his nation of suppressed servants as deliverer and judge, but he foolishly and frivolously squandered his physical potency on pagan Philistine fillies. One of his loose lovers was also a liberal liar who loved money more than muscles. Certainly Samson's safety was not her primary priority. Her treacherous tears tricked Samson into telling her the truth about the source of his superior strength. She cuddled him, then coerced him into getting clipped, captured, and conquered. His physical power fell prey to the trap of Philistine female flesh and flirtation because he was a weak-willed wimp when it came to spiritual strength.

Isn't it interesting that the first recorded words of Samson are, "I saw a woman – get her for me!"? When the Philistine warriors captured him they burned out his eyes with a hot poker so he could never again see a woman. (Friend, it is wise for us to keep our eyes on Jesus, don't you think?) After binding him and blinding him, they tied him to a millstone to use him for grinding grain. Let's remember that silly Samson suffered subjugation because he squandered his supernatural strength on sinful satisfaction. Let's never forget that sin binds, sin blinds, and sin grinds!

Sin will lead you farther than you intended to go away.

Sin will keep you longer than you intended to stay.

Sin will cost you more – much more – than you ever intended to pay! God allowed devious, deceitful Delilah to bring Sinful Samson down. He played with fire and got burned!

The good news is that a story is not over till it's over! There is a strong suggestion that Samson submitted to the Savior and repented. When he cried out to God at the Philistine festival, the Almighty renewed Samson's strength and restored his resolve. In his death, Samson conquered more pagan Philistines than he did in his life.

Now let's take a look at some insightful excerpts from Ravi Zacharias' article, "Evicting the Sacred":

Evicting the Sacred from Society

"… I am a Christian. When I came to America decades ago, I was thrilled to see Christmas celebrated and the reason for the season so obvious: the birth of Jesus Christ. Did I assume that every American was thus a Christian? Certainly not. But I expected the charitable heart of even the dissenter to allow that which has been practiced in this country historically and traditionally to continue.

But alas, it is not so. In Thailand and Indonesia Christmas carols are sung in shopping centers and Christmas trees adorn airports. But in America the anti-Christian bias of silly advertisements like Bloomingdales' 'Merry, Happy, Love, Peace' reflect ideas firmly planted in midair and proclaim no reason for the season.

Who is offended by a public celebration of Christmas? The anti-Christian secularist who lives under the illusion that values are cradled in a vacuum. Peace and love for what? What do these terms really mean? Are they self-evident? Not by any means.

America may not be a Christian nation per-se, but only the Judeo-Christian worldview could have framed such a nation's ideas and values: 'All men are created equal, that they are endowed by their Creator with certain unalienable Rights.' No other religion or secular assumption can affirm such a statement except the Judeo-Christian worldview. But today that very worldview, on which our systems of government and law are based, is expelled from the marketplace.

Democracies that are unhinged from all sacred moorings ultimately sink under the brute weight of conflicting egos. Freedom is destroyed not just by its retraction, but more often by its abuse.

Is it not odd that whenever it has power, liberalism is anything but liberal, both in the area of religion and politics? We now have something called 'spirituality' because people don't like the word 'religion.' What does spirituality mean? It means you may believe anything you wish to believe but regarding ultimate things, 'No absolutes, please.' The relativism and spirituality with which our society lives have one thing in common: they are both sophisticated ways of self-worship.

It is not accidental that even as Christian values have been jettisoned, the world is economically and morally on the verge of bankruptcy. Oh, but Jesus' Name still surfaces in the West. Maybe more often than any other name. Why? Because profanity still reigns. Oh yes, and God still figures in our philosophy: even when 'Mother Earth' quakes and thousands die, we still blame 'Father God.' The banishment of Christmas may be the anti-theists' great longing. But they still want the gifts of Christmas – love, joy, peace, and reason. Malcom Muggeridge once opined that we have educated ourselves into imbecility.

What are we celebrating at Christmas? What is the message of Christmas? It is the birth of the One Who promised peace, joy, and love. Try as we will, we cannot realize such values without acknowledging the point of reference for these absolutes: the very person of God and His gift to us of a changed heart and will. **That message needs to be heard around our world that is reeling with problems and rife with hate. For we have proven we are not fit to be God.**

G.K. Chesterton was right: '**The problem with Christianity is not that it has been tried and found wanting, but that it has been found difficult and left untried.**'

Some years ago, I walked into the Forbidden City in Beijing. It was a cold and grey January. I paused as I saw deep inside its walls a shop with the banner still fluttering, 'Merry Christmas.'

That which was happily displayed in the Forbidden City is now all but forbidden in our cities. A Chinese professor once remarked to me, 'You Christians need to thank God for Communism, because we left the souls of our people empty, making room for the gospel.'

Maybe someday we will thank the rabid secularists as well, when Merry Christmas will no longer be forbidden in our cities. **Exhausted and disappointed in self-worship, we may turn to God again and hear His story afresh.**" – Dr. Ravi Zacharias is the president and CEO of Ravi Zacharias International Ministries (rzim.org), a speaker and author of Why Jesus? Rediscovering His Truth in an Age of the Mass marketed Spirituality. ("Samaritan Ministries", December 2012, pp. 1, 7. Used by permission.)

Secularism is bias against the sacred.

Know Thyself

I want to pick up and expand on Ravi's sentence, *"Exhausted and disappointed in self-worship, we may turn to God again and hear His story afresh."*

Was it Socrates or Plato who wrote, "Know thyself!"? Do you realize that this is part of the foolish pagan philosophy which contradicts the truth revealed to us by Almighty God? Are you a committed Christian? A semi-committed Christian? If so, why follow the pagan advice to "Know thyself"? Do you realize that you can waste hours, days, months, even years seeking to find yourself? If you do accomplish that goal of "finding yourself", what will you find? You will find a fool who has been wasting much time with such a futile pursuit! Suddenly you will realize that it was a foolish, self-centered pursuit impossible to attain because the only one who knows your heart is God Himself. *"The heart is deceitful above all things, And desperately wicked; Who can know it?"* Jeremiah 17:9. Your search to know yourself has likely degenerated into searching for love and meaning in all the wrong places – power, prestige, and pleasure (sexual immorality). Wouldn't it be so much wiser to follow the example of the apostle Paul who, even years after his dramatic conversion, made it his goal and passion to know Christ? Could this be the reason he became the second most influential man in history? (Jesus is the first – no doubt about it!!!) *"But what things were gain to me, these I have counted loss for Christ. Yet indeed I also count all things loss for the excellence of the knowledge of Christ Jesus my Lord, for whom I have suffered the loss of all things, and count them as rubbish, that I may gain Christ and be found in Him, not having my own righteousness, which is from the law, but that which is through faith in Christ, the righteousness which is from God by faith;* **that I may know Him and the power of His resurrection,** *and the fellowship of His sufferings, being conformed to His death, if, by any means, I may attain to the resurrection from the dead. Not that I have already attained, or am already perfected; but I press on, that I may lay hold of that for which Christ Jesus has also laid hold of me. Brethren, I do not count myself to have apprehended; but one thing I do, forgetting those things which are behind and reaching forward to those things which are ahead.* **I press toward the goal for the prize of the upward call of God in Christ Jesus.** *Therefore let us, as many as are mature, have this mind; and if in anything you think otherwise, God will reveal even this to you."* Philippians 3:7-15.

The Beautiful and the Ugly, The Exciting and the Boring

There is nothing so beautiful as that which is good. There is nothing so ugly and boring as that which is evil.

Satan uses fiction and our vivid imaginations to turn that around. He makes evil look exciting, fascinating, intriguing, and attractive. Revival preacher, Archie Word, warned us not to be captivated by the liquor ads with beautiful women dressed in black velvet. Look under the billboard to see the drunk wallowing in his own vomit for the true picture. Sin has pleasure for a season – then comes the bitter payoff. Yes, there will be payday someday!

Christ candidly warns us of trials and hardship when we take up our cross to follow Him, but the rewards are out of this world!!!

WARPED OR WONDERFUL?

Satan appeals to the imagination by making evil appear intriguing, exciting, and fun. He also lies to us that following Christ is boring. The opposite is true! Would you like to join me in the exciting adventure of following Jesus? *"You therefore, my son, be strong in the grace that is in Christ Jesus. And the things that you have heard from me among many witnesses, commit these to faithful men who will be able to teach others also. You therefore must endure hardship as a good soldier of Jesus Christ. No one engaged in warfare entangles himself with the affairs of this life, that he may please him who enlisted him as a soldier."* 2 Timothy 2:1-4

It is Likely That a Liberal Has More Confidence in His Dog than in Our God – or Our Kids!

Recently on a "Breakpoint" radio program one of the speakers told that when they were promoting abstinence education instead of the Planned Parenthood Program of so-called "comprehensive sex education" (which is **definitely** not comprehensive because they spurn and mock abstinence education) a listener responded by saying that the kids need condom education because they are going to do it anyway. "To think otherwise is foolish," he told them. Obviously the one who responded has absorbed and adopted the liberal lie that the kids are going to follow their natural urges and fornicate no matter what we say or do to prevent it. Why am I so brazen as to label this a "liberal lie"? Because it is, that's why!

1. Are you aware that Uganda adopted abstinence education to stem the tide of death by AIDS – and in just a few years have been hugely successful? If I remember correctly, they lowered the number of AIDS cases by somewhere between 60% to 80%! Yet to our shame as a nation our Former Secretary of State, Hillary Clinton, went to Uganda and threatened to withdraw our financial support unless they switch to the Planned Parenthood program of promiscuous

perversion. How outrageous!!!

2. Are you aware that abstinence only education courses here in the US have been amazingly successful in lowering unwed pregnancies, abortions, and sexually transmitted diseases?

3. Are you aware of the fact that some liberals own house-trained dogs? Isn't that amazing? **These liberals have confidence that they can train their dogs to control their natural urges – yet strongly declare that we cannot train our kids to control their natural urges!!!** They have more confidence in their dogs than their kids – and our kids! **Are you outraged yet? If not, why not?**

By the way, who is it who is being foolish?

Are we Setting the Right Example?

If we are going to train our children to control their sexual urges, to respect their own bodies and the bodies of those of the opposite sex as amazing creations of Almighty God, and to save their intimate expressions of affection for the one and only person he or she marries, then we must set the right kind of example.

Hot Clothes and Burning Feet

(The Path of Destruction and How to Avoid It)

"For the commandment is a lamp, and the law a light; reproofs of instruction are the way of life, to keep you from the evil woman, from the flattering tongue of a seductress. Do not lust after her beauty in your heart, nor let her allure you with her eyelids. For by means of a harlot a man is reduced to a crust of bread; and an adulteress will prey upon his precious life. **Can a man take fire to his bosom, and his clothes**

not be burned? Can one walk on hot coals, and his feet not be seared? *So is he who goes in to his neighbor's wife; whoever touches her shall not be innocent. People do not despise a thief if he steals to satisfy himself when he is starving. Yet when he is found, he must restore sevenfold; he may have to give up all the substance of his house. Whoever commits adultery with a woman lacks understanding; he who does so destroys his own soul. … And there a woman met him, with the attire of a harlot, and a crafty heart. … Do not let your heart turn aside to her ways, do not stray into her paths; for she has cast down many wounded, and all who were slain by her were strong men. Her house is the way to hell, descending to the chambers of death."* Proverbs 6:23-32; 7:10, 25-27

"You, therefore, who teach another, do you not teach yourself? You who preach that a man should not steal, do you steal? [22] You who say, "Do not commit adultery," do you commit adultery?" Romans 2:21-22

Abstain

"Beloved, I urge you as sojourners and exiles to abstain from the passions of the flesh, which wage war against your soul. Keep your conduct among the Gentiles honorable, so that when they speak against you as evildoers, they may see your good deeds and glorify God on the day of visitation. … For this is the will of God, that by doing good you should put to silence the ignorance of foolish people. Live as people who are free, not using your freedom as a cover-up for evil, but living as servants of God. … For what credit is it if, when you sin and are beaten for it, you endure? But if when you do good and suffer for it you endure, this is a gracious thing in the sight of God. For to this you have been called, because Christ also suffered for you, leaving you an example, so that you might follow in his steps. He committed no sin, neither was deceit found in his mouth. When he was reviled, he did not revile in return; when he suffered, he did not threaten,

but continued entrusting himself to him who judges justly. He himself bore our sins in his body on the tree, that we might die to sin and live to righteousness. By his wounds you have been healed." 1 Peter 2:11-12; 2:15-16, 20-24 (ESV)

"So live that you would not be afraid to sell the family parrot to the town gossip!" ~ Will Rogers

If I listen to things that are ungodly;

If I look at things that are ungodly;

If I run with people that are ungodly. . .

then I am sowing to the flesh and I will reap destruction – not only in my life, but also in my children's lives! So remember – and **never** forget: *"No temptation has overtaken you except such as is common to man; but God is faithful, who will not allow you to be tempted beyond what you are able, but with the temptation will also make the way of escape, that you may be able to bear it. . . Therefore, whether you eat or drink, or whatever you do, do all to the glory of God."* 1 Corinthians 10:13, 31.

How can a young man cleanse his way? By taking heed according to Your word. With my whole heart I have sought You; oh, let me not wander from Your commandments! Your word I have hidden in my heart, that I might not sin against You. Psalm 119:9-11

Our Potent, Pertinent, Powerful Purity Principle

I want to bring this chapter to a conclusion with powerful excerpts from the most potent power for purity in this world –the Word of God inspired by the Spirit of God. The Psalmist wrote, *"How can a young man cleanse his way? By taking heed according to Your word. Your word I have hidden in my heart, that I might not sin against You."* Psalm 119:9, 11

Actually, I really need to clarify more completely that at the time the Psalmist wrote Psalm 119:11, the most potent power for purity was the Word of God hidden in the heart, but now we who are Christians have even far more potent power – the Holy Spirit Himself dwelling in our hearts to empower us to obey His Word hidden in our hearts. That's amazing! That's liberating! That's victorious!

The Sign and Seal of the New Covenant

Do you realize what is the sign and seal of the New Covenant? Do you realize what the New Covenant actually is? On the Passover eve before He was crucified, Jesus instituted the New Covenant. *"And He took bread, gave thanks and broke it, and gave it to them, saying, 'This is My body which is given for you; do this in remembrance of Me.' Likewise He also took the cup after supper, saying, 'This cup is the new covenant in My blood, which is shed for you.'"* Luke 22:19-20.

So, what is the New Covenant (New Testament)? Note that it is not a book!!! I realize that we have printed copies of the New Covenant Scriptures with New Testament printed on the cover. In Jesus' own words we have the clarification that the New Covenant is in His blood. It is a blood covenant relationship with God through the sacrifice of Jesus Christ. We enter this covenant of grace by faith in His blood sacrifice for our sin when we repent and are baptized into Christ. The sign of the New Covenant is the cup containing fruit of the vine representing the blood of Jesus and the seal of our entrance into this New Covenant is the gift of the Holy Spirit. The Sabbath was the sign and seal of the Old Covenant between God and the nation of Israel. (Please see Exodus 31:12-18.) The

Sabbath is not the sign and seal of the New Covenant.

Please carefully and prayerfully read these Scriptures:

"Then Peter said to them, 'Repent, and let every one of you be baptized in the name of Jesus Christ for the remission of sins; and you shall receive the gift of the Holy Spirit. For the promise is to you and to your children, and to all who are afar off, as many as the Lord our God will call.'" Acts 2:38-39.

"There is therefore now no condemnation to those who are in Christ Jesus, who do not walk according to the flesh, but according to the Spirit. For the law of the Spirit of life in Christ Jesus has made me free from the law of sin and death . . . But you are not in the flesh but in the Spirit, if indeed the Spirit of God dwells in you. Now if anyone does not have the Spirit of Christ, he is not His. And if Christ is in you, the body is dead because of sin, but the Spirit is life because of righteousness. But if the Spirit of Him who raised Jesus from the dead dwells in you, He who raised Christ from the dead will also give life to your mortal bodies through His Spirit who dwells in you." Romans 8:1-2, 9-11.

"Now He who establishes us with you in Christ and has anointed us is God, who also has sealed us and given us the Spirit in our hearts as a guarantee." 2 Corinthians 1:21-22.

"Now He who has prepared us for this very thing is God, who also has given us the Spirit as a guarantee. So we are always confident, knowing that while we are at home in the body we are absent from the Lord. For we walk by faith, not by sight. We are confident, yes, well pleased rather to be absent from the body and to be present with the Lord." 2 Corinthians 5:5-8.

"In Him you also trusted, after you heard the word of truth, the gospel of your salvation; in whom also, having believed, you were sealed with the Holy Spirit of promise," Ephesians 1:13.

Live a life of Truth, Beauty, Victory and Purity!

If you truly want to live a life of truth, beauty, victory, and purity then keep your eyes on Jesus, your heart filled with the Holy Spirit, and your feet on the straight and narrow!

More than Conquerors in Cultural Clashes

1. **Eyes** on Jesus

    a. *"Therefore we also, since we are surrounded by so great a cloud of witnesses, let us lay aside every weight, and the sin which so easily ensnares us, and let us run with endurance the race that is set before us, looking unto Jesus, the author and finisher of our faith, who for the joy that was set before Him endured the cross, despising the shame, and has sat down at the right hand of the throne of God. For consider Him who endured such hostility from sinners against Himself, lest you become weary and discouraged in your souls."* Hebrews 12:1-3.

    b. *"But we all, with unveiled face, beholding as in a mirror the glory of the Lord, are being transformed into the same image from glory to glory, just as by the Spirit of the Lord."* 2 Corinthians 3:18.

2. **Heart** Filled with the Holy Spirit

    a. *"Therefore do not be unwise, but understand what the will of the Lord is. And do not be drunk with wine, in which is dissipation; but be filled with the Spirit, speaking to one another in psalms and hymns and spiritual songs, singing and making melody in your heart to the Lord, giving thanks always for all things to God the Father in the name of our Lord Jesus Christ, submitting to one another in the fear of God."* Ephesians 5:17-21.

    b. *"But above all these things put on love, which is the bond of perfection. And let the peace of God rule in your hearts, to which also you were called in one body; and be thankful. Let the word of Christ dwell in you richly in all wisdom, teaching and admonishing one another in psalms and hymns and spiritual songs, singing with grace in your hearts to the Lord. And whatever you do in word or deed, do all in the name of the Lord Jesus, giving thanks to God the Father through Him."* Colossians 3:14-17.

3. **Feet** on the Straight and Narrow

"'Enter by the narrow gate; for wide is the gate and broad is the way that leads to destruction, and there are many who go in by it. Because narrow is the gate and difficult is the way which leads to life, and there are few who find it."
Matthew 7:13-14.

DOES GOD HAVE A SENSE OF HUMOR?

Many years ago I walked into a small fast-food restaurant in Nampa about mid-afternoon to order a hamburger. There were no other customers and only one employee – a beautiful young lady. She was both waitress and cook, so she came over to my table, took my order, and walked back over to the grill. Even though I was already a happily married man, her beauty caught my attention, and without thinking about what I was doing I was staring at her as she walked back over to the grill. Then I noticed the sign posted directly above the stove where she was standing – "Keep Your Eyes on Jesus!" Suddenly I diverted my eyes from her to Jesus and said, "Yes, Sir!" (Silent prayer.) Does God have a sense of humor? What do you think?

A TIME TO FLEE!

In that case I didn't flee – I stayed and ate my sandwich I had ordered. However, I want to tell you about another incident that took place a few years later at a water park in Boise on a hot summer day. I supplied lighting for the water park business and went there to check needs. On my way in, I walked past an attractive young lady wearing a swim suit she had outgrown. As I exited the building, she winked at me as I went by. The thought did occur to me that I should take her a tract and witness to her, but the Holy Spirit reminded me that there was a time to flee. I prayed, "Lord, please send a woman to witness to her. I'm getting out of here!" There is a time to fight a time to flee!!!

I hope you hide some of these portions of His Word in your heart.

"What shall we say then? Shall we continue in sin that grace may abound? Certainly not! **How shall we who died to sin live any longer in it? Or do you not know that as many of us as were baptized into Christ Jesus were baptized into His death?** *Therefore we were buried with Him through baptism into death, that just as Christ was raised from the dead by the glory of the Father, even so we also should walk in newness of life. For if we have been united together in the likeness of His death, certainly we also shall be in the likeness of His resurrection,* **knowing this, that our old man was crucified with Him, that the body of sin might be done away with, that we should no longer be slaves of sin.** *For he who has died has been freed from sin. Now if we died with Christ, we believe that we shall also live with Him, knowing that Christ, having been raised from the dead, dies no more. Death no longer has dominion over Him. For the death that He died, He died to sin once for all; but the life that He lives, He lives to God.* **Likewise you also, reckon yourselves to be dead indeed to sin, but alive to God in Christ Jesus our Lord. Therefore do not let sin reign in your mortal body, that you should obey it in its lusts.** *And do not present your members as instruments of unrighteousness to sin, but present yourselves to God as being alive from the dead, and your members as instruments of righteousness to God. For sin shall not have dominion over you, for you are not under law but under grace."* Romans 6:1-14.

"And we know that all things work together for good to those who love God, to those who are the called according to His purpose. *For whom He foreknew, He also predestined to be conformed to the image of His Son, that He might be the firstborn among many brethren. Moreover whom He predestined, these He also called; whom He called, these He also justified; and whom He justified, these He also glorified...* **Yet in all these things we are more than conquerors through Him who loved us."** Romans 8:28-30, 37.

Remember, it does **not** say that we **can be** more than conquerors – we **are** more than conquerors! **Let's be who we are!**

"*Now the Lord is the Spirit; and where the Spirit of the Lord is, there is liberty.* **But we all, with unveiled face, beholding as in a mirror the glory of the Lord, are being transformed into the same image from glory to glory, just as by the Spirit of the Lord.**" 2 Corinthians 3:17-18.

"*Brethren, join in following my example, and note those who so walk, as you have us for a pattern. For many walk, of whom I have told you often, and now tell you even weeping, that* **they are the enemies of the cross of Christ: whose end is destruction, whose god is their belly, and whose glory is in their shame—who set their mind on earthly things.** *For our citizenship is in heaven, from which we also eagerly wait for the Savior, the Lord Jesus Christ, who will transform our lowly body that it may be conformed to His glorious body, according to the working by which He is able even to subdue all things to Himself.*" Philippians 3:17-21.

Our part is not to glory in our shame, but to glory in our God! **"Rejoice in the Lord always. Again I will say, rejoice! Let your gentleness be known to all men. The Lord is at hand.** *Be anxious for nothing, but in everything by prayer and supplication, with thanksgiving, let your requests be made known to God; and the peace of God, which surpasses all understanding, will guard your hearts and minds through Christ Jesus. Finally, brethren, whatever things are true, whatever things are noble, whatever things are just, whatever things are pure, whatever things are lovely, whatever things are of good report, if there is any virtue and if there is anything praiseworthy— meditate on these things.*" Philippians 4:4-8.

Let us not be ashamed to stand up and speak out for purity, truth, righteousness and the glory of God as Paul did. "*And since we have the same spirit of faith, according to what is written, 'I believed and therefore I spoke,' we also believe and therefore speak, knowing that He who raised up the Lord Jesus will also raise us up with Jesus, and will present us with you. For all things are for your sakes, that grace, having spread through the many, may cause thanksgiving to abound to the glory of God.*" 2 Corinthians 4:13-15.

The Power of a Positive NO!

If you are going to protect your purity – and the purity of your potential partner for life – you need to set boundaries!

- ✓ Boundaries on where and when you meet.

- ✓ Boundaries on what you look at and listen to.

- ✓ Boundaries on how much time you spend together – especially alone.

- ✓ Boundaries on how late you will be together.

- ✓ Boundaries on where you spend time together.

- ✓ Boundaries on the companions you spend time with. Remember: *"Do not be deceived: 'Evil company corrupts good habits.'"* 1 Corinthians 15:33

- ✓ Boundaries on kissing each other.

- ✓ Boundaries on where and how you touch each other.

I have 2 pertinent examples for you:

1. Biblical courtship should and can be a wonderful season of life – with no regrets. Years ago when Jim Dietrich started dating Connie Strubhar, Gary and Sandra's youngest daughter, he told her that he would never kiss her until and unless he intended to ask her to marry him. Why? Because he did not want to stir up passions it was not time to fulfill, **and** he did not want to break her heart or his own if they realized that it would not be a wise option for them to marry. One evening when he brought her home she bounced into the house brimming with excitement she

could not contain – "Mom! Dad! Jim kissed me!" They all understood what that meant. Gary and Sandra were almost as excited as Connie because they had observed what an honorable young man Jim was, and would be glad to see him as their son-in-law – the spiritual leader and provider for their daughter.

How many teenage girls do you think are excited to come home to their parents to share the joy of saying, "He kissed me"? This type of openness builds strong family relationships instead of suspicion, mistrust, and aggravations. It's a beautiful thing!

Jim and Connie have been married for many years, have a grown son and daughter who love the Lord, and they serve as mentors for other couples on building strong marriage and family relationships.

2. On the radio, I heard Paul Shepherd share an illustration about a couple who nearly lost control when they were alone watching a movie with the lights turned low. They had failed to set the boundaries where they should have, and she was the one who got so stirred up she started putting the move on him. (Men aren't always the aggressive ones when it comes to inappropriate touching.) Fortunately – by the grace of God – this young man knew the power of a positive NO! He understood they were in spiritual and moral danger. He stood up, turned up the lights and said to her, "If you ever touch me like that again, you won't see me again!" The couple is now married, so his bold action probably saved their relationship. It definitely saved them from the sin of fornication! If they had compromised their convictions to their passions they would have trespassed on private property without a license, and would have committed a sin against God, against each other, and against their own bodies. *"Do you not know that your bodies are members of Christ? Shall I then take the members of Christ and make them members of a harlot? Certainly not!*

Or do you not know that he who is joined to a harlot is one body with her? For 'the two,' He says, 'shall become one flesh.' But he who is joined to the Lord is one spirit with Him. **Flee sexual immorality.** *Every sin that a man does is outside the body, but* **he who commits sexual immorality sins against his own body. Or do you not know that your body is the temple of the Holy Spirit who is in you, whom you have from God, and you are not your own? For you were bought at a price; therefore glorify God in your body and in your spirit, which are God's.**" 1 Corinthians 6:15-20

Often the guilt which ensues after an immoral compromise destroys the relationship. The antidote for this nagging guilt is the grace of God with His forgiveness through the blood of Jesus Christ. Have you received this forgiveness? He will cast your sin into the sea of His forgetfulness to be remembered no more! "Then Peter said to them, "*Repent, and let every one of you be baptized in the name of Jesus Christ for the remission of sins; and you shall receive the gift of the Holy Spirit.*" Acts 2:38

Learn the power of a positive NO! (Ladies, your NO may need to be accompanied with the power of a positive slap in the face!)

TAKING A STAND

When you take a stand on a standard – someone may call you a legalist. That's not legalism! Be careful what you do with grace. "*For the grace of God that brings salvation has appeared to all men, teaching us that, denying ungodliness and worldly lusts, we should live soberly, righteously, and godly in the present age, looking for the blessed hope and glorious appearing of our great God and Savior Jesus Christ, who gave Himself for us, that He might redeem us from every lawless deed and purify for Himself His own special people, zealous for good works.*

Speak these things, exhort, and rebuke with all authority. Let no one despise you." Titus 2:11-15.

"Because the sentence against an evil work is not executed speedily, therefore the heart of the sons of men is fully set in them to do evil." Ecclesiastes 8:11

Purity - Not Perversion is the Alternative Lifestyle!

Jesus said, ***"Blessed are the pure in heart, for they shall see God."*** Matthew 5:8.

God Does Want Me to be Happy – Doesn't He?

This is a common question in our corrupt culture. It came to my attention again recently when a believer told me that a man used this loaded question to her when she told him that she believes homosexuality is wrong. He responded, "God does want me to be happy, doesn't He?" How should we answer this question? Why not ask the questioner a counter question – "What makes you happy?" Or ask, "What is your definition of happiness?" If sinful behavior is your definition of being happy, then the answer is, NO!!!

It is true that there is in sinful behavior a fleeting fulfillment – then come the devastating, deplorable, degrading, destructive consequences! It is Satan who wants you to be happy – for a season – then reap the miserable consequences of sin in this life for the long term and in eternity forever. God wants you to practice self-control now and be happy now, next week, next month, next year – and forever!

Those who search for significance, self-worth, and satisfaction through sexting or any other perversion of their sexuality may find fleeting fun in flirting and following physical passions, but they will ultimately reap the bitter consequences. *"Do not be deceived, God is not mocked; for whatever a man sows, that he will also reap. For he who sows to his flesh will of the flesh reap corruption, but he who sows to the Spirit will of the Spirit reap everlasting life."* Galatians 6:7-8.

Yes, God Does Want You To Be Happy! Here's How!

(Note: The word "blessed" literally means "happy or blissful")

THE JESUS MANIFESTO

"Then He opened His mouth and taught them, saying:

"Blessed are the poor in spirit,
*   For theirs is the kingdom of heaven.*
Blessed are those who mourn,
*   For they shall be comforted.*
Blessed are the meek,
*   For they shall inherit the earth.*

Blessed are those who hunger and thirst for righteousness,
*   For they shall be filled.*
Blessed are the merciful,
*   For they shall obtain mercy.*
Blessed are the pure in heart,
*   For they shall see God.*
Blessed are the peacemakers,
*   For they shall be called sons of God.*
Blessed are those who are persecuted for righteousness' sake,
*   For theirs is the kingdom of heaven.*

"Blessed are you when they revile and persecute you, and say
all kinds of evil against you falsely for My sake. Rejoice and be
exceedingly glad, for great is your reward in heaven, for so they
persecuted the prophets who were before you." Matthew 5:2-12.

These wonderful words are from the Master Messenger's Superb Sermon spoken on the side of a mountain. I call this The Jesus Manifesto. What a strong contrast to the Humanist Manifesto! (Humanist is very different from humanitarian.) The Jesus Manifesto produces humanitarians who reach out to suffering humans. The Humanist Manifesto produces secular sectarians like the Freedom From Religion Foundation and the American Civil Liberties

Union. They expend a huge amount of time, money, and energy fighting God and undermining Christian influences in our nation – but where are their humanitarian projects? They want to tear down crosses, rip "Under God" from our Pledge of Allegiance, and "In God we Trust" from our money, and knock Ten Commandment monuments out of public view. **Their focus is on tearing down – not building up! They spurn the purity principle and promote all manner of sexual immorality, deviation, and perversion.**

My friend, weigh carefully what worldview you choose to accept, live by, and promote. Look both at the roots and the fruits of the philosophy which will define your life and your destiny!

The Jesus Manifesto – known by multitudes as The Beatitudes – has been praised and promoted by statesmen and scholars as the greatest manifesto ever given, and The Sermon on the Mount in which Jesus delivered His Manifesto as the most powerful message ever delivered. The Humanist Manifestos (both 1933 and 1973 versions) are a couple of duds in comparison. Not only are they duds – they are devious, deadly and destructive.

The Commitment

Finally, I want to share this concise, clear, crisp quotation from the late Adrian Rogers:

> **"The church is not the servant of the state!**
> **The church is not the master of the state!**
> **The church is the conscience of the state!**
> **We will be civil – but WE WILL NOT BE SILENT!!!"**

The Bottom Line

Courage is not the absence of fear – it is conquering of fear! "For God has not given us the spirit of fear, but of love and of power and of a sound mind." 2 Timothy 1:7.

WE ARE MORE THAN CONQUERORS.

WE WILL BE CIVIL - BUT

WE WILL NOT BE SILENT!!

SUPPLEMENT

I highly recommend you read these two articles, both found in the December 2012 issue of *afaJournal*:

"The Morally Heroic and the Rescue of Culture," by Ed Vitagliano (pp. 20-21)

"Christians Respond to Cries for Freedom," by Teddy James (pp. 22-23)

Questions for Chapter 5

1. What three vitally important tests was Nicole Pramik overlooking in her article, "Listening with Open Ears"?

2. Do you believe that watching a movie like *Titanic* is wholesome entertainment for believers? Why or why not?

3. What is the underlying motive for adopting evolutionism (or other non-Christian worldviews and religions)?

4. What is the real Planned Parenthood?

5. Why is secularism intent on evicting the sacred from society?

6. Is the Greek philosophy, "Know thyself", a Biblical teaching and an aspect of true wisdom? Why or why not?

7. Why is it likely that a liberal has more confidence in his dog than in our God?

8. What is our potent, pertinent, powerful purity principle?

9. What three things can we do to live a life of truth, beauty, victory, and purity?

10. Does God most want us to be happy or holy? Does God's description of what it takes to be truly happy (joyous) different from most human expectations?

"Covenant Eyes" software with accountability partners is highly recommended by Dr. James and Ryan Dobson for recovery from Pornography addiction.

CHAPTER 6:

WHY ARE THERE SCHOOL SHOOTINGS AND TERRIBLE TRAUMAS?

One mother leaving the murder scene of the horrible school shooting massacre in Newtown, Connecticut, on December 14, 2012, was heard sobbing, "Why?" This is the common cry of the human heart when pondering terrible tragedies, especially when perpetrated intentionally by human evil. Multiple factors can play a role in these tragedies, but there is a common denominator to all of them and a solid Biblical answer to that common question, "Why?" The contributing factors may be as diverse as disrespect for the sanctity of life, abortion, evolutionism, humanistic philosophy, divorce, separation from parents, teasing and mocking, occult practices, harboring anger and building up bitterness, traumatic TV and movies, violent video games, sadistic music and false religion – but **the bottom line answer is still sin**. Hold on! Before you turn away and write off this answer as too simplistic and naïve, please keep reading and openly, honestly pray about this potential answer. With a sincere heart, consider the evidence presented in this chapter.

Before we delve deeper into the ultimate root cause of all these tragedies, let's at least consider the insights from a few pertinent articles about the Newtown slaughter, etc.

"Rampant School Violence"

Ken Ham

"From Connecticut to California, horrible school violence is on the rise in America. Ultimately, sin is the cause of such violence, but we suggest there's an underlying education problem that has a great deal to do with the growing number of school shootings.

You see, the secular schools have all but banned God and the teaching of creation from the classroom. Prayer and Bible readings are no longer part of the curriculum. And Darwinian evolution is taught as fact.

The more that students believe there's no God, and that they're just animals, the more they will also believe there's no purpose and meaning in life...and that humans have no real value.

This is the underlying influence on the culture that's greatly contributed to why violence – including in schools – is on the rise in this nation." (**Answers Update**, Volume 20, Issue 3, p. 16, adapted from the March 18, 2013 broadcast of the *Answers...with Ken Ham* radio program).

"WHY?"
by Ray Hawk

"How can a twenty year old walk into a classroom of Kindergarten children and begin shooting and murder all twenty of them, in addition to six adults? The first adult was his own mother!

Someone asked, "Where was God?" Don't blame Him. This nation kicked Him out of our public schools fifty years ago. People are asking, "Why?" From a biblical standpoint, there is an answer to that question.* Jesus said the devil fell from heaven (Luke 10:18). Revelation 12:9 tells us that he was cast down to the earth and that he deceives the whole world. Paul tells us he is the god of this world and blinds the mind (2 Corinthians 4:4). He entered Judas Iscariot to betray Jesus and today he enters anyone who opens his heart to him (Luke 22:3). Many have.

My heart goes out to everyone in Newtown, CT affected by this tragedy. We have all seen the god of this world at work! Since our country is turning its back upon Jehovah God and His Anointed one Jesus, the void will be filled by Satan.

The President expressed his sorrow and sympathy on national TV and mentioned this and other events where lives were lost due to firearms. He hinted about more gun control as a solution. Guns are not the problem, **sin is.** The same would be true if one used a kitchen knife, baseball bat, tire tool, his hands, explosives, or a brick to end another's life. We already have clinics where babies are being murdered "legally," far outnumbering the Newtown tragedy! Those who publicly shed tears for the twenty children murdered at Newtown, don't do so for the millions who are aborted every year.* In fact, they condone it. Satan is alive and well! Satan has hardened hearts to the murder of millions of babies. He is now doing so in the hearts of a few, like Adam Lanza, by eliminating the "age" factor!

The school at Newtown, CT, like all others in this nation, are known as "Gun Free Zones." That means it is against the law for anyone to enter that school with a weapon on his person. Law abiding citizens will respect and obey that law. A criminal appreciates such "zones," knowing that he is the only one with a gun. He can murder without interference. Because of that ruling and the wickedness that prevails, we may expect more and more occurrences like this.

Some may incorrectly think that if the government forces everyone to turn in his guns, no one will have one and everyone will be safe. That is wishful thinking of the deceived. Guess who is deceiving them? Only the law abiding will turn them in. They are not the ones who initiate such horror. The criminals will not obey that mandate. In fact, they will get more, in illegal ways.

It is interesting that the news media, in the majority of cases, refuses to print those events where a citizen, who had a permit to carry, stopped criminals from a killing rampage. According to the FBI, each year around a million such events take place, where 98 times out of 100, the criminal gives up just by seeing someone else with a gun pointed in his direction. Some citizens do find it necessary to shoot, like a grandfather did by wounding one gun welding criminal and driving him and his partner from the store. They were later apprehended. An employee of an auto parts store saw a criminal was holding his manager at gun point and threatening to kill him. He ran out to his car, retrieved his weapon, and disarmed the perpetrator. His reward? He was fired by the manager he saved, because he brought a weapon onto the premises, which was forbidden by the store's strict "no gun" policy! Is something wrong with that picture?

Not just schools, but universities, libraries, civic centers, post offices, movie theaters, hospitals, all federal and state government offices, as well as private businesses that are "Gun Free Zones" **are continually at risk and an invitation** to the criminal to repeat what happened in Connecticut! It would seem that some of our laws benefit the criminal more than they help the law abiding.

If politicians do not believe you and I have a right to protect ourselves and our loved ones, let them be an example to us and dismiss those who guard and protect them with guns, bullet proof vest, and armored cars. We pay for their protection. Is our life inferior to theirs?

Our sympathy is extended to the families of the victims in this tragedy of Friday, December 14 in Newtown, Connecticut.

*My thanks for nuggets of truth, which I borrowed from last Sunday's sermon by Kenneth Grizzell and a short article by Jon Gary, which I have included within this article." (Ray Hawk, *My Thoughts*, Sunday, December 23, 2013. Used by permission.)

NEWTOWN SHOOTING VICTIMS

Charlotte Bacon, 6	James Mattioli, 6	TEACHERS/OTHERS:
Daniel Barden, 7	Grace McDonnell, 7	Rachel Davion, 20
Olivia Engel, 6	Emilie Parker, 6	Dawn Hochsprung, 47
Josephine Gay, 7	Jack Pinto, 6	Nancy Lanza, 52
Ana Marquez-Greene, 6	Noah Pozner, 6	AnneMarie Murphy, 52
Dylan Hockley, 6	Caroline Previdi, 6	Lauren Rousseau, 30
Madeleine F. Hsu, 6	Jessica Rekos, 6	Mary Sherlach, 56
Catherine V. Hubbard, 6	Avielle Richman, 6	Victoria Soto, 27
Chase Kowalski, 7	Benjamin Wheeler, 6	
Jesse Lewis, 6	Allison n. Wyatt, 6	

"Massacre in Newtown

Q & A With Dr. James Dobson"

"*Q. Dr. Dobson, I am extremely concerned about my children, ages six and seven, in the aftermath of the horrible killings in Newtown, Connecticut. They don't' know the details, but they've heard at school that 'something awful' happened to many boys and girls. They are asking about it and I don't know what to tell them. How should I handle this tragic situation?*

A. The massacre of children that occurred recently is almost beyond comprehension. Parents everywhere are grieving and trying to decide how to respond to their children's unanswerable questions. Maybe these suggestions will be helpful.

I think it is important to tell your young children that there are some very bad people in the world who do hurtful things to others. Sometimes boys and girls are the ones who get hurt by these people, and that is what recently happened. I wouldn't tell them that children were killed, or murdered, or that something else unthinkable happened at a school. Don't overstate it in a way that will terrify them. But they do need answers.

At this point, you have to walk a very narrow path. On the one hand, you want to teach them to stay away from strangers and to tell you if anything scares them. On the other hand, you can't afford to make them feel like the world is out to get them and that they are in constant danger. You want them to be cautious without being fearful of all adults.

Everything depends on your demeanor. If you are anxious and fearful, they will be too. Children take their cues from their parents. Try to discuss the subject without showing that you are extremely upset. Don't cry or make your kids think you are not able to protect them. Their security is in your hands. They also need to know that the crisis is over.

Tell them, 'Police came to get the bad man and he will never hurt anyone again.' Assure your children of your love and remind them that God gave them mommies and daddies to protect them, and that you watch out for them every hour of every day. This is why you sometimes have to say 'no' to their requests.

If you have a strong faith, I think you should then turn to Jesus. Tell them He cares for each of us and that He will hear us when we ask for protection. He knows our names and is with us at all times. The Bible also tells us He especially loves little children.

My six-year old grandson, Lincoln, has been having some bad dreams about monsters and wakes up crying at night. When he told his dad about it two weeks ago, Ryan began reading the 91st Psalm with him every night before going to sleep. This is a comforting passage, and Lincoln has had very few nightmares since they began reading.

I have paraphrased Psalm 91 below, taken from 'The Message.' You might want to use it, or any other version. The Message is written for adults, obviously, and might need to be edited for children as I have done:

Those who sit down in God's presence will spend the night in His shadow. He's my protection. I trust in Him and I'm safe! He rescues me from hidden traps, and shields me from every danger. His huge arms encircle me – under them I'm perfectly safe; His arms protect me from harm. I fear nothing – not even wild animals at night.

Bad people who try to scare me will get pushed away. Even evil can't get close to me. It can't get through the door. God ordered His angels to guard me wherever I go. If [I] stumble, they'll catch me; their job is to keep me from falling. I'll walk unharmed among lions and snakes, and kick them out of my way. 'If I hold on to God,' He says, 'I'll get you out of trouble. I'll give you the best of care if you'll only get to know and trust me.'

Call me and I'll answer. I'll be at your side in bad times. I'll rescue you and give you a long life, and give you a long drink of salvation!'

I've taken some liberties with the Scripture, here, but I think I've been faithful to the context. After you have read this Psalm, I suggest you pray together and thank Jesus for loving and caring for us. Thank them also for the angels that stand guard over us as we sleep. And thank them for mommies and daddies who also love and take care of their children. Ask Jesus to help us learn to trust Him more. Finally, on alternative nights, read or quote the 23rd Psalm with your children. You might memorize it together.

Every circumstance is different and the suggested wording offered here should vary with the age, maturity, and security of each child. What I've written was designed for kids in elementary school, and is just a guide to be modified to meet the needs of a particular boy or girl.

I hope this is helpful. What a shame that we have to deal with tragedies like this, but I'm afraid it is the world we live in.

Q. What do you think caused the killer in Newtown to do such unthinkable things?

A. I am not familiar with the particulars of this massacre but I can speak to the question generally. America has become a dangerous place partially because of the violence we tolerate. Even young children grow up today playing violent video games, watching unwholesome cable television, wretched Hollywood movies and MTV, and many other depictions of dramatized murder, rape, drug usage, etc.

Children are exposed to these influences from early ages. Millions of kids come home to empty houses every afternoon and watch unsavory stuff that they should never be allowed to witness.

Harmful examples of this violent nature are evident everywhere, even at the highest levels of society. On December 9, 2012, President Barack Obama invited the rapper, Psy, to the white House for a performance. This is the man who has sung at anti-American concerts featuring his own lyrics. One of them reads, 'Kill those _____ Yankees who have been torturing Iraqi captives; Kill those _____ Yankees who ordered them to torture; Kill their daughters, mothers, daughters-in-laws and fathers; Kill them all slowly and painfully.' Despite his history, the President brought Psy into the 'people's house,' and honored him as a great entertainer. No wonder violence is so deeply woven into the fabric of the American culture.

The sponsors and creators of unwholesome entertainment have insisted for decades that children are not harmed by dramatized violence. How foolish! Why would advertisers spend billions of dollars to get their products before the public, including children, if they thought no one was paying attention? We have to acknowledge that what kids see and hear directly influences how they think and behave. One quick glance at Reece's Pieces in the movie E.T sent America's kids rushing out to buy the candy. How outrageous to pretend that a steady depiction of raping and torturing and knifing innocent victims will not warp the morals and character of the nation's children. Some of them as adults make society pay for its negligence and abuse when they were young and impressionable.

There is another dimension that should be noted. Some adults who commit violent crimes were sexually and verbally abused or horribly neglected when they were young. These tragic experiences produce prodigious amounts of the stress hormone, cortisol. It floods the brain during times of severe distress or fear and causes irreversible damage to receptors in the brain. One of the consequences of this damage is an inability of teens and young adults to 'feel' for others. Many of them can kill without any emotional response to what they are doing. They have no conscience.

Millions of dollars have been invested in behavioral research to understand this phenomenon. It's clear from these studies that childhood terror and emotional distress can create violent psychopaths. These individuals who were not cared for when they were babies and toddlers grow up to wreak havoc on innocent victims. We can do a much better job with the children entrusted to our care.

I also want to share a letter from Pastor Jim Carlson, which conveys the heartache we all feel.

Friends,

The heart-wrenching events in Connecticut today make us all feel sad and angry. Evil brings out these emotions. We weep with the parents who lost their precious little ones and recoil at the thought that one deranged individual could cause so much pain for so many families. The first Christmas, when Herod ordered the killing of every child two years of age and under within a 15 mile radius of Bethlehem, must have felt the same way. 'A voice is heard in Ramah, weeping and great mourning, Rachel weeping for her children and refusing to be comforted, because they are no more (Matthew 2:18).' There are usually no answers to the 'why' questions of life after a tragedy like this. However, one thing is sure. We desperately need the Christ of Christmas in our world and in our lives. It is only because of His atoning death and resurrection that righteousness will ulti-

mately win the day and His justice will prevail. As we pray for those who are grieving in Newtown, may we all find new hope and inner peace in the presence of Jesus this Christmas season." (Dr. James Dobson's Family Talk, "A Nation Shaken by the Sandy Hook Tragedy" broadcast)

Now let's delve deeper into the ultimate cause of all these tragedies from Jack Cottrell's pertinent perspective: R.D.

The Cosmic Curse

By Jack Cottrell

"The corruption and condemnation resulting from sin are experienced not only by human beings but also by the entire universe. Man as the image of God is designed to stand in a particular relationship with both God and the world. When sin corrupts the image, these relationships are also distorted. Thus when the human race fell into sin, in a real sense the physical creation as a whole experienced a *fall*. The penal consequences of sin apply not only to human beings, but also to the whole of creation. Thus in addition to human death there is a kind of cosmic death, a cosmic curse.

The cosmic curse affects the world in two ways. One is the distorted relationship with mankind, which was intended by God to be the world's ruler (Gen 1:28) but has ended up being its slave. The other is an actual state of disorder, disruption, and decay into which the universe as such has fallen...

The alien character of this fallen age is also reflected in Col 3:2, 'Set your mind on the things above, not on the things that are on earth [ges].' First John 2:15 is similar: 'Do not love the world [kosmos] nor the things in the world.' That John is not referring to the cosmos as created but as fallen is seen in his following explanation: 'For all that is in the world, the lust of the flesh and the lust of the eyes and the boastful pride of life, is not from the Father, but is from the world. The world is passing away, and also its lusts' (1 John 2:16-17).

Thus does the Bible describe this world or this age as *evil*, or as alien to man's best interests. This does not mean that the physical world is inherently evil; it means that it has become evil because it shares in the corruption that has been caused by human sin and in the condemnation that God has poured out upon it."

THE FUTILITY OF THE CREATION

"The text that most clearly and forcefully describes the cosmic curse is Rom 8:18-22.

'For I consider that the sufferings of this present time are not worthy to be compared with the glory that is to be revealed to us. For the anxious longing of the creation waits eagerly for the revealing of the sons of God. For the creation was subjected to futility, not willingly, but because of Him who subjected it, in hope that the creation itself also will be set free from its slavery to corruption into the freedom of the glory of the children of God. For we know that the whole creation groans and suffers the pains of childbirth together until now.'

Here Paul speaks of 'the creation,' the physical or natural world; and he personifies it as experiencing an 'anxious longing' for, or 'eager expectation' (NIV) of, the day when the sons of God will be revealed. This is the day when God's family of believers will be raised from the dead (v. 23). Why is the universe earnestly, breathlessly awaiting this day? Because it is not just the human race that is under the curse of death and in need of redemption; the whole cosmos likewise has been plunged into a state of corruption and stands in need of healing.

This text presents the status of this condemned world in three vivid pictures. First, it has been 'subjected to futility' (v. 20), or 'subjected to frustration' (NIV). This takes us back to Genesis 1-3. When God placed the human race in charge of the rest of the material creation (Gen 1:26-28), from that point on the fate of the latter was tied to that of the former. When Adam sinned, God declared, 'Cursed is the ground because of you' (Gen 3:17). Instead of being man's servant, the earth became his antagonist. Instead of perpetuating man's life indefinitely, it is forced to engorge man's dead body into its dusty maw (Gen 3:18-19)…"

THE PROBLEM OF EVIL

"The fact that both mankind and the cosmos as a whole lie under the corruption and condemnation of sin gives rise to what is commonly known as 'the problem of evil.' Even to the casual observer it is obvious that the world as it presently exists cannot be consistently called 'very good' (Gen 1:31). There is still much beauty and wonder in it, but it is also permeated with pain, ugliness, and disaster – collectively called 'evil.'

Two kinds of evil are usually distinguished: moral and natural. Moral evil is the sin or wickedness which originates in the hearts of free moral creatures (human beings and fallen angels) and which expresses itself in their sinful actions. Examples include greed, hatred, selfishness, deceit, stealing, lust, and envy. Natural evil (sometimes called physical evil) is that which originates from natural processes or the perversion thereof. Examples are genetic defects, diseases, insanity, famine, suffering, and death; also any natural event – flood, lightning, earthquake, tornado, hurricane – that results in suffering or death. Sometimes moral evil and natural evil may be combined into a single event. For example, an act of murder is a moral evil on the part of the murderer which results in a natural evil (i.e., death) for the victim. Other examples are torture; rape; spouse and child abuse; and drug or alcohol abuse that results in birth defects, injury, or death.

The presence of such elements in the universe can be understood by those who accept the Biblical teaching concerning sin, death, and the cosmic curse. But for those who do not view the world with this understanding, it is easy to see how evil can be a problem. Actually there are two separate problems. One has to do with the cause of particular instances of evil, e.g., 'Why did my baby die?' or 'Why did lightning strike my neighbor?' The other has to do with the origin of evil as such, e.g., 'why is there such a thing as human death in the first place?' "Why are there such things as birth defects at all?' 'Why does any sort of weather disaster occur?' The latter are the more basic kinds of questions that constitute 'the problem of evil.'...

The best answer to the problem of evil is what is called the free-will defense. It says in essence that God created the world with neither moral evil nor natural evil existing in it; everything was originally 'very good' (Gen 1:31). But he did create free-will beings for whom moral evil was a possibility. Why did God do this? The Bible does not give an explicit answer to this question; but we infer from other teaching in Scripture that God's chief purpose and desire were to have creatures who would love, serve, and glorify him of their free choice and not by coercion or manipulation. We infer this, for example, from the fact that the first and greatest commandment is that we should love God with all our hearts and minds (Matt 22:37). That this is the most important thing we can do suggests this freely chosen love is what God desires from his creation more than anything else. Giving his creatures free will was a necessary means to this end.

The capacity to freely love God, though, also requires the capacity to choose to hate and reject God. Thus in a sense the creation of free-will beings entailed a risk. But God was willing to risk the free choice of evil in order to have freely chosen love and worship. Here is the extent of God's responsibility for evil: he is responsible for its possibility, but not its actuality. He made the free creatures who had the potential for choosing evil.

Sadly, God's creatures have chosen to use their free will to commit sin. And as a consequence of this free choice, all the evil that exists in the world has come into existence, the physical as well as the moral. It is not difficult to see how moral evil is the result of free will. Angels and men were created with the capacity to sin; some of the angels and the first human beings exercised that capacity under the permissive will of God, and moral evil became a reality.

But what about physical evil? Free will can explain the presence of moral evil in the world, but how do we explain evils such as birth defects, disease, and death? The answer is that free will is the ultimate origin of physical evils, too. Physical evils are present in the world because of sin, and sin is present because of free will. This point must be explained very carefully. Even though it is a very important truth it is easily misunderstood. **Here is the best way to say it: all physical evils are ultimately the consequence of sin, but they do not all derive from sin in the same way...**

Thus we see that evil in both its forms (moral and physical) is the consequence of the free-will choices of men and some angels to commit sin against God. It is not a necessary element of God's creation. But given the existence of free-will beings, it was from the beginning a possibility. As it happened, it was a possibility that became a reality.

It is safe to say that most of the individual instances of evil in the world are not caused by God but are allowed to happen according to his permissive will. This is in keeping with his commitment to the relative independence of his creation, including the relative independence of the natural processes and creaturely free will. This applies to all moral evil, including the first sins in the Garden of Eden. **God allows man the integrity of free choice. When evil is chosen, he allows the evil consequences that flow from it to pour out their cup of suffering upon mankind, and does not choose to intervene and prevent it.**

Thus in the face of personal calamity and suffering it is probably improper to ask, 'Why is God doing this to me?' In all likelihood God himself is not doing it; it is probably the result of somebody's free-will choice, either directly or indirectly. A baby born with a birth defect, for example, may be suffering the direct consequence of his mother's drinking alcohol during her pregnancy. Or the genetic flaw may go back much further, perhaps even to the garbling of nature that occurred with Adam's sin.

In view of the sovereignty of God's permissive will, it is proper to ask, 'Why did God *allow* this to happen?' This is so because nothing happens without God's foreknowing it and deciding not to prevent it. To say that God permits something to happen means that he *could* have prevented it if he had chosen to do so, if he had had a good reason for doing so It is true, then, that God could have prevented this birth defect or that accident or that disease. When a saint of God in the throes of undeserved suffering cries out, 'Why is God allowing this to happen?' this is indeed one of the most difficult questions to answer.

Two considerations are relevant. **First, we must remember that the possibility of evil is the price of free will.** Now that creaturely freedom has made evil a reality, there is no turning back. God cannot overrule every evil choice of man and every evil consequence therefrom without contradicting his own purposes in creating beings with free will. This is part of the price we pay for freedom, and which God himself pays for creating us thus. **When a child lies suffering from an incurable illness and his parents stand beside him in grief, do we think that God suffers any less than the child or his parents? Yet God has decided that having creatures with free will is worth the price of suffering, even the suffering of sacrificing his own Son on the cross.** If we cannot penetrate the mystery of a particular experience of suffering, at least we can appreciate the fact that God is suffering with us and in his wisdom and goodness has judged the final result to be worth it.

The second thing to remember is that God has promised that all things will work together for good to those who love him and are called in accordance with his purpose (Rom 8:28). Thus even the suffering which he permits can be used for the benefit of those who experience it or for the benefit of those whose lives are touched by it. See Rom 5:3-4; 2 Cor 1:3-6; Jas 1:2-4.

This may be one reason why God does not always answer our prayers for protection and deliverance from evil. Sometimes he does protect and deliver us, of course; so we should never fail to pray for God's special providence in these matters. But sometimes he does not intervene; rather he allows the affliction to occur or to continue. **In these cases we must trust that the wisdom of God has discerned a higher good that will come from the affliction.** Perhaps we ourselves will observe or experience this higher good;

perhaps it will take place without our ever being aware of it. **After all, God sees the whole pattern of providence while we see only small parts of it, often just the darker parts. In such cases there is no alternative to trusting and goodness and wisdom of the Sovereign Ruler of the universe.**" (Jack Cottrell, "The Faith Once for All", Chapter 12, College Press. Used by permission.)

Corruption resulting from rebellion brought on condemnation = the Cosmic Curse!

I want to finish this section on The Problem of Evil with a quotation from an astute reviewer and my personal friend, D. Lloyd Thomas (who has a whole string of degrees after his name). R.D.

"Satan walks to and fro throughout nature to see whom he may devour. He goes before the throne of God to challenge the restrictions God has placed on him, and tries to gain permission to torment individuals. God allows this to show the faithfulness of individuals (ref Job). God does not, however, necessarily tell the individual what is going on nor why it is permitted. The torment is just as real, and just as undesirable, and may result in Satan winning the battle/war when the individual turns his/her back on God through a lack of faith."

"Meaninglessness does not come from being weary of pain – it comes from being weary of pleasure."

~ Ravi Zacharias

THE PROPAGANDA ABOUT "THE POPULATION BOMB" BOMBED

"U.S. 'overpopulation' a fraud for political ends an excuse for abortion and other social causes"

By Norm Fox

"The Centers for Disease Control in the United States have issued a statistical update that adds to the evidence against alleged 'overpopulation' trends and points instead to a looming underpopulation crisis. The population Research Institute (PRI), meanwhile, continues its studies on the over-urbanization of America which is not the same as overpopulation.

Promoters of abortion-on-demand, or course, have the most to gain from convincing the public that a growing population will lead to food shortages and general poverty as too many people compete for too few resources. But the nationalized health care law was sold to the public on a similar argument, that as 'population soars,' people will become less capable of providing for their own medical needs and will need government assistance. End-of-life medical care and the committees called 'death panels' by the critics also connect with alleged overpopulation.

CDC's 2011 statistics confirm that the U.S. birth rate has fallen sharply below the population replacement rate of 2.1 live births per woman and is now 1.9. LifeNews.com calls this 'not a baby boom but a birth dearth.' The number of babies born in the nation plummeted by 10% between 2007 and 2011. Economically this portends a generational problem, especially in a nation that has committed itself to the socialist model of 'entitlements' for the elderly paid for by a strong population base of younger citizens. The numbers also show that over 40% of births in 2011 were to unmarried women, up from 18% in 1980 which likely forecasts fewer of the next generation being contributors and more being receivers of entitlement funds.

PRI says that worldwide, half the global population has

moved from country to city creating an appearance of overpopulation while actually translating into fewer food producers per capita. Their website, at overpopulationisamyth.com, provides scientific information on this premise as well as a series of simple videos that make the subject understandable and entertaining." (*The Times and the Scriptures*, Weekly Bulletin for December 16, 2012)

(Note: I have used many pertinent quotations from other authors to set the stage for my major points in this chapter.) R.D.

"All those who Hate Me Love Death!" Proverbs 8:36

Do you realize:

1.   That so-called "hate crimes" (usually the fact that some Christian called homosexuality a sin) are splashed all over our news media in America while real hate crimes – the brutal persecution of millions of Christians – and the brutal murder of thousands of them in Islamic, Hindu, Buddhist and Communist regions of our world are shunned and ignored by the established media sources? Why?

2.   That the promotion of "comprehensive sex education" in our public schools funded by our government produces **far more** pregnancies and abortions than no sex education? That the most effective sex education courses are abstinence courses – positively proven by Uganda – yet our government shuns and down-plays abstinence education and gives millions of dollars to Planned Parenthood – the biggest baby killer in America? Why?

> I can personally testify that the Biblical abstinence education I learned from my home town conservative Christian Church (now Life Bridge Church in Longmont, CO) had a potent, positive effect in my life as a teen.

3.   That some so called "ethics professors" are now promoting "after birth abortion" – the right to kill your baby for a few months after it's born if you decide you don't want it?

4.   That PETA (People for the Ethical Treatment of Animals) promotes abortion while campaigning for protecting all forms of animal life? In other words, "Save the whales (or snails, owls, etc.) – but kill the babies!" Why?

5.   That the average life expectancy of a practicing homosexual is 42 years – yet the normal age of death in the US is 75? Yet homosexuality is being relentlessly advertized through Hollywood, promoted in government and business "diversity" seminars (often mandatory), and being upheld in court decisions as normal and healthy behavior. Why?

6.   That physician assisted suicide laws (so called death with dignity) have produced a rash of even more suicides in Oregon – yet they are still being promoted. Why?

7.   That Ted Turner (and other media moguls) promotes a **reduction** of world population to no more than a half billion? That means wiping out approximately six and a half billion people from the face of the earth!!! Why?

8.   That overpopulation is the rallying cry for reducing world population – yet the entire population of the world could stand in the area covered by Jacksonville, Florida, and suburbs. (There are vast unpopulated areas in our own USA – and other areas of our world. So if it's too crowded where you are – MOVE!)

9.   That some of the most popular symbols and tattoos in our rock music culture are death symbols (like the skull and crossbones). Why?

10.   That these facts are usually ignored in major media sources but easily verifiable through statistics available through Family Talk (drjamesdobson.org), Focus on the Family (focusonthefamily.com), Break Point (breakpoint.org), American Family Association (americanfamilyassociation.com), Alliance Defending Freedom (alliancedefendingfreedom.org), and *The Times and the Scriptures* (www.timesandscriptures.com).

What is the Basic Cause?

What is behind all of this emphasis on death? Our corrupt culture has rejected Almighty God and His truth and adopted a philosophy of death. Evolutionism is a philosophy in which deep time and death become the heroes of the story! (See "Catastrophic Consequences of Evolution" – Chapter 3 in my book, *Ready to Give an Answer*). Witchcraft and vampires are now being glorified in books and movies. Why? Why is it that God's Word and prayer have been banned from so many schools (including ball games and graduation ceremonies) while Paganism, Hinduism, Islam, Witchcraft and vampires are "in"? Because wisdom personified in Proverbs says, *"But he who sins against me wrongs his own soul; All those who hate me love death."' Proverbs 8:36.* Isn't it ironic that those who reject the wisdom of God because they don't want Him controlling their lives end up falling for almost anything? They often fall into the death traps of addictions, parapsychology (occultism) and other humanistic (atheistic) philosophies that glorify death rather than glorifying God. It's true that those who reject God will fall for something sinister and perverse. Why? **Because they have rejected the wisdom of God and therefore fall for the lies of Satan.**

What are We Celebrating at Halloween?

It seems that Halloween is almost more important to Americans than Christmas, in recent years. It definitely gets more advertising than Thanksgiving. I wonder what the secular humanists are going to do when they realize that the word really means hallowed eve. Probably nothing as long as God Himself is not the one being hallowed (honored). Has it occurred to you that Halloween is not a hallowed eve – except for Satanists and witches covens – it's their high Sabbath? Hasn't Halloween degenerated into a celebration of death? What are the decorations we see – some starting in September? Witches. Goblins. Black cats. Skeletons. Skulls and crossbones. Jack-o-lanterns. Spiders and spider webs. Ghosts. What do they symbolize?

Once in Ukraine, when I was invited to speak in a school for their English classes during October, the teacher asked me to speak about Halloween. They were studying American holidays, and wanted me to tell them my perspective as an American. They had the classroom decked out like American classrooms in October. It was one of my most difficult assignments, because I like to bring something positive and uplifting in my lessons. I did tell the students that I agree with many churches in America that have harvest parties to celebrate the goodness of God in bringing the harvest. Let's celebrate the Hallowed One and His Harvest – not Halloween! Too many are celebrating death and devious doctrines of demons already!

Would you like a couple of suggestions about how to make a positive impact for Christ out of a negative influence holiday?

1.   How about changing how we greet people to "Happy Harvest Eve" instead of "Happy Halloween"?

2.   How about turning the Trick or Treat tradition into an opportunity for sharing truth by giving illustrated Christian booklets and a church invitation along with the candy? My favorite two of these booklets are:

> a. "Big Daddy" available from Chick Publications, Phone: 909-987-0771 - www.chick.com
>
> b. "The Atheist Test" available from Living Waters Publications, Phone 562-920-8431 www.livingwaters.com

"The thief does not come except to steal, and to kill, and to destroy. I have come that they may have life, and that they may have it more abundantly." John 10:10 Let's celebrate life!

Think about it – in a nation founded predominantly by Christian believers on Biblical principles there has been one lawsuit after another by bitter God-haters like Madelyn Murray O'Hare and Michael Newdow to undermine and destroy those foundations. This concerted effort by atheists to destroy the foundations like Bible reading and prayer in schools has been highly effective. Schools were originally started in this nation by believers to teach their children to read the Scriptures.

Do You Know?

Do you know that the Ivy League colleges and universities in America (Yale, Harvard, Princeton, etc.) were founded by Bible believers to train ministers of the gospel? Consider these standards for graduation from Harvard in the early years. The laws of President Dunster of Harvard, adopted in 1642, indicate the scope of the first college curriculum in America. The opening of the document is as follows: *"Every scholar that on proof is found able to translate the original of the Old and New Testament into the Latin tongue, and shall be imbued with the beginnings of natural and moral philosophy, withal being of honest life and conversation . . . may be invested with his first degree."* How many would graduate now if those were still the standards? Probably not one! Zero! Why? Because now these same colleges and universities have been infiltrated by those who hate God and mock His Word.

In spite of the fact that the "Mayflower Compact" was the covenant document of a Christian congregation which began with the words, "In the Name of God, Amen!", and the fact that the "Mayflower Compact" was the basic foundation for our national constitution, Michael Newdow and other atheists repeatedly bring lawsuits to delete "Under God" from our "Pledge of Allegiance" and strike out "In God We Trust" as our national motto. Why should we pay attention to atheists? Do you realize that an atheist cannot by any stretch of imagination be a loyal American? Why not? Because our "Declaration of Independence" is even more basic to our existence as a nation than our "Constitution." It preceded the

"Constitution"! Within the first few sentences of our "Declaration of Independence" are these powerful words: *"We hold these truths to be self-evident, that all men are created equal, that they are **endowed by their Creator** with certain unalienable Rights, that among these are Life, Liberty and the pursuit of Happiness."* An atheist is one who denies that we have a Creator; therefore he denies the source of our unalienable rights. **Do you know that an atheist is a traitor to the most basic, foundational principle of the American nation – that our rights come from God – not from government?** Michael Newdow, if you don't like the fact that America was founded upon God and His Word, why don't you move to communist China or North Korea? You probably wouldn't like it there – but you are trying to pull America down to their style of government – where an individual has no rights except that which the government allows him to have.

Do you know that Roger Baldwin, the founder of the ACLU was a communist? (You can also check the documentation for this in the resources I gave earlier). The ACLU is one of several organizations (like Freedom from Religion Foundation) which encourage atheist lawsuits, but the ACLU is the biggest and most powerful. The ACLU is supposed to mean American Civil Liberties Union, but would be more accurately described as the American Communist Legal Union or Anti Christian Liars Union. Did you know that the Scopes Trial in Dayton, Tennessee in 1925 was planned and orchestrated by the ACLU to open the door for the teaching of evolutionism in America's public schools? Do you know that macro-evolution (Darwinism) is a basic doctrine of the religion of Humanism? Yes, humanism (a cloak name for atheism) has been recognized by our US Supreme Court as a religion! The religion of Humanism is now deeply entrenched in our public schools – and it doesn't like competition from those who contradict its doctrines. Do you know Humanism is in – Christianity is out? Humanists like to use the false cloak that "evolutionism is science and creationism is religion." **No! That is a false premise. They are both religious – both are belief systems.** No human being was there to see what happened "in the beginning" – but God inspired Moses to tell what happened. **They are opposite and opposing worldviews.** Humanism teaches that "man is the measure of all things"; Creation teaches that God is the measure of all things. Humanism teaches that in the beginning there was nothing – but then it exploded and became everything – with no design (because there was no Designer) – no purpose – no meaning – no hope – and no moral standards outside of the ones we make up for ourselves and call values. We send our American kids into this indoctrination, into humanism and then wonder why depression, immorality, homosexuality, and suicide rates among teens have skyrocketed over the past fifty years. **Isn't it time to wake up?** (For careful documentation of the planned infiltration of our school system with humanism by Horace Mann and John Dewey, see the books by Samuel Blumenfeld, *Is Public Education Necessary?* and *N.E.A.: Trojan Horse in American Education*, and the DVD documentary, "Indoctrination" by Colin Gunn.

The Hope

Do you know that at the time of Brezhnev's death he was probably the most prominent atheist in the world – yet when his wife leaned over the casket to give him her final farewell kiss those standing nearby saw her put the sign of the cross on his chest? Why would she do that? **Because in that final desperate moment of truth she couldn't help but realize that atheism (humanism) has no hope. She realized that Jesus Christ is The Hope of this world and she demonstrated that with the universal symbol of Christianity – the cross.**

Following World War II, when Billy Graham was still a young evangelist, he was invited to meet with Konrad Adenhauer. Adenhauer stood looking out over the devastation of the city of Berlin, then turned to Billy and asked, "Mr. Graham, do you truly believe that Jesus Christ arose from the dead?" Billy paused just a brief moment, and then replied, "Mr. Adenhauer, if I did not believe that Jesus rose from the dead, I would have nothing to preach!" Mr.

Adenhauer nodded, then turning back to look out the window he said, **"If Jesus Christ did not arise from the dead, I see no hope for mankind!"**

The Apostle Paul wrote: *"And if Christ is not risen, your faith is futile; you are still in your sins! Then also those who have fallen asleep in Christ have perished. If in this life only we have hope in Christ, we are of all men the most pitiable. But now Christ is risen from the dead, and has become the firstfruits of those who have fallen asleep." 1 Corinthians 15:17-20* In his purpose statement to the Colossians, Paul wrote, *". . .Christ in you, the hope of glory. Him we preach, warning every man and teaching every man in all wisdom, that we may present every man perfect in Christ Jesus. To this end I also labor, striving according to His working which works in me mightily." Colossians 1:27-29*

The Major Theme

Now that we have briefly viewed the contrast between Christianity and Humanism, let's come back to our major theme for this chapter, "All Those Who Hate Me Love Death" and look at this statement in its context. The book of Proverbs is a book of contrasts, such as good versus evil, obedience versus disobedience – but especially wisdom versus foolishness. In chapter 7 a foolish man is portrayed who falls into the trap of an adulteress (a crafty harlot) and is led into destruction, but in chapter 8, wisdom is personified and portrayed as a woman crying out from a high hill for people to listen, forsake their foolishness, and choose wisdom. Please carefully consider these pertinent excerpts: *"**I, wisdom, dwell with prudence, and find out knowledge and discretion.** The fear of the LORD IS TO HATE EVIL; Pride and arrogance and the evil way and the perverse mouth I hate. Counsel is mine, and sound wisdom; I am understanding, I have strength. By me kings reign, and rulers decree justice. By me princes rule, and nobles, all the judges of the earth. **I love those who love me, and those who seek me diligently will find me.** Riches and honor are with me, enduring riches* *and righteousness . . . Now therefore, listen to me, my children, for blessed are those who keep my ways. Hear instruction and be wise, and do not disdain it.* **Blessed is the man who listens to me,** *watching daily at my gates, waiting at the posts of my doors.* **For whoever finds me finds life, and obtains favor from the LORD; but he who sins against me wrongs his own soul; all those who hate me love death."** Proverbs 8:12-18, 32-36

What Happens to a Society that Rejects God?

Now let's move to the first chapter of Romans and look at what happens to a society that rejects the wisdom of God and chooses the foolishness of worldly "wisdom". Paul wrote: *"I am a debtor both to Greeks and to barbarians, both to wise and to unwise. So, as much as is in me, I am ready to preach the gospel to you who are in Rome also. For I am not ashamed of the gospel of Christ, for it is the power of God to salvation for everyone who believes, for the Jew first and also for the Greek. For in it the righteousness of God is revealed from faith to faith; as it is written, 'The just shall live by faith.' For the wrath of God is revealed from heaven against all ungodliness and unrighteousness of men, who suppress the truth in unrighteousness, because what may be known of God is manifest in them, for God has shown it to them. For since the creation of the world His invisible attributes are clearly seen, being understood by the things that are made, even His eternal power and Godhead, so that they are without excuse, because, although they knew God, they did not glorify Him as God, nor were thankful, but became futile in their thoughts, and their foolish hearts were darkened. Professing to be wise, they became fools, and changed the glory of the incorruptible God into an image made like corruptible man—and birds and four-footed animals and creeping things. Therefore God also gave them up to uncleanness, in the lusts of their hearts, to dishonor their bodies among themselves, who exchanged the truth of God for the lie, and worshiped and served the creature rather than the Creator, who is blessed forever. Amen. For this reason God gave them up to vile passions. For even their women exchanged the natural use for what is against nature. Likewise also the men, leaving the natural use of the woman, burned in their lust for one another, men with men committing what is shameful, and receiving in themselves the penalty of their error which was due. And even as they did not like to retain God in their knowledge, God gave them over to a debased mind, to do those things which are not fitting; being filled with all unrighteousness, sexual immorality, wickedness, covetousness, maliciousness; full of envy, murder, strife, deceit, evil-mindedness; they are whisperers, backbiters, haters of God, violent, proud, boasters, inventors of evil things, disobedient to parents, undiscerning, untrustworthy, unloving, unforgiving, unmerciful; who, knowing the righteous judgment of God, that those who practice such things are deserving of death, not only do the same but also approve of those who practice them." Romans 1:14-32* (Note that the very things God condemns have become the themes of many talk shows and Hollywood movies.)

The Heart of the Problem

is the Problem of the Heart

When God is spurned and His Word is banned from a society, calloused hearts and seared consciences become the rule rather than the exception. In our travels, my wife, Della and I have visited three of the Nazi concentration death camps – Dachau and Buchenwald, Germany and Salaspils, Latvia. There is a blood chilling presence of evil in those places that punctuates the pertinence of God's truth that "the heart is deceitful above all other things, and desperately wicked – who can know it?" Jeremiah 17:9. Dostoyevsky was absolutely right when he wrote that if there were no God – anything would be permissible. How else can we explain how Nazi doctors could perform horrible experiments on Jewish men, women and children (as well as others they considered sub-human), then go to their homes and families and attend Wagner concerts as though performing a normal days' work? Seared consciences! Calloused hearts! Corrupt minds! **Where there are no absolutes from God, Satan becomes absolute master!!!** No wonder these camps were called "when hell was in session!"

Perilous Times

I hope you read these passages carefully and prayerfully. Here is one more – a very sobering passage which Paul wrote to his younger coworker, Timothy, who was like a son to him. These words were penned shortly before Paul was executed – he was sharing what were the deepest concerns of his heart. *"But know this, that in the last days perilous times will come: For men will be lovers of themselves, lovers of money, boasters, proud, blasphemers, disobedient to parents, unthankful, unholy, unloving, unforgiving, slanderers, without self-control, brutal, despisers of good, traitors, headstrong, haughty, lovers of pleasure rather than lovers of God, having a form of godliness but denying its power. And from such people turn away!"*   *2 Timothy 3:1-5 (NKJV)*

As you have considered these sobering passages of Scripture, do you see more clearly what is happening to our beloved country of America? To our own families? To the majority of American children who have been brainwashed by the corruption all around us?

Humanistic Psychology

On a broadcast recently, I heard Ravi Zacharias share a poem that went something like this:

At the age of three I was mocked by my brothers
So in retaliation – I poisoned all my lovers!
A class in psychology taught me how to justify my assault:
So everything I do that's wrong is someone else's fault!

Such humanistic psychology is really nothing new – it actually started in the Garden of Eden. I once heard Zig Ziglar summarize the story from Genesis 3 this way (approximately):

When God confronted Adam for his sin, he blamed Eve – and God Himself. "**Lord**, that **woman You** gave me – **she** gave me the forbidden fruit." When God confronted Eve, she blamed the serpent. When God confronted the serpent – he didn't have a leg to stand on!!!

When you read Genesis 3, don't miss the fact that God pronounced the curse of judgment on the serpent (as Satan's instrument), then on Eve (and all her female descendants), then on Adam – and through him on all humanity because he was the corporate head of the human family. Not one escaped responsibility. Excuses do **not** work with God.

Liberal Philosophy

The stark reality of the "liberal" philosophy is that there is often more sympathy for the perpetrator of a crime than for the victim. The net result is that capital punishment for capital crimes has almost disappeared – with a few rare exceptions. Please consider the duration of the covenant God made with Noah after the flood. Also, please note that the rainbow is God's symbol (sign of the covenant). **"Gay rights" activists have stolen and perverted God's symbol! We need to recapture it for God's intended purpose!**

"So God blessed Noah and his sons, and said to them: 'Be fruitful and multiply, and fill the earth. And the fear of you and the dread of you shall be on every beast of the earth, on every bird of the air, on all that move on the earth, and on all the fish of the sea. They are given into your hand. Every moving thing that lives shall be food for you. I have given you all things, even as the green herbs. But you shall not eat flesh with its life, that is, its blood. Surely for your lifeblood I will demand a reckoning; from the hand of every beast I will require it, and from the hand of man. From the hand of every man's brother I will require the life of man. Whoever sheds man's blood, By man his blood shall be shed;

For in the image of God He made man. And as for you, be fruitful and multiply; Bring forth abundantly in the earth And multiply in it.' Then God spoke to Noah and to his sons with him, saying: 'And as for Me, behold, I establish My covenant with you and with your descendants after you, and with every living creature that is with you: the birds, the cattle, and every beast of the earth with you, of all that go out of the ark, every beast of the earth. Thus I establish My covenant with you: Never again shall all flesh be cut off by the waters of the flood; never again shall there be a flood to destroy the earth.' And God said: 'This is the sign of the covenant which I make between Me and you, and every living creature that is with you, for perpetual generations: I set My rainbow in the cloud, and it shall be for the sign of the covenant between Me and the earth. It shall be, when I bring a cloud over the earth, that the rainbow shall be seen in the cloud; and I will remember My covenant which is between Me and you and every living creature of all flesh; the waters shall never again become a flood to destroy all flesh. The rainbow shall be in the cloud, and I will look on it to remember the everlasting covenant between God and every living creature of all flesh that is on the earth.' And God said to Noah, 'This is the sign of the covenant which I have established between Me and all flesh that is on the earth.' Genesis 9:1-17.

"God Keeps His Promise"

By Jeff Vines

"I do not have an answer for why God allows so much pain into some people's lives. What I do know is that whatever God calls us to endure, he assumes the responsibility to equip us to endure it (1 Corinthians 10:13; 2 Corinthians 12:9). God will give you exactly what you need in every circumstance, if you run to Him.

But sometimes what you need is endurance, courage, or faith – not the absence of hunger or need. **A greater purpose, an eternal one, is at stake.** God may have orchestrated your season of scarcity for purposes greater than yourself. God's kingdom may be glorified through your times of want. Even Paul said that he had learned to be content 'in plenty or in want' (Philippians 4:12). There were seasons in Paul's life when, despite much prayer, his physical needs remained unmet. And yet he discovered contentment. In other words, God gave him what he truly needed – the strength to endure those times and the peace that would, even in the darkest moments, keep him from despair.

In some unseen way God will use our unmet need to glorify himself and expand his kingdom here on the earth. That's the real promise! God works everything together for good (Romans 8:28).

Martyred missionary Jim Elliot once said, 'He is no fool who gives what he cannot keep to gain that which he cannot lose.' For the authentic follower of Jesus Christ, giving up what he cannot keep in order to gain what he cannot lose becomes commonplace. Life is the greatest need of all; yet some are asked to give it up. Though we all die, because of Christ we will live again; and the life we now have doesn't even compare with the life that shall be. **God will ultimately give us all that we need. You can count on it!**

My friend Ajai Lall lives in India and leads pastors who are turning the world 'right side up' with the gospel. He brought me to tears as he described the faith and commitment of his young preachers Each new day brings the threat of death: they are torched, beaten with iron rods, dipped in hydrochloric acid, raped, and tortured...on a daily basis! **Yet their request to the American church is not for prayer that the persecution will end, but for prayers that these pastors will be brave and courageous enough to endure it – because that is how the kingdom grows. They are praying that God will give them what they need – courage.**

God is granting their request. Those pastors are relentless in the face of danger. Why? Because they live for a purpose greater than themselves and truly believe that whatever they give up in this life, God will more than make up for in the next. **The most important thing in the here and now is that the kingdom of God is expanded on the earth through their lives.**

Perhaps Corrie Ten Boom said it better than anyone else. During their horrific experience in the concentration camps of the

Third Reich, she and her sister learned: 'There is **no pit so deep that God's love is not deeper still.**' Even in our darkest hour we must never despair. God says that he will always give us what we truly need. And that's a promise." (Jeff Vines, "Unbroken – 8 Enduring Promises God will Keep". Used by permission.)

Here is the Promise

"And we know that all things work together for good to those who love God, to those who are the called according to His purpose. For whom He foreknew, He also predestined to be conformed to the image of His Son, that He might be the firstborn among many brethren." Romans 8:28-29

PERSONAL TESTIMONY

How God has Given us Beauty for Ashes

(A Recent Letter to Dr. James Dobson)

Dear Dr. Dobson,

I feel like we know you personally. Why? Because in the 1970's, when we were missionaries in Germany (Alpine Christian Mission) we were uplifted and inspired continually by Earl Lee's messages (through cassette tapes) and yours, because he interviewed you and shared some of your messages. In 1977 we returned to Boise where I served as missions' professor at Boise Bible College and we started listening to your radio broadcasts on KBGN. (Isn't 1977 when you started Focus on the Family?) I also feel like we know you personally because you interviewed two personal friends of ours on Focus on the Family – Bill Putman and Donnalee Velvick.

You see, in 1980 we moved to Nampa to help out with a new church that Bill Putman was planting and Della became his church secretary. Angela, who later said to Bill, "Daddy, I'm pregnant" at age 15 in New Plymouth, was one of my Sunday school students when they were in Nampa. (She was a really sweet, compliant young girl – I called her Angel. Do you know that she is now married to a pastor in California?) Donnalee, founder of Hope House, was a member of the church Bill planted. Hope House has grown a lot and I often speak at Hope Chapel on their big campus, where her son-in-law, Keith Croft, is pastor and also house dad for one of the houses of kids.

We relate to those you have interviewed with great struggles and heartaches. Thank you for sharing their inspiring stories of triumphant faith. Troubles often come in bunches like bananas, but we shouldn't be surprised because Jesus warned us in John 16:33 – "In this world you will have tribulation, but be of good cheer, I have overcome the world."

Our heaviest series of troubles came in 1989 - '90:

January '89 – My mother died in Longmont, Colorado (my home town) and we had blizzard conditions for travel.

February '89 – Our daughter, Sandy, got married and we had the empty nest heartache to deal with.

March '89 – My older brother called from California heartbroken that his wife left him and was quote: "shacking up with a worse drunk than I ever was." This came after he quit drinking to please her.

May '89 – Our first granddaughter, Rachel, was born severely handicapped – Trisomy 18. The doctor callously told our son, Randy, that she probably wouldn't live more than six months – then walked out leaving Randy to tell his wife, Patti, the tragic news. (Rachel actually lived ten years – but Randy and Patti's marriage deteriorated and fell apart under the strain.)

May '89 – While Della was in Florida to help Randy and Patti with the baby I totaled our son-in-law's motorcycle and landed spread eagle on the pavement.

June '89 – My co-worker in our literature ministry, Kendall Bauer, died. He was my fishing friend and had become like another father to me.

October '89 – My older brother, Don, was heartbroken that his wife had spurned his efforts to win her back and their divorce was final.

December '89 – Don's house burned and the fire was started by his grandson (on his ex-wife's side).

January '90 – Don's son committed suicide by hanging himself in his closet. No one in the family knew that he had gotten hooked on crack cocaine. I flew down to California to spend a week with Don and invited him to come live with us.

January '90 – Our church died and I got blamed for it. It was like another death in the family. This was Nampa Valley Christian Church – the congregation that Bill Putman planted. After two years Bill moved to New Plymouth to plant another new congregation in nearby Ontario, Oregon. Sam Harsin became our preaching minister, but he and his family left in 1988 – very discouraged because of those who had undermined his ministry and caused strife. I was serving as an elder and working a full time job besides, but took on the preaching ministry part time. I did not have the leadership ability to get it turned around, so after consulting with other leaders – including Bill Putman, Gary Strubhar, and Steve Holsinger – we decided we had to disband rather than going deeper and deeper in debt. Steve Holsinger, who had taken Bill Putman's place as director of Intermountain Church Planters Association, told me, "Rick, it isn't fair, but you are getting blamed – even though you and Della stuck it out while so many others were leaving the church like rats off a sinking ship."
Summer '90 – I personally learned the truth of Steve's words by the rejection I experienced at our sister congregation where we transferred. The chairman of the elders asked me on one occasion,

"Why don't you just forget about being an evangelist?" He may as well have asked me, "Why don't you just forget about breathing?" Later he told me, 'I don't want anything Rick Deighton has to offer!" (Several years later, after we had moved away, he apologized to me on the phone.)

Summer '90 – The toughest confrontation of my life was with my older brother. Don accepted my invitation to come to Nampa to live with us, but returned to his drinking. One evening when I came home from an evangelistic Bible study with a couple, Della told me that Don came home drunk and was acting strange. She was afraid of him, so I realized what I had to do. The next morning I told him Della had been afraid of him when he was drunk and that I could not allow my wife to live in fear in our own home, therefore he had a choice. I told him that his addiction would continue to get progressively worse unless he got help – so he could either get the help to stop his drinking, or he would have to find another place to live. He was really angry at first, but later thanked me for forcing him to do what he realized he had to do.

Now here is the great news: God allowed all these heart-rending problems in our lives to move us through the doors He would open to the best and most productive ministry of our lives – Overseas Outreach. We love what God has led us into by our move to Gresham, Oregon. Our very good friends, Gary and Sandra Strubhar invited us to come to Gresham for me to serve as his associate minister. Gary told me, "You and Della need healing time. You might make it through another bad experience – but Della won't.' The music, led by Greg Strubhar (their son) and the messages were so healing, inspiring, and uplifting that the tears flowed freely – usually from Della, but sometimes from both of us. Gary would often ask Della, "Was that a four or a five hanky service?" From Gresham God began opening more and more doors to us – but that is another story.

Thank you again for your inspiring and challenging programming – and for taking time to read this epistle (I never intended it to be so long).

May Almighty God continue to multiply your godly influence in this nation and around the world.
Yours & His,
Rick

Note: I see Dr. James Dobson as a hero and courageous champion for Christian social values, but I don't agree with him on some important issues, even as he does not agree with some of my strongly held convictions. Therefore, I believe it may be wise and appropriate to point out that Almighty God reserves the right to use people who disagree with me. He also reserves the right to use people who disagree with you. We are both fallible human beings with limited understanding and perspectives. Only God and His Word are infallible.

So if you read something you disagree with in this chapter, please forgive me, be patient, and keep reading. If you are inclined to write to me about your concerns, please do. You will find contact information at the end of the book. **If we are patient and forgiving we can use the "iron sharpens iron" principle and learn from each other.**

"God does not comfort us to make us comfortable but to make us comforters." ~ Billy Graham

"Blessed be the God and Father of our Lord Jesus Christ, the Father of mercies and God of all comfort, who comforts us in all our tribulation, that we may be able to comfort those who are in any trouble, with the comfort with which we ourselves are comforted by God." 2 Corinthians 1:3-4

The Triangle of Triumph

In early October of 2001, I flew to Germany first, on my way to Ukraine for the second time. In May, I had been a presenter for my first time at the Man and the Christian Worldview Symposium, and

I was returning for the Man and the Christian Worldview Conference. This was only about three weeks after the terrible 9/11 attacks in America and shortly after air travel began to function again. While in Germany, I got emails from Della telling me that my sister, Elinor's husband died and Reggie and Esther Thomas' son had committed suicide. Reggie is the founder of White Fields Overseas Evangelism and the evangelist who had invited me to become an associate evangelist. While at the airport, I saw the TV news report about a flight of Russian Jews from Israel who were on their way to Russia to visit their relatives when their plane went down in the Black Sea. I don't think there were any survivors. The camera showed close-up pictures of the grieving relatives' anguished expressions. To top off the flood of bad news reports, I opened a newspaper at an airport and read about one husband in Liverpool, England who murdered his own wife and another in Munich, Germany who had also committed such an atrocity. The thought occurred to me that if I focused on the flood of bad news, I would be functioning under such a cloud of doom and gloom that I would be of no positive benefit to anyone on this mission trip. I decided to intentionally change my focus to be able to minister to others and myself. I remembered that Peter's message to scattered believers who were suffering from intense persecution was about "**joy indescribable and full of glory**". "*In this you greatly rejoice, though now for a little while, if need be, you have been grieved by various trials, that the genuineness of your faith, being much more precious than gold that perishes, though it is tested by fire, may be found to praise, honor, and glory at the revelation of Jesus Christ, whom having not seen you love. Though now you do not see Him, **yet believing, you rejoice with joy inexpressible and full of glory, receiving the end of your faith—the salvation of your souls.**"* 1 Peter 1:6-9

This is the background into which God intervened to give me the idea for developing my signature sermon, 'The Triangle of Triumph." The text is 1 Thessalonians 5:16-18. "*Rejoice always, pray without ceasing, in everything give thanks; for this is the will of God in Christ Jesus for you.*"

The diagram (which is my outline) looks like this:

Rejoice Always   Pray without ceasing

In everything give thanks; for this is
the will of God in Christ Jesus for you.

DO YOU CONTROL YOUR EMOTIONS – OR DO YOUR EMOTIONS CONTROL YOU?

Do you recognize that it is much easier to act yourself into feeling better than to feel yourself into acting better??? Are you functioning and flourishing by faith, or floating and floundering by feelings???

It is essential to a victorious Christian life to remember that emotions are a wonderful servant, but a terrible master. We only have one Master!!! Live your life to the audience of One! The decision to rejoice is your choice!

"This is the day that the Lord has made; we will rejoice and be glad in it." Psalm 118:24

The Necessity of Personal Application

I shared this message at a church in Germany on the following Sunday, then on Monday flew to Ukraine for the conference. Once again I was staying as a guest in the home of Sergei and Olga Golovin in Simferopol, the capital city of Crimea (the southern peninsula of Ukraine). I was scheduled for some pre-conference lectures in universities and institutes in the area for a few days before the conference, and again (at my request), Vlad Devakov would be my interpreter. Tuesday a.m. was my first speaking appointment, and Vlad came to Sergei's home to meet me. As we were planning for a taxi, Vlad mentioned that the institute where we were scheduled was only a 15 or 20 minute walk from Sergei's home, so I said, "Let's walk!" I was excited to see Vlad again, so in my joy of conversing with him, I did a foolish thing – I kept looking at Vlad instead of watching where I was walking. There was a missing bar in a grate over a drain in the street and I stepped where that bar should have been. Since I can't walk on water – or air – I went down hard! It scraped my shin and hurt like crazy, but didn't break my leg. Vlad helped me up and Sergei came running with two other co-workers. They helped me back to Sergei's home where Olga cleaned the wound, put on antiseptic and bandaged it. A few moments later as Vlad and I were riding in a taxi to the institute, my leg was still throbbing and I was thinking, "**Lord, is this a test?**" Wasn't it a bit ironic that two days before this, I had preached, "Rejoice always! Pray without ceasing! In everything give thanks!" I even remembered proclaiming, "This is the will of God for you!" I didn't feel like rejoicing. I didn't feel like praying. I didn't feel like giving thanks – but I had told the German Christians: "So what? Are we only going to obey God when we feel like it? Do you allow your children to disobey you because they don't feel like obeying you???" So I began to think about what I could give thanks for. At first, the only thing I could think of was that my leg wasn't broken, so I thanked God for that fact. (Later when I went back and looked at that grate, I felt deeply grateful because if I had fallen either a slight bit to the right or left my heel would likely have caught on another bar, and my fall would have snapped my leg below the knee.) After beginning the thanksgiving process, I remembered where we were going – a secular institute in a Russian speaking, formerly communist nation where I would have the privilege to share a Christian worldview message. This was the fulfillment of a deep dream on my heart for years! Praise God! Thank you, Lord! By the time we arrived at the institute a few minutes later, even though my leg was still hurting, my attitude was healed, my heart was rejoicing, and my spirit was soaring. **God gave me a test – and His Spirit within gave me the victory!** Remember, the same trial is both a test and a temptation. What is the difference? God wants you to pass! Satan wants you to fail! Even if you fail, remember that by grace we are saved and by grace we are sanctified. **Jesus paid for our sins to give us another chance – and another – and another. His Sprit and His grace turn the stumbling blocks of failures into the stepping stones of stunning successes!**

The Triangle of Triumph is the basis for victory upon victory through obedience to His Word. Learn to listen to the clear instructions of the Spirit through the Word. Obey Him for victory! Reject the subtle suggestions of Satan to submit to subjective feelings! "*Rejoice always! Pray without ceasing! In everything give thanks!; for this is the will of God in Christ Jesus for you.*" 1 Thessalonians 5:16-18

Our Strength!

"*The joy of the Lord is our strength!*" Nehemiah 8:10

Joy is even deeper than happiness. In the English language, the word "happiness" comes from the same root as the word "happenings." Our joy comes from our relationship with Almighty God as His beloved children – it does not depend on happenings. However, we should also note that when the word "blessed" is translated "happy," as in the Beatitudes, it is not dependent on happenings either. Perhaps "joyous" would be a more accurate synonym for "blessed".

Swedish Plaque
Shared joy is double joy!
Shared sorrow is half a sorrow!

What About You?

What about you? Do you choose to love the wisdom of God? Do you choose to love God Himself? To accept Jesus Christ as your Lord and Savior? He is the One who conquered death and offers hope. (If you want confirmation of these truths, please contact us and ask for *Is the Bible without Any Errors?* It's a booklet of about 60 pages and I will give it to you if you will read it. You may also request *Ready to Give an Answer.* Or you can read either of them online at www.overseasoutreach.com.)

I hope and pray that you will be one who chooses "The Fellowship of the Unashamed" and will say with Paul: *"For I am not ashamed of the gospel of Christ, for it is the power of God to salvation for everyone who believes, for the Jew first and also for the Greek." Romans 1:16*

Fellowship of the Unashamed

"I am part of the fellowship of the unashamed. I have Holy Spirit power. The die has been cast, I have stepped over the line. The decision has been made. I won't look back, let up, slow down, or back away. My past is redeemed. My present makes sense. My future is secure. I am finished and done with low living, sight walking, small planning, smooth knees, colorless dreams, tainted vision, mundane talking, cheap giving, and dwarf goals. I no longer need preeminence, prosperity, position, promotion, or popularity. I don't have to be first, I don't have to be right, I don't have to be recognized. I don't have to be praised, regarded or rewarded. I live by faith, lean on His presence, walk by patience, live by prayer and labor by power. My face is set, my gait is fast, my goal is heaven, my road is narrow, my way is rough, my companions are few, my mission is clear. I cannot be bought, compromised, detoured, lured

away, turned back, deluded or delayed. I will not flinch in the face of sacrifice, hesitate in the presence of the adversary, negotiate at the table of the enemy, ponder at the pool of popularity or meander in the maze of mediocrity. I won't give up, shut up, or let up, until I have stayed up, stored up, prayed up, paid up and preached for the cause of Christ. I must go 'til He comes, give 'til I drop, preach 'til all know, and work 'til He stops me. And when He comes for His own, He won't have any problem recognizing me."

~ Bob Moorehead.

The Commitment

Finally, I want to share this concise, clear, crisp quotation from the late Adrian Rogers:

"The church is not the servant of the state!

The church is not the master of the state!

The church is the conscience of the state!

We will be civil – but WE WILL NOT BE SILENT!!!"

The Bottom Line

Courage is not the absence of fear – it is conquering of fear!
"For God has not given us the spirit of fear, but of love and of power and of a sound mind." 2 Timothy 1:7.

WE ARE MORE THAN CONQUERORS.

WE WILL BE CIVIL - BUT

WE WILL NOT BE SILENT!!

QUESTIONS FOR CHAPTER 6

1.   After reading and pondering the article in the opening part of this chapter, how would you reply to the question, "Why did he kill all those children?"

2.   What is "the cosmic curse," and what difference does it make in our worldview and our perception of God?

3.   How would you answer the probing question, "If God is love and God is all powerful, why does He allow terrible evil and traumatic trials in our world, especially in our lives as believers?"

4.   What is the propaganda about "The Population Bomb"?

5.   Proverbs 8:36 says, "all those who hate me love death." Please explain who is speaking in this verse, and what relevance this has to our American culture in the 21st century.

6.   What are some of the evidences of the truth of Proverbs 8:36?

7.   What is behind all this emphasis on death?

8.   What is the only hope for mankind? Give your reasons for your answer.

9. What happens to a society that rejects God?

10. What is the Triangle of Triumph and what difference should it make in our lives?

Chapter 6: Why Are There School Shootings...

CHAPTER 7:

WHICH WAY, AMERICA?

Contemplation on Cultural Clashes

("Politically Correct" Radicalism Rejected and Refuted)

The apostle Paul was a Hebrew of the Hebrews with a passion for his own people, Israelites, yet Almighty God ordained and appointed him as apostle to the gentiles (nations). If you have read the New Testament Scriptures, especially in the book of Acts and in Romans chapter 9-11, you have probably noticed that he never lost his passion for the salvation of Israel. Consider his words recorded in Romans 9:1-4a: *"I tell the truth in Christ, I am not lying, my conscience also bearing me witness in the Holy Spirit, that I have great sorrow and continual grief in my heart. For I could wish that I myself were accursed from Christ for my brethren, my countrymen according to the flesh, who are Israelites, to whom pertain the adoption, the glory, the covenants, the giving of the law, the service of God, and the promises;"*

I am a bi-vocational missionary with a primary focus on the former Soviet Union nations, especially Ukraine, but I am an American and I do also have a passion for America. I do not claim to have the intensity or effectiveness of outreach that Paul had, but I do care deeply about reaching lost souls for Christ here in America. Perhaps even more, I long to help believers here at home as well as overseas become bold witnesses for Jesus. Then He transforms lives and cultures one heart at a time.

In this chapter I am sharing excerpts from issues of our Overseas Outreach prayer letters over the past few years. Since my heart aches for spiritual awakening here in America, I share these articles that pertain to being "More than Conquerors in Cultural Clashes".

July 2009

Dear Friends and Prayer Partners,

On Saturday, July 4th, we celebrated the 233rd anniversary of our Declaration of Independence for the United States of America. We had a great time with our family, enjoying a barbeque and games, and we are so thankful to have them living nearby, but we do have very deep concerns for their future – and the future of our nation. Last year at this time I wrote that we "thanked God for the freedom we still enjoy in America, and prayed for the multitudes of deluded souls who haven't a clue about the true liberty in Christ, the price Jesus paid for our liberty, nor the sacrifices made by our founding fathers (and mothers) to give us a nation built on Christian principles and the sacrifices being made still today by those defending our freedom. So with these emotions still surging in my soul, my first request is to pray for America." Please, please pray for America! The erosion of our freedoms just since last year is appalling!

The Surging Stream of Social Stupidity

(The "Warp" and "Woof" of it all)

Another good alternative title for this article would be "Whatever Became of Sin?" but this title was already used for an influential book by Dr. Karl Menninger, published in 1973. Unfortunately its influence was not strong enough to stop the surging stream of social stupidity. Now in America, as in ancient Israel, every man does that which is right in his own eyes. The results are just as chaotic. Christians need to follow the courageous example of Karl Menninger to expose and label sin "sin". This article is written to Christians to challenge us to arise from apathy to anger and from anger to action – appropriate action. May we become like the sons of Issachar, *"who understood the times and knew what Israel should do..." 1 Chronicles 12:32.*

Chapter 7: Which Way, America?

Does it also seem to you that we are surrounded with a strange, warped, perverted, degraded and distorted society now? Adultery is politely called "an affair"; sodomy is politely called "gay"; the murder of unwanted, unborn babies is called "choice" or "reproductive freedom" (in spite of the fact that, in most cases, the choice was already made to indulge in sexual promiscuity). If the child is unwanted, it is called a "blob of tissue"; if it is wanted, it is called a baby! Isn't that unjust discrimination? In the case of rape, the innocent baby is usually executed for the crime of his or her father – and the perpetrator may or may not be punished. Word manipulation is rampant! We are told by the "tolerant" liberals that we must be polite and "politically correct" instead of calling these crimes and atrocities by their true names – or we are guilty of "hate crimes" because we use "hate speech". Then the "tolerant" crowd rages intolerantly about our intolerance. Why don't the major media sources label the homosexual activists "intolerant" or "hateful" for calling Carrie Prajean filthy names verbally and in writing, threatening her, and discriminating against her for her viewpoint? What was her social blunder? She honestly answered a direct question from a blatant homosexual activist judge by saying that she believes marriage is between a man and a woman. This same judge (of the Miss America Pageant) called her filthy names on his blog and stated that if Carrie (Miss California) had won, he would have marched up on stage and snatched the crown from her head. (Of course, if she pushed him away or slapped him, she could be charged with a hate crime!) Ministers of the gospel in Sweden, Canada, and the U.S.A. have been jailed or falsely charged with hate speech for teaching that the Word of God labels homosexuality as an abomination, but I have not read about any homosexual activists being jailed for practicing sodomy (which is still a crime on the books of some states) or for practicing hate speech by sending death threats to the Christian leaders and other organizational leaders who promoted Proposition 8 (and similar marriage amendments in other states). How ironic! Have you read of any sodomites being charged with hate speech or hate crimes?

Why is it with the "politically correct" philosophy that killing babies is called "choice", but practicing sodomy is not a choice? Some say, "They can't help it—they were born that way. It's not a choice!" Friends, every human being is born with an instinctive urge to lie—but when we practice lying, it's because we choose to tell a lie! Those who choose to lie are liars. Those who choose to practice sodomy are sodomites. (By the way, do you know what's wrong with "politically correct"? It isn't! It's politically warped! It's morally bankrupt! It's intellectually stagnant!)

The claim that it is impossible for homosexuals to change is a glaring lie. Difficult, yes! Impossible, no! Thousand have repented, changed their habits, and left the homosexual lifestyle behind. I know some of them personally. The apostle Paul wrote to the Christians in Corinth: *"Or do you not know that the unrighteous shall not inherit the kingdom of God? Do not be deceived; neither fornicators, nor idolaters, nor adulterers, nor effeminate, nor homosexuals, nor thieves, nor the covetous, nor drunkards, nor revilers, nor swindlers, shall inherit the kingdom of God. And such were some of you….." 1 Corinthians 6:9-11 (NASV).* Yes, Jesus is the answer. He has the power to change us and transform us more and more into His image.

Wake Up to Reality!

When are we going to gain the guts to wake fellow Americans up to reality by calling sin by its proper name, instead of politely (cowardly) tiptoeing around the "politically correct" crowd using their own flowery terms? Let's get real! The evangelists whose sermons the Holy spirit used to strike conviction to the hearts of thousands during the "Great Awakening" did not tiptoe around the issues of their times – they called sin by its first name. Where is our courage? "For God has not given us the spirit of fear; but of power and of love, and of a sound mind." 2 Timothy 1:7. Let's bag the word manipulation and throw it in the trash can where it belongs! Friends, if you put whipped cream and strawberries on a cow pie and call it a pancake, you still have cow manure! I've heard that Abe Lincoln once said to a boy, "A dog normally has four legs, doesn't it?" "Yes." "What if we call his tail a leg – how many legs does he have?" "Five!" "No!" replied Lincoln. "The dog still has four legs and a tail. Calling his tail a leg does not change the facts!" "Woof! (We have already looked at the "warp").

On May 30, 2009, a man shot and killed an infamous abortion doctor, George Tiller. That man is a murderer because he acted as a vigilante, usurped authority, and committed a crime. Every major pro-life organization has denounced his action, yet some pro-abortion groups insist on labeling pro-life people as "dangerous", "terrorists" or "hate mongers". Why are they not exposed by major media sources and charged with distortion, discrimination and hate mongering? (Maybe because they are part of the "politically correct", "tolerant" crowd, do you think?) The pro-abortion crowd ignores the fact that George Tiller is guilty of murdering about 60,000 innocent babies in his clinic and causing suffering to so many women with his unsanitary and inhumane practice, while they extol him as though he were a hero. In reality he fits in the same category with the Nazi doctors of Hitler's Third Reich. To top it off, he served as an usher in his liberal Lutheran church. How ironic! How putrid! How sick our society! Pray for America!

What is Gay Marriage?

I grew up in Longmont, Colorado, on Pratt Street – and two blocks away was "Gay Street". One of the cutest girls in our eighth grade class was named "Gay". About 30 miles from our home in Nampa is "Gayway Junction" in Fruitland, Idaho. Our 1964 Webster's Dictionary defines "gay" as

"1. joyous and lively; merry; happy; light-hearted." Why have we allowed the homosexual activists to steal and distort this pleasant word? What a shame to read this word twisted from a synonym for joy into a synonym for sodomy! (However, if we go down to the fourth and last definition for gay, it says, "wanton, licentious: as a gay dog." Here, friends, is the "warp" and "woof" of the homosexual lifestyle.) This is reality.

So what is "gay marriage"? If we take the true, first meaning of the word "gay", it would be the happy union of one man with one woman in the legal bond of marital bliss. You can read about it in "The Song of Songs" in your Bible. It is the celebration of romantic, marital love with God's smile of approval. God never smiles on homosexuality. If you want to read about it, see Genesis 19 and Leviticus 18:22. "It is abomination." The penalty for both sodomy and adultery under Old Testament law was death by stoning. God is the Creator who "made them male and female". He invented sexuality, designed woman as man's helper, companion, and sexual partner in the marriage. Family is His creation, and He does not take it lightly when arrogant human beings botch up and ruin His design while trying to re-invent marriage and family to their own liking. *"Marriage is honorable among all, and the bed undefiled, but fornicators and adulterers God will judge." Hebrews 13:4.*

Throughout history, cultures around the world have recognized marriage and family as the first and most important unit of society. Centuries before Christ, the Greek philosopher Aristotle wrote, "In the first place there must be the union of those who cannot exist without other; namely of male and female…the first thing to arise is the family." Sodomy existed in their depraved culture, but at least they were not stupid enough to label it "marriage".

Some say, "Ignorance is bliss". Maybe that's why so many Americans sit in front of the TV set, laughing over sordid sitcoms that mock Christians and ridicule Biblical morality. They should be grieving and repenting.

According to political correctness, it is intolerant and terrible to discriminate against homosexuals, dark-skinned people, Muslims, witches and warlocks, but it is fine to mock Christians or light-skinned American males. By their standards it is also fine to discriminate against abstinence education (even though the only safe sex is abstinence until marriage and faithfulness in marriage), so most public schools and some private schools are promoting pornography and promiscuity. Often they become recruiting centers for homosexual activists in their comprehensive sex education programs. God said, *"Woe unto them who call evil good and good evil; that put darkness for light, and light for darkness; that put bitter for sweet, and sweet for bitter!" Isaiah 5:20 (KJV).*

Beyond Stupidity

A man who raped and sodomized a four-year-old girl was sentenced to only one year incarceration. Kent Hovind, a godly and effective creation evangelist, was sentenced to ten years in prison on distorted charges by the IRS, and yet this pedophile gets one year! That is outrageous! Asinine! Social stupidity run rampant! Pray for the criminal to repent! Pray for the judge to repent! Pray for Kent Hovind and his wife, Jo, to be released!

In America it is certainly social stupidity to allow atheists like Michael Newdow to determine policy. He, and other atheists, want to remove crosses, our national motto, "In God We Trust", and "under God" from our pledge of allegiance. They are making strong inroads, in spite of the fact that it is impossible for an atheist (humanist) to be a loyal American. Why? Because by denying that we have a Creator, he is rejecting the very basis of our unalienable rights. *"We hold these truths to be self-evident, that all men are created equal. That they are endowed by their Creator with certain unalienable rights, that among these are life, liberty and the pursuit of happiness."* Declaration of Independence, 1776. A few years later, in 1781, Thomas Jefferson wrote: *"God who gave us life gave us liberty. And can the liberties of a nation be thought secure when we have removed their only firm basis, a conviction in the minds of the people that these liberties are a gift of God? That they are not to be violated but with His wrath? Indeed, I tremble for my country when I reflect that God is just; that His justice cannot sleep forever."*

The Epitome of Stupidity

Perhaps the epitome of stupidity is seen in churches that are celebrating "The Year of Darwin", calling the science-fiction of evolutionism true science, teaching theistic evolution, and claiming that these polar-opposite faith systems are compatible. You could as easily freeze water on the surface of the sun as to logically harmonize the blatant contradictions between Biblical creationism and Darwinian evolutionism. To say, "I believe the Bible, but I also believe Darwin wrote truth about evolutionism is the epitome of stupidity! It is ignorance on parade! It is true that Charles Darwin was a seminary student before he went on his famous Beagle voyage, but on that journey he took Charles Lyell's "Principles of Geology", which rejected the Biblical account of Creation and the Flood. In his autobiography, Darwin wrote, *"Whilst on board the Beagle, I was quite orthodox...But I had come, by this time, to see that the Old Testament from its manifestly false history of the world...was no more to be trusted than the sacred books of the Hindoos, or the beliefs of any barbarian." ("The Autobiography of Charles Darwin, 1809-1882, New York: WW Norton, 1958, p. 71).* Obviously Charles Darwin was either very confused or intentionally lying when he called himself "quite orthodox", even though he rejected the Old Testament as true history – but then many seminary professors do the same.

"Rejection of the Bible leaves mankind with no source of truth and reality other than what he himself chooses to believe or invent. It should be no surprise that any society where evolution is taught and believed is also a society where immorality, selfishness, violence, and hatred inevitably increase." (from A CLOSER LOOK AT THE EVIDENCE by Richard & Tina Kleiss).

When we look at the causes of school shootings (venting anger and hostility), increased teen pregnancies, immorality and adultery (indulging lusts), etc., let's not overlook the obvious. For decades in our schools, museums, state parks, etc. the religion of humanism, with Darwinism, as a basic tenet, has been training us to think we are nothing but animals. If we teach children long enough that they are nothing but animals, why are we surprised when they act like animals? In Germany, Hitler and the Nazi Party could never have done what they did without the philosophies of Darwin and Nietche. At Columbine School Eric and Devin acted out their evolutionary belief system of survival of the fittest while wearing swastikas. Wake up! Let's get real! For too long we have tolerated sordid social stupidity!

Ironically, atheists often understand the conflict between Christian faith and evolutionary faith better than many professing Christians. In "The American Atheist" magazine, G. Richard Bozarth wrote concerning the meaning of evolution: *"Christianity has fought, and still fights science, and will fight science to the desperate end over evolution, because evolution destroys utterly and finally the very reason Jesus' earthly life was supposedly made necessary. Destroy Adam and Eve and the original sin, and in the rubble you will find the sorry remains of the Son of God. Take away the meaning of His death; if Jesus was not the Redeemer who died for our sins, and this is what evolution means—then Christianity is nothing."*

Although I strongly disagree with G. Richard Bozarth in his concept of evolutionism as science, I do believe that he has clearly defined the conflict between evolutionary faith and Biblical faith. In order to clarify further why I refer to evolutionism as science fiction, we should look at the definition of terms.

Definition of Terms

Science: It is important to note that the definition of the word "science" has shifted meaning since the publication of Darwin's "Origin of Species" in 1859. This shift is from "operational science", based on empirical evidence, to "origin science", based on evolutionary philosophy. Actually "origin science" is philosophy, not science. We should return to the original definition of operational science as the field of study dealing with empirical evidence. To be truly science, it must be **observable**, **repeatable**, and **demonstrable.** What happened in the distant past cannot be observed, repeated, or demonstrated; therefore, theories about the past belong in the field of philosophy.

Macro-evolution: When I speak of the theory of evolution, I am referring to "molecules to man" macro-evolution as popularized by Charles Darwin in "Origin of Species" (1859). Others had promoted the basic concept of evolution for centuries, but Charles Darwin and his colleagues created a wave of popular acceptance like never before. Therefore, I will use the term "Darwinism" as a synonym for the theory of evolution, even though modern evolutionists have rejected some of Darwin's ideas.

Micro-evolution: "Micro-evolution is defined as small changes in the genome of an organism caused by random mutations in the DNA. The mechanisms claimed for micro-evolution as well as macro-evolution are random genetic mutations coupled with natural selection. Despite claims to the contrary, mutations have never been observed to result in a net increase in genetic information." ~Dr. Bob Compton.

Since mutations and small changes are observable, repeatable, and demonstrable, micro-evolution is science. However, it takes a major leap of faith to believe that these minor changes within fixed limits are proof of macro-evolution. Micro-evolution is fact; macro-evolution is faith.

What committed evolutionists fail to recognize or refuse to admit is that they have no evidence to show that it is even possible for either mutations or natural selection to add new information to the genetic pool. **And without new information added to the gene pool, macro-evolution is impossible because the idea of upward progress is basic and essential to the theory of evolution.** So the bottom line is that micro-evolution does not produce a build up of new information in the DNA, which would be essential in order for macro-evolution to occur. (To pursue this deeper, I highly recommend the book, "In the Beginning Was Information" by Dr. Werner Gitt.)

Slipping into Heresy

It is true that many people have slipped into the heresy of theistic evolutionism with the flippant attitude, "I believe God created....I just don't care how He did it." The root of the problem here may be blatant ignorance because of being too indifferent or too lazy to study the facts, or it may be intentional deception. The fact is that evolutionism is <u>not</u> a way that God created—it is a diametrically opposite and opposing worldview to creationism. Creation is <u>not</u> evolution; evolution is not creation! If you want to know how God created, don't read Darwin's distortions—read God's Word. God tells us how He did it. We choose to believe Him or not to believe Him.

Here is God's clear, unmistakable truth: *"The Lord merely spoke, and the heavens were created. He breathed the word, and all the stars were born. He gave the sea its boundaries and locked the oceans in vast reservoirs. Let everyone in the world fear the Lord, and let everyone stand in awe of him. For when he spoke, the world began! It appeared at his command." Psalm 33:6-9 (NLT)*. When God speaks, things happen! Please also carefully and prayerfully read Genesis 1 and 2. This is not a matter of interpretation—it is a matter of belief or unbelief.

Throughout this article I have been using the term "stupidity" in its colloquial sense, but in reality many of the people pushing this social stupidity are highly intelligent, but diabolically or delusionally motivated. The proper term is foolishness. *"The fool has said in his heart, 'There is no God.'" Psalm 14:1*. Blatant atheists openly declare their unbelief; practical atheists profess to believe in God, but live as though He doesn't exist. We are sinking into the quagmire of quicksand—a nation governed by fools. Does it not seem evident that God is withdrawing His hand of protection from this once great nation?

Taproots

Reams of paper full of glaring examples of our slide into the surging streams of social stupidity could be written. However, these examples would mostly be the fruits of this tree of foolishness; what are the roots? Although there are many roots, I believe the two taproots are: 1. the depravity of the human heart and 2. the subtlety of Satanic seductions. Concerning the human heart, Jeremiah 17:9 says: *"The heart of man is deceitful above all other things and desperately wicked..."* James wrote, *"Let no one say when he is tempted, 'I am tempted by God'; for God cannot be tempted by evil, nor does He*

Himself tempt anyone. But each one is tempted when he is drawn away by his own desires and enticed." James 1:13-14 (NKJV). Concerning the Satanic seductions, Genesis 3:1 says, *"Now the serpent was more subtle (cunning) than any beast of the field..."*

Cutting the Taproots

We can use the Sword of the Spirit to cut the taproots of personal sin and social stupidity, for the Word of God tells us, *"No temptation has overtaken you except such as is common to man; but God is faithful, who will not allow you to be tempted beyond what you are able, but with the temptation will also make the way of escape that you may be able to bear it." 1 Corinthians 10:13 (NKJV).* Of course, this promise was written to Christians (those in covenant union with the Father through Jesus). If you do not yet have this wonderful union, here are God's instructions and promises:

"Believe on the Lord Jesus Christ and you will be saved..." Acts 16:31. "Repent and let each of you be baptized in the name of Jesus Christ for the forgiveness of your sins, and you shall receive the gift of the Holy Spirit." Acts 2:38 (NASV).

Where Do We Go From Here?

(What Shall We Do?)

1. Wake up to reality and believe the Truth. Jesus said, *"I am the way, the truth, and the life." John 14:6.* Believe Him! Follow Him!

2. Speak up! Let's speak up now in this country while we still retain a measure of the freedom of speech we once knew. And may we have the courage to speak up for Jesus even when it can cost us our lives. Church leaders are often afraid to speak up about creation, abortion, or homosexuality because they don't want to offend anyone, they don't want to be accused of being "too political", and they are afraid

they may lose their tax exempt status. Brothers, let's remember that when a moral issue becomes political, it does not stop being a moral issue. Nearly 500 years ago Martin Luther wrote that if a man of God speaks the Word of God on every other topic except the most burning issue of the time, **he has not yet spoken the Word of God!** I believe he was right. Paul told Timothy, *"Preach the word of God. Be persistent, whether the time is favorable or not. Patiently correct, rebuke, and encourage your people with good teaching."* 2 Timothy 4:2 (NLT). Earlier in that same book Paul reminded him that *"God has not given us the spirit of fear; but of power, and of love, and of a sound mind."* *2 Timothy 1:7 (KJV).* Let's remember the One to whom we must give account. When we stand before the throne of God, the issue will not be, "Did I lose our tax exempt status?" Rather it will be, "Did I faithfully declare the whole counsel of God?"

3. When we speak, let's remember, *"Whoever speaks, let him speak, as it were, the utterances of God..." 1 Peter 4:11 (NASV).* The New Living Translation says, "Then speak as though God Himself were speaking through you." Remember that when we speak the oracles (utterances) of God, we are speaking true wisdom. The well-meaning leaders who tell Christians not to use the Bible or quote scripture to unbelievers (since they don't believe it) are wrong. They are deluded! They are telling the soldier to put away his sword. That's foolishness. Paul wrote, *For I am not ashamed of the gospel of Christ, for it is the power of God to salvation..." Romans 1:16 (KJV).*

Those who do not fear God speak foolishness. Wisdom personified in Proverbs 8 says, *"All those who hate me love death." Proverbs 8:36.* No wonder the skull and crossbones has become so popular with rock groups, and those who hate God's wisdom promote abortion and euthanasia. Listen and focus: *"My son, if you will receive my sayings, and treasure my commandments within you, make your ear attentive to wisdom, incline your heart to understanding;*

For if you cry for discernment, lift your voice for understanding; If you seek her as silver, and search for her as for hidden treasures; then you will discern the fear of the Lord, and discover the knowledge of God. For the Lord gives wisdom; From His mouth come knowledge and understanding. He stores up sound wisdom for the upright; He is a shield to those who walk in integrity, guarding the paths of justice, and He preserves the way of His godly ones. Then you will discern righteousness and justice and equity and every good course. For wisdom will enter your heart, and knowledge will be pleasant to your soul; Discretion will guard you, understanding will watch over you, to deliver you from the way of evil, from the man who speaks perverse things; from those who leave the paths of uprightness, to walk in the ways of darkness; who delight in doing evil, and rejoice in the perversity of evil; whose paths are crooked, and those who are devious in their ways." Proverbs 2:1-15 (NASV).

4. Pray for a new, "Great Awakening". Pray! Pray! Pray! Fasting and prayer is in order to see social stupidity transformed into spiritual strength. *"If My people, who are called by My name will humble themselves, and pray and seek My face, and turn from their wicked ways, then I will hear from heaven, and will forgive their sin and heal their land." 2 Chronicles 7:14 (NKJV).*

5. Practice Purity! If you have allowed yourself to drift into entertainment containing foul language, nudity, immorality and the glorifying of the wrong types of heroes, please consider these strong, clear teachings from the Word of God: *"Therefore, I urge you brothers, in view of God's mercy, to offer your bodies as living sacrifices, holy and pleasing to God—this is your spiritual act of worship. Do not conform any longer to the pattern of this world, but be transformed by the renewing of your mind." Romans 12:1-2. "...Let us throw off everything that hinders and the sin that so easily entangles, and let us run with perseverance the race marked out for us. Let us fix our eyes on Jesus, the author and*

perfecter of our faith…" Hebrews 12:1-2. "Finally, brothers, whatever is true, whatever is noble, whatever is right, whatever is pure, whatever is lovely, whatever is admirable—if anything is excellent or praiseworthy—think about such things." Philippians 4:8. "Do not love the world or anything in the world. If anyone loves the world, the love of the Father is not in him. For everything in the world—the cravings of sinful man, the lust of his eyes and the boasting of what he has and does—comes not from the Father, but from the world." 1 John 2:15-16. "Blessed are the pure in heart, for they will see God." Matthew 5:8. Why not exercise the discipline of "Just say No!" to unfit forms of entertainment? Actually, if we get busy doing the positive commands (like visiting widows and orphans and taking the gospel to the world), we won't have time to indulge our minds and hearts in filthy forms of entertainment. The bottom line is, "Lord, what would You have me do?"

6. In spite of the surging stream of social stupidity, praise God anyway! No matter how bad our circumstances, if we obey God, we can and will live victorious lives in the "Triangle of Triumph". The three sides of the triangle are: 1) Rejoice evermore. 2) Pray without ceasing. 3) *In everything give thanks, for this is the will of God in Christ Jesus concerning you."*

   1 Thessalonians 5:16-18 (KJV).

7. Remember whose side you are on. He who is in us is greater than he who is in the world. One plus Almighty God makes the winning team. Read to the end of the Book. We win! When you look at how entrenched social stupidity is in our culture, remember Goliath. The bigger they are, the harder they fall!

   Besides, remember, you are not alone; when you look beneath the turbulent waters on the surface, you will see that God is on the move with His people—right here in America.

For example:

1) In the prayer arena there is a movement developing of such magnitude that I've never seen before: prayer concerts, prayer and fasting, pastors and leaders prayer retreats.

2) In the youth arena there are the "See You at the Pole" prayer meetings, Bible clubs, Extreme Devotion meetings, True Love Waits, etc.

3) In the legal arena The Rutherford Institute, The American Center for Law and Justice, Christian Law Association, Alliance Defense Fund, Foundation for Moral Law, and others are battling the social stupidity and intimidation of the ACLU in court—and winning! (Not always, but the majority of cases).

4) On the global scale, the world Christian movement is growing exponentially in South America, Africa, Asia, and Eurasia. Thousands of new believers are coming to Christ daily! Watch out world! The Christians are coming! Look up believer! Jesus is coming!

In conclusion, I want to share an amazing and powerful portion of Scripture from *2 Corinthians 4:3-7 (NLT)*: *"If the Good News we preach is veiled from anyone, it is a sign that they are perishing. Satan, the god of this evil world, has blinded the minds of those who don't believe, so they are unable to see the glorious light of the Good News that is shining upon them. They don't understand the message we preach about the glory of Christ, who is the exact likeness of God. We don't go around preaching about ourselves; we preach Christ Jesus, the Lord. All we say about ourselves is that we are your servants because of what Jesus has done for us. For God, who said, 'Let there be light in the darkness,' has made us understand that this light is the brightness of the glory of God that is seen in the face of Jesus Christ. But this precious treasure—this light*

*and power that now shine within us—is held in perishable contain-
ers, that is, in our weak bodies. So everyone can see that our glorious power is from God and is not our own."*

Yours & His,
Rick

*How long will these freedom symbols still stand – here in
our beloved homeland?*

+ + + + + + + + + +

December 2012

At the Risk of Being Politically Incorrect:

Merry Christmas

This is a statement I have been hearing on the radio recently.
My response emotionally is, "So what? Why should I want to
be 'politically correct' according to our current corrupt culture?
Risk??? We here in America still have such tender skin when we
need tough hide! Try being politically incorrect in Saudi Arabia
or North Korea. That is risk! Why should I bow to current corrupt culture to comply with political correct doctrines when I still
have so much fleeting full freedom to fight for fullness of truth and
righteousness? Do I want to be politically correct by refusing to say
'Merry Christmas' or refusing to call sin 'sin'? (Remember, it's just
an 'alternative lifestyle.')" Where is the grit and courage of a Patrick

Henry to say, "I know not what path others may take, but as for me, give me liberty or give me death!"?

Do you know what is wrong with "politically correct'? It isn't! It is politically, morally and spiritually corrupt. Do you know where the politically correct doctrine originated? Probably not – I didn't either until very recently, but I did have enough Biblical and historical and philosophical information to identify politically correct doctrine as raw, unvarnished Marxism. An acquaintance in a local business told me that political correctness comes directly out of the little red book entitled, "Quotations from Chairman Mao Tsetung"! He also told me the book is still available on Amazon, and I should look on page 147. I ordered my own copy. Here are a couple of sentences from page 147: *"Without the style of hard struggle, it is impossible to maintain a firm and correct political orientation."* ..... *"What really counts in the world is conscientiousness, and the Communist Party is most particular about being conscientious."* Page 1 of this little book says, *"The force at the core leading our cause forward is the Chinese Communist Party. The theoretical basis guiding our thinking is Marxism-Leninism."*

Do you realize that Mao was the worst mass murderer in history? Yes, he orchestrated the murder of far more people than Hitler and Stalin! Why should we want to compromise God's inspired Word to comply with "political correctness"?

"Beware lest anyone cheat you through philosophy and empty deceit, according to the tradition of men, according to the basic principles of the world, and not according to Christ. For in Him dwells all the fullness of the Godhead bodily; and you are complete in Him, who is the head of all principality and power." Colossians 1:8-10 (NKJV). Remember, "in Him dwells all the fullness of the Godhead bodily." "In the beginning was the Word, and the Word was with God, and the Word was God......And the Word became flesh and dwelt among us, and we beheld His glory, the glory of the only begotten of the Father, full of grace and truth."

John 1:1 and 14 (NKJV). Approximately 750 years before the apostle John wrote those words the prophet Isaiah wrote, "For unto us a Child is born, Unto us a Son is given; And the government will be upon His shoulder. And His name will be called Wonderful, Counselor, Mighty God, Everlasting Father, Prince of Peace." Isaiah 9:6 (NKJV). Therefore, in the name of Jesus (Whose name is politically incorrect to mention), Who is Emmanuel (God with us), I want to wish you a wonderful *MERRY CHRISTMAS!!!*

Polluted "Politically Correct" Christmas

'Twas the month before Christmas when all through our land, Not a Christian was praying nor taking a stand. The reason for the season no one could say – the PC Police had taken that away!

The children were told by the schools not to sing About Shepherds and Wise Men and Angels and things. It might hurt people's feelings, the teachers would say. December 25th is just a "Holiday".

~ Author unknown

From Our Mailbox

Hi, Rick and Della!

We share your serious disappointment in the election results. Obama bought his re-election. Imagine that: I thought he'd steal it!

As you have encouraged me, I'd like to encourage you: God is still in control! He lifts up leaders, and brings them down (we can only hope!)

"By me kings reign, and princes decree justice. By me princes rule, and nobles, even all the judges of the earth. I love them that love me; and those that seek me early shall find me." (Proverbs 8:15-16)

"The king's heart is in the hand of the LORD, as the rivers of water: he turneth it whithersoever he will. Every way of a man is

right in his own eyes: but the LORD pondereth the hearts. To do justice and judgment is more acceptable to the LORD than sacrifice." (Proverbs 21:1-3)

The following verse (Prov. 21:4) describes our President - who acts more like a king than a president -quite well, I think: "An high look, and a proud heart, and the plowing of the wicked, is sin." Obama looks down his nose when he talks, and seems to think he's better than anybody.

We must keep our Country in prayer, and remember that God is still on the Throne; He is still in control. And, He loves us. We must continue to pray for the Church, and even more so for the unsaved, that in this time of stress and ignorance, they will have a personal encounter with the True and Living God.

Keep looking up!
Love in Jesus Christ,
Sam O'Leary

+ + + + + + + + +

"God Sent Us a Saviour"

"If our greatest need had been information,
God would have sent us an educator.
If our greatest need had been technology,
God would have sent us a scientist.
If our greatest need had been money,
God would have sent us an economist.
If our greatest need had been pleasure,
God would have sent us an entertainer.
But our greatest need was forgiveness,
So God sent us a Saviour." ~Roy Lessin

The Focus Factor

"But Our Eyes Are Upon You"

Dear Friends and Prayer Partners,

"Know your enemy" is a strategically important part of any battle plan, and spiritual warfare is certainly no exception. Those of you who regularly read these prayer letters know that I've been sounding the warning repeatedly concerning the fact that "politically correct" is actually politically corrupt, and the moral depravity and degradation of our entire society is due to some degree (perhaps a huge degree) to the apathy of professing Christians and the cowardice of many church leaders to call sin "sin", and to stand for the foundational truths of the first 11 chapters of Genesis. When the light is hidden under the bushel (cloistered inside church buildings) and the salt has lost its flavor (and its sting), it is good for nothing! How else can we explain the fact that America has more professing Christians and more Christian colleges, universities, seminaries, and bookstores than any other nation on earth, yet our country is shedding its Christian heritage like a horse sheds its winter coat in springtime? When will more and more Christian leaders choose to be strong, to be bold, to courageously proclaim the truth of God's Word from the very first word of Genesis to *"even so, come Lord Jesus"* of Revelation? The apostle Paul wrote to the Romans:

"And do this, knowing the time, that now it is high time to awake out of sleep; for now our salvation is nearer than when we first believed. The night is far spent, the day is at hand. Therefore let us cast off the works of darkness, and let us put on the armor of light. Let us walk properly, as in the day, not in revelry and drunkenness, not in licentiousness and lewdness, not in strife and envy. But put on the Lord Jesus Christ, and make no provision for the flesh, to fulfill its lusts." Romans 13:11-14 (NKJV)

Most of you also know that the ominous danger from foreign powers is not nearly so threatening as the rot in the gut of America. Osama bin Laden is not nearly as dangerous to us as Obama bin Lyin' because so many gullible Americans still swallow his line, in spite of the fact that his lies have been publicly exposed time after time (although cleverly concealed by most major media outlets because of their liberal love affair with Barak Hussein Obama). Even internationally, he was given the Nobel Peace Prize – for what???? Our pseudo president has spent thousands of dollars fighting multiple lawsuits demanding he produce a legitimate birth certificate*, has openly declared that America is no longer a Christian nation, has ignored the National Day of Prayer in May, then declared June national homosexual month, has apologized to the world for America, has demanded that the name of Jesus and the cross be covered at his speaking appointments, has refused to honor the American flag with his hand over his heart, yet has bowed before the king of Saudi Arabia and before the emperor of Japan, has placed 32 radical rogue, unelected "czars" in positions of great power, has plunged our country more deeply in debt than any nation in history, has ram-rodded his Marxist agenda through Congress, has usurped the authority of free enterprise by taking over the banking industry, the auto industry, and the health care industry, has more aggressively promoted abortion than any former president, has nullified the Mexico City Policy so that now our tax dollars promote foreign abortions and has extended rampant immorality through Planned Parenthood, yet he professes to be a Christian. Jesus said, *"by their fruits ye shall know them."* Isn't hypocrisy in the White House just as despicable as hypocrisy in the church house?

(*Note: According to the Constitution, the President must be a natural born U.S. citizen. Barak Obama claims he was born in Hawaii, but his grandmother says she was present at his birth in Kenya.)

Brothers and sisters – this tends to be very distressing to those of us who love God and our country (which was definitely founded on Christian principles!) But I have very good news for you. The winds of positive change are blowing! For example:

1. Hundreds of thousands of church leaders and church members are waking up and signing on to the Manhattan Declaration.

2. Many – perhaps thousands or hundreds of thousands of us are participating in 40 days of fasting and prayer for our nation from January 4 – February 12.

3. More outspoken leaders are exposing the apathy in our churches and corruption in our country – boldly speaking truth. Many of them defied the recently passed "Hate Crimes" law by teaching the Biblical truth publically about homosexuality in front of the Supreme Court (or was it the Justice Department?). This was led and inspired by Alliance Defense Fund to test the freedom of speech and to challenge the administration to take them to court. So far I haven't heard about the administration taking up the challenge.

4. Recently an Obamania editor declared that Barak Obama will do more for humanity than Jesus Christ. Do any of you remember what happened to the Beatles after John Lennon said, "The Beatles are more popular than Jesus?"

On January 1st I was reading the story of Judah facing the huge threat from the combined forces of Moab, Ammon and Edom. Here is what the record says:

"And Jehoshaphat stood in the congregation of Judah and Jerusalem, in the house of the Lord, before the new court, and said, O Lord God of our fathers, art not thou God in heaven? and rulest not thou over all the kingdoms of the heathen? and in thine hand is there not power and might, so that none is able to withstand thee? . . . O our God, wilt thou not judge them? for we have no might against this great company that cometh against us; neither know we what to do: but our eyes are upon thee. . . . And he said, Hearken ye, all Judah, and ye inhabitants of Jerusalem, and thou king Jehoshaphat, Thus saith the Lord unto you, Be not afraid nor dismayed by reason of this great multitude; for the battle is not yours, but God's. . . . Ye shall not need to fight in this battle: set yourselves, stand ye still, and see the salvation of the Lord with you, O Judah and Jerusalem; fear not, nor be dismayed; tomorrow go out against

them: for the Lord will be with you. And Jehoshaphat bowed his head with his face to the ground: and all Judah and the inhabitants of Jerusalem fell before the Lord, worshipping the Lord. . . . And when he had consulted with the people, he appointed singers unto the Lord, and that should praise the beauty of holiness, as they went out before the army, and to say, Praise the Lord; for his mercy endureth for ever. And when they began to sing and to praise, the Lord set ambushments against the children of Ammon, Moab, and mount Seir, which were come against Judah; and they were smitten."

2 Chronicles 20:5-6, 12, 15, 17-18, 21-22 (KJV)

Lord, our eyes are on You! We look forward with anticipation to what You are going to do in our nation, in our world, and in our own hearts! We praise You and revel in Your majesty, Your power, and Your wisdom. Your Name will be exalted and Your Truth will prevail!

Conclusion

My thoughts for this prayer letter were sparked this morning by both the story of King Jehoshaphat's prayer and trust and by Dietrich Bonhoeffer's prayer and trust. Dan Johnson wrote: "German Lutheran pastor Dietrich Bonhoeffer's fiery denouncement of Adolf Hitler's anti-Semitism led to his imprisonment in 1943. While there, he ministered to and held services for his fellow prisoners." He wrote this prayer just before his execution.

"O God, early in the morning I cry to you, help me to pray and to concentrate my thoughts on you: I cannot do this alone, in me there is darkness, but with You there is light: I am lonely, but you do not leave me; I am feeble of heart, but with You there is help; I am restless, but with You there is peace, in me there is bitterness, but with You there is patience; I do not understand Your ways, but You know the way for me."

Dietrich Bonhoeffer was imprisoned the same year I was born, which sparked for me more reflections. Was the threat he faced in Germany over 60 years ago so different from the threat we now face in America? I don't think so. Remember, last month I mentioned that I have two articles written by elderly Germans now living in the USA, who both say that what is now happening in America, they saw before in Germany when the Nazis were taking over. You may think, "It can't happen here." Oh? Really? Christians are being severely persecuted in many nations and sarcastically mocked in mainline media in America. Also, when Barak Obama was an Illinois senator he voted "NO" repeatedly on the "Born Alive Protection Act", which was designed to save the lives of infants who survived botched abortions. (This is one of the facts he brazenly denied during his election campaign.) Any man so cold-blooded toward innocent babies is capable of any and all of the atrocities perpetrated by Hitler and his henchmen. These issues motivate me to speak out against the evil of the current administration as Dietrich Bonhoeffer did in his day. The legacy of Nevil Chamberlain and most German pastors was cowardly compromise, but the legacy of Dietrich Bonhoeffer and a few other bold believers was and is courageous conquest. The Nazis killed his body – but not his spirit! His stirring words and example live on to inspire us to look up and say again to the Lord, "but our eyes are upon You"! What kind of legacy will we leave to our children and grandchildren in these tumultuous times? Will they see in us the courage of commitment plus the jubilation of joy in the trauma of tough trials?

Yours & His,
Rick

****

A Note from Della

I want to suggest that we make Romans 12:12 our theme or motto for the year 2010:
"Be joyful in hope, patient in affliction, faithful in prayer."
Once again as we consider the seriousness of the things Rick has written, it needs to be balanced with joy and hope in order

for us to survive and not give in to discouragement or despair. A phrase from an old hymn came to mind – it says: *"Many things about tomorrow, I don't seem to understand; but I know Who holds tomorrow, and I know Who holds my hand."*

Lord, as a father holds the hand of his little child, help me to remember that You are holding my hand. May I always trust You and never let go of your hand – even in times of affliction!

"Many sorrows come to the wicked, but unfailing love surrounds those who trust the Lord. So rejoice in the Lord and be glad, all you who obey him! Shout for joy, all you whose hearts are pure!"

Psalm 32:10-11 (NLT)

You are trustworthy, God. May I be "faithful in prayer," place my complete trust in You, and keep my heart pure! Then I can be "joyful in hope"!

May you, our friends, be richly blessed with joy in 2010! May the smile of our Father rest on each of you!

+ + + + + + + + +

February 2010

Alarmed, But Encouraged – Simultaneously!

Dear Friends and Prayer Partners,

I realize that for the past 6 months (and often before) I have returned to the theme of sounding a wakeup call to my fellow Americans, and especially my fellow Christians in America because of the accelerating moral deterioration of our nation. Sometimes I feel like Jeremiah, whose heart was broken over the moral rot of Judah and came to be known as the weeping prophet. However, Jeremiah's writings also contain some of the most beautiful expressions of hope and encouragement in the Word of God. For example, here is a favorite of mine:

"For I know the thoughts that I think toward you, says the Lord, thoughts of peace and not of evil, to give you a future and a hope. Then you will call upon Me and go and pray to Me, and I will listen to you. And you will seek Me and find Me, when you search for Me with all your heart." Jeremiah 29:11 (NKJV)

Searching for Him with all our hearts – that is the key issue! Now consider this gem from *Jeremiah 33:3: "Call to Me and I will answer you, and show you great and mighty things which you do not know."* Wonderful! Let's call to Him with all our hearts!

"Judge Not" – Does This Mean "Don't Be Discerning – Be Gullible"?

We have received many highly appreciative calls and notes in response to our December and January letters from friends feeling the same Jeremiah burden, but we've also received a couple of very negative responses. Here is the response from someone who sent back our January prayer letter with this note at the bottom but did not sign it, and did not put a return label on the envelope: "I find your 'newsletter' very inappropriate in the religious sense so I'm returning it to you! Jesus was neither Republican nor Democrat!" I have three responses to this one.

1. I have very little respect for someone who is too cowardly to sign what he writes. Once, Dwight L. Moody was handed a note by a co-worker who told him someone asked him to give Moody the note before he preached. When he opened the note it contained only one word, "Fool!" Moody publically responded by saying, "I have often received notes from people who refused to identify themselves, but this evening I received a note from someone who identified himself but did not give me a message."

2. It is a foolish statement to say, "Jesus was neither Republican nor Democrat", because those political parties didn't even exist when Jesus lived on earth.

3. This misses the point – the point is that moral issues <u>do</u> matter to God and should matter to us. The fact is, however, that the Democratic Party has enshrined "pro-choice" into their official party platform and the Republican Party has "pro-life" in their party platform. Is God pro-choice or pro-life? He is <u>both</u>! And He told us how to choose! Consider what Moses said to Israel: *"I have set before you life and death, blessing and cursing; therefore choose life. . .that you may love the Lord your God, that you may obey His voice, and that you may cling to Him, for He is your life. . . "* Deuteronomy 30:19-20 (NKJV).

When does human life begin? Again, let's turn to Jeremiah, who wrote, *"Then the Word of the Lord came to me saying: 'Before I formed you in the womb I knew you; Before you were born I sanctified you; and I ordained you a prophet to the nations."* Jeremiah 1:4-5 (NKJV). Can it be more clear? One of the seven things God hates is the shedding of innocent blood, yet the Democratic Party officially endorses the brutal murder of millions of innocent babies – and they are intent on using our tax dollars to do it. There are a few pro-life Democrats, but they are fighting their party's policy. The biggest problem with the Republican Party is their "big tent" policy of allowing rank liberal pro-abortion individuals to continue as members. If you are going to stand for something – stand for it! Clean house! By the way, that is what Paul wrote to the Corinthian church in chapter five of his first epistle.

In fourth century Rome, Telemachus was shocked when he witnessed the bloody brutality of the gladiatorial games and saw the blood lust of the crowd. He jumped into the arena shouting, "In the Name of Christ – stop!" At first the crowd jeered and mocked him, but he persisted his pleading. However, when a gladiator cut him down, the crowd suddenly sat in stunned silence. Then one man got up and walked out, then another – and another. Thousands silently walked out of the coliseum. That ended the gladiatorial games! One man's conviction, his willingness to stand up and speak out, and his personal sacrifice, made the difference. With about 1.5 million abortions every year since the infamous Roe vs. Wade decision January 22, 1973, America now has, as a nation, bloodier hands than Nazi Germany – over 50,000,000 abortions. That is outrageous! Horrible! Christian, your voice matters! Stand up! Speak out! Stop the bloodshed! (Note: There are varying reports about Telemachus, but this is the one I read in *Voice of the Martyrs* and heard from Ravi Zacharias.)

Abortion is not the only moral issue – but it is one of the "big three" addressed in "The Manhattan Declaration." The last report I read says over 370,000 have signed on just since November 20. Wow! The goal is one million. Have you signed on yet? You can do so at ManhattanDeclaration.org.

The next response I want to share came from friends who did give their names. I will not tell their names, but I want to share my reply to help answer common false concepts which many other Christians have also absorbed from our corrupt culture.

Dear Friends,

Your first line in this latest letter is, "After reading your latest newsletter and many prior to this one, we have decided we would like you to take us off your mailing list." Your last paragraph says, "After a lot of discussion between the two of us we composed this e-mail. Even though we are not near as educated in God's word as you are, we know you will respect both our views and wishes."

For my response, I want to say first of all that we will respect your wishes and honor your request. I do respect both of you, remember our good times together, and treasure our friendship. Concerning your views expressed in this last letter, that is another matter – I truly feel sad and falsely accused. Here's why:

You wrote, "As Luke 6:37 states, '*Do not judge, and you will not be judged…*,'" yet just before that in the same paragraph you wrote, "Anyway, we just feel that you've gotten on a pretty high horse with

your views about Obama but then it's your newsletter." Apparently you feel it is fine to judge me about my views and your entire letter was written to express why you believe I'm wrong. So if Luke 6:37 means what you seem to imply it means, then the sword is double-edged and cuts both ways. This has become perhaps the most often quoted verse in America, while most people ignore the context and the fact that Jesus also commanded *"judge righteous judgment."* *John 7:24.* Why isn't this the most quoted verse? I want to share with you Ray Comfort's brief commentary on this in "The Evidence Bible".

The world often takes this verse out of context and uses it to accuse Christians of being "judgmental" when they speak of sin. In the context of the verse Jesus is telling His disciples not to judge one another, something the Bible condemns (Romans 14:10: James 4:11). In Luke 6:41, 42 He speaks of seeing a speck in a brother's eye. In John 7:24 He said, "Judge not according to the appearance, but judge righteous judgment." If someone steals, lies, commits adultery or murder, etc., the Christian can make a (righteous) moral judgment and say that the actions were morally wrong, and that these sins will have eternal consequences. Chuck Colson said, "True tolerance is not a total lack of judgment. It's knowing what should be tolerated – and refusing to tolerate that which shouldn't."

Concerning my views about Obama, I have two comments: 1. If I'm doing the same things he's doing, you have every right – and the duty - to confront me and quote "judge not that you be not judged." That fits the context of what Jesus said. 2. I am not ashamed or repentant about expressing my views about Obama's actions. In fact, they are matter of public record. May I send you the documentation? Remember that I mentioned the two articles written by elderly Germans now living in America who tell in detail the things they are now seeing happen here that they saw happening in Germany when the Nazis were taking over. Will you read them if I send them to you? Do you believe Dietrich Bonhoeffer was "high horse" and wrong for confronting Hitler and exposing the evil Nazi regime? You wrote, "Also the president doesn't legislate, the Congress does." Yes, you are right – according to our

Constitution. However, now the reality is that Barak Obama has been aggressively ram-rodding his Obama-care through Congress with high pressure tactics that are even offending some Democrats. You wrote, "We no longer want to read your personal view mixing religion and politics." So is mixing religion and politics wrong? This is another very commonly held misconception in America. I want to remind you that John the Baptist confronted King Herod with his immorality by boldly declaring, "It's not right for you to have her." King Herod was a political leader and not a true believer. The chief priests and Pharisees were both political and religious leaders, yet Jesus exposed their evil deeds, confronted them, and called them hypocrites. Were John the Baptist and Jesus wrong for "mixing religion and politics"?

One statement I do thoroughly agree with you about is "We do find limiting federal government not only Biblical but desirable from a Christian point of view" – but then you proceeded to say, "rather than attacking the beliefs about homosexuality and abortion." The apostle Paul wrote that we are to expose the unfruitful works of darkness! And concerning limiting federal government, it is ironic that you would write that, because Barak Obama is expanding the reach of federal government faster than any president in the history of our nation! That is a big part of my alarm – and the alarm of millions of other Americans (mostly Christians). I also have some deep disappointments about George Bush – mainly about his big spending, his expansion of federal government, and his promotion of the socialist program of the super highway to unite Mexico and Canada with USA in one North American Union. (This would destroy our Constitution, which is solidly based on Biblical principles.) However, to his credit, George Bush stood up for two of the most critical moral issues of our time – the sanctity of life and the sanctity of marriage (one man for one woman). In fact, Citizen Magazine honored him for being the most pro-life president in the history of our nation. (Citizen Magazine is published by Focus on the Family and I highly recommend you get it and American Family Association Journal, rather than relying on the major media news sources alone. You can find them at Focus on the Family, 8605 Explorer Dr., Colorado Springs, CO 80995-7450, www.CitizenMagazine.com and P.O. Drawer 2440, Tupelo, MS 38803, www.afa.net).

The Word of God says, "Righteousness exalts a nation, but sin is a reproach to any people". You wrote, "It is not our responsibility to demand righteousness from and dole out punishment to those who are unsaved." The fact is that according to our Constitution it is our responsibility. We are the government. Those who hold office are only to be our representatives.

The Word of God also says, *"If the foundations be destroyed, what can the righteous do?" Psalm 11:3.* The Creation – Evolution debate is the most foundational issue. Yes, the foundations are being destroyed here in America as they have been in Europe. Would you consider watching the "State of the Nation" DVD by Ken Ham and an insightful CD "Have We Forgotten" by Coral Ridge Ministries? I have extra copies for our book table and will be glad to send them to you.

Probably the most serious matter from your letter is that you missed or overlooked the most important points and special emphasis in the past issues of Overseas Outreach – especially December and January. There are two major points:

1. It is primarily because of the apathy of Christians (and professing Christians) that we are in this rut in America. It's a wake-up call!

2. Besides the wake-up call to the apathetic, these issues were written to encourage the alert – those who are awake and increasingly distressed with the degradation and direction of our nation. The lead-in article for December was entitled "The Main Thing." And what is "The Main Thing"? The pre-eminence of Jesus Christ as Lord! We are to worship and exalt and enjoy Him no matter what else is going on in our world. The lead-in article for January was "The Focus Factor" – which is to focus our eyes on Jesus and remember that no matter how powerful are the enemies and how desperate

the situation , "*the battle is not yours, but God's . . . see the salvation of the Lord." 2 Chronicles 20:15-17.* (Jehoshaphat did send his army into battle, but ahead of the army he sent the singers praising the Lord). Likewise, we are to engage the enemy in spiritual warfare – but not downhearted and defeated – rejoicing in the Lord.

We got very positive responses from a number of appreciative readers. I'm really sorry you missed the message.

In the love of our Lord Jesus Yours & His,
Rick

P.S. Would you consider reading my letter to a friend why socialism is evil?

Questions for Chapter 7 – First Half

1. How does the changing of terminology enhance the "Surging Stream of Social Stupidity"?

2. What did I label as "The Epitomy of Stupidity"? Do you agree? Why or why not?

3. How has the definition of the word "science" shifted from its original meaning? Also, why is it important to clarify this difference?

4. Please explain the difference between macro-evolution and micro-evolution.

5. What are several (at least 3) things that you can do to cut the taproots of personal sin and social stupidity?

6. The Focus Factor is vitally important. Where should we keep refocusing our attention?

7. Della wrote that Romans 12:12 should be our theme (or motto) for 2010. Perhaps it should be our theme for every year. What do you think and why?

8. Is it possible to be "Alarmed, But Encouraged – Simultaneously!"? Why or why not?

9. What is the Manhattan Declaration and what difference can it make? Have you signed it? (Do you suppose there is a connection with the Declaration of Independence?)

10. Do you believe it is "gossip" to expose the lies and outrageous corruption of our current administration – even specifically naming the leaders involved? Why or why not?

+ + + + + + + + + +

PURPOSE DRIVEN – BUT WHOSE PURPOSE?

"And we know that all things work together for good
to those who love God,
to those who are called according to His purpose." Romans 8:28

It is vitally important to live purpose driven lives and to understand that God causes ALL THINGS to work together for GOOD to those WHO LOVE GOD and are called ACCORDING TO HIS PURPOSE! This verse has for years been an anchor to my soul. Believing God's promises – specifically this – is definitely a frustration extractor in my life. Sometimes I just bow and pray like this: "Lord, I don't see how You are going to bring any good out of this situation, but I don't have to see it. You promised, and I believe You. Thank You for the good You are going to bring out of this." When He does bring the good, will I recognize it and praise Him for it? Only if I am focused on living my life ACCORDING TO HIS PURPOSE!!! To truly bring glory to God in my life, I must keep focused on living out His purpose, not my purpose. Balaam, Alexander the Great, Karl Marx, Adolf Hitler, and Josef Stalin all lived purpose driven lives, but brought death and devastation to millions because each was living for his own warped purpose instead of God's purpose. And what is God's purpose? It's no secret! God inspired Paul to reveal it to us in the next verse: *"For whom He foreknew, He also predestined to be conformed to the image of His Son..." Romans 8:29.* Here is the mystery of predestination revealed! Whatever God allows in my life – and in yours – is for the purpose of shaping me – and you – to become more and more like Jesus! Therefore, let's focus on faith, not frustrations – on Jesus, not injustices! We become what we think about. So *"let us lay aside every weight, and the sin which so easily ensnares us, and let us run with endurance the race that is set before us, LOOKING UNTO JESUS, the author and finisher of our faith, who for the joy that was set before Him endured the cross, despising the shame, and has sat down at the right hand of the throne of God." Hebrews 12:1-2 (NKJV). "Finally, brother, whatever is true, whatever is noble, whatever is right, whatever is pure, whatever is lovely, whatever is admirable – if anything is excellent or praiseworthy – THINK ABOUT SUCH THINGS." Phil. 4:8 (NIV)*

+ + + + + + + + + +

March 2010

The Danger of Compromise with Cultural Corruption

We are to be in the world but not of the world – and we are to separate ourselves from the deceptive philosophies and evil practices of this "cosmos" – worldly system. Kenneth Beckman consistently drilled into us – his students at BBC – "When you compromise, you become part of the problem you once sought to solve." Thank you, Kenny! It's so true. Are you on the fence?

CONSIDER THESE SCRIPTURES:

"I beseech you therefore, brethren, by the mercies of God, that you present your bodies a living sacrifice, holy, acceptable to God, which is your reasonable service. And do not be conformed to this world, but be transformed by the renewing of your mind, that you may prove what is that good and acceptable and perfect will of God." Romans 12:1-2 (NKJV)

"Therefore 'come out from among them and be separate, says the Lord. Do not touch what is unclean, and I will receive you. I will be a Father to you, and you shall be My sons and daughters, says the Lord Almighty.'" 2 Corinthians 6:17-18 (NKJV)

Chapter 7: Which Way, America?

"Beware lest anyone cheat you through philosophy and empty deceit, according to the tradition of men, according to the basic principles of the world, and not according to Christ. For in Him dwells all the fullness of the Godhead bodily; and you are complete in Him, who is the head of all principality and power." Colossians 2:8-10 (NKJV)

"Do not love the world or the things in the world. If anyone loves the world, the love of the Father is not in him. For all that is in the world – the lust of the flesh, the lust of the eyes, and the pride of life – is not of the Father but is of the world. And the world is passing away, and the lust of it; but he who does the will of God abides forever." 1 John 2:15-17 (NKJV)

It was compromise with corrupt culture that ruined the worship and morals of Israel and led to the destruction of the nation by foreign powers over and over. Likewise, with God's people in Christ's church through the ages, the corruption of cultural compromise has been, and continues to be more devastating than the external forces of persecution and ridicule.

When discussing Biblical topics it is a wise practice to call Bible topics by Bible names. In fact,

1 Peter 4:11 says, "If anyone speaks, let him speak as the oracles of God." (NKJV) The footnote for oracles says, "utterances." God speaks about homosexuality as the practice of sodomy and as an abomination – never as "being gay." The common re-definition of the word "gay" to mean homosexual came out of the homosexual activists' propaganda tool book to change America's thinking. They also taught that "being gay" is a matter of "being born that way," and cannot be changed. How strange – I have friends who are ex-homosexual, but I don't have any friends who are ex-black. Skin color is genetic. Committing sodomy is sinful practice. True repentance brings change. All human beings are born with a corrupted nature that is attracted to sin. Some temptations are stronger to one than another – but we are all responsible for our choices.

However, I don't read of "Thief Pride Parade," "Liar Pride Month," or "Celebrate Adultery Week." Truly "they glory in their shame," as the Bible says.

I've noticed that instead of accepting the clear teaching of Leviticus 18:22 that homosexuality is an "abomination," and the teaching of 1 Corinthians 6:9-11 that those who practice such things "shall not inherit the kingdom of God," some choose to re-interpret the Word of God according to "science" in order to arrive at what they choose to believe. It is interesting that Paul wrote, *"O Timothy! Guard what was committed to your trust, avoiding the profane and vain babblings and contradictions of what is falsely called knowledge (science / KJV) by professing it, some have strayed concerning the faith. Grace be with you. Amen."* 1 Timothy 6:20-21 (NKJV) And since that verse ends with grace, it is also appropriate to remember that "God resists the proud, but gives grace to the humble." 1 Peter 5:5 (NKJV) Parading with pride in our rebellion will always meet the resistance of God – and ultimately His wrath – but when we humbly repent and confess our sin and need to Him – then His arms are open to receive us and forgive us by the power of the blood of Jesus Christ.

We received the following quote by email recently, and it just seems to fit with what I have been writing about.

"I believe...that our background and circumstances may have influenced who we are, but we are responsible for who we become."

+ + + + + + + + +

April 2010

"My Times Are in Your Hands"

Psalm 31:14-15 (NKJV)

Dear Friends and Prayer Partners,

True Christians in America are already dealing with the persecution of despicable discrimination, media mockery, ridiculous ridicule, contemptuous court cases, and sometimes violent vitriol (as in the cases of Cassie Bernall and Rachel Scott at Columbine, and the violent attacks by homosexual activists against the promoters of Proposition 8 in California), but it is likely to get much worse and widespread far sooner than most Americans realize. Last summer our home congregation had a guest speaker from Voice of the Martyrs, and after the service, some ladies asked him if he believes such violence is coming here, as many Christians in other countries now experience and endure. His response was immediate – "Oh, it's inevitable!" In full view of the impending danger to believers, I want to share three responses:

1. Don't be surprised – be prepared! The apostle Paul wrote, *"Yes, and all who desire to live godly in Christ Jesus will suffer persecution."* II Timothy 3:12 (NKJV). Jesus said, *"Then they will deliver you up to tribulation and kill you, and you will be hated by all nations for My name's sake."* Matthew 24:9 (NKJV)

2. Don't be afraid – trust God! It is an amazing, but well established fact that the best church growth takes place in spite of persecution (or because of persecution). There has been phenomenal growth in China and Sudan parallel with powerful pressure and persecution. Let's pray like David did. *"But as for me, I trust in You, O Lord; I say, 'You are my God.' My times are in Your hand; deliver me from the hand*

of my enemies, and from those who persecute me. Make Your face shine upon Your servant; save me for Your mercies' sake." Psalm 31:14-16 (NKJV)

3. Don't miss the blessing – rejoice! Let's remember the words of wisdom from our Wonderful Counselor. *"Blessed are those who are persecuted for righteousness' sake, for theirs is the kingdom of heaven. Blessed are you when they revile and persecute you, and say all kinds of evil against you falsely for My sake. Rejoice and be exceedingly glad, for great is your reward in heaven, for so they persecuted the prophets who were before you."* Matthew 5:10-12 (NKJV)

+ + + + + + + + + +

July/August 2010

An Open Letter to a College Student struggling with doubts about God, the Bible, Christ, and Christianity

Dear "Mike", (His name is changed to protect his identity)

Test Everything

The Bible tells us to *"test everything – hold on to the good. Avoid every kind of evil." 1 Thessalonians 5:21-22.* God encourages us to check things out – to test them, but He also tells us to avoid every kind of evil. I'm writing this to commend you for wanting to test everything – but to warn you that the writings of the Buddhist critic of the Bible are <u>not</u> the writings of an honest skeptic. They are evil, wicked, dishonest distortions of the Bible and Christian writers. I'll give you a couple of examples to show you what I mean, but first I want to point out that this wicked author is willingly ignorant and intentionally distorting truth. Besides, what does Buddhism have to offer? It is a hopeless, skeptical, atheistic philosophy. It is empty – devoid of meaning and joy.

Willingly Ignorant

Why do I say that the author is willingly ignorant? Because he parades himself as a philosophical and Biblical scholar, yet ignores the fact that every good Christian apologist has already thoroughly answered and demolished his infantile arguments.

Have you read *Mere Christianity* by C.S. Lewis? *More than a Conqueror* by Josh McDowell? *The Case for Christ* by Lee Strobel? All of these were atheists or agnostics who were converted by the powerful evidence for Christ and the accuracy of the Bible when they did the research. I was also once an atheist, but God captured my heart by a dramatic answer to prayer and turned me around. I am so thankful for that. *Ready to Give an Answer* is my book. Did we send you a copy? Other outstanding books are *A Closer Look at the Evidence, Censored Science* and *Search for the Truth*. Will you read these if we send you copies? I also want to highly recommend that you read the article, "Tackling Charges of Biblical Inconsistency" by James J. S. Johnson in the July issue of *Acts & Facts*. In fact, I even more highly recommend that you subscribe to this outstanding magazine. (Institute for Creation Research, P.O. Box 59029, Dallas, TX 75229, 214-615-8300, www.icr.org)

I've had a lot of experience answering critics and skeptics on college and university campuses, as well as at "Man and the Christian Worldview" symposiums attended by many Ph.D. professors, scientists and philosophers. Sometimes I write to an author to try to engage him, but I will not try to contact the Buddhist author because he has demonstrated to me by his writings that he is a dishonest mocker. The Word of God says, *"Whoever corrects a mocker invites insult; whoever rebukes a wicked man incurs abuse. Do not rebuke a mocker or he will hate you; rebuke a wise man and he will love you. Instruct a wise man and he will be wiser still; teach a righteous man and he will add to his learning." Proverbs 9:7-9 (NIV)*

What are you Searching For?

Mike, if you are sincerely searching for truth, you won't find it in the writings of the Buddhist mocker – so why waste your time? The only reason I can see why you would choose to continue to read his writings (or those of blatant atheists like Sam Harris, Christopher Hitchens or Richard Dawkins) is if you are looking for excuses not to believe in God or His Word because you don't want to repent. Mike, what are you looking for? Are you willing to pray, *"Search me, O God, and know my heart; test me and know my anxious thoughts. See if there is any offensive way in me, and lead me in the way everlasting."? Psalm 139:23-24*

Now I'll give you a couple of examples of the Buddhist author's distortions. He often uses the "straw man" tactic, which is to distort an argument of Christians and set up this distorted "straw man" then cut it down and tear it apart. Then he crows over his triumph – when in reality he hasn't dealt with the real issue at all. Here is an example:

Does Everything have a Cause?

He wrote, "Christians will sometimes say that <u>everything</u> has a cause..." **False! False! False!** Christian apologists point out that it is a scientific law that every <u>effect</u> must have an adequate cause. This makes a huge difference because God is <u>NOT</u> an effect – He is the cause! He is the first cause.

He also wrote, "This old argument contains its own refutation, for if everything has a first cause, then the first cause must also have a cause." This argumentation is so weak it is ridiculous, because he continues to build on the fallacy of "<u>everything</u>" instead of the true argument "<u>every effect</u>", <u>plus</u> he commits the logical fallacy of saying that the <u>first</u> cause must also have a cause. **If it is the <u>first</u> cause it cannot also have a cause!** If it did, it wouldn't be the <u>first</u> cause. Duh!!!

Who Made God?

Sometimes a small child will ask the question, "Who made God?" – which only reveals the child's ignorance about the definition of who God is. God is the eternal, almighty Creator of everything and everybody. **If someone made God, He wouldn't be God.** The one who made him would be God. But then the child could ask, "Who made that God?" Such questioning could go on forever. That would be infinite regression – another logical fallacy.

Does a Wise Man Ridicule Solomon?

The cynical critic ridicules the Song of Solomon as worthless erotic poetry. Actually, he is just too dense in his cynicism to recognize it as a beautiful love poem which celebrates marriage and harmonizes perfectly with other portions of Scripture which warn against immorality. See Proverbs chapters 5 through 7, and 1 Corinthians chapter 7. Proverbs 18:22 says, *"Whoso finds a wife finds a good thing, and obtains favor of the Lord."* Hebrews 13:4 says, *"Marriage is honorable in all, and the bed undefiled: but whoremongers and adulterers God will judge."* Marriage is God's invention and plan for male-female sexual satisfaction and fulfillment emotionally as well as physically. It was God Himself who created them male and female and designed one man for one woman for life as the basic unit of family and society. Family, faithfulness, fidelity and friendship for life are all part of His beautiful plan. Della and I are still enjoying the richness of His plan after all these years. The "Song of Songs" is also a beautiful picture of the intimate love and sacrifice of Christ for His bride, the church.

The only Worldview Which Explains the Origin of Evil

Biblical Christianity (with the possible exception of Orthodox Judaism which accepts the Old Testament as true history) is the only worldview which has a logical consistent explanation for the existence of evil. Many people blame God – ignoring the fact that He created everything perfect and peaceful and put human beings in a beautiful garden in the beginning. Now we live on a cursed earth full of evil, heartache and suffering because of man's rebellion against God!

Do you understand why I say he uses infantile arguments? Do you want a man like this to be your mentor? Why not look to your father's godly example and choose him as your mentor?

Mike, please openly and honestly consider what the apostle Paul wrote: *"I am not ashamed of the gospel, because it is the power of God for the salvation of everyone who believes: first for the Jew, then for the Gentile. For in the gospel a righteousness from God is revealed, a righteousness that is by faith from first to last, just as it is written: 'The righteous will live by faith.' The wrath of God is being revealed from heaven against all the godlessness and wickedness of men who suppress the truth by their wickedness, since what may be known about God is plain to them, because God has made it plain to them. For since the creation of the world God's invisible qualities – his eternal power and divine nature – have been clearly seen, being understood from what has been made, so that men are without excuse." Romans 1:16-20 (NIV)*

Who do You want as a Mentor?

Do you want the apostle Paul (a converted skeptic with a powerful intellect) to be your mentor – or do you want wicked fools who are without excuse to be your mentors? By the way, why don't you ask those wicked fools to logically explain why Saul of Tarsus, the passionate persecutor of Christians, was converted and became the most motivated missionary of the first century (perhaps of all time – except for Jesus Himself)? How do they explain that? They don't! They ignore it! **But it is solid historical fact. How do you explain it?**

Too Harsh?

Do you think I am too harsh in my evaluation of the Buddhist critic and the other blatant atheists I mentioned? Please consider what God says: *"The fool has said in his heart, 'There is no God.' They are corrupt, they have done abominable works, there is none that does good." Psalm 14:1; 53:1.* Besides, the Word says, *"The fool has said in his heart there is no God"* and these guys blab it right out loud and put it in print. *Proverbs 15:1 says, "…the mouth of fools pours out foolishness"!* I was also one of these wicked fools who blabbed it out loud. **I am so thankful God convicted me of my sin and drew me out of that web of wickedness.**

Is Human Nature Basically Good?

Did you notice that the last part of the verse says, *"…there is none that does good"*? This destroys the humanistic doctrine that mankind is basically good by nature. Jeremiah 17:9 says, *"The heart is deceitful above all things and desperately wicked…"* Do you know that the rejection of God, His Word, and His Son is a moral issue (often covered up with an intellectual smokescreen)? The root of the problem is not intellectual (concerning our unanswered questions, etc.). Please consider John 3:16 in its context! *"For God so loved the world, that he gave his only begotten Son, that whosoever believes in him should not perish, but have everlasting life. For God sent not his Son into the world to condemn the world; but that the world through him might be saved. He that believes on him is not condemned: but he that believes not is condemned already, because he has not believed in the name of the only begotten Son of God. And this is the condemnation, that light is come into the world, and men loved darkness rather than light, because their deeds were evil. For every one that does evil hates the light, neither comes to the light, lest his deeds should be reproved. But he that does truth comes to the light, that his deeds may be made manifest, that they are wrought in God." John 3:16-21 (KJV)* The basic fact is that either you will repent and allow the Holy Spirit to shape your desires to the truth, or you will reject the truth and warp God's Word to fit your desires. Which will it be? *"Come now, and let us reason together, says the LORD: though your sins be as scarlet, they shall be white as snow..." Isaiah 1:18*

Is there Actually Solid Evidence that Jesus Arose from the Dead?

Do you know who Simon Greenleaf was? He was the head of the law department at Harvard and the professor who wrote a three volume set on how to gather and evaluate evidence. His set became the world-wide standard for training lawyers and judges. He was the man who knew more about how to evaluate evidence than any other individual. One day in the 1800's a student asked him, "Professor Greenleaf, do you believe Jesus Christ arose from the dead?" Because he was raised in a Jewish home where he was constantly told that Jesus was an imposter who was not the Messiah and did not rise from the dead, he said, "No." Then the student had the audacity to ask, **"Professor Greenleaf – have you examined the evidence?"** This left him embarrassed before the entire class because he had often told his students, "Never make any important decision without examining the evidence." Simon Greenleaf began an intense study of the evidence originally to prove he was right, but was converted to Christ by the overpowering evidence. He wrote a book on the evidence for the resurrection of Christ and said that any honest jury would have to say that Jesus Christ arose from the dead. He also wrote that the four evangelists Matthew, Mark, Luke and John were totally accurate in all their historical references and that their writings are valid historical documents. If you look up Simon Greenleaf on the internet, you can read for yourself what he wrote about the four gospel writers. It's hard to wade through because of the technical terms and verbiage style of the 1800's, but I've done it. His testimony is powerful – and irrefutable!

The question is, What will you do with this evidence? With Jesus? Today He is our Savior. One day He will be our judge. Do you want Him as your Savior – both now and then? He has left the choice with you. I hope you choose wisely.

"To Him Who is able to keep you from falling and to present you before His glorious presence without fault and with great joy – to the only God our Savior be glory, majesty, power and authority through Jesus Christ our Lord, before all ages, now and forevermore! Amen." Jude 24-25

Yours & His,
Rick

+ + + + + + + + +

September 2010

"Don't Mix Religion with Business"

Dear Friends & Prayer Partners,

Have you heard the popular proverb, "Never talk about religion or politics – especially in business"? I'm sure you have, and I have been directly reminded of it several times (but not as often as I would expect). My observation is that those who mandate this piece of worldly wisdom are very adamant about it and not open to consider another viewpoint. One manager cut me off from making a lighting bid because I offered her an inspiring flyer. She said, "I don't believe in mixing religion with business." (In other words,

"Don't talk about anything really important!") I told her that my relationship with my Lord has priority and is more important to me than business, but I wish that I had asked her this question: "Jesus taught me to treat other people as I want to be treated, so it is a vital part of my faith. Do you not wish for me to mix this principle of my faith with business when working with you?"

At any rate, I reject the above-mentioned popular proverb because it is not a Biblical proverb. Jesus told us to share His truth, His Good News with everyone. I have a higher commission and His wonderful promise, "Lo, I am with you always." I realize that I will lose a few accounts this way, but my thankful heart rejoices in the fact that God is blessing and providing for us in Deighton Lighting, even during these tough economic times. Perhaps you are struggling with tough times financially, physically or emotionally. Here are some tremendous verses that inspire and sustain me. (All are from the New King James Version).

"Plead my cause and redeem me; Revive me according to Your word." Psalm 119:154

"Great peace have those who love Your law, And nothing causes them to stumble." Psalm 119:165

"My lips shall utter praise, for You teach me Your statutes. My tongue shall speak of Your Word, for all Your commandments are righteousness. Let Your hand become my help, For I have chosen Your precepts." Psalm 119:171-173

"Our help is in the name of the Lord, Who made heaven and earth." Psalm 124:8

"The Lord has done great things for us, whereof we are glad." Psalm 126:3

"Those who sow in tears shall reap in joy. He who continually goes forth weeping, bearing seed for sowing, shall doubtless come again with rejoicing, bringing his sheaves with him." Psalm 126:5-6

June 2011

Christians Only! No Creed But Christ!

I believe my heritage from the Restoration Movement churches is a great advantage to have opportunities to speak in a variety of denominational churches in Ukraine, because I come simply as a Christian with no denominational program to push. At a school where I was asked, "What confession are you?" (meaning "what denomination do you belong to?") I answered, "Jesus is Lord! That is my confession. I don't belong to a denomination – I belong to Jesus Christ, my Lord." They had a hard time grasping this, but I told them I want to be just a Christian – nothing more, nothing less.

Yes, friends, I believe the Biblical principles of the American and Russian Restoration Movements are still valid – and are a great heritage! These principles are easier to understand than to practice, but let's remember: "We are not the only Christians – but we are Christians only!" Let's remember and practice:

"In essentials – unity

In opinions – liberty

In all things – charity"

Let's also remember that when God opens the doors, He expects us to walk through!

During this spring trip I had open doors to preach, share my testimony and Della's, and distribute our books in Russian at two very large congregations, First Baptist Church in Odessa and Christian Hope Church (Pentecostal) in Kiev. In both of these and other congregations the messages were received enthusiastically and invitations were extended for me to return. Let's boldly walk through the doors God opens to us and clearly "speak the truth in love."

This spring Victor Knowles wrote an excellent article entitled,

"Is the Restoration Plea Still Valid?" As I reflect on that question, I ask myself, "How could it be invalid?" I understand the essence of the Restoration Movement to be the restoration of faith in God and His absolute truth. The Bible is **His revelation** – and therefore, it is the inerrant Word of Almighty God! *"Forever, O Lord, thy Word is settled in heaven." Psalm 119:89.* **Our part is to restore people's trust in Him Who has already told us the truth** – not to make up our own "truth" about the foundational truths of creation, the fall of man, the worldwide flood, or marriage or salvation or the church, etc. If we don't believe what He said, then let's be honest enough to stop pretending to be Christians. That is the essence of hypocrisy!

When I recognize that I have sinned, and I repent – **"He restores my soul."**

When I am frustrated and troubled – **He restores my peace!**

When I am heartbroken over rebellion and sin – **He restores my joy!**

When I am bone tired and weary of "contending earnestly for the faith" – **He restores my strength** so that I can "mount up with wings as eagles, run and not be weary, walk and not faint."

Do I believe the restoration plea is still valid? Absolutely! I hope to restore your trust too. **Let's restore people's absolute trust in Christ and in doing things His way instead of our way!**

July 2011

Pertinent Points on Truth and Consequences

Following are some quotes that are pungent and pointed:

"Speak your mind – and ride a fast horse!" Anonymous
"Tolerance is a virtue for those who have no convictions." ~ G. K. Chesterton

These next 5 points I believe came originally from Adrian Rogers:

Thoughts on Truth and Unity:

- *It is better to be divided by truth than united in error.*

- *It is better to tell the truth that hurts and then heals than to tell a lie that comforts and then kills.*

- *It is better to be hated for telling the truth than to be loved for telling a lie.*

- *It is better to stand alone with the truth than to be wrong with a multitude.*

- *It is better to succeed ultimately with the truth than to succeed temporarily with a lie.*

Evolutionism is Satan's monumental lie! Let's expose it!!! ~ Rick Deighton

August 2011

The Atheists are Coming!

Dear Friends & Prayer Partners,

On Saturday, July 30th, about 7:30 a.m. Stan Lutz (our Northwest Science Museum director) called me and asked for prayer because the "Free-Thinkers" Club had invited the Atheists of Idaho to come with them that day to discredit our museum. We were in Keizer, Oregon, and prayed earnestly for God to give Stan wisdom, and many other believers were praying too. That afternoon we attended Becky Cherry's wedding at Central Christian Church in Portland, and when we checked my cell phone afterwards, we had a message from Stan praising God for the encounter. Stan has an incredible mind full of scientific facts, but he was relying on the power of God. Even though there was a whole group of atheists opposed to what Stan had to present, God put the right words in his mouth at the right time with the right documentation, and the atheists were dumbfounded. At least one of them told Stan, "This isn't what we expected!" Stan's young apprentice, Sam Harper, chuckled over the encounter after they left. **What an amazing God we serve!** Are you praying, "Lord, please fill me with Your Spirit and put me in the right place at the right time with the right words to honor You"? Try it! Then observe how He works. **You may be amazed.**

Later Stan told me that one member of the group gave $1.00 for offering – and the group took about $200.00 worth of books. Praise God! Please pray with us that they will read and be converted. Somehow Stan also got a copy of an email intended only for their group. Here are some excerpts. Notice the tone in it.

"Alright Everyone – this trip to the Creation Museum is being hosted by Dan Thering and his group WVFT (West Valley Free Thinkers.) He's inviting Idaho Atheists – and any other secular groups in town that are interested in attending. This event is free, but of course – you have to pay

for your own laundry after _____ yourselves laughing at the 'creation exhibits.'

~ Mike"

Here is the info Dan provided for the event:

"At approximately 12:30 – 1 p.m., we will drive over to Zion Christian School, the facility currently housing the NW"S"(C)M. As representatives of the secular community, please try to remain as respectful as possible. Criticisms and the odd giggle may be hard to avoid, but please treat their exhibit as you would want them to treat any public museum."

Perhaps our flyers given out at the "God and Country Rally" just before the 4th of July were what got the attention of the atheists. We distributed nearly 2,000 copies of a flyer.

+++++++++++++++

January 2012

Fearlessly Facing the Future with Faith!

What fears and uncertainties do we Americans face as we stare ahead at 2012?

What about: Economic uncertainties…Political uncertainties…Security uncertainties…Terrorist attacks...War with Iran and Russia…World War 3…Hostility toward and persecution of Christians?

What shall we learn from Paul's perspective?

"Not that I have already attained, or am already perfected; but I press on, that I may lay hold of that for which Christ Jesus has also laid hold of me. Brethren, I do not count myself to have apprehended; but one thing I do, forgetting those things which are behind and reaching forward to those things which are ahead, I press toward the goal for the prize of the upward call of God in Christ Jesus." Philippians 3:12-14 (NKJV).

I. **Forget the Past**

    A. Fumbles and Foul-ups

    B. Awards and Attainments

What can we learn from a befuddled football player?

The following illustration about Roy Riegels is from an excellent message by Rich McQuinn.

"On January 1, 1929, the Golden Bears faced the Georgia Tech Yellow Jackets at the Rose Bowl in Pasadena, California. Midway through the second quarter, Riegels, who played center, picked up a fumble by Tech's Jack 'Stumpy' Thomason. Just 30 yards away from the Yellow Jackets' end zone, Riegels was somehow turned around and ran 65 yards in the wrong direction. He could have scored a touchdown for his own team, but life turned him around and he was confused on the direction he should travel. Ever been there?

".....Riegels was so distraught that he had to be talked into returning to the game for the second half. Riegels turned in a stellar second half performance, including blocking a Tech punt. Lom passed for a touchdown and kicked the extra point, but Tech would ultimately win the game and their second national championship by a final score of 8-7. The example of how the distraught Riegels

was persuaded to pick himself up, return to the field and play so hard during the second half is sometimes used by motivational speakers to illustrate overcoming setbacks.

"Despite the nationwide mockery that followed, Riegels went on to live a normal life, serving in the United States Army Air Forces during World War II, coaching high school and college football, including time at Cala, and running his own chemical company. In 1991, Riegels was inducted into the Rose Bowl Hall of Fame. Riegels died in 1993 at the age of 84. In 1998, he was posthumously elected to Cal's Hall of Fame.

"In the locker room at half time, Roy Riegels sat in the corner with his face buried in his hands, crying. The room was silent. The Coach didn't make his usual half-time speech, but shortly before the team was to take the field for the second half, he said, 'The starting team is going back onto the field to begin the second half.'

"The whole team left the locker room, except for Riegels, who remained in the corner with his face in his hands. 'I can't do it, Coach,' he said. 'I can't play. I ruined the team.' The Coach said, 'Get up, Riegles. The game is only half over. You belong on the field.'

"Guess what? Our game is only half over. Regardless of the past, we still have the rest of the game to play. So what if the enemy scored off of you in the past! God is willing to forget about the mistakes of the first half. And He expects us to do the same!!! Remember that the game is only half over!"

Application: Track runners know they can't win the race by looking back. Forget the past! Look unto Jesus and move forward!

II.   **Focus on the Future!**

    A. Be glad for <u>all</u> that God is planning for you!

    B. Keep asking, "Lord, what would <u>You</u> have me to do?"

    C. Keep praying, "Lord, fill me with Your Spirit and put me in the right place at the right time with the right words to honor You!"

    D. Keep forgetting those things which are behind and reaching forward to those things which are ahead.

    E. Keep pressing towards the goal for the prize of the upward call of God in Christ Jesus.

III.   **Find Fulfillment in the Present!**

    A. Don't wait to begin! Do it now!

        1. Cancel your "if only" excuses – remember Mary and Martha.

        Trust Jesus now – in your circumstances!

        2. Realize things are never going to settle down.

        3. Realize we are living on a cursed earth, so we must choose to enjoy life and thank God under adverse circumstances.

    B. Praise God for whatever abilities and whatever spiritual gifts He has given you – use them to His glory! You are a masterpiece in the making! Eph. 2:10.

    Stir up the gift that is in you!

    C. Remember the ultimate goal – to become like Christ.

God may need lots of sandpaper for some of us! (A master Carpenter must use lots of sandpaper to turn rough lumber into fine furniture!)

Conclusion: What perspective does God want us to have as we face an uncertain and fearsome future? Consider these powerful passages of Scripture:

"Only be strong and of good courage, for to this people you shall divide as an inheritance the land which I swore to their fathers to give them. Only be strong and very courageous, that you may observe to do according to all the law which Moses My servant commanded you; do not turn from it to the right hand or to the left, that you may prosper wherever you go. This Book of the Law shall not depart from your mouth, but you shall meditate in it day and night, that you may observe to do according to all that is written in it. For then you will make your way prosperous, and then you will have good success. Have I not commanded you? Be strong and of good courage; do not be afraid, nor be dismayed, for the Lord your God is with you wherever you go." Joshua 1:7-9 (NKJV).

"You will keep him in perfect peace, whose mind is stayed on You, because he trusts in You. Trust in the Lord forever, for in YAH, the Lord, is everlasting strength." Isaiah 26:3-4 (NKJV).

"For thus says the Lord God, the Holy One of Israel: 'In returning and rest you shall be saved; In quietness and confidence shall be your strength.'" Isaiah 30:15 (NKJV).

"For God has not given us a spirit of fear, but of power and of love and of a sound mind."

2 Timothy 1:7 (NKJV).

December 2011

The Grinch and the Christmas Wars

The true story of our most memorable Christmas, which we shared with you last year, took place long before the "politically correct" crowd set out to steal Christ from Christmas and the culture wars began over the term "Merry Christmas" or "Christmas tree." Who doesn't recognize that "Holiday Tree" is simply a lame attempt to avoid using a term that contains Christ at its core? In a recent *Knowlesletter*, Victor wrote that even some Christian organizations are leaving out the name of Christ – to avoid offending someone! What??? Years ago liberal churches stopped singing about the blood of Jesus and expunged that phrase from their hymnals because it was offensive. What? The Word of God still says *"knowing that you were not redeemed with corruptible things like silver or gold from your aimless conduct...but with the precious blood of Christ..." 1 Peter 1:18-19.* Let's sing "Power in the Blood" again – and crank up the volume!!

+ + + + + + + + + +

February 2012

Truth + Trust =Triumph and Tranquility

Dear Friends & Prayer Partners,
In this prayer letter I plan to share with you some thoughts from other writers about the degeneration of America, but first I want to focus your attention on the truth that Almighty God is the one and only Sovereign! He is almighty! It is important to be aware of the giants before us – but even more important to keep in

focus the Majesty and Power above us and within us (if we are "in Christ", He is in us by His Spirit)! "'Not by might nor by power, but by my Spirit' says the Lord Almighty.'" Zechariah 4:6 (NIV). David triumphed over Goliath because he did not compare Goliath with himself – he compared Goliath with God. If we focus our total attention on our problem, it looms bigger, so let's always assess our problems in the proper perspective. *"Oh Lord my God...How Great Thou Art!"* Isaiah's prayer expresses this thought perfectly: *"You will keep him in perfect peace whose mind is stayed on You, because he trusts in You. Trust in the Lord forever, for in YAH, the Lord, is everlasting strength." Isaiah 26:3-4 (NKJV).*

"For thus says the Lord God, the Holy One of Israel: 'In returning (repentance) and rest you shall be saved; in quietness and confidence shall be your strength.'" Isaiah 30:15 (NKJV).

+ + + + + + + + + +

March 2012

What Is Your Perspective?

The giants of humanism, evolutionism, and materialism are intent on ousting God from government, schools, and society. Their proponents are temporarily willing to allow those crazy "Bible thumpin' Christians" to go huddle in their churches – "but don't you dare try to speak your convictions openly or impose your morals on our culture!" Have you noticed the hypocrisy of the humanist, abortionist, homosexual activist crowd? They are blatantly and aggressively imposing their jaded immorality on society while telling us that Christians are intolerant if we dare speak out against their agenda. They don't believe in a level playing field, and they are willing to lie to distort the historical facts about the beliefs of the founding fathers of America. The fact is that it is impossible for an atheist to be a loyal American – so why are schools and government agencies bowing to the whims of the atheists? Our Declaration of Independence is even more basic than our Constitution, and it clearly states, "We hold these truths to be self evident – that all men are **created** equal and are endowed by their **Creator** with certain unalienable rights – life, liberty and the pursuit of happiness." Since the atheist denies that we have a Creator, he denies the fountain from which our unalienable rights come. From his perspective, rights do not come from God – they come from government. That spells tyranny!!! Therefore, an atheist <u>cannot</u> be a loyal American! Why are we paying attention to atheists who want to take down the crosses, remove "In God We Trust" from our money, and throw out "under God" from our Pledge of Allegiance?

Is man the measure of all things? Are you the master of your own soul and the captain of your own fate? No! A thousand times NO!! This is a lie from Satan. **Majesty is the measure of all things!** *"O Lord, our Lord, how excellent is Your name in all the earth, You who set Your glory above the heavens." Psalm 8:1 (NKJV).* Let's get things in proper perspective! The Bible teaches that the fear of God is the beginning of knowledge [science] (Proverbs 1:7), and the fear of God is the beginning of wisdom. (Proverbs 9:10). Therefore, one who does not fear God is willfully ignorant – (Romans 1:18-22) – why should we pay attention to him? "The fool has said in his heart, 'There is no God.'" (Psalm 14:1 and 53:1). It is repeated twice – that is God's emphasis! So why should we pay attention to the rantings and writings of Richard Dawkins, Christopher Hichins, Sam Harris, Isaac Asmov, Michael Newdow, and their colleagues? *"Behold, the fear of the Lord, that is wisdom; and to depart from evil is understanding." (Job 28:28) KJV.*

Let's get even closer to home. Are your eyes on the Rock of Ages or your own resources? Are you a professing Christian, yet a practicing atheist? **Where is your trust in troubled times like these? Is your perspective mesmerized, measured and monitored by money?** You cannot – <u>cannot</u> – worship money and Majesty! Worship His Majesty! He will measure and monitor your money. **Don't love money and use people! Love people and use money – to His glory!** Be mesmerized by Majesty – not money!

Our Lord says, "Be **still and <u>know</u> that I am God.**" (Psalm 46:10) KJV. Money is not God. It can be gone with the wind – but the Eternal One remains. Men are not God – even those who like to pretend that they are. Where is your focus – on God or on Goliath?

+ + + + + + + + + +

June 2012

"Lord, What Do You Want Me to Do?"

This is one question Saul of Tarsus asked when, on the road to Damascus to persecute more Christians, he was confronted with the amazing, powerful Lord Jesus Christ, Who appeared to him as a light from heaven. However, notice Saul's first question:

"Then he fell to the ground, and heard a voice saying to him, 'Saul, Saul, why are you persecuting Me?' And he said, 'Who are You, Lord?' And the Lord said, 'I am Jesus, whom you are persecuting. It is hard for you to kick against the goads.' So he, trembling and astonished, said, 'Lord, what do You want me to do?'" Acts 9:4-6a (NKJV)

Perhaps you already know that Saul was dramatically converted to Jesus and became Paul the Apostle, who wrote approximately half of our New Testament Scriptures. Even the adamant evolutionist author and historian, H.G. Wells, admitted that Jesus Christ of Nazareth impacted history far more than any other man who has ever lived. In fact, He divides history in half – B.C. and A.D. **Truly history is His Story!** When you talk with skeptics, ask them, "**If Jesus did not rise from the dead, how do you explain this fact?**" And since Paul the Apostle is second only to Jesus in his impact upon history, ask them, "**How do you explain the conversion and extreme zeal of Paul from persecutor of Christians to persecuted proclaimer of the gospel if Jesus did not rise from the dead?**" By his own testimony Paul declared that his encounter with the risen Christ is what changed his course – and the course of history.

Also, please notice the first question Saul asked, "**Who are you, Lord?**" (Since he addressed Jesus as "Lord", he must have already known – but he needed to hear it.) Is Jesus your Lord – your Master? First you need to recognize Who He really is – Immanuel (God with us), Creator, Redeemer, Resurrected Lord. Then you are ready to ask the second question, "**Lord, what do You want me to do?**"

These are the two most pertinent and important questions you can ask. Why? Concerning the first question, Jeremiah wrote: *"But the Lord is the true God, He is the living God and the ever lasting king."* Jeremiah 10:10 Concerning the second question he wrote *"O Lord, I know the way of man is not in himself, it is not in man who walks to direct his own steps."* Jeremiah 10:23

One of the most often asked questions among Christians is, "How do I know the will of God for my life?" Usually this has to do with some specific detail – but if you follow the clearly revealed commands of Scripture, God's Holy Spirit will guide you in discerning His will in the details, *"for as many as are led by the Spirit of God, these are sons of God." Romans 8:14*

Often in Ukrainian University classes I tell my students that Almighty God has given them the right to choose which worldview to follow. If they choose evolutionism, then they are nothing but evolved animals with no intelligent designer, no plan, no purpose, no meaning and no hope, because evolutionism (by Frank Peretti's clear definition) is "from the goo to you by way of the zoo". (Besides, who started life in the goo anyway? Evolutionism believes many miracles and one of them is spontaneous generation – which Louis Pasteur scientifically showed to be false.) On the other hand, I tell my students that **I no longer have enough faith to believe evolutionism** and choose to believe "that Almighty God has specifically designed and created each one of you uniquely different from every other human being who has ever lived. He has given you a unique blend of talents, interests and abilities so that no one else can fulfill the purpose for which He has designed you. **Your greatest joy in life is to discover and fulfill the purpose for which He designed you.**

If you are asking, "Lord, what do You want me to do?" here are the basics:

1. *"Believe on the Lord Jesus Christ and you will be saved."* Acts 16:31

2. *"…Repent, and let every one of you be baptized in the name of Jesus Christ for the remission of sins; and you shall receive the gift of the Holy Spirit."* Acts 2:38 (NKJV)

3. *"Then Jesus came and spoke to them, saying, 'All authority has been given to Me in heaven and on earth. Go therefore and make disciples of all the nations, baptizing them in the name of the Father and of the Son and of the Holy Spirit, teaching them to observe all things that I have commanded you; and lo, I am with you always, even to the end of the age.' Amen."* Matthew 28:18-20 (NKJV)

4. *"Be very careful, then, how you live – not as unwise but as wise, making the most of every opportunity, because the days are evil. Therefore do not be foolish, but understand what the Lord's will is. Do not get drunk on wine, which leads to debauchery. Instead, be filled with the Spirit. Speak to one another with psalms, hymns and spiritual songs. Sing and make music in your heart to the Lord, always giving thanks to God the Father for everything, in the name of our Lord Jesus Christ. Submit to one another out of reverence for Christ."* Ephesians 5:15-21 (NIV)

5. *"For this is the will of God, your sanctification: that you should abstain from sexual immorality; that each of you should know how to possess his own vessel in sanctification and honor, not in passion of lust, like the Gentiles who do not know God; that no one should take advantage of and defraud his brother in this matter, because the Lord is the avenger of all such, as we also forewarned you and testified. For God did not call us to uncleanness, but in holiness. Therefore he who rejects this does not reject man, but God, who has also given us His Holy Spirit."* 1 Thessalonians 4:3-8 (NKJV)

6. *"Rejoice always, pray without ceasing, in everything give thanks; for this is the will of God in Christ Jesus for you."* 1 Thessalonians 5:16-18 (NKJV)

7. *"You will show me the path of life; In Your presence is fullness of joy; at Your right hand are pleasures forevermore."* Psalm 16:11 (NKJV). Since "the joy of the Lord is your strength", you will continue to gain strength and joy by basking in the presence of Almighty God.

As you abide in His presence and obey Him, you will experience His leading in the answers to your prayers about the details not given in Scripture.

Since we are to be "redeeming the time for the days are evil", remember that every day God grants us 11,400 seconds, which must be invested or lost. **As you ask, "Lord what do You want me to do?" and wait on His answer, how are you now investing those valuable seconds?** Since it is much easier to steer a car that is already moving, doesn't it make sense that it will be much easier for God to guide you if you are already moving on the instructions He has already given you?

+ + + + + + + + + +

July 2012

"TRUTH IS THE NEW HATE SPEECH"

Perhaps you remember the brief article we shared by Ray Hawk with this title in our April letter (If you save our letters, I encourage you to look back and read it – or you can look it up on our website at www.overseasoutreach.com or write to us for another copy.) The article is clear, concise, convicting – and true! I recently received a letter which vividly demonstrates the complete accuracy of Ray Hawk's allegations. Here is the background for the letter:

I was in one of the businesses we have provided lighting for, and I offered the owner's wife our May letter. She obviously didn't want it (I guess she read some of our other letters) and began to severely criticize Mitt Romney. I told her I'm not enthused with Mitt Romney either. **Then she dropped the bombshell statement by saying that the man who now occupies the White House is the most honest man who has ever been there.** Believe it or not – I held my tongue (amazing, isn't it!). I did walk out very soon after that!

A short time after that I read Dr. James Dobson's *Family Talk* newsletter for April in which he documents and exposes with direct quotations some of the lies Barack Obama has been caught in concerning abortion, free speech, freedom of religion and freedom of conscience for pro-life doctors, pharmacists, etc. I decided to send her a copy with the question, "If he is the most honest man to occupy the White House, how do you explain these blatant contradictions?" Here is her reply – word for word. (I'm deleting the author's name to protect the guilty. I am offering the letter to my friend, Rich Schell, to use in his counseling classes as an example of multiple violations of logical communication.)

"Mr. Rick H Deighton,

Anyone that used the pulpit to spread hate needs to think over what the Lord must think of that. We are all his children. He didn't say 'come ye little children unto me, no not you, not you and not you.' Let him be the judge and love mankind.

The world is so full of hate. I stand by what I said to you and I know the name President Obama. Who is James Dobson? I raised six children, two adopted. I didn't abort any of mine but considering what some people have to offer, drug homes ECT. That is between them and God. I am so sick of people that go around looking down their noses at people that aren't the replica of themselves.

I help the man with a cup on the corner and I don't ask him his political status or his religion or if there are any warrants out for him. If he is hungry he should be fed. I or you are not his judge or jury.

Freedom of Choice allows me to write you. Freedom of Choice is what America stands for. I refuse to be caught up in hate."

She used huge, bold print – then hand wrote the last three sentences – with the underlining – apparently to express her strong emotions. I did not send her a reply – what's the use? However, here is what I felt like writing:

"Thank you! Your overwhelming love for Dr. Dobson, for me, and for all other conservative Christians is so evident from this letter! By the way, you didn't attempt to answer my question. Why not?

Yours & His,
Rick Deighton"

Here are some observations:
1. I did not speak to her from a pulpit – I sent her a well documented letter. (If you want a copy, please write. We will gladly send you a copy.) However, I will say that I am not afraid or ashamed to say from a pulpit what is documented in James Dobson's letter. I believe that Barack Obama is a false prophet with a huge ego and a Messiah complex who needs to be exposed. If Christian leaders don't do it – who will? Shall we leave that to the conservative Jews, Mormons and Catholics? Be strong! Be bold! Tell the truth! Remember, when a moral issue becomes a political issue, it does not stop being a moral issue. In the early years of American history most preachers had election sermons to expose the moral issues and the candidates' positions. In 1954 Senator Lyndon Johnson designed a bogus law to threaten preachers with the loss of the tax exempt status of the church if they dared to preach election sermons again. He didn't want preachers fouling up his socialist plans and programs. That law passed. Now many preachers are afraid to speak up because they may lose their tax

exemption. What about being more afraid of Almighty God? He inspired Paul to write to Timothy: *"I charge you therefore before God and the Lord Jesus Christ, who will judge the living and the dead at His appearing and His kingdom: Preach the word! Be ready in season and out of season. Convince, rebuke, exhort, with all long-suffering and teaching. For the time will come when they will not endure sound doctrine, but according to their own desires, because they have itching ears, they will heap up for themselves teachers; and they will turn their ears away from the truth, and be turned aside to fables. But you be watchful in all things, endure afflictions, do the work of an evangelist, fulfill your ministry."* 2 Timothy 4:1-5 (NKJV)

Alliance Defense Fund has been encouraging pastors to challenge this bogus law as a blatant violation of the constitutional right to freedom of speech. They **want** the IRS to take a pastor to court so they can openly expose this law as unconstitutional. On Freedom of Speech Day three or four years ago, about fifty challenged the law by preaching on moral issues that have become political and sending copies of their sermons to the IRS. This year over four hundred did so. To date, the IRS has not attempted to rescind the 501c3 status even once! **Could it be they know better than to try?** (In 2013 there were over 1,600 challenges! R.D.)

2. I believe that Barack Obama is a highly dangerous hypocrite, not only for America, but for all Christians – both domestic and foreign. Why do I say this? Because Barack Obama professes to be a Christian, yet by his actions he denies and blasphemes the Name of our Sovereign Lord Jesus Christ. Jesus said, *"By their fruits you will know them."* Matthew 7:20. He was speaking about false prophets. Barack Obama is the man who spurned the National Day of Prayer in May, then declared the entire month of June as a celebration of homosexuality his first year in office. This year, along with Eric Holder, he denounced the Defense of Marriage Act as unconstitutional – then called it Defense Against Marriage Act when going public with his endorsement of "gay marriage". Barack Obama adamantly promotes the murder of the innocent unborn (and even some who are born), the agenda of the homosexual rights

campaign (which God labels abomination), and the agenda of
Islam, both foreign and domestic, (he even bowed before the king
of Saudi Arabia). Maybe you have also wondered why a committed Marxist who trained under activist demonstrator Saul Alinsky
would want to team up with Islam. Precisely because both Marxists
and Islamists hate America, hate Israel, and hate Christians. Both
philosophies follow the maxim that the end justifies the means.
Therefore, by either of these anti-Christ philosophies it is right
and good to lie, cheat, steal – even murder – if it promotes their
"greater cause". Unless we understand this we cannot understand
what is going on. This helps us realize why Obama has appointed
at least thirty nine Czars (Caesars) who answer to him – not to the
American voters (and one of these – his "Green Czar" was removed
after being exposed as a card-carrying communist). This also helps
us realize why he and his administration speak of the "freedom
of worship" (private) rather than the freedom of religion (public)
which our United States constitution guarantees. The late Chuck
Colson pointed out on one of his latest broadcasts that the **only**
time he ever heard Barack Obama speak of "Freedom of religion"
was when he was promoting the building of a gigantic mosque at
the New York City site of 9/11. To Islamists everywhere such a
mosque is a symbol of victory and claim to ownership.

Earlier I mentioned that Barack Obama not only believes in and
promotes abortion (the murder of the unborn), but also infanticide
(the murder of babies already born). That is because as a senator he
repeatedly voted against the "Born Alive Act", which was designed
to save the lives of infants who have survived botched abortions.
During his campaign he lied to cover this up – in spite of obvious
exposure by his recorded voting record. It is my sincere conviction
that any man this cold hearted is capable of any of the atrocities
committed under the Nazi regime. In fact, if you want to look carefully at the parallels between the United States of America now and
Germany in the 1930's you will find them striking and startling. I
highly recommend that you consider reading Eric Metaxis' carefully documented biography, *"Bonhoeffer"* and Erwin Lutzer's, *"When
a Nation Forgets God"*.

You may notice that I never use the title "President Obama". That is intentional – because I don't believe he legitimately deserves the title. He is the man who has spent hundreds of thousands of dollars for legal defense to avoid producing a valid birth certificate and refused to show up in court in Memphis when subpoenaed to appear to validate his claim that he was born in Hawaii in spite of strong evidence that he was born in Kenya. He apparently believes that he is above the law. It is a fact that his father is not an American citizen, which already nullifies his legitimacy for the presidency.

3. What about hate? Do I hate Barack Obama? I confess that I've sometimes struggled with the temptation to hate him, but I've asked God to deliver me from such hatred by realizing:

A. That he is a soul for whom Jesus died. On the cross Jesus prayed for His enemies, *"Father forgive them – they know not what they do."*

B. That he is a blind man spiritually. You don't hate a blind man for walking in darkness – you pray for God to open his eyes, convict him of sin, and bring him to deep and true repentance, baptism, forgiveness of sin and receiving of the gift of the Holy Spirit. That is what I'm doing. Therefore, I do not hate Barack Obama – I love him with the love of Christ by praying for his conversion for his sake and for the sake of the nation. Even though I hate what he is doing and sometimes feel intense anger, I do not hate him. (Every parent should also relate to such feelings!) For example, when I see the Obama administration taking the State of Arizona to court for protecting their own borders, encroaching more and more on constitutional freedoms by power grabs and executive orders, and intentionally driving America to bankruptcy with outrageous pork barrel spending (which will hurt our kids and grandkids more than us)

I do feel angry – intensely angry. I am not ashamed of that fact. I believe more Christians need to wake up and get angry. Anger itself is not sin – it's what we do with it that matters. The Word of God says, "*...be angry – and sin not.*" Ephesians 4:26, and *"God is a just judge, and God is angry with the wicked every day."* Psalm 7:11. Sometimes anger is the most godly emotion we can experience – and apathy the most ungodly! I'm reminded of a story I heard about a preacher who approached an elder and said, "We have two huge problems in this congregation – ignorance and apathy. What do you recommend we do to solve these?" The elder replied, "I don't know – and I don't care." These are huge problems in most American churches – and too many don't know and don't care. **Believers, earnestly pray for revival and prepare for persecution.** Hopefully the revival will come before the persecution – but it may not. Already there is intense hostility toward Biblical Christianity in Hollywood, in the media, in academia, in the school system, in the court system and in many businesses – yet many Christians are asleep with the attitude that it can't happen here.

I'm first a Christian, but I'm also a husband, a father, a grandfather, a missionary, a business owner and a citizen of the United States of America. There are responsibilities in each realm of my life and influence. **Abraham Lincoln spoke of government of the people, by the people, and for the people. In this nation politics is my business – my responsibility.** If you are an American citizen – **it's yours too!** If you are a Christian, your responsibility is heightened, not diminished because **we** are the ones to be salt and light in a dark world. **What are you going to do about it?**

4. I also realize that Barack Obama is simply the front man for some other powerful, shadowy figures – billionaires like George Soros, Ted Turner, and Tom Gill who share his godless philosophy. I also pray for their conversion.

5. The real battle is spiritual. *"For though we walk in the flesh, we do not war according to the flesh.* **For the weapons of our warfare are not carnal but mighty in God for pulling down strongholds, casting down arguments** *and every high thing that exalts itself against the knowledge of God,* **bringing every thought into captivity to the obedience of Christ,** *and being ready to punish all disobedience when your obedience is fulfilled."* 2 Corinthians 10:3-6.

Does the fact that I do not agree with the political agenda of the left wing elitists mean that I hate them? Does the fact that James Dobson rips the mask off and exposes some of Barack Obama's false promises and outright lies mean that he is propagating hate? This must be an effective tactic – they keep using it as their trump card. **If their charge is true then we must face the inevitable conclusion that our Lord Jesus Christ was guilty of "hate speech" as well.** The chief priests were both political and religious leaders in Israel, yet Jesus ripped the mask off their lies and false doctrines, exposed them as false prophets, and called them hypocrites! (See Matthew 23). Jesus was even more severe with them than the Old Testament prophets were with the corrupt leaders in their times. Yet in Acts 6:7 we read, *"And the word of God spread, and the number of the disciples multiplied greatly in Jerusalem, and* **a great many of the priests were obedient to the faith."** Finally, the truth penetrated their calloused hearts! **Many of the priests repented and obeyed the gospel!** Praise God! It took the severity of Jesus' love, plus overwhelming evidence to convict and convince them. **Sometimes love must be tough!** Paul was the man God chose to pen the most potent description of true love in all literature (see 1 Corinthians 13), yet Paul is the man who exposed a false prophet with harsh words: *"But Elymas the sorcerer (for so his name is translated) withstood them, seeking to turn the proconsul away from the faith. Then Saul, who also is called Paul,* **filled with the Holy Spirit,** *looked intently at him and said, 'O full of all deceit and all fraud, you son of the devil, you enemy of all righteousness, will you not cease perverting the straight ways of the Lord? 'And now, indeed, the hand of the Lord is upon you, and you shall be blind, not seeing the sun for a time.'*

And immediately a dark mist fell on him, and he went around seeking someone to lead him by the hand. Then the proconsul believed, when he saw what had been done, being astonished at the teaching of the Lord." Acts 13:8-12. This exposure led to the salvation of the proconsul. **That's tough love in action! Where is the tough love today in our churches?** In our politically **incorrect** society? (How can it be "politically correct" when it is morally wrong?) Why was Joe Wilson pressured by his Republican colleagues to apologize for shouting, "You lie!" when he spoke the truth? James Dobson used more polite terminology, such as duplicity and deception, but the bottom line is that he exposed some of Barack Obama's lies (which the liberal media refuses to expose).

Are we willing to speak truth about abortion? About marriage? The Word of God says, *"Marriage is honorable among all and the bed undefiled, but fornicators and adulterers God will judge."* Hebrews 13:4. So called "gay marriage" is not gay (happy)! It is not marriage! It is not honorable! It is not undefiled! It is homosexual perversion which God calls an abomination. **What right does anyone have to call "marriage" what God calls abomination?** Friends, it's time to wake up! It's time to call a spade a spade and a sin a sin! How else will sinners be convicted by the Word of God and come to repentance? **Tough love is real love – Biblical love!** Ravi Zacharias has a message entitled, 'The Intolerance of Tolerance". Is the letter I received a classic example of this message? One university professor opposing Christians on campus for rejecting his viewpoint (about homosexuality, I believe) said, "We don't tolerate the intolerable!" We shouldn't be surprised. Biblical Christianity was "intolerable" in the first century also. Jesus said, **"If *they hated me they will hate you.*"**

October 2012

Which Way America?

"In God We Trust" – or "In Government We Trust"

Almighty God says, *"Those who honor me I will honor"* 1 Samuel 2:30. I certainly believe this applies to individuals, but I also believe it applies to nations, for the Word of God also tells us, *"Righteousness exalts a nation, but sin is a reproach to any people"* Proverbs 14:34. Today as I write this (October 6) it is exactly one month before the most critical election in the history of this constitutional republic. Remember – this is a constitutional republic which was intentionally founded by our forefathers – not a democracy! Do you remember our pledge? *"I pledge allegiance to the flag... and to the **republic** for which it stands, one nation **under God**, indivisible, with liberty and justice for all."* Plato wrote over 300 B.C. that a pure democracy could never last because the people would bankrupt the treasury when they discovered they could vote themselves more and more money from the public treasury. The current administration is not only bankrupting the treasury, but also seeking to obliterate God from government, from schools, from morals, and from public life. Do you remember that Barack Hussein Obama leaves God out of the Declaration of Independence? He says "endowed with certain..." instead of "endowed by our Creator with certain inalienable rights". If our rights are not "endowed by our Creator" but by our government, then the government can take them away (which is already happening to an alarming degree).

November 2012

Reflection on the Election

On November 7th, as I was struggling with deep disappointment and a sick feeling in the pit of my stomach, God directed my attention to some passages in the book of Daniel that I believe are very pertinent. This is the context of how God was dealing with the proud and pompous potentate, Nebuchadnezzar, king of Babylon – who thought he was the ruler of the world and deserved to be worshipped. Following is a portion of what Nebuchadnezzar wrote after God humbled him and brought him low:

> *"Nebuchadnezzar the king, To all peoples, nations and languages that dwell in all the earth: Peace be multiplied to you. I thought it good to declare the signs and wonders that the Most High God has worked for me. How great are His signs, and how mighty His wonders! His kingdom is an everlasting kingdom, and His dominion is from generation to generation.....In order that the living may know that the Most High rules in the kingdom of men, gives it to whomever He will, and sets over it the lowest of men." Daniel 4:1-3 & 17 (NKJV).*

The King James Version says "the basest of men." Amen. God is in control. I'm reminded of Solomon's words that "there is nothing new under the sun." As it was in the days of Daniel, about 2600 years ago, so it is today.

Nebuchadnezzar became a God-honoring believer and his letter concludes with these amazing words:

> *"Now I, Nebuchadnezzar, praise and extol and honor the King of heaven, all of whose works are truth, and His ways justice. And those who walk in pride He is able to abase." Daniel 4:37 (NKJV).*

How did God punish and prune Nebuchadnezzar for his pride before promoting him back to his position as potentate? He knocked his sense out in order to pound some sense into him. Nebuchadnezzar went from insomnia to insanity to insight! (I thank Chuck Swindoll for this insightful observation.)

Here are Daniel's words to Belshazzar in reminding him of his grandfather's experience:

> *"O king, the Most High God gave Nebuchadnezzar your father a kingdom and majesty, glory and honor. And because of the majesty that He gave him, all peoples, nations, and languages trembled and feared before him. Whomever he wished, he executed; whomever he wished, he kept alive; whomever he wished, he set up; and whomever he wished, he put down. But when his heart was lifted up, and his spirit was hardened in pride, he was deposed from his kingly throne, and they took his glory from him. Then he was driven from the sons of men, his heart was made like the beasts, and his dwelling was with the wild donkeys. They fed him with grass like oxen, and his body was wet with the dew of heaven, till he knew that the Most High God rules in the kingdom of men, and appoints over it whomever He chooses. But you his son, Belshazzar, have not humbled your heart, although you knew all this." Daniel 5:18-22 (NKJV).*

Note that God punished and pruned Nebuchadnezzar by making him a wild man and sending him out to live with the wild donkeys. Please fervently pray for our "president" to have the pride knocked out so he becomes a bona fide bold believer! God did it with Nebuchadnezzar – He can do it again!

Final Article

My final article for Chapter 7 (the number of completion) does not come from one of our prayer letters. This article comes from a lesson I prepared for a business seminar in Ukraine. "Integrity Wins" in business and in life! It fits perfectly with the theme, "More than Conquerors in Cultural Clashes."

INTEGRITY WINS!
By Rick Deighton

Introduction:

In a small town in southern U. S. A. there were two brothers who were known all over the country as notorious scoundrels. After one brother died, the other went to the preacher of the small congregation and offered him $1,000 to do the funeral and declare his brother a saint. The preacher, as a man of integrity, knew he could not lie, but he and his church could really use the money. "Give me 24 hours to think and pray over this. I'll give you an answer tomorrow," he told the man. The next day the preacher called back and agreed to do the service.

At the funeral, to the shock and chagrin of the living brother, the preacher declared, "Honestly, I must tell you that the man in this coffin was a liar, a cheater, and a womanizer. Actually, he was a rotten scoundrel, but compared to his brother, he was a saint!!!" In this way, the young preacher fulfilled the requirement, yet maintained his integrity. Integrity is the foundation of all inter-personal relationships.

Some excuse lying or cheating by saying, "Oh, it's just business—that is how it's done. NO! Build on rock—not on sand! I'm not talking about refusing to make a profit. There must be a profit, or there will be no business. But when you agree on a price or a service, keep your word!

Purpose Statement:

The first purpose of this paper is to answer the questions, "Is honesty the best policy in business?" and "Do the honest business-men come in last?"

My second purpose is to clarify what integrity is and why it is worth any price to build integrity into your life and your business. **You cannot have integrity in your business, if you don't have it in your life!** What you are is basic to what you do. The Bible says concerning a miser: **"For as he thinks in his heart, so is he."** Proverbs 23:7 (NKJV).

I. The Essence of Integrity *(What is it?)*

My dictionary gives three definitions for integrity, and they are all closely related:

1. "The quality or state of being complete; unbroken condition; wholeness; entirety."

2. "The quality or state of being unimpaired; perfect condition; soundness."

3. "The quality or state of being of sound moral principle; uprightness, honesty, and sincerity."

A. Strength of Character

Of course, we want to focus on definition number three, but the other two will illustrate the meaning for us. When carpenters speak about the integrity of wooden beams or rafters, they mean that there are no visible knot holes or cracks to weaken the wood. Wood with integrity does not break under pressure; so also, businessmen with integrity are sound—they do not break under the pressure of bribes or threats.

We find an outstanding example of such strength of character in Genesis 39. Joseph was the favored son of his aging father, and his jealous brothers sold him into slavery. Potiphar, the captain of Pharaoh's guard in Egypt, bought him. When Potiphar noticed how God blessed Joseph with success and saw that he could be trusted, he elevated Joseph to become manager of his entire estate. The problem arose when Potiphar's wife also noticed that Joseph was well built and handsome. She lusted for him and said, "Come to bed with me!" The temptation was real, and Potiphar's wife was probably beautiful. Joseph may have felt flattered that she would want him, a slave. He could have rationalized, "After what my brothers did to me, I deserve some rewards." But Joseph was a businessman of integrity, so he refused her advances. He told her, "With me in charge, my master does not concern himself with anything in the house; everything he owns he has entrusted to my care. No one is greater in this house than I am. My master has withheld nothing from me except you, because you are his wife. How then could I do such a wicked thing and sin against God?" Genesis 39:8-9 (NIV). Joseph was a man of integrity!

What gave Joseph the strength of character to resist her constant attempts to seduce him? Notice his focus. He was focused on others—not on self! He would not betray his master's confidence, nor would he sin against God. When we look to how our actions will affect others and how we can please God, we strengthen character and build integrity. Reputation is what others think I am; integrity is what I am in the dark when no one else is looking. What I am in the dark, however, will sooner or later come out into the light.

What I believe or don't believe about God will directly affect my actions, my character, my integrity. King David of Israel recognized this fact, therefore, he prayed: "I know, my God, that You test the heart and are pleased with **integrity**." 1 Chronicles 29:17 (NIV).

What results came from Joseph's integrity? At first, the results seemed awful. Potiphar's wife became incensed at the rejection and falsely accused Joseph of attempting rape. Joseph ended up demoted and locked in prison. (We can assume, however, that Potiphar trusted Joseph's integrity more than his wife's, or Joseph would have been executed.) By God's blessing, Joseph was raised up from prison to prime minister of Egypt—second in command only to Pharaoh. **From the pit to the pinnacle by providential power!** That is Joseph's story. **Integrity wins!**

B. **What Qualities Demonstrate Integrity?**

1. **Be reliable—keep your word!** My father was a carpenter and contractor, who owned his business (along with a partner). At twelve years of age, I began working with him and never observed him cheating anyone but himself. The reason he cheated himself was that he often bid jobs too low, and they took longer than he estimated, but when he gave someone a price for a job, he stuck by it. Although my dad was not a Christian, he adopted this Christian principle into his life and his business. Because people knew he was reliable, they gave him their business.

   Recently in our lighting business, I bid on a job, estimating sixteen hours electrician time, but our electrician was able to finish in twelve and a half hours. I could have charged Brown Bus Company the full amount of the bid, but I believe I had told Brad, "It won't be more than this, but it could be less." When I told him that the actual amount he owed was less than the bid, he was pleasantly surprised and said, "That's different! It usually turns out to be twice as much!" I believe we will get his business again. **Integrity wins!**

2. **Be virtuous and faithful, even in little things. Remember to be flexible with your personal opinions, but stand solid on your principles.** I've read that the reason Abraham Lincoln was nicknamed "Honest Abe" was because he had walked back a long distance to return five cents he was overpaid. Another story I've heard that is reported to be based on a true account was about a preacher who received too much change from a bus driver. When the preacher returned the extra change to the driver, he told him, "I believe you gave me too much change by mistake," the driver said, "No, it was not by mistake. **It was a test. I heard you speak yesterday, and I wanted to know if you practice what you preach. I will be back to hear you again."** Integrity wins!

II. THE PRICE OF INTEGRITY

A. **Integrity may cost you your position.** My wife, Della, once quit her job when we really needed the money because I was still in college. Why did she quit? Because the supervisor at the business she worked for was expecting (demanding) that she lie for them.

B. **Integrity may cost you lots of time** because it takes longer to do a job right than to take short cuts.

C. **Integrity may cost you your life.** Queen Esther was willing to risk her life by going to the king without his bidding in order to save her people, but she said, "**If I perish, I perish.**" Her people were saved and she didn't have to sacrifice her life. **Integrity wins!**

III. THE REWARDS OF INTEGRITY

A. A Clear Conscience

"The man of integrity walks securely, but he who takes crooked paths will be found out." Proverbs 10:9 (NIV). What a wonderful peace there is to lie down and sleep with a clear conscience, instead of lying awake wondering who else knows what you have done.

B. Peace and Security

"You will keep him in perfect peace, whose mind is fixed on You..." Isaiah 26:3 (NKJV).

"Righteousness guards the man of integrity, but wickedness overthrows the sinner." Proverbs 13:6 (NIV). If you choose to discard integrity "be sure your sin will find you out."

C. Guidance

"The integrity of the upright guides them, but the unfaithful are destroyed by their duplicity." Proverbs 11:3 (NIV). It is so much easier to make decisions on many matters when strong principles of integrity guide you.

Examples: Before my closing illustration, I want to share a few examples of these rewards. My formal education was in theology and philosophy, not business, and I am an ordained minister of the gospel of Christ. For twelve years I functioned full time in the area of my professional training as a minister in a local church, as a missionary and co-founder of Alpine Christian Mission, and as a Bible College professor. However, for nearly 30 years I have functioned as a bi-vocational evangelist by earning our primary income in business. My research in business comes from training seminars, writings and recordings of highly successful entrepreneurs, who have learned how to build a prosperous business. Three of the most outstanding of these trainers are Zig Ziglar, Paul J. Meyer, and Tom Hopkins. All of them have come from very humble financial backgrounds, including hand-to-mouth poverty.

Tom Hopkins started out earning his income carrying steel beams on a construction site after dropping out of college. Paul J. Meyer began earning his income picking fruit in the orchards of southern California. Zig Ziglar's mother was a widow with a large family, and it took all of them working together to have enough to eat during the Great Depression of the 1930's in America. Now each of these men is a highly skilled business entrepreneur with multi-million dollar business investments. What do all of them have in common? Integrity! Every one of these men built his life and his business on integrity. And every one of them is a committed Christian, who attributes his integrity and his success to Jesus Christ, our Lord!

Paul J. Meyer wrote a book several years ago entitled, "Unlocking Your Legacy", in which he tells of starting 100 businesses during his life. Sixty five of those businesses are no longer functioning, but he doesn't consider any one of them a failure, because he learned something valuable from each one. He still owns 35 functioning, profitable businesses. The best known of these is "Success Motivation Institute", which in itself is a multi-billion dollar enterprise. I would say this man is a successful businessman, wouldn't you? But do you know what he considers his greatest accomplishment? His faith transmitted to his family! His legacy and his joy is that he is still married to the wife of his youth, they both love God and each other, and all of their grown children are committed Christians. **What a legacy! Integrity wins!**

Conclusion:

A pertinent story we recently received by email is an excellent illustration:

"*A few years ago, a group of salesmen went to a regional sales convention in Chicago. They had assured their wives that they would be home in plenty of time for Friday night dinner. In their rush, with tickets and briefcases in hand, one of them inadvertently knocked over a table which held a display of apples. Apples flew everywhere. Without stopping or looking back, they all managed to reach the plane in time for their nearly missed boarding. ALL BUT ONE!!! He paused, took a deep breath, got in touch with his feelings, and experienced a twinge of compassion for the girl whose apple stand had been overturned. He told his buddies to go on without him, waved good-bye, told one of them to call his wife when they arrived home, and explain why he was taking a later flight. He then returned to the terminal, where the apples were scattered all over the floor. He was glad he did, because the display of apples, which was now in total disarray, belonged to a young lady who was totally blind! She was softly crying, tears running down her cheeks in frustration, and at the same time helplessly groping for the spilled produce as the crowd swirled about her. No one stopped to help, and no one seemed to care about her plight.*

"*The salesman knelt on the floor with her, gathered up the apples, put them back on the table, and arranged them into a display. As he did this, he noticed that many of the fruits had become battered and bruised. These he set aside in another basket. When he had finished, he turned to the blind girl and asked, 'Are you okay?' She nodded through her tears. He then took out his wallet, pulled out a few bills, and said, 'Please take this $40 for the damage we caused. I hope we didn't spoil your day too badly.'*

"As the salesman started to walk away, the bewildered girl called out to him, 'Mister...' He paused and looked back. Then, she asked, 'Are you Jesus?' Without responding, he slowly made his way to the departure gate to catch the later flight with the question burning in his mind: 'Are you Jesus?' Do people mistake you for Jesus?"   ~ *Author Unknown*

Why did the blind girl mistake this salesman for Jesus? Integrity! He acted with integrity and showed her kindness. Paul J. Meyer said, **"No legacy is as rich as integrity." Integrity wins!**

The Commitment

Finally, I want to share this concise, clear, crisp quotation from the late Adrian Rogers:

"The church is not the servant of the state!

The church is not the master of the state!

The church is the conscience of the state!

We will be civil – but WE WILL NOT BE SILENT!!!"

The Bottom Line

"I'm tired of being inhibited! I want to be inhabited! Lord, live your life through me!"

~ *Adrian Rogers*

Courage is not the absence of fear – it is conquering of fear! "For God has not given us the spirit of fear, but of love and of power and of a sound mind." 2 Timothy 1:7.

WE ARE MORE THAN CONQUERORS.

WE WILL BE CIVIL - BUT

WE WILL NOT BE SILENT!!

Questions for Chapter 7 – Second Half

1. What is the danger of compromising with cultural corruption?

2. What two points were most significant to you in the open letter to a college student struggling with doubts?

3. Does everything have a cause? Why or why not?

4. What is the only worldview which explains the origin of evil? Why?

5. Is there actually solid evidence that Jesus arose from the dead? Explain your answer.

6. Do you believe the folk proverb, "Don't mix religion with business"? Why or why not?

7. What happened when the atheists (humanists) came to discredit our display for Northwest Science Museum?

8. What can we learn from a befuddled football player?

9. What is your perspective about the cultural wars? What do you see as God's leading for you to make a difference – a positive impact for truth and righteousness?

10. Do you, deep down in your soul, believe that integrity wins? Why or why not?

Chapter 7: Which Way, America?

Final Thoughts

When a family of skunks takes up residence under your house it is very difficult to get them out without a fight and without raising a stink. This is perhaps the best illustration I can think of for our political situation in America today. I believe we need not just a battalion, but an entire army of prayer warriors who will pray fervently, love profusely, give generously, and fight unashamedly for truth and righteousness in the powerful name of Jesus Christ our Lord. For example, in the midst of a plethora of bad news reports I recently heard this uplifting report: In Florida, a group of ladies were in a home for a jewelry party when a robber walked in, pulled a handgun, and ordered them to put all their money, jewelry, and cell phones in a bag. One lady thought it was just a joke and said, "Oh, it's only a squirt gun!" The robber was incensed. He assured them it was no joke and said he would kill one of them to prove it. Then he pointed the pistol at one lady's temple. At this, the hostess looked directly at him and said, "Get out of my house! In the Name of Jesus Christ I command you to get out of my house!" Several other ladies started saying, "Jesus! Jesus! Jesus!" The man turned and ran out of the house. **There is power in the name of Jesus!**

In the concluding section of this book I want to first address my fellow Americans who have also committed their lives to the Lord Jesus Christ. John 1:18 says, *"No one has seen God at any time. The only begotten Son, who is in the bosom of the Father, He has declared Him." In Him we have both grace and truth!* **We are empowered by the Holy Spirit**, Who dwells in our hearts in order for us to live victorious Christian lives and speak the truth in love to our fellow Americans who have not yet committed their lives to Jesus. **We hold the keys to conquest in cultural clashes! In fact, we are "more than conquerors in cultural clashes!!!"**

We know Him who is the Way, the Truth, and the Life! We have His power, His love, and His truth by the indwelling of His Spirit. The issue is this – **Do we have the passion to boldly speak the truth in love and fervently pray for true revival in our churches and deep conviction and spiritual awakening in our nation so that millions bow their knees and hearts to the Lord Jesus Christ?** That is the question!

Is the Harvest Past?

For America?

For you?

"'The harvest is past, the summer is ended, and we are not saved!'" Jeremiah 8:20

The truth is that it is very late – but NO! – the harvest is not past, but I believe the greatest harvest of souls for America is still ahead of us. Let's lift up the hands that hang down, strengthen the feeble knees, and get with it!! Remember: *"The LORD HAS DONE GREAT THINGS FOR US, and we are glad. . . Those who sow in tears shall reap in joy. He who continually goes forth weeping, bearing seed for sowing, shall doubtless come again with rejoicing, bringing his sheaves with him." Psalm 126:3, 5-6.*

"And do this, knowing the time, that now it is high time to awake out of sleep; for now our salvation is nearer than when we first believed. The night is far spent, the day is at hand. Therefore let us cast off the works of darkness, and let us put on the armor of light. Let us walk properly, as in the day, not in revelry and drunkenness, not in lewdness and lust, not in strife and envy. But put on the Lord Jesus Christ, and make no provision for the flesh, to fulfill its lusts." Romans 13:11-14

Now I want to share an outline I got from Adrian Rogers, plus a few of my own comments:

The Exaltation of a Nation

"Righteousness exalts a nation, but sin is a reproach to any people." Proverbs 14:34

I. The Exaltation of Our Nation

This is the past! It came on the wave of the first Great Awakening!

II. The Deterioration of Our Nation

This is the present. It has come about through the undermining, ungodly philosophies of Darwin, Freud, Marx, Engels, Nietzsche, Kane, Hume and a few others! *"Beware lest anyone cheat you through philosophy and empty deceit, according to the tradition of men, according to the basic principles of the world, and not according to Christ. For in Him dwells all the fullness of the Godhead bodily; and you are complete in Him, who is the head of all principality and power." Colossians 2:8-10*

What shall we do about it? That, my friend, is the main purpose of this book!

III. The Rejuvenation of Our Nation

This is our future – if we, the people of God, choose to obey Him! *"...if My people who are called by My name will humble themselves, and pray and seek My face, and turn from their wicked ways, then I will hear from heaven, and will forgive their sin and heal their land." 2 Chronicles 7:14.*

"Confess your trespasses to one another, and pray for one another, that you may be healed. The effective, fervent prayer of a righteous man avails much. Elijah was a man with a nature like ours, and he prayed earnestly that it would not rain; and it did not rain on the land for three years and six months. And he prayed again, and the heaven gave rain, and the earth produced its fruit. Brethren, if anyone among you wanders from the truth, and someone turns him back, let him know that he who turns a sinner from the error of his way will save a soul from death and cover a multitude of sins." James 5:16-20.

Now in the wake of these powerful truths, let's ask ourselves, "Are we going to cringe, cower and complain, or are we going to live and act on the fact of who we really are? **We ARE "More than conquerors!!!"**

Now I'm going to let some excellent writers clinch the conquering concepts in your hearts. They have already said it better than I can.

The July 2010 *afaJournal* has an excellent article entitled "Deism and the Declaration: Fact-checking Jefferson's theology", which is an interview with American historian David Barton. Here are the last 3 questions and answers:

"AFAJ: Why have most of us never heard these things in our history classes?

DB: We use an approach in history today called deconstruction and post-structuralism. Deconstruction points out all the negatives and makes the exception into the rule. Post-structuralism divides people into groups and makes them part of the group rather than part of the full unit.

For instance, out of the 56 signers of the Declaration, textbooks will only mention Jefferson and Franklin. They will point out the least religious and say all the Founding Fathers were like those two. That's the exception, not the rule.

We are taught the Founding Fathers were rich, elitist, land owners. This isn't true. Sam Adams was so poor he didn't even have a suit to wear in Congress. His friends had to take a collection so he could buy his first suit.

Then there is post-structuralism. We don't teach all the black founders who were there during the Revolution. We don't show all the pictures of whites and blacks together. We don't point out that the heroes of Bunker Hill and Yorktown were black soldiers who received more commendations than any others. We don't point out Massachusetts never had a time when blacks could not vote, or that women voted throughout the colonial period. Back then, we were all Americans. Whether black or white, man or woman, red or brown.

AFAJ: How can people educate themselves?

DB: The best way to educate yourself is to read books before progressives got ahold of textbooks. They got into the education system in the 1920s. If you want to get a good historical view, you have to read any book prior to 1900. The good thing about Google books is that you can read all these great books online. Groups like Wallbuilders and others are reprinting history books that have been used for generations because they are unbiased.

AFAJ: Do you think America can get back to the ideals of the Declaration?

DB: Absolutely. I'm convinced of it. I have more optimism today than I've had in 30 years. Look at the best sellers right now. They are things like David McCullough's book *John Adams*. Americans are willing to pay money to learn what they were supposed to learn in school. All the information in that book used to be in the textbooks. Now we are willing to pay good money on the free market, and that's very healthy. We are getting back to a hunger for knowledge of who we were, what made us who we are and knowing the men who started our country.

So read the old stuff. I recommend everyone read George Washington's Farewell Address. We used to require that in public schools. In that Washington says you cannot have political prosperity if you separate religion and morality from politics. That's what seculars are trying to do, and it will destroy our political and economic prosperity." (*afaJournal*, July 2010 www. afajournal.org)

"CHOOSE YOUR ATTITUDE"
by Charles R. Swindoll

"He who trusts in his own heart is a fool, but he who walks wisely will be delivered. Solomon: Proverbs 28:26

This may shock you, but I believe the single most significant decision I can make on a day-to-day basis is my choice of attitude.

It is more important than my past, my education, my bankroll, my successes or failures, fame or pain, what other people think of me or say about me, my circumstances, or my position.

Attitude . . . keeps me going or cripples my progress. It alone fuels my fire or assaults my hope.

When my attitudes are right, there's no barrier too high, no valley too deep, no dream too extreme, no challenge too great for me.

Yet, we must admit that we spend more of our time concentrating and fretting over the things that can't be changed in life than we do giving attention to the one thing that can, our choice of attitude.

'I think the most significant decision I can make today is my choice of attitude.' —Chuck Swindoll"

(Excerpted from Charles R. Swindoll, *Wisdom for the Way* (Nashville: J. Countryman, a division of Thomas Nelson, Inc., 2001). Copyright © 2001 by Charles R. Swindoll, Inc. All rights reserved. Used by permission.)

INSIGHTS FROM ALEXIS DE TOCQUEVILLE

"The American Republic will endure until the day Congress discovers that it can bribe the pubic with the public's money."

"Democracy and socialism have nothing in common but one word, equality. But notice the difference: while democracy seeks equality in liberty, socialism seeks equality in restraint and servitude."

"The greatness of America lies not in being more enlightened than any other nation, but rather in her ability to repair her faults."

"Life is to be entered upon with courage."

"When the past no longer illuminates the future, the spirit walks in darkness."

"The Americans combine the notions of religion and liberty so intimately in their minds, that it is impossible to make them conceive of one without the other."

"The main business of religions is to purify, control, and restrain that excessive and exclusive taste for well-being which men acquire in times of equality."

ALL AUTHORITY BELONGS TO CHRIST*

by D. James Kennedy

"All authority has been given to Me in heaven and on earth – Matthew 28:18b (NKJV)

All power is given unto Jesus Christ. After His ascension, He sat down at the right hand of God until His enemies be made His footstool (Psalm 110:1 and Hebrews 1:13). Through these last 2,000 years, Jesus Christ has been continually gaining the victory, a victory which began at the time of His death and resurrection and which continues on through the ages.

In AD 363, Julian the Apostate, the emperor of Rome who tried to relight the fires on pagan altars and overthrow the newly established Christian faith, marched against the Persians. One of his soldiers, a Christian, was sorely derided and persecuted by some of the heathen soldiers. They mocked him, beat him, threw him to the ground, and said, "Tell us, where is your carpenter now?"

He responded, "He is busy constructing a coffin for your emperor." A few months later, a mortal wound in his side, Julian the Apostate took his hands, grasped a handful of his own blood, flung it against the sky, and said, "Thou has conquered, O Galilean." The Carpenter of

Galilee is busy constructing coffins for all the ungodly kings and kingdoms of this earth.

Christ is Lord of all."

(*This commentary is selected from the daily devotional* Beside Still Waters. Used by permission.)

+ + + + + + + + +

"Caesar or Christ?"

Surely the message of the Revelation encourages believers to envision the eternal glory beyond the present terror.

"The Revelation of Jesus Christ is not a revelation *about* Christ, it is a revelation *from* the living Christ. He sent it by His angel to His servant John, who was doing time on the isle of Patmos for the word of God and for the testimony of Jesus Christ. John, in turn, shared The Revelation of Jesus Christ with the seven angels of the seven churches in Asia. Today churches around the world are blessed, as were they, by the reading, hearing and application of the powerful message contained in the prophetic book. Homer Hailey said, "The grand theme of Revelation is that of war and conflict between good and evil resulting in victory for the righteous and defeat for the wicked...**It is a war to the death for one, and eternal victory for the other."**

In his *Daily Bible Study Series* on Revelation, William Barclay describes Domitian, who ruled Rome from AD 81-96, as 'a devil ... a cold-blooded persecutor.' He was the first to seriously demand 'Caesar worship.' Everyone who addressed Domitian in speech or letter had to begin with the words 'Our Lord and God.' Barclay writes, 'Here is the background of the Revelation. All over the Empire men and women must call Domitian god –or die. Caesar worship was the deliberate policy; all must say: 'Caesar is Lord.' There was no escape. What were the Christians to do? What hope had they? They had not many wise and not many mighty. They had no influence or prestige. Against them had risen the might of Rome which no nation had ever resisted. **They were confronted with the choice – Caesar or Christ.**'

'It was to encourage men in such times,' says Barclay, 'that the Revelation was written. John did not shut his eyes to the terrors; he saw dreadful things and he saw still more dreadful things on the way; **but beyond them he saw glory for those who defied Caesar for the love of Christ.** The Revelation comes from one of the most heroic ages in all the history of the Christian Church ... The Revelation is a clarion call to be faithful unto death in order to win the crown of life ... it contains the blazing faith of the Christian Church in the days when life was an agony and men expected the end of the heavens and the earth as they knew them, **but still believed that beyond the terror was the glory and above the raging of men was the power of God.**'

History repeats itself. Today, Christians in many parts of the world are experiencing terror and dreadful treatment. **Many believe that more Christians have been killed by 'cold-blooded persecutors' in the 20th century than in all the previous centuries since the days of the Caesars** in ancient Rome. In many Muslim nations today it is 'Muhammad or the sword.' Nearly every day we read or hear of believers being killed and church buildings being burned by fanatical followers of Muhammad or Hindu extremists. Surely the message of the Revelation encourages believers to envision the eternal glory beyond the present terror.

Who would have dreamed of a day in America where the government was no longer supportive of religious liberty, biblical marriage, and the sanctity of life? The largest religious institution in the United States, the Roman Catholic Church, is being forced to offer insurance with contraception services, including the 'morning after' pill. The same vile directive is being forced upon Wheaton College, an evangelical college, and Hobby Lobby, a Christian-based business. 'Caesar or Christ' all over again.

Following the re-election of President Obama, entertainer Jaime Foxx praised the president at the 2012 BET Soul Train Awards, saying, 'It's like church in here. First of all, give an honor to God and our Lord and Savior Barack Obama.' **To this day the White House has not denounced this outright blasphemy.** It is one thing to be narcissistic; it is quite another to have a Messianic complex. Earlier, the May 14, 2012 cover of *Newsweek* magazine declared Obama 'the first gay president,' placing a rainbow halo over his head. **Are the times we live in merely disgusting ... or are they extremely dangerous?**

But no matter the resident in the White House, John saw a Rider on a white horse (Rev 19:11)! The armies of heaven followed Him on white horses (19:14), the beast and the false prophet were captured and cast into hell (19:20), and Satan himself was hurled into hell (20:10). God shall dwell with us and wipe away every tear (21:4), Jesus is coming quickly (22:7, 12), and we shall have the right to the tree of life and enter through the gates into the beautiful city (22:14). **Beyond the terror of man is the glory of God.**"

(Victor Knowles, *One Body*, Spring 2013. Used by permission.)

+ + + + + + + + + +

"Stand Your Ground, Oh Church"

by Dr. Bob Moorehead

"**Stand your ground, O Church! The enemy is on the rampage again! Stand your ground! Let neither fear of public opinion or criticism by the ungodly daunt your mission!**

Final Thoughts

The cesspools of immorality, perversion, and filth are belching up sewage again, but stand your ground! The deceiving twins of lethargy and apathy are working overtime, but stand your ground, O Church, stand your ground. The volcanic ash of addictions and abuse is falling like never before, but stand your ground, dear Church! As Satan shreds marriages, fractures families, and rains domestic violence on homes, stand your ground. While greed, lust, anger, murder, rape, perversion, drunkenness, pornography, lying, adultery, fraud and despair all have their heyday, stand your ground, O Church, stand your ground! As your prophets adjust the truth to save their faces and their jobs, dear Church, don't retreat, or back away. While much of your membership continue their materialistic lifestyle, and continue to be 'at ease in Zion,' still, stand your ground, O Church, stand your ground!

While liberal politicians continue to separate God and government, and you are unfairly restricted, don't give up or give in, but stand your ground.

Though you are criticized, damned, hated, cursed, ignored, and reluctantly tolerated, still, stand your ground! Remember who you are, a Kingdom that cannot be shaken, a holy nation, a royal priesthood, the people of God, an indestructible organism, a mighty army, a kingdom of priests, a household of faith, a company of the committed, and a fellowship of the unashamed. So, stand your ground, stand your ground. You will be laughed at, scorned, ridiculed, written off, spit upon, and put down, but stand your ground!

Keep your vision high, your pride low, your faith undaunted, your work consistent, and your tenacity unflinching, because you are the Body of Christ.

Dear Church, when the battle's done, the blood of your last martyr has dried, the noise of war has abated, and the dust has settled, you, dear Church will stand! Scarred? Yes! Bruised? Absolutely. Thrashed? Most assuredly, but victorious and invincible, knowing that the gates of hell can't stand against you. When the trumpet is blown, and the last enemy has surrendered, you, dear Church, will stand victorious and triumphant, ready to meet your Groom when He comes for His bride. **Then you will stand, crown in place, sword of victory drawn, the enemy slain, and the long battle won!**

So stand your ground, O Church, stand your ground!"

MORE THAN CONQUERORS

"Beloved, do not think it strange concerning the fiery trial which is to try you, as though some strange thing happened to you; but rejoice to the extent that you partake of Christ's sufferings, that when His glory is revealed, you may also be glad with exceeding joy. If you are reproached for the name of Christ, blessed are you, for the Spirit of glory and of God rests upon you. On their part He is blasphemed, but on your part He is glorified. But let none of you suffer as a murderer, a thief, an evildoer, or as a busybody in other people's matters. Yet if anyone suffers as a Christian, let him not be ashamed, but let him glorify God in this matter. For the time has come for judgment to begin at the house of God; and if it begins with us first, what will be the end of those who do not obey the gospel of God? Now 'If the righteous one is scarcely saved, Where will the ungodly and the sinner appear?' Therefore let those who suffer according to the will of God commit their souls to Him in doing good, as to a faithful Creator." 1 Peter 4:12-19

"Finally, my brethren, be strong in the Lord and in the power of His might. Put on the whole armor of God, that you may be able to stand against the wiles of the devil. For we do not wrestle against flesh and blood, but against principalities, against powers, against the rulers of the darkness of this age, against spiritual hosts of wickedness in the heavenly places. Therefore take up the whole armor of God, that you may be able to withstand in the evil day, and having done all, to stand. Stand therefore, having girded your

waist with truth, having put on the breastplate of righteousness, and having shod your feet with the preparation of the gospel of peace; above all, taking the shield of faith with which you will be able to quench all the fiery darts of the wicked one. And take the helmet of salvation, and the sword of the Spirit, which is the word of God; praying always with all prayer and supplication in the Spirit, being watchful to this end with all perseverance and supplication for all the saints— and for me, that utterance may be given to me, that I may open my mouth boldly to make known the mystery of the gospel, for which I am an ambassador in chains; that in it I may speak boldly, as I ought to speak." Ephesians 6:10-20

"And we know that all things work together for good to those who love God, to those who are the called according to His purpose. For whom He foreknew, He also predestined to be conformed to the image of His Son, that He might be the firstborn among many brethren. Moreover whom He predestined, these He also called; whom He called, these He also justified; and whom He justified, these He also glorified. What then shall we say to these things? If God is for us, who can be against us? He who did not spare His own Son, but delivered Him up for us all, how shall He not with Him also freely give us all things? Who shall bring a charge against God's elect? It is God who justifies. Who is he who condemns? It is Christ who died, and furthermore is also risen, who is even at the right hand of God, who also makes intercession for us. Who shall separate us from the love of Christ? Shall tribulation, or distress, or persecution, or famine, or nakedness, or peril, or sword? As it is written: 'For Your sake we are killed all day long; We are accounted as sheep for the slaughter.' Yet in all these things we are more than conquerors through Him who loved us. For I am persuaded that neither death nor life, nor angels nor principalities nor powers, nor things present nor things to come, nor height nor depth, nor any other created thing, shall be able to separate us from the love of God which is in Christ Jesus our Lord." Romans 8:28-39

"Hear me when I call, O God of my righteousness! You have relieved me in my distress; Have mercy on me, and hear my prayer. How

long, O you sons of men, will you turn my glory to shame? How long will you love worthlessness and seek falsehood? Selah. But know that the LORD HAS SET APART FOR HIMSELF HIM WHO IS GODLY; The LORD WILL HEAR WHEN I CALL TO HIM. Be angry, and do not sin. Meditate within your heart on your bed, and be still. Selah.

Offer the sacrifices of righteousness, and put your trust in the LORD. There are many who say,
"Who will show us any good?" LORD, LIFT UP THE LIGHT OF YOUR COUNTENANCE UPON US. You have put gladness in my heart, More than in the season that their grain and wine increased. I will both lie down in peace, and sleep; For You alone, O LORD, MAKE ME DWELL IN SAFETY." Psalm 4.

The Commitment

Finally, I want to share this concise, clear, crisp quotation from the late Adrian Rogers:

"The church is not the servant of the state!
The church is not the master of the state!
The church is the conscience of the state!
We will be civil – but WE WILL NOT BE SILENT!!!"

The Bottom Line

"I'm tired of being inhibited! I want to be inhabited! Lord, live your life through me!"
~ Adrian Rogers

Courage is not the absence of fear – it is conquering of fear! "For God has not given us the spirit of fear, but of love and of power and of a sound mind." 2 Timothy 1:7.

WE ARE MORE THAN CONQUERORS.

WE WILL BE CIVIL - BUT

WE WILL NOT BE SILENT!!

Remember ... "We are all faced with incredible opportunities cleverly disguised as impossible situations." ~ Chuck Swindoll

"God sometimes lets us get to a point where no one can help you but Him."
~ Paul Shepherd

"We are more than conquerors

Through Him who loved us so.

The Christ who dwells within us

Is the greatest power we know!"

~ Ralph Carmichael

Closing Thought

Now I want to remind my fellow Christians once again to be bold witnesses for our Lord Jesus.

Final Thoughts for You Who are Not Saved – or are Unsure of your Salvation

My friend, I truly do appreciate the fact that you have taken your valuable time to read what I have written – and I compliment you for sticking it out with me to the end (of this section). Now I want to ask you some probing questions – and I hope you will be asking your-self, in all honesty, these questions:

1. Do you know that you have eternal life? If you die today, or if Jesus returns this evening – are you ready to meet Him face to face? The prophet Joel said, "Prepare to meet your God!" Are you prepared?

2. Do you know that God wants you to have rock solid assurance of His forgiveness and the gift of eternal life? *"Then Peter said to them, "Repent, and let every one of you be baptized in the name of Jesus Christ for the remission of sins; and you shall receive the gift of the Holy Spirit." Acts 2:38. "And this is the testimony: that God has given us eternal life, and this life is in His Son. He who has the Son has life; he who does not have the Son of God does not have life. These things I have written to you who believe in the name of the Son of God, that you may know that you have eternal life, and that you may continue to believe in the name of the Son of God." 1 John 5:11-13.*

3. Do you know at least one major difference between Christ and antichrist? Christ is the Good Shepherd who calls His sheep by name. Antichrist is a tyrant who calls his servants by a number. *"When Jesus returns will He call you by name – or will your number be up?" ~Adrian Rogers*

4. Do you realize that when the last trumpet sounds and Jesus bursts through the clouds in splendor and great glory that He will be coming as conquering King – not as the suffering Savior? He already came, paid the price for your sin as your Savior, and said,"It is finished!" Have you accepted that payment for your sin? He paid your penalty and offers you eternal life –but he will not force you to receive it.

5. When you stand before Almighty God on that great Judgment Day, will you hear, "Well done, good and faithful servant" – or "Depart from Me – I never knew you!"? Will your destiny be in the "Smoking" or "Non-Smoking" section? Please consider very carefully and prayerfully these potent, pertinent, persuasive passages:

BEWARE!

There Is A Point of NO Return!

"Beware, brethren, lest there be in any of you an evil heart of unbelief in departing from the living God; but exhort one another daily, while it is called 'Today,' lest any of you be hardened through the deceitfulness of sin. For we have become partakers of Christ if we hold the beginning of our confidence steadfast to the end, while it is said: 'Today, if you will hear His voice, do not harden your hearts as in the rebellion.'" Hebrews 3:12-15.

"The foolishness of a man twists his way, and his heart frets against the LORD." Proverbs 19:3

"He who is often rebuked, and hardens his neck, will suddenly be destroyed, and that without remedy." Proverbs 29:1

"Do not boast about tomorrow, for you do not know what a day may bring forth." Proverbs 27:1

"And behold, I am coming quickly, and My reward is with Me, to give to every one according to his work. I am the Alpha and the Omega, the Beginning and the End, the First and the Last.' Blessed are those who do His commandments, that they may have the right to the tree of life, and may enter through the gates into the city. But outside are dogs and sorcerers and sexually immoral and murderers and idolaters, and whoever loves and practices a lie. 'I, Jesus, have sent My angel to

testify to you these things in the churches. I am the Root and the Offspring of David, the Bright and Morning Star.' And the Spirit and the bride say, 'Come!' And let him who hears say, 'Come!' And let him who thirsts come. Whoever desires, let him take the water of life freely." Revelation 22:12-17

"THE MASTERPIECE"

by Michael Youssef, Ph.D.

"There is a story about a wealthy man and his only son who travelled the world together collecting priceless paintings by Van Gogh, Monet and many other masters. Tragically, the son died at war while rescuing others. Distraught and lonely, the old man dreaded the upcoming Christmas day.

Christmas morning, a young soldier knocked on his door and said, 'I'm a friend of your son. I'm one of the ones he rescued.' Then the soldier presented a picture he had painted of the son. Though the picture lacked genius, the brokenhearted father saw the features of his precious son and immediately valued this painting above all the masterpieces in his home. Every day, the father gazed at the portrait and told his housekeeper of his great love for it.

When the father died, the art world buzzed with excitement over the sale of his extraordinary art collection on Christmas day.

The first item offered was the painting of the son, but no one in the self-important crowd would bid on the amateurish portrait. The auctioneer insisted that the terms of the will required the portrait must be sold before any other paintings could be offered. Finally, the housekeeper, tears streaming down her cheeks, said to the auctioneer, 'May I pay ten dollars for it? That is all the money I have. I knew the son, and I know how much the father treasured that portrait.' The auctioneer said, 'The bid is ten dollars. Going once, going twice, gone,' and the gavel fell.

The auctioneer then announced that the auction was over. 'What do you mean?' said the stunned audience. 'There must be hundreds of millions of dollars of art here.' The auctioneer replied, 'It is very simple. **According to the will of the father, whoever takes the son gets it all.'**

Like the art collectors, not everyone can see the real value of a relationship with Jesus. John 1:11 tells us that Jesus came to His own but His own received Him not. **They did not accept the precious gift of God's Son, a gift that brings with it all the blessing and love of God.**

If you are not intentional about recognizing and receiving Jesus Christ, you will have nothing in the end, and there will be no negotiation of God's terms. God's Son may have been born in the most humble of circumstances in a manger in Bethlehem, but He is coming back in power and glory. **The next time we see Jesus, things will be very different from His first coming. Not only will He be the King of kings, but He will be a judge and we will be held accountable for our lives**.

Read John 3:18-36 and Revelation 3:16. Clearly, there are two categories of people: those who fully accept the Son as the only means to the Father and those who don't. People who are indifferent or neutral about the Son will miss the opportunity to live eternally with the Father in Heaven. It is not enough to believe Jesus was a good man or a prophet; James 2:19 says that even the devil believes and 'trembles.'

Have you said 'Yes' to the Lord Jesus Christ as your Savior? Luke 15:7 says there will be joy in Heaven when you do. **Tell the Father today about your love for His son. Ask God to protect your heart from being neutral or complacent about your devotion to Jesus. Is there someone you know who needs to acknowledge Jesus as Savior? Pray about being intentional about introducing them to the Son."** (From "Leading the Way". Used by permission.)

SUPPLEMENT

Don't Quit

When things go wrong, as they
sometimes will,
When the road you're trudging
seems all uphill,
When the funds are low and the
debts are high,
And you want to smile, but you
have to sigh,
When care is pressing you down
a bit –
Rest if you must, but don't you
quit.

Life is queer with its twists and
turns,
As every one of us sometimes
learns,
And many a person turns about
When they might have won had
they stuck it out.

Don't give up though the pace
seems slow –
You may succeed with another
blow.

Often the struggler has given up
When he might have captured the
victor's cup;
And he learned too late
When the night came down,
How close he was to the golden
crown.

Success is failure turned inside
out –
So stick to the fight when you're
hardest hit, -
It's when things seem worst that
you mustn't quit.

Questions for Final Thoughts

1. There is a true account about an attempted robbery in the first paragraph. What did the hostess do and what was the result?

2. Do you believe that there is hope left for America to be rejuvenated and exalted by God once again? Why or why not?

3. How did historian David Barton answer the question, "Do you think America can get back to the ideals of the Declaration"?

4. What does Charles Swindoll believe is the single most significant decision he can make on a day-to-day basis? Do you agree?

5. What, to you, was the most significant point Victor Knowles brings out from the book of Revelation in his article, "Caesar or Christ"?

6. What stirred you most in Bob Moorehead's article, "Stand Your Ground, Oh Church"?

7. What does God assure us we can know in Romans 8:28-29?

8. How do you intend to implement in your life the truth that in Christ we are "MORE THAN CONQUERORS IN CULTURAL CLASHES"?

9. Do you believe that we can truly be confident about our salvation? Can we actually know that we have eternal life? Do you have that confidence personally?

10. What is the significance of the story, "The Masterpiece"?

APPENDIX I:

REVIEWER COMMENTS

~

"Rick, I know your heart for the Lord and the lost. I have always had deep admiration for you for your heart and life. I do not find you offensive nor overly blunt. I look forward to reading what you have to say. We do live when the USA is falling apart. I don't know how much longer it can survive, not long I believe with the current direction. Something needs to be done to warn people. I have just been studying the Persian Empire and have observed that there were many similarities with them and the USA. They lasted 200 years and ruled the world. We have lasted just over 200 years and have been the strongest nation in the world's history. But we are now bankrupt financially and morally. I cannot believe what people are willing to accept from our national and state leaders. It is a huge mess....."

(Next paragraph is after he reviewed Chapter 2):

"Rick: This is SUPER great!!! I find no fault with it, wish it could be widely circulated and read. I did not read it for punctuation and proper English, but for content. As you know, I am very busy at the present, with more work every week than I can accomplish. But in reading it I find it is right on target and conveys in a very clear way my own views. God Bless you and Della.

Your friend and brother;
Charles Crane, Eagle Christian Church"

"Rick: I have read Chapter 4 and agree with you and your stand for Biblical morality and against perversion. I am impressed

with your knowledge of the subject and ability to state clearly the issues involved. I thank God for your willingness to stand for right and truth....I heartily endorse this excellent work.

Your brother,
Charles Crane"

* * * * * * * * * *

"This is all great material that is powerful truth as a Christian apologetic! We can pray God will use this to spread His gospel message!" ~ Rich Schell

* * * * * * * * * *

"This chapter is a very strongly worded and forceful declaration of what needs to be heard in the USA. I think your wording and message is very appropriate and clear without being condescending. Did not find anything I would suggest you change. The chapter is strongly worded for patriotic presentation, but the message cannot be diluted and be effective.....I very much enjoyed reading your thoughts. Your comments are things I have felt for a long time need to be expressed to America." ~ D. Lloyd Thomas

* * * * * * * * * *

"Very good once again. I agree with you completely. Get this published and I pray everyone reads it. I couldn't improve on it at all. Couple minor comments. Page 4: I agree about 'gay'. I hate it that the homosexual community has spoiled a good word that used to mean happy and care-free...Page 5: My pastor says, 'What you compromise to keep, you will lose.'.....
Thanks, Blessings,
Stan Brower"

* * * * * * * * * *

"Hi bolder soldier!

"Wow, what a powerful exposé of the enemy's strategy. It's hard to imagine how far our country has moved from her 'roots'! From the president on down, we are being pressured to actively endorse the abomination of homosexuality. Culture has turned from sinning with a tight fist to celebrating sin we ought to be ashamed of. Great reminders of who is tolerant. This chapter is on the money--- what's coming in your next chapter? Your illustrations are relevant; your comparisons are accurate, your metaphors are powerful. Chapter 3 nearly melted down my computer screen.

A fellow soldier,
Gary Strubhar"

* * * * * * * * *

"With regard to More than Conquerors in Cultural Clashes I have read each installment. As I recall, your concern was to present your readers with truthful but sensitively delivered information present in a balanced format. I believe you have achieved that goal so far.

Best regards, Drew

APPENDIX II:

15 CORE CONVICTIONS OF

RICK DEIGHTON

~

1. I believe that Jesus Christ is the Way, the Truth, and the Life. He was God manifested in flesh and is the only hope of the world.

2. I believe that God has revealed Himself as Father, Son, and Holy Spirit; that in Jesus dwells all the fullness of the Godhead bodily; and that in Him are hidden all the treasures of wisdom and knowledge.

3. I believe that the Bible from Genesis to Revelation is the inerrant Word of God. Its truths are worth diligently studying, accurately teaching, and doggedly defending. To doggedly defend the truth, however, does not give us license to spew venom on our opponents, for we must always "speak the truth in love."

4. I believe that all Christians are commissioned to share the gospel and to be ready always to give an answer for the hope that is within us, and to do so with humility and godly fear (not arrogance and antagonism).

5. I believe that Christian leaders are called to equip all believers to minister in order to fulfill the great commission and the great commandment.

6. I believe that God is the perfect balance of absolute love and absolute justice; therefore, the accurate proclamation of the gospel will reveal the true nature of God.

7. I believe the proclamation of the gospel includes the death, burial, resurrection and appearances of Jesus Christ as evidence of who He is.

    I Cor. 15. It is also necessary with proper timing to share how to respond to the gospel in faith, repentance and baptism for the forgiveness of sin.

    (Mark 16:16; Acts 2:38)   We are saved by grace through faith, not by our good works, for our own best works look like filthy rags next to God's righteousness. We are created in Christ Jesus unto good works (the result of our salvation). Eph. 2:8-10

8. *I believe that the key to proclaiming the good news to non-Christian and post-Christian cultures is creation evangelism, i.e. we must begin with God as Almighty Creator to declare Him as Adequate Redeemer as Paul did at Mars Hill. Acts 17*

9. I believe that we of the Restoration Movement are Christians only, but we are not the only Christians. We should not alienate other believers by acting like we consider ourselves the only Christians.

10. I believe that every person on earth is valuable to God and is worth saving. This of necessity includes enemies of the gospel like hostile editors, evolution devotees, abortion doctors, Marxist professors, Muslim terrorists, pimps and pornographers. We are to be wise in the way we treat outsiders. We must remember that our real enemy is Satan and that the love-filled apostle Paul was the hate-filled Saul of Tarsus before his conversion.

11. I believe that prayer is our first and most dynamic strategy in breaking down Satan's strongholds. Prayer is not the only thing we are called to do, but until we have prayed and waited on God for direction we are foolish to charge ahead on our own.

12. I believe that after prayer, love is our most powerful weapon to melt cold hearts and open closed doors. I believe that the New Covenant pivots on two commandments--Faith which works by love! Gal. 5:6

13. I believe that Jesus' prayer in John 17:20-21 teaches us that unity in the Body of Christ is the most vital factor in reaching the world for Jesus. The world doesn't need us to teach them how to fight—that is one thing they are really good at. The world needs to look to God's church with longing eyes and say, "Behold how they love one another."

14. I believe that we cannot promote Christian unity by compromising God's truth, for in the same high priestly prayer Jesus said *"Sanctify them in thy truth. Thy Word is truth!" (John 17:17).* In our culture, the only virtue is tolerance. The ungodly wisdom of this world is pressuring us to conform and fit into its mold by tolerating the intolerable. To faithfully follow Jesus means having the backbone to oppose evil. Was Jesus always gentle and mild? Apparently the money changers in the temple, the Pharisees and the chief priests didn't think so. Jesus Himself said, *"If they have hated Me, they will hate you."* We must be willing to be misunderstood, hated and slandered for Jesus' sake.

15. Therefore, I believe that to effectively evangelize our lost, confused, hostile world we must carefully balance and prayerfully walk the tightrope stretched between truth and unity. *"Lord, fill us with Your Spirit, for we cannot accomplish this on our own."*

CREATIVE CHRISTIAN FAMILY LIFE SEMINARS

~*Laugh! Learn! Love! Live!*~

Family Life Seminars in Ukraine and Russia are proving to be an effective evangelistic outreach, as well as a means of strengthening families. If your church is interested in a weekend seminar, please let us know, and we will give you more information and check on scheduling.

The following themes are available.

Relationship Messages:

1. How to Build Strong Relationships

2. The Biblical View of Sexuality

3. How to Win Over Temptation

4. How to Win Over Bitterness

5. Monstrous Problems—Awesome God!

6. Three Shades of Love

7. How to Restore Romance in Marriage

8. How to Improve Communication in Marriage

9. How to Train Children to Obey

10. Training Positive & Productive Kids

11. Love & Respect (for powerful progress in relationships)

12. Grace, the Foundation of our Faith

Christian Evidence Messages:

1. Why I Believe in God

2. Jesus, The Carpenter

3. Creation or Evolution—What Difference Does It Make What We Believe?

4. Genesis or Jurassic Park—Which?

5. Monstrous Problems—Awesome God!

6. The Reality of the Resurrection

7. Does the Bible Contradict Itself Concerning Salvation?

8. The Source of Freedom

9. The Power of Perspective

10. Catastrophic Consequences of Darwinism

11. The Place of Creationism in Scientific Knowledge

Other topics:

1. The Church Has Power!

2. The Reality of Hell

3. The Reality of Heaven (Don't Miss Heaven for the World!)

4. Living the Abundant Life

5. Victorious Christian Living (Two messages)

6. Triangle of Triumph

7. Geometry of Joy

8. The Source of Joy

9. The Sufficiency of Jesus Christ

10. The Superiority of Jesus

11. Look Who's Watching You!

12. What is Your Purpose in Life?

13. Worldviews in Conflict

Rejoicing in Jesus,

Rick Deighton

OVERSEAS OUTREACH

Rick & Della Deighton
P. O. Box 1224
Nampa, ID 83653-1224
overseasoutreach@earthlink.net

www.overseasoutreach.com